The Honest Heretique

For

William Thomas (Pennar) Davies
1911–96

and

Stanley L. Greenslade
1905–77

Ministers of the Gospel

The Honest Heretique

The Life and Work of William Erbery (1604–1654)

John I. Morgans

With thanks to Norah who has shared my life with William Erbery since 1962

I wish to express my gratitude to Eirian Jones, Lefi Gruffudd and the staff of Y Lolfa for their encouragement, advice, patience and skill.

First impression: 2012

Cover design: Y Lolfa

ISBN: 978 184771 485 5

Published and printed in Wales
on paper from well maintained forests by
Y Lolfa Cyf., Talybont, Ceredigion SY24 5HE
website www.ylolfa.com
e-mail ylolfa@ylolfa.com
tel 01970 832 304
fax 832 782

IF THIS BE HERESY…

PERSONAL CONVICTIONS

All that he knows of God is that he is known of God

Love believes all things, and hopes all things;
believes the best of all, and hopes they will be better

My Religion is, to be of no Religion, with man;
that is, to have fellowship with none,
and yet to have fellowship with all in God

These particular forms of religion,
and private opinions must fall…
that the power of righteousness may appear to All

This is all he hath now to say. That as he first professed he knew nothing, nor maintained any thing as dogmatical, so he confesseth himself not yet carried out of the way of further enquiry and sees himself be-wildernessed as a way-faring man

Let silent Truth, and these
Speaking times interpret these Scriptures

LIBERTY OF CONSCIENCE

That as the three chief Religions in the world, are the Christians, Jews and Turks; so this Christian Common-wealth appearing so favourable to the Jews, why not to the Turks? And if for unbelieving Jews, why not for misbelieving Christians, who in their utmost knowledge love the Truth and Peace? Why may not honest Papists have the like Liberty of Conscience, in due time, amongst Protestants in England, when our Governours see good

We think of converting the Heathens, and the Heathens are at hand to convert us Christians and Churches, from our forms of religion to the power of righteousness

God shall appear not onely thy light, but the light of the World, the light of every man, and the light of every creature

Hold forth Christ from the appearance of God in the world, from the light of the world that is in them, from inward experiments, from outward providences, from the writings of Poets and prophane Authors; yea, from all the Creation

THE CHURCH AND ITS MISSION

The Church is a free Company, or Society of Friends

My neighbour is not only one of the next house, or of my own family, my friend; but every man is my flesh

All the people of God shall become one Land, one Continent, wherein the Lord alone shall live

None but the Women, the weakest saints, see the resurrection at hand, which the present apostles and Ministers of the Gospel laugh at, and look upon as idle tales

'Tis not the black raven, but the Dove; that brings an olive-branch in her mouth, a message of peace and gladness to men. 'Tis not the Cock, but the female Dove goes forth. The feeble, the weakest saints God will most glorifie

SOCIAL AND POLITICAL CONCERN

Ease the oppressed of their burthens,
release the prisoners from their bonds, and relieve poor Families
with bread by a publick stock

God will find a way to feed the poor out of the bellies of the
rich, who shall not only make restitution according to their
substance, but shall vomit up all that they have swallowed

These kinds, with their Nobles, Lords, and Dukes,
all proceeded from a cursed pedigree

Why may not rich Citizens, racking Landlords in the Country,
and mighty moneyed men, be made immediately to rise in
their payments, that poor Farmers, Labourers,
and honest Tradesmen may be spared?

The Defendant reserving to himself all the liberty
to a free-born subject of England and Wales

To do to every one as we would that men would do unto us.
This is the sum of All Religion, that is truly Christian and noble

CONTENTS

PREFACE

IT SEEMS A long time ago. It is a long time ago! Nearly fifty years ago, in 1962, I was a 23-year-old student, training for ministry. Dr Pennar Davies, Principal of the Congregational Memorial College in Swansea suggested I take a college scholarship and embark on research at Oxford. I was interested in seventeenth-century puritanism. "What or whom should I study?" I asked. "William Erbery" came the response, "an intellectual and moral giant."[1] Pennar was convinced that Erbery had been grossly neglected and misunderstood. Pennar had sympathy for this man who, like him, was prepared to push the boundaries. He too was prepared to be a nonconformist, true to himself and his experience of God.

Six months later, in October 1963, my research began at Mansfield College, Oxford, supervised by Stanley Greenslade, Canon of Christ Church and Regius Professor of Ecclesiastical History at Oxford. The start was not encouraging. Dr Geoffrey Nuttall, the most eminent English Puritan historian at that time, had justified excluding Erbery from his series of four lectures (published as *The Welsh Saints* in 1957) by referring to an anonymous tract of 1685 in which the author had stated that "Mr Erbury was taken ill of his Whimsies… Mr Erbury's Disease lay in his Head, not in his Heart." Dr Nuttall concluded that "In my own judgement a perusal of Erbury's writings unfortunately confirms these statements, and I do not propose to consider him further. He was not of the same calibre, mentally or spiritually, as the other three men, however much they may all have owed to him."[2]

Would it be worth spending several years of my life on a wild-goose chase? Did Erbery have anything of value to say to his contemporaries and to ours? What did 'taken ill of his Whimsies' mean?, this 'disease in his Head'? Should I begin the exploration? It was to get worse before it got any better.

I turned to the standard histories of the Puritan period. Dr Nuttall's view reflected the general impression made by Erbery. Benjamin Brook in 1813 had written that Erbery "laboured under a sore affliction, which had deeply affected his head."[3] Thomas Rees in 1883 summed up that "Mr Erbery, several years before his death, was visited by a sore affliction, which to some degree deranged his mind" and, commenting on Erbery's writings, stated "Here and there we find in it flashes of wit, and some of the most correct, sublime, and telling ideas, but interspersed with such a mass of religious nonsense, as none but a mentally deranged man would have penned."[4]

More hopeful was the estimate in 1920 of Thomas Richards, Wales' pioneer Puritan historian: "Erbery's answer to the charges before the C.P.M. [Committee for Plundered Ministers in 1653] is full of the subtle arguments of a master of controversy. It should be said that his was a wonderfully versatile but somewhat unbalanced mind whose high ideals set up impossible standards for an age of transition."[5]

That is where the matter stood when I started my work in 1963. The thesis, submitted three years later, presented a different stance from that of Brook, Rees and Nuttall. The thesis needed to be defended at the examination schools at Oxford and the *viva* took place in July 1966. The internal examiner was Dr Barry White of Oxford, and the external examiner was no other than Dr Nuttall of London. After an hour's examination, I was aware I had not done well. In fact it was not as bad as it could have been. There could have been three possible results: acceptance, failure, referral. The thesis was referred, and two years later, in 1968, I returned to Oxford, to the same examination schools and to two examiners. The Oxford examiner, Dr White, was there, but this time the external examiner was Dr Ernest Payne of London. At the close of the hour, I was asked "Do you still disagree with Dr Nuttall's position?" What could I say, but "Yes, I still believe Erbery is a most interesting man, who deserves careful appraisal."

As I left the room, Dr Payne said, "And so do we." The thesis was accepted.

Is that the end of the story? A copy of the thesis was placed in the Bodleian Library in Oxford and from 1968 until April, 2010, I had neither time nor opportunity to return to the thesis. I was invited to speak about Erbery to the congregation at Canton Uniting Church, Cardiff, a church tracing its origins in 1640 to the ministry of Erbery. I dusted down the thesis, and picked up where the 29-year-old had left off in 1968.

Much has happened in the last 40 years. Many scholars have read the thesis. Above all, Christopher Hill, late Master of Balliol and one of the pre-eminent historians in the field of seventeenth -century England had discovered Erbery and described him as a pioneer of radical thought and action.[6] Erbery is coming into his own after 350 years. All these writers agree that Erbery was not mentally deranged.

Erbery rocked the boat, he thought outside the box, he was a presser forward in a period often described as the Puritan Revolution. By many he would have been admired as a pioneer who challenged the orthodoxies of his day. Unfortunately he became known to future generations not through his own work, but through the writings of those who saw him as schismatic, a turbulent antinomian, a heretic and a blasphemer. Some went further and described him as a madman, probably buried in bedlam.

The intention of this book is to enable Erbery to speak for himself. There are extracts from all his writings, presented consecutively from *The Great Mystery of Godliness* of 1639, to *The Great Earthquake* published in July 1654, three months after his death. There is a sketch of Erbery's life and thought, and introductions to each tract. For the first time, the general public can decide whether Erbery was 'taken ill of his whimsies' or was 'an intellectual and moral giant'.

John I. Morgans
December 2012

PART ONE

AN INTRODUCTION TO THE LIFE AND WORK OF WILLIAM ERBERY

A SKETCH OF ERBERY'S LIFE

ERBERY'S EARLY LIFE 1604–1643

LITTLE IS KNOWN of the first thirty years of Erbery's life. He stepped into the spotlight for the first time only when Archbishop Laud wrote to Charles I, that the new vicar of St Mary's in Cardiff had been 'very disobedient to your Majesty's Instructions'. From 1633 onwards, Erbery seemed to court controversy. He was forced to resign his Cardiff living and at the outbreak of the Civil War, when his Cardiff property was plundered by the Royalists, he served as an Army chaplain first under the Earl of Essex and then under General Fairfax. When Oxford fell to the parliamentary forces, Erbery was in the limelight in instructing and supporting the rebellious students and soldiers. He defended his position vigorously against six Presbyterian visitors sent by parliament to force Erbery and his followers to submit to orthodoxy. He was obliged to leave the city at the instruction of General Fairfax. Finally in 1653, he was accused and tried for heresy at Westminster before a congregation of 500. This man of Roath, Cardiff did not live a quiet life. The last twenty years of his life often saw him hit the headlines, but after his death in 1654, he has been quietly forgotten.

William Erbery was born in 1604 in Roath-Dagfield, Cardiff. His father, Thomas Erbery, was a merchant who had probably come across from the West Country of England to establish an iron foundry in the Merthyr Valley before moving to Cardiff. It is probable that Thomas married Elizabeth, daughter of Rees David, a Cardiff cordwainer.[1] William entered Brasenose College, Oxford in 1619, graduated in 1623 and proceeded to Queens' College, Cambridge where he earned a second degree in

1626. He subscribed for deacon's orders in the diocese of Bristol on December 23rd 1626 and became curate in St Woolos in Newport in 1630.

Erbery admits to suffering from a sensitive Puritan disposition when he writes to a Puritan commissioner in 1652, 'I have been afflicted from my youth, and suffered the terrors of the Lord to distraction.'[2] However, there is no evidence of his activities or views when he was at university or while he served in Bristol and Newport. There is one ambiguous reference to his Newport ministry: 'Being called by the Lord to preach at Newport, the Town where I was a Preacher first.'[3] Although Erbery was familiar with the work of William Wroth and the saints at Llanfaches, again there is no evidence of when that contact began.

He remained at Newport until 1633 when he became vicar of St Mary's in Cardiff. He had been presented with the living by Sir Thomas Lewis of Penmarc, a member of the influential Puritan Lewis family of Y Fan. The Lewis family were patrons of William Wroth and business associates of Erbery's father.[4]

He was instituted in Cardiff on the 7th of August, 1633. Almost immediately his Puritan views resulted in his being viewed as a dangerous schismatic. The King had instructed that *The Declaration of Sports,* issued on October 18th, 1633 should be publicly read from every pulpit at Sunday worship. The declaration was targeted at 'Puritans and precise people' and encouraged 'lawful recreations and honest exercises upon Sundays, and other Holy-days'. The injunction ordered 'that the Bishop of that Diocese take the like strait order with all Puritans and Precisians within the same, either constraining them to conform themselves or to leave the county.'[5]

Erbery refused to read the royal commandment and there followed a lengthy struggle between Erbery and William Murray, Bishop of Llandaf. The controversy may have begun with Murray, but it soon reached the ear of Laud, Archbishop of Canterbury, and even the King. In his annual reports to Charles, Laud referred to his struggles with the schismatic Erbery. Ultimately Erbery was summoned to appear before Laud at the Court of High

Commission at Lambeth. Laud's reports to the King present important and intriguing reading.[6]

REPORT FOR 1634

The Bishop of Landaff certifies, That this last Year he Visited in Person; and found that William Erbury, Vicar of St. Maries in Cardiff, and Walter Cradocke his Curate, have been very disobedient to your Majesty's Instructions, and have Preached very Schismatically and Dangerously to the People. That for this he hath given the Vicar a Judicial Admonition, and will further proceed, if he do not submit. And for his Curate, being a bold ignorant young Fellow, he hath Suspended him, and taken away his License to serve the Cure. Among other things he used this base and Unchristian passage in the Pulpit, That God so loved the world, that for it he sent his Son to live like a Slave, and dye like a Beast. (p.533)

The King (Charles Rex) wrote in the margin of his copy of the report for 1634. **C.R.** 'This is not much unlike that which was not longe since uttered elsewhere, viz. That the Jewes Crucified Christ like a Damned Rogue between Two Theeves, &c.'

Erbery and Cradock were now marked men. Cradock was suspended immediately and lost his Licence, but Erbery's case dragged on year after year. In the following years his name was linked with William Wroth, the vicar of Llanfaches in Monmouthshire. By 1638, Wroth 'hath submitted', but in the following year he founded, with several others, the first Independent Church in Wales.

REPORT FOR 1635

In this Diocess, the Bishop found, in his Triennial Visitation the former Year, two noted Schismaticks, Wroth and Erbury; that led away many simple People after them. And finding, that they wilfully persisted in their Schismatickal course, he hath carefully preferred Articles against them in the High-Commission Court; where, when the Cause is ready for Hearing, they shall receive according to the Merits of it. (p.537)

REPORT FOR 1636

For Landaff, there is very little found amiss; Only the Bishop complains, that whereas Mr. Wroth and Mr. Erbury are in the High-Commission for their Schismatical proceedings; the slow prosecution there against them, makes them both persist in their By-ways, and their Followers judge them Faultless. But for this, I humbly present to your Majesty this Answer, That now the loss of two Terms by reason of the Sickness, hath cast the Proceedings of that Court, as well as of others, behind-hand; [7] And there is no Remedy, where all things stay as well as it. (p.544)

REPORT FOR 1638

There were in this Diocess the last year but two Refractory Ministers known to the Bishop, Mr. Wroth and Mr. Erbury: The former hath submitted; but the other would neither submit, nor satisfie his Parishioners, to whom he had given publick offence; so he resigned his Vicarage, and hath left therby the Diocess in peace. (p.555)

The 1638 report records that Erbery would not submit 'nor satisfie his Parishioners' and was forced to resign his living. Erbery later infers that he also resigned at that time from the ministry of the Church of England. The first report (1634) had pointed out that the charges against Erbery had included his refusal to read the *Book of Sports*, but all the reports point out that he 'Preached very Schismatically and Dangerously to the People' (1634), 'wilfully persisted in their Schismatickal course' (1635), and continued with his 'Schismatical proceedings' (1636). By 1638 he had 'resigned his Vicarage'.

Further evidence for Erbery's Puritan ministry at Cardiff comes from Christopher Love, a young man converted under Erbery's ministry at St Mary's.[8] Love, a Presbyterian, was writing in 1651, days before his execution for supporting the Scots' attempt to restore Charles II to the throne, states:

As for Master Erbury, though he is fallen into dangerous opinions, yet, he being my spirituall Father, I do naturally care for him, as Timothy did for Paul, my heart cleaves to him in love, more than to

> any one man in the World; I speake to the praise of God, he was the instrument of my conversion, near twenty years agoe, and the means of my education also in the University, for which kindnesse, the half I have in the World, I could readily part with for his reliefe.[9]

Vital information about Erbery's ministry in Cardiff was discovered by an extraordinary piece of good fortune. In 1964, books were being re-bound in Queen's College Library, Oxford.[10] A librarian at the Bodleian Library, Mr Paul Morgan, discovered that a letter had been used as a pastedown the last time that particular book on law was being bound. Dated August 1637, it is a letter from Francis Harvey of Bristol to Webb, the Oxford bookseller, and refers to the possible printing of a book by William Erbery. Harvey claims, 'I doe thinke that I shall sell 600 in his own towne of card/iff'. This is the earliest reference to the first of Erbery's publications. A year later, on the 24th January, 1638/9, there is an entry in the Stationers' Register:

> Master Milborne Entred for his Copie under the handes of Master Wykes and Master Mead warden a book called 'The Misticall union of Christ and his Church' by Master Earbury.[11]

In 1639, Robert Milbourne published the first printing of '*The Great Mystery of Godliness* at the Unicorne neere Fleet-Bridge in 1639, followed by a second print in 1640 in Little Britain, at the signe of the Holy Lamb'. The subtitle to the book is 'The Mysticall union of Christ and his Church'. Probably the book was not published earlier because Erbery's case was still continuing at the Court of High Commission.

The book is of considerable importance because it reveals Erbery to be an orthodox Calvinist Puritan.[12] An emphasis on the Word and Sacraments are central to the personal nurture of the Christian. Erbery's theological stance at this time would have been perfectly acceptable to both Christopher Love, a Presbyterian and Walter Cradock, an Independent.

There is uncertainty about Erbery's actions between 1638 and the outbreak of the Civil War in 1642. It is difficult to gauge his attitude towards Christian ministry and church government. He had resigned from the Church of England in 1638, and because of his respect for the 'Saints' at Llanfaches, he had helped form a similar 'new modelled Church' in Cardiff, probably in 1640. However, in retrospect, he described this as a retrograde step. He believes he should have encouraged these disaffected Anglicans to remain 'scattered Saints'.

> I Was first your Preacher, then your Pastor; and this last, not out of light in myself, but in love to the Saints of Lanvaghes, who being then gathered into a new modelled Church, never left me, till I and mine came into the same form with them: so we walked, they in the light, because I believe that led them into fellowship; but I in darkness, because contrary to my own light, in love only (as I said) I followed them, because I would not offend; but see the judgment of God lesse love and more offences fell out between us as after we came into a brotherhood, or combination of Churches, then when we were at first a company of scattered Saints. Well, gathered Churches we must be, and so we were, till the sword scattered us all into England.[13]

Writing in retrospect, Erbery suggests that his formation of a new modelled church in Cardiff was in deference to the Llanfaches saints rather than an adherence to his own principles. However, recent research[14] reveals that Erbery 'preached Independency' during the period of the early 1640s. Erbery was in Bristol in October and November 1640 and was invited to preach at Burrington and Chew Stoke in Somerset. John Cole of Chew Magna was in the congregation one Sunday afternoon and gave his evidence to the Court of the Bishop of Bath and Wells:

> He desired the congregation to pray to God that they might have a Christian Church here in England. And farther he said that a Christian Church did consist in these three particulars, the Members, the Pastors, and the Administration of God's Ordinances. For the first, the Members, he said they must be saints by calling, the pastors he said they must be chosen by those members, and the administration of

> God's ordinances he said must be administered to none but those that are saints by calling.[15]

The wardens of the two parishes were summoned to the bishop's court after these disorderly services. Chew Stoke Church was so full that people had to stand in the graveyard. Erbery preached twice in each place and each sermon lasted two hours. He prayed in his own words; from the pulpit in Chew Stoke, he asked some of his listeners what they had learned and they answered him. He did not read evening prayer from the prayer book in Chew Stoke although it was a Sunday afternoon. After the service in Burrington (on a working day), Erbery met some of the congregation in a house in the village.[16]

At the same time, further recent research[17] has revealed the critical role played by Erbery in petitioning the House of Commons about the need for a godly ministry in Wales.

> The first indication of the Welsh radicals pressing their case for reform came in December 1640, when William Erbery submitted a petition to the Commons... he, and the clique of Puritan ministers associated with him, saw his role to be that of a spokesman for the whole of Wales... It was noted on the surviving copy of this petition that it was granted on 12 January 1641, and liberty was given by the Commons to a closely-associated group of Welsh radicals – quite possibly those mentioned as attending on parliament – to preach throughout Wales. They were Erbery himself, Walter Cradock, Henry Walter, Ambrose Mostyn and Richard Symonds.[18]

Dr Bowen's research points out that on the 16th February, 1641, a further and longer petition was delivered to the Commons.

> It was submitted in the name of 'many subjects in the principality of Wales', and was headed by the subscriptions of seven 'preachers of the Word of God' and just over three hundred others. The seven preachers were William Wroth, William Erbery, Walter Cradock, Henry Walter, Richard Symonds, Ambrose Mostyn and Robert Hart.[19]

Erbery was clearly a key figure in the Puritan circle seeking the reform of the Church. It is no surprise then that at the outbreak of war, Erbery's home in Cardiff was confiscated by the Cavaliers. 'Having been a Sufferer from the beginning; first, by the Prelates, in the High-Commission: next, by the Royall-Party for my affection to the parliament, being the first Plundered Minister in Wales.'[20]

Like his fellow Puritans in south-east Wales, Erbery was forced to flee from the Royalist forces because 'the sword scattered us all into England'. Erbery made his way to Windsor Castle where he sought help from Christopher Love who was serving as chaplain to John Venn, Governor of the castle. Love later wrote movingly of his relationship with Erbery:

> It is true, about eight or nine years since, he was plundered in Wales, and did come to see me at Windsor Castle, but a Sonne could not make more of a Father, than I made of him, according to my ability; when I had not twelve pounds in all the World, I let Master Erbury have six of it, indeed he afterward gave me a horse, for which I received not much above forty shillings; yea I procured him a place in the Army, to be Chaplaine to Major Generall Skippons Regiment where he had eight shillings a day.[21]

ERBERY'S ARMY EXPERIENCE 1643–1649

The Army exerted a revolutionary experience upon Erbery's thought. This is no surprise when one notes Richard Baxter's description of the New Model Army. After the Battle of Naseby, Baxter visited the Army and abhorred the multifarious opinions amongst the chaplains and soldiers. Sects, schisms and chaos abounded. He deplored that many were:

> For State Democracy, and sometime for Church Democracy; sometimes against Forms of Prayer, and sometimes against Infant Baptism, (which yet some of them did maintain); sometimes against Set-times of prayer, and against the tying of our selves to any Duty before the Spirit move us; and sometimes about Free-grace and Free-will, and all the Points of Anti-nomianism and Arminianism.[22]

Erbery's connection with the Army began in 1643 and continued until 1649, although he also served civilian congregations in London during this period. In August 1643 he was paid £20 arrears as chaplain to Major-General Skippon's regiment of foot in the Earl of Essex's Army. In January 1644/5 the Commons ordered him to be paid £50 arrears. From August 1646 to January 1646/7, he was chaplain to Col. Richard Ingoldsby's New Model regiment of foot while it was garrisoning in Oxford. In January 1646/7 to April 1647 he served as chaplain to Col. Lambert's New Model regiment of foot. He was sometime chaplain to Fairfax's regiment of horse for which he received £31:13s:9d arrears in 1650.[23] While serving in the Army, Erbery became associated with a circle of radical chaplains. Amongst them were William 'Doomsday' Sedgwick, the apostle of the Isle of Ely; Joshua Sprigge, a retainer of Fairfax during the war who became fellow and senior bursar at All Souls, Oxford; and John Saltmarsh, a forerunner of the Quakers. Evidence of Erbery's activities during this period comes particularly from the vitriolic pen of Thomas 'Gangraena' Edwards. A strict orthodox Presbyterian, his writings are heavily coloured, but his information on Erbery's whereabouts and actions are probably accurate.[24]

> There is one Mr. Erbury that lived in Wales, who in the beginning of the Parliament was an Independent, but by degrees is fallen to many grosse Errors, holding universal Redemption, &c. and now a Seeker, and I know not what. This man was a Chaplain in the Earl of Essex's Army a great while, and did broach there many Antinomian Doctrines, and other dangerous Errors; but having left the Army a good while since, he was about London, and did vent his opinions here; but about Spring last he hath betaken himself to the Isle of Ely for his ordinary residence, from whence he takes his progresse into one county or another in private houses, venting his opinions amongst well-affected people under the habit of holinesse. In July last he was at Berry, where he Exercised in private, some forty persons being present, he declared himself for general Redemption; that no man was punished for Adams sins; that Christ died for all; that the guilt of Adams sin should be imputed to no man; He said also, that

within a while God would raise up Apostolical men, who should be extraordinary to Preach the Gospel, and after that shall be the fall of Rome: He spake against gathering Churches, the Anabaptists Re-baptizing, and said men ought to wait for the coming of the Spirit, as the Apostles did; look as in the Wildernesse they had Honey and Manna, but not circumcision and the Passeover till they came into Canaan; So now we may have many sweet things, Conference and Prayer, but not a Ministery and Sacraments: And then, after the fall of Rome, there shall be new heavens, and new earth; there shall be new Jerusalem, and then the Church shall be one, one street in that city and no more. Not long after he had been at Berry, he went into Northamptonshire, and came to Northampton, where in a private meeting the main scope of his Exercise was, to speak against the certainty and sufficiency of the Scriptures, alledging there was no certainty to build upon them, because there were so many several copies; he was also at Oundel, Newport-Pagnel, and appointed shortly to return again to Berry.[25]

There is one Master Erbury spoken of in my first part of Gangraena, who about June or the beginning of July last, as he was going to Wales, lay at Marlborough one night; and being in the Town he came to a house where commonly once a week many good people of that Town meet together to confer and discourse of good things; and there Master Erbury spake to them (many being there present) to this purpose, that he knew not what they might expect, but he came neither to pray nor to preach, but to learn of Christ and of his Saints, and making a discourse to them, he declared his opinions, venting himself against Christ being God, affirming he was only man, pleading for universall Redemption, speaking against Baptism & all ministry, using words to this effect, that he knew not how they stood affected, or how it was with them; but with many Christians it was thus with them, that they knew not what to do with a man in black cloathes, or a black man among them; but that was for the time when Christians were Babes and Children, but now they were all taught of God, and needed not that any one should teach them: When he had done speaking, some of the company stood up and opposed him as not being satisfied in what he had said, telling him it was not only Errour, but Blasphemy to deny Christ to be God, and brought some Scriptures to prove it, as in I John 5.7 speaking of the Father, Word,

> and Holy Ghost, the Apostle saith, These Three are One; unto whom Master Erbury replyed, It was not so in the Originall; but some of the people re-joyned they knew not the Originall, but they beleeved it was so; and however they were assured that he was the Sonne of God: Master Erbury objected again, those words were not in the Greek but put in by some who were against the Arrians; and so the meeting broke up, the people who met, being much offended at him.[26]

Edwards was describing events of 1645. During the following summer of 1646, Oxford, headquarters to the King and his court, fell to the parliamentary Army. Erbery was there as a chaplain and his lectures proved popular with rebellious students and with the victorious, sectarian troops. Because things seemed to be getting out of hand, parliament sent six Presbyterian ministers to restore order. Four separate accounts survive of the debates between the Presbyterians, led by Francis Cheynell, and Erbery, and all make fascinating reading.[27]

The Oxford debates reveal that Erbery had changed dramatically during the seven years since the publication of *The Great Mystery of Godliness* in 1639 and 1640. When Erbery had begun writing his first treatise, he was still serving as vicar of St Mary's in Cardiff, but was being tried at the Court of High Commission. The following turbulent years saw him resign his living; form the first Independent Church cause in Cardiff; suffer the loss of his home at the outbreak of the Civil War and be forced to flee from Wales. Penniless, he had appealed to Christopher Love who helped him become an Army chaplain. The following years saw him serve in the Army and learn from the radical movements in the Army and in the London congregations. The national revolutionary political and social events were paralleled by Erbery's exploration of a new experience of God. The external 'providences' and the 'internal discoveries' resulted in Erbery's new theology first expressed in his *Nor Truth nor Errour* (1647). A significant exploration of the revolution in Erbery's theology is to be found in an article by Prof. M. Wynn Thomas. He also recognizes the importance of Erbery's Army experience.[28] Both Prof. Thomas and Dr Medwin

Hughes[29] reflect creatively on Erbery's theological radicalism, and of his influence particularly on Morgan Llwyd. By the time Erbery arrived at Oxford in 1646, the foundation of his faith and theology had been firmly laid and it served as the springboard for his further explorations during the following eight years of his life.

ERBERY'S LATER EXPERIENCE 1649–1654

At Oxford, Erbery had served as chaplain to Colonel Lambert's New Model regiment of foot. Although General Fairfax ordered his removal from Oxford, Erbery served as chaplain to Fairfax's regiment of horse for which he received payment in arrears as late as 1650.[30]

Leaving Oxford in 1647, Erbery spent his time between his Cardiff home and London. Anthony à Wood suggests that his London base was Christ Church, Newgate.[31]

> After the surrender of the Garrison of Oxon in 1646, we find him there to be Chaplain to a Regiment of Parliamenteers, to keep his Conventicles for them in an house opposite to Merton Coll. Church, (wherein afterwards in the time of Oliver, the Royal Party had their religious Meetings) and to study all means to oppose the Doctrine of the Presbyterian Ministers sent by the members of Parliament to preach the Scholars into obedience, as I have (Vide Hist. &c. Antiq. Univ. Oxon. Lib. 1. an. 1646.) else here told you. But being desir'd to depart thence (where he had maintained several Socinian opinions), he went soon after to London, where venting his blasphemies in several places against the glorious divinity and blood of Jesus Christ, especially in his Conventicle at Christ Church within Newgate, where those of his opinion met once, or more in a week.[32]

Towards the end of 1648, Erbery published his third tract. It appeared under two different titles: *The Lord of Hosts* and *The Armies Defence*.[33] Both were published in London by Thomas Newcomb for Giles Calvert at the sign of the Black Spread-Eagle at the west end of St Pauls. Much of Erbery's work after 1648 was published by Calvert whose home and shop became a centre for radical thinkers.[34] Erbery's theological principles first expressed in *Nor Truth nor Errour* were expanded in *The Lord of Hosts* to reflect his views on the changing political and social scene.

At the beginning of January 1648/9, the month on which the King was executed at Whitehall, Erbery attended the Whitehall debates of the General Council of the Army.[35] Both the Putney and Whitehall debates centred on the discussion of the 'Agreement of the People', in which the Levellers embodied their constitutional theories. At Whitehall were the chief Army officers, and two officers and two agitators from each regiment. The higher officers, like Cromwell and Ireton, tended to be more conservative, particularly on social questions, while the lower officers were more radical. The debates lasted for two weeks in December and January 1648/9, after which the officers and agitators were sent back to their regiments. Erbery's position was that freedom of religion, and a righteous society were more important than theoretical discussions about constitutional reform. His speeches were recorded during the discussions which took place on the 8th, 10th and 11th of January 1649.

By 1648, Erbery had published only three tracts. While serving as an orthodox Puritan clergyman in Cardiff, he had been working on *The Great Mystery of Godliness*. There is no record of further writing until his response to the Oxford debates of late 1646 and early 1647. *Nor Truth nor Errour* is the production of the new, radical Erbery who had broken free from the thought-forms and practices of a minister of the Church of England. These fresh ideas were re-expressed in *The Lord of Hosts* of 1648, but it was not until 1652 that Erbery began to produce a spate of writings which continued unabated until his death in April 1654.

From 1652 until Erbery's death, Calvert and others published collections of Erbery's letters to friends and fellow-travellers, polemical and humorous writing, theological and ecclesiological tracts, and political pamphlets. They were aimed at audiences in Wales and in England, and give a rare and contemporary insight into the fierce debates of the period. They reveal that Erbery was active as a speaker (he did not regard himself as a preacher), particularly in south Wales where he was engaged in several disputations. This was as true of the time he spent in London where he reports of attending and reporting on meetings and debates.

The consequence of his disputes in London resulted in his being charged of heresy. This resulted in house arrest and his appearance before the Committee for Plundered Ministers in late 1652/3. The trial, held in the Chequer Chamber in the Palace of Westminster before an audience of more than 500, was a major event in the religious calendar of February 1652/3. It was recorded by Sir William Clarke, Secretary to the Council of the Army.[36] Erbery was accused of heresy and blasphemy, but answered the charges with clarity and passion. His defence, which Erbery later produced for publication (*The Honest Heretique*), was prepared with great care. He answered every charge with precision and intelligence, was declared innocent of all charges and released from house arrest. For some reason, *The Honest Heretique* remained unpublished until after Erbery's death when John Webster[37] his friend and colleague, collected his works in *The Testimony of William Erbery* in 1658.

His release was the trigger for a new lease of life, and Erbery continued to write with even greater enthusiasm and energy. Fourteen tracts appeared in what was to prove his final year. His last work, published three months after his death was *The Great Earthquake*. It has many similarities to *The Honest Heretique*, in that it also presents a systematic presentation of his convictions.

Erbery died in 1654. Wood suggests 'that he died in the beginning of the year (in April I think) sixteen hundred fifty and four, and was, as I conceive, buried either at Ch Church before mentioned, or else in the Cemiterie joining to Old Bedlam near London.'[38]

Further evidence of his death was given in an elegy written by J.L.:

> A small Mite, In Memory of the late deceased (yet still living, and never to be forgotten) Mr. WILLIAM ERBERY. April 20, 1654.

What if thy flesh hath lost its form?
In us thou living art:
Light that's of God in thee was born,
Love centred in thy heart.
In and through storms thou hast been led:
All clouds before thee fell;
Man true, that's one with God the Head,

Even in thy life will dwell.
Right Resurrection do we own;
Believe's, you need not fear't:
Eternally it shall be known;
Risen Erbery's light will clear't.
Yet many real hearts could weep,
'Cause thus thy flesh doth seem to sleep.

But if the Envious do rejoyce,
Thinking thy life hath lost its voice,
They'll be deceiv'd: for it will live,
Their Serpent mortal wounds to give.

Most of Erbery's works were later collected by John Webster and published by Giles Calvert in 1658. It was only after the death of Erbery that his family step out of the shadows. His widow, Mary, and his daughter Dorcas belonged to the Quaker meeting in Cardiff as early as 1655, and became followers of James Naylor. In 1667 Mary gave an orchard for a Quaker graveyard at Sowdrey in Cardiff. Another daughter, Lydia, married Henry Fell and they served as Quaker missionaries in Barbados. Erbery's son, Mordecai, married Elizabeth Chapman, daughter of Mary Chapman, a prominent Cardiff Quaker who gave land for the Quaker graveyard at Quaker's Yard.[39] It seems that Erbery's children reached the destination of Erbery's journey.

THE CONTRIBUTION OF WILLIAM ERBERY

FOUR YEARS AFTER Erbery's death, Webster published *The Testimony of William Erbery* (1658). His purpose was to produce 'a collection of the writings of the aforesaid author, for the benefit of posterity'. Webster's *To the Christian Reader* ends with the words, 'To conclude, Thou hast here presented to thee, some fragments of this Author, That his Testimony may not be lost, but may remain upon Record against the backslidings of this age.' (p. ix.)

Sadly, *The Testimony* seems to have been effectively lost for the next three centuries. His reputation was permanently blighted by the anonymous author who in 1685 wrote that 'Mr Erbury… was taken ill of his Whimsies… Mr. Erbury's Disease lay in his Head, not in his Heart.' This was taken up like a mantra. He 'laboured under a sore affliction,' (Benjamin Brook in 1813) and 'Here and there we find in it [*The Testimony*] flashes of wit, and some of the most correct, sublime, and telling ideas, but interspersed with such a mass of religious nonsense, as none but a mentally deranged man would have penned' (Thomas Rees in 1883). Even Geoffrey Nuttall, the foremost scholar of puritanism, referring to the anonymous tract, concluded that 'in my own judgement a perusal of Erbury's writings unfortunately confirms these statements' (1957). This is where the reputation of William Erbery lay until the beginning of a rehabilitation process which began with my unpublished thesis, 'The Life and Work of William Erbery' (1968) and particularly and popularly with the later work of Christopher Hill – especially *The World Turned Upside Down* (1972), *The Experience of Defeat, Milton and Some Contemporaries*

(1984) and *The English Bible and the Seventeenth-Century Revolution* (1993).

When I first studied Erbery, the physical process involved reserving the copy of *The Testimony* in the Bodleian Library, and using paper and pen to copy extracts each day. It was a time-consuming, arduous process which demanded sitting in a static position for many hours, a sharp eye and a firm pen. Because there were relatively few copies of *The Testimony* in existence, the work was open only to those who had the opportunities and time to almost live in one of the few libraries where there was a copy of the book.

Recently all has changed. All of Erbery's works can be read online through the website of Early English Books Online. They can be downloaded and read at leisure. It is now possible to compare the original publications with Webster's *The Testimony*. In 2009, Kessinger Publishing reprinted *The Testimony* in its collection of rare reprints. For the first time, the writings of Erbery are accessible to the world. He can speak for himself for the first time since 1654 – even *The Testimony* did not contain all his works.

I have had the privilege of spending time with Erbery on two lengthy occasions. I was first introduced to William Erbery by Dr Pennar Davies in 1963 and five years later successfully submitted a thesis at Oxford, under the supervision of Dr Stanley Greenslade. Forty years later and now in retirement, I have had the renewed privilege of returning to Erbery. I have read him with *new* older eyes. When I first studied Erbery, I was eager to rehabilitate this maligned thinker. He was not mad! He was not a heretic! He was as sane, and as orthodox as you and me! This was the unconscious agenda of a young research student anxious that his thesis would be approved.

Now as I read him a second time, my agenda is very different. My sole purpose is to give Erbery the opportunity to speak for himself. I am now confident that he was a true radical and 'an intellectual and moral giant' (Pennar Davies). He needs no-one to defend him. He only needs the opportunity to share his views.

This has been my motive in producing *The Honest Heretique,* the title Erbery gave to his own defence in 1653 against the charge of heresy and blasphemy

What have I learned from my being alongside William Erbery? I am no longer the young student seeking Erbery's rehabilitation. As I look back on my lifetime of ministry, I am awed by his bold attempt to express his developing, radical experience of God, his determination to fulfil God's justice, his demand for liberty of conscience, and his confidence in the destiny of humankind.

TRUST YOUR EXPERIENCE OF THE LIVING CHRIST

Erbery's education at Oxford and Cambridge and his entry into the ministry of the Church of England was challenged by his introduction to the Puritan movement. We cannot be certain when that happened, but certainly by the time he became vicar of St Mary's in Cardiff in 1633, he was a doughty opponent of the Laudian attempts to bring the Church back to its Catholic roots. He formed conventicles in Cardiff; he spoke against the *Book of Sports*; he was tried before the Court of High Commission; he was forced to resign from the ministry of the Church of England.

However, he remained resolute in his Puritan, Calvinist heritage and expressed this with clarity and passion in *The Great Mystery of Godliness* of 1639 and 1640. Although his theology remained constant, his ecclesiology was being transformed, in that he now approved of the congregational way and founded the first Independent cause in Cardiff in 1640 – only a year after the formation of Llanfaches (the first such cause in Wales). By the early 1640s, when he was nearly 40 years of age, Erbery was at ease with a Calvinist-based theology and an Independent ecclesiology. This stance would have served him well throughout a decade which saw the Independents replace the Presbyterians as the leaders of the rebellion against King and episcopacy.

The Oxford debates of 1646 and 1647 reveal that Erbery had changed radically during the seven years since *The Great Mystery of Godliness.* The changes in Erbery's external circumstances had, of course, been dramatic. Forced to resign his living, he initiated the Congregational cause in Cardiff. At the outbreak of the Civil War, he was 'the first plundered minister in Wales' and lost his home. Forced to flee to Windsor, he was aided by Christopher Love to become an Army chaplain and, as such, he participated in radical movements in the parliamentary Army, in London congregations and with groups of searchers throughout the country. These formative factors resulted in the new theology he expressed at the Oxford Disputations. By this time the foundation of Erbery's faith and theology had been firmly laid and they served as the springboard for his further explorations during the following eight years of his life.

What had persuaded Erbery to change his views? What was at the heart of this converting experience? Why had it come about? In what way did he express this new experience? He discovered two central, radical convictions. He had come to experience the immanence and the imminence of God.

THE IMMANENCE OF GOD

The war had given Erbery a new experience of God and humankind. He no longer had any truck with a theological system which centred on a deity with power but without grace.

As an Anglican he had accepted that 'Predestination to Life is the everlasting purpose of God, whereby (before the foundations of the world were laid) he hath constantly decreed by his counsel secret to us, to deliver from curse and damnation those whom he hath chosen in Christ out of mankind, and to bring them by Christ to everlasting salvation, as vessels made to honour.' (*Articles of Religion,* Article XVII)

As an orthodox Calvinist he concurred with: 'Those of mankind that are predestinated unto life, God, before the foundation of the world was laid, according to His eternal and immutable purpose, and the secret counsel and good pleasure of His will, hath chosen, in Christ, unto everlasting glory... The rest of mankind God was pleased, according to the unsearchable counsel of His own will... to ordain them to dishonour and wrath for their sin, to the praise of His glorious justice.' (*Westminster Confession* Chapter III, articles V and VII)

He had himself written 'O how miserable and wretched is that man or woman that lives and dies (as many doe, Mat 7.13) in this corrupt and cursed condition without Christ!' (*The Great Mystery of Godliness*) Did his ministry as chaplain during brutal warfare convince him of the blasphemy of dividing humankind eternally into election either for salvation or damnation? What divine power would operate like this? Erbery's experience of the war convinced him those beliefs were religious nonsense.

Erbery's view of God was now founded on a love and power expressed in the death and resurrection of Christ, and on the gift of the Pentecostal Spirit of fire and power. God who was in Christ was also in the saints, in full measure but not in the same manifestation. 'Christ in you' and 'the glory I have given them' were Pauline and Johannine convictions inspiring Erbery's exploration of 'divinity within humanity'.

> That the fulnesse of the Godhead dwels in the Saints, as in the Son, in the same measure, though not in the same manifestation, he being in this last sense anointed above his fellows, and God manifest in the flesh: But seeing we are his Brethren, we have the same Divine nature, our Fathers nature as full in us as he: and we being his body and fulnesse also, though the oyl first appear poured forth on the Head, yet it runneth down to his hem, all his Members are annointed with him. (*Nor Truth, nor Errour*)

This living, loving God could not be enchained in rigid scholastic formulae or in repetitive, dreary liturgical patterns. Erbery made no compromise with contemporary stereotypes or with his own past! His service as an Army chaplain gave him a new experience of the living 'Christ in you, the hope of glory'. This personal sense of the presence of God convinced him that the being of God in Christ was also discovered within the saints and the whole of humankind. The divine essence existed within God's people and the whole of creation. The universe exists because of its divine origin, it participates in the divine nature, is being shaped by divine power and is to be fulfilled 'when God himself shall dwell gloriously in the midst of his people'.

The Gospel mystery of 'Christ in you' had remained hidden since the Apostasy and would be fully manifested at the fulfilment of the ages. Erbery, like most of his contemporaries, was convinced that the Day of the Lord was close at hand. This was clear from the evidence of these 'speaking times'.

THE IMMINENCE OF GOD

Erbery's personal experience of 'the inwardness of God' was coupled with his conviction that the nations were 'providentially guided towards the fulfilment of God's purposes'. The revolutionary political period of the Civil War was a precursor of the imminence of the Kingdom. Erbery reflected the millenarian vision of most of his fellow Puritans. Most of the twice-monthly sermons preached before parliament in the 1640s encouraged the Members that they were God's agents in bringing in the Final Kingdom. The earlier part of that decade was dominated by Presbyterian ministers and the latter half by Independents. They shared a common conviction that they were God's elect hastening the last and glorious Day. Contemporary events reinforced their Biblical interpretation. It was only when the enthusiasm of the main-line Puritan waned that there was room for the Fifth Monarchist party to recapture the vision.[1] These were halcyon days. England (or Scotland or Wales, or Britain) served as the ensign of God's final great act of providence. During the revolutionary decade following 1640, Puritans tried to clarify their certainty that everyday events were being shaped by the expected last Day. These were the final battles of Christ in which the saints exercised a specific and critical role.

Erbery understood history as shaped into Three Ages or

Dispensations. It is possible that Erbery was influenced by the thinking of the twelfth-century Joachim of Fiore, current during seventeenth-century puritanism.[2] For Erbery, the three ages were (1) Law and Forms, expressed in the Old Testament; (2) Gospel and the Apostolic Church of the New Testament; (3) Spirit when the New Jerusalem would be established. Between the Second and Third Dispensations came the long period of Apostasy which had begun 'when Kingdoms came to be Christian, then Kingdoms began to be Churches; yea Churches came to be Kingdoms, and National Churches began'. This had begun in the second century, was continuing until the present, and was now reaching its completion. Then would follow 'the acceptable year of the Lord, the day of Christ, the new heaven and new earth, when the saints begin to reign.'

Because Erbery rejected a physical interpretation of the second coming of Christ, it is more difficult to visualise his picture of the end time. It will be when the destiny of humankind is fulfilled, when there is the revelation of the unity of person with person, for 'all the people of God shall become one Land, one Continent, wherein the Lord alone shall live.' It will be when saints are recognized as united with God:

> ...for 'tis the glorious liberty of the children of God, the manifestation of the sons of God, the appearing of the great God in us, when we shall be like him, see him as he is, know him as we are known, see him eye to eye; as he sees us, we shall see him, see his Face, and his Name on our foreheads; that is, we shall not only see God, but men shall see God in us; for all that see us shall acknowledge that we are the seed which the Lord hath blessed: the blessed seed is Christ the Son of God, so all the Saints shall be in the glory of the Father, when the Son shall be subject, and God be All in all. (Letter to Morgan Llwyd in *A Call to the Churches*.)

It will be when the saints, humankind and the whole of creation will reflect their oneness in divine power, justice and grace. In the culmination of the purposes of the Trinitarian God, no one and no thing is left out. At the heart of Erbery's theology is a confidence in the fulfilment of God's purposes for the whole of creation. It is a breathtaking vision of universalism:

> ...when thy light shall be the Lord God in thee, then God, thy Sun, shall not go down; and God, thy Moon, shall not be with-drawn: yea, God shall appear not onely thy light, but the light of the World, the light of every Man, and the light of every Creature: thou shalt then clearly see the invisible things of God, even the Eternal Power and Godhead in the whole Creation, and no more Sun or Moon shining in the Heaven, but God himself shining in both, and his glory filling the Earth also, and every thing in Heaven and Earth, as the appearance of God. (*The Great Earthquake*)

During the final days of the Apostasy, the saints were called to exercise a service of faithfulness and suffering throughout this period of persecution. Erbery drew a golden line of martyrs from the reign of Mary to those who, like himself, were now tarred with the brush of being 'Sectaries, Hereticks, and Blasphemers'. The saints were the forerunners of the Final Age.

> In Queen Maries daies, the Saints suffered as Protestants; in Queen Elizabeths, as Professors; in King James's, as Puritans: in King Charles's, as Separatists; in our days, as Sectaries, Hereticks, and Blasphemers: But the Lord will give us a new name shortly himself... (*Nor Truth, nor Errour*)

The dominating themes of the *immanent* and *imminent* Christ resulted in Erbery's breaking loose from the shackles of contemporary orthodoxy. Erbery's personal experience of the 'inwardness of God' was coupled with his conviction that God was 'providentially guiding the nation towards the Third Dispensation'.

A THEOLOGICAL REVOLUTION

Erbery's new and radical experience of God which emerged during the Civil War demanded a similar revolution in his theology. The old wineskins could not hold the new wine. How could he communicate this experience of the immanent and imminent God? God was a living, loving presence. Like other radical Puritans, particularly Army chaplains like William Sedgwick, Peter Sterry and Joshua Sprigge,[3] Erbery explored the sense of the reality of the Spirit, in opposition to the calcified form in which the church had become fixed. Puritan thinking and practice had often trapped itself within scriptural legalism, theological inflexibility, ecclesiological formalism and ethical Pharisaism.

Many Puritans stressed the letter of Scripture. It could be interpreted only by professional expositors. Radicals, like Erbery longed for Scripture to be freed from the shackles of legalistic literalism. Erbery used all the tools of contemporary Biblical scholarship, but insisted that Scripture became alive only with a meeting of human spirit and divine Spirit.

Erbery approached traditional theological positions from this existential position. For example, he emphasized the unity of the purposes of God:

> … yet in truth God is unchangeable in his Essence, not being (as men conceive) first in love, then in wrath, then in love again, first pleased, then offended, then reconciled; but as the Attonement was not made to God, but received by men, in the Ministry of the Gospel; so it was manifested then that God was not to be reconciled to men, but men to be reconciled to God… wrath is not of Gods part, but of Mans… (*The Honest Heretique*)

He opposed the traditional satisfaction theory of the Atonement: 'his death was the manifestation of Gods love, and the love of God brought forth Christ to live, and to die for us… as Gods wrath to be pacified is not written in Scripture, so God is not to be reconciled to Man, but Man to God'. (*The Honest Heretique*)

In his determination to emphasize the eternal graciousness of the living God, Erbery emphasizes the unity of God in order to avoid the perils of believing in tritheism.

> Thus the Scripture (speaking of God, and Christ, and the Spirit) must be spiritually understood; not in a carnal sense, as three distinct persons, but as a threefold discovery, or making forth of that one God to Man. God in himself, of whom are all things, is the Father: the same God and Father manifest in flesh, is the Son; that mighty God powerfully acting and exerting himself in flesh, is the Spirit... (*The North Star*)

Because of his insistence that God was unwavering in his eternal purposes of bringing the whole of creation to fulfilment, Erbery rejected a traditional doctrine that Christ's death fulfilled the justice of God. How could a cruel Father demand such a sacrifice from a loving Son? Erbery's experience of God convinced him that the divine Spirit is eternally creative, reconciling in the Son Christ and fulfilling through the saints, humankind and the whole of creation.

Christian confidence lay at the heart of Erbery's remarkable demand for the broadest expression of a liberty of conscience 'for unbelieving Jews... for misbelieving Christians, who to their utmost knowledge love the Truth and Peace... the Turks do (in their righteous ways) worship the Son in the Father, though not naming Christ as Christians do... the Apostles were in love... with men of all Religions... why may not honest Papists have the like liberty of Conscience.' (*The Honest Heretique*)

Therefore it is no surprise that Erbery was accused of heresy by the Anglican Ralph Farmer, the Baptist Edmund Chillenden, the Independent Henry Nichols and the Presbyterians Francis Cheynel and Thomas Edwards. While all differed violently over issues of church government, they shared a similar theological stance.

AN ECCLESIOLOGICAL REVOLUTION

Because Erbery believed the seventeenth century was experiencing the death throes of the age of the Apostasy, the ministry, ordinances and government of all formal Churches were no longer valid.

Although Erbery had been ordained into the Church of England, the Civil War saw him move dramatically from his Anglican and Puritan positions. Even before the outbreak of war, he had formed the first Congregational cause in Cardiff, according to the 'New England Way'. That was only the first stage in his pilgrim's progress. He courageously rejected the payment of tithes for the sustaining of ministry (including his own ministry) and saw himself as one of the scattered saints, a seeker, and one who should wait in peace and patience. He sympathizes with New lights, Notionists, and with 'John's Spirit in the North of England, and the Spirit of Jesus rising in North-wales'. 'What is the meaning of those honest men and women in the North, that so many of them are taken with that power, that they can do nothing else but quake and tremble?' (*The Children of the West*)

Erbery directed his writings towards the churches of his day, and wrote knowledgeably and forcefully about the history and practice of Papists, Prelates, Presbyterians, Independents and Baptists. He dismissed their differing forms of government, ministries, sacraments and prayers. Having rejected all their stances, he reached the enigmatic position of 'My religion is, to be of no religion, with man; that is, to have fellowship with none, and yet to have fellowship with all in God.' His personal position was one of 'retiring into the inner world, waiting in silence, seeking the truth, walking in light and being a wayfaring man.' That his wife and children became members of the Society of Friends, and were associated with James Naylor, suggests the way they thought Erbery's ideas were moving. Whether Erbery would have become a Quaker must remain a matter of conjecture, but he certainly shared much of their theology and ecclesiology.

A POLITICAL AND SOCIAL REVOLUTION

During this period of social and political revolution, Erbery served as a chaplain first under the Earl of Essex, and later under General Fairfax. He was present at the Whitehall debates in January 1649, the very month when the King was executed. He wrote a great deal about contemporary history and described the rule of monarchy, aristocracy in parliament and democracy in the Army. He referred to cavaliers and roundheads. However he was not convinced that constitutional change would necessarily meet the underlying needs of the governed. 'The reign of men, whether Monarchy, Aristocracy, or Democracy, or whatever else, hath been for the destruction of men.'

What was the function of government? It was 'to breake in pieces the oppressor, to ease the oppressed of their burdens, to release the prisoners of their bondes, and to relieve poore familys with bread.' Erbery put this New Testament text into practice in his daily life. One of the reasons for his rejection of payment by tithes was 'the oppression of Tithes came to my ears, and the cry of the oppressed filled my heart, telling me, That I and my children fed on their flesh, that we drunk their blood, and lived softly on their hard labour and sweat.' The poor should be supported by the government taxing the rich, and providing a 'treasury for the poor'. In the words of Sir Charles Firth, 'Erbury, to use a modern phrase, demanded social reforms, and refused to be satisfied with improvements in the machinery of government.'[4]

Despite Erbery's agnosticism towards constitutional forms of government, he remained convinced that God was appearing in the present powers. The saints already 'begin to reign'. There will be 'no new forms of religion, but a power of righteousnesse is expected newly to arise in the Nation'. Just as religion would be replaced by righteousness, ministers would be succeeded by magistrates. After the collapse of the Nominated Parliament in November 1653, he wrote to the disillusioned Fifth Monarchists, Christopher Feake, Vavasor Powell and John Rogers, that 'so 'tis like the Lord will blesse the present Government, because 'tis now as 'twas never before… our Nobles begin to be of our selves, and our Prince or Governour to proceed from the midst of us.' What proved to be almost his final words were written in *The Man of Peace* in February 1654, 'surely he is stark blind who hath not seen God already, rising in the Nation, in Parliament and Army before; and I hope higher hereafter in the present Powers.'

FINAL THOUGHTS

Erbery's ecclesiological and theological movement led him from a Puritan and Anglican position to a spiritualist and secular emphasis. He was a radical thinker in revolutionary times. He was one of a group who were thinking out their position *de novo* during a civil war. They did not retreat to university desks or monastic cells. They knew the heat of battle and the intrigue of political life.

Erbery is typical of a movement within puritanism from Calvinist orthodoxy to a theology of immediacy. He was dissatisfied with much of contemporary theology and ecclesiology, and his radical experience of God drove him to explore in new directions. Was Erbery a precursor of movements that flourished later in the history of the Church? His emphasis upon the living Spirit and upon a Christ whose return was imminent foreshadows Pentecostalism. By insisting upon religious experience, he parallels the growth of Pietism in Germany and in its descendant, English Methodism. His sense of divine immanence shares much with late seventeenth-century Platonism. His Biblical criticism served as a springboard for Rationalism. He shared much with the emerging Quaker movement, especially in the revolt against the formalism of the contemporary church.

Does the thinking of Erbery have relevance for our own age? Both the seventeenth, and the late twentieth and early twenty-first centuries are periods of flux and many of Erbery's ideas find their parallel today. Although Erbery was severely critical of unbending formalism in the spheres of theology, liturgy, ethics and church government, he never abandoned the Christian faith. He explored new ways of expressing the 'good news' in his combination of the immanent and the imminent God. He was unwavering in his demand for toleration and justice.

Erbery's theological radicalism was the result of his attempt to reinterpret his experience of God in Christ. To him, the orthodox rigorously defined and straightjacketed a severe God who had no relationship with the Word made flesh in Jesus Christ. Erbery's points of reference were consistent: an immediate, personal experience of Christ in you, and an assurance that the events of contemporary history were a foretaste of the arrival of the Last Times, the Third Dispensation.

Erbery feared that this living God was being stifled by contemporary ecclesiology and orthodox theology. Any call to a futile repetition of a theology centred on infallible Scripture, or upon a vain restoration of a New Testament pattern of church life would be a call to retreat from the challenges and opportunities of the present age. Allow God who had spoken in Christ to make himself known through the saints.

His continuing search to present and live his faith resulted in many accusations of heresy and blasphemy. Although he lived with these attacks all his life, it was not until early 1653 that he was formally charged with heresy and appeared before the Committee for Plundered Ministers in London. After his defence and acquittal, his enemies seemed to have adopted a fresh tactic. They attempted to undermine his credibility by slandering him as insane. It would seem that Erbery may have successfully defended himself against heresy, but was defenceless against the posthumous stigma of his 'being ill of his Whimsies'.

Was Erbery not of the same calibre, mentally or spiritually as the other Welsh Puritans? Or was he an intellectual and moral giant? At least now, Erbery can speak for himself and the reader can make a decision.

PART TWO

THE WRITINGS OF WILLIAM ERBERY

1

The Great Mystery of Godlinesse 1639 and 1640

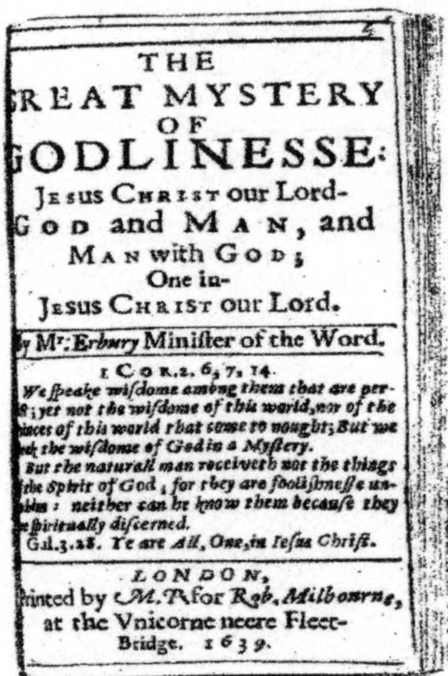

THE GREAT MYSTERY OF GODLINESSE: JESUS CHRIST our Lord-GOD and MAN, and MAN with GOD; One in- JESUS CHRIST our Lord.

By Mr. Erbury Minister of the Word.

1 Cor.2.6,7,14.

We speake wisdome among them that are perfect; yet not the wisdome of this world, nor of the Princes of this world that come to nought; But we speak the wisdome of God in a Mystery.

But the naturall man receiveth not the things of the Spirit of God; for they are foolishnesse unto him: neither can he know them because they are spiritually discerned.

Gal.3.28. *Ye are All, One, in Iesus Christ.*

LONDON, Printed by M.P. for Rob. Milbourne, at the Vnicorne neere Fleet-Bridge. 1639.

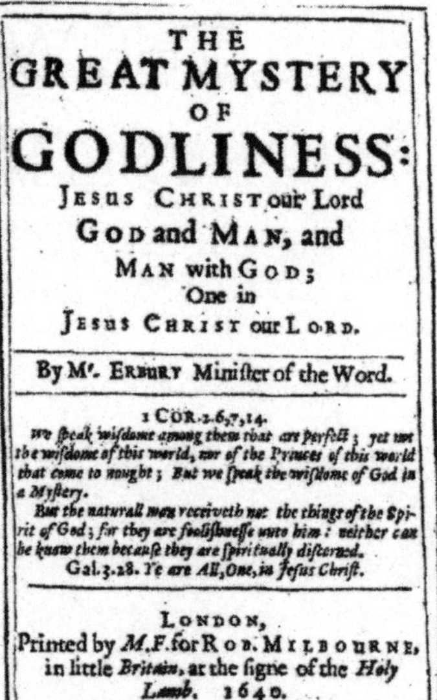

THE GREAT MYSTERY OF GODLINESS: JESUS CHRIST our Lord GOD and MAN, and MAN with GOD; One in JESUS CHRIST our LORD.

By Mr. ERBURY Minister of the Word.

1 COR.2.6,7,14.

We speak wisdome among them that are perfect; yet not the wisdome of this world, nor of the Princes of this world that come to nought; But we speak the wisdome of God in a Mystery.

But the naturall man receiveth not the things of the Spirit of God; for they are foolishnesse unto him: neither can he know them because they are spiritually discerned.

Gal.3.28. *Ye are All, One, in Jesus Christ.*

LONDON, Printed by M.F. for ROB. MILBOURNE, in little *Britain*, at the signe of the *Holy Lamb.* 1640.

THE GREAT MYSTERY OF GODLINESSE:
JESUS CHRIST our Lord-GOD and MAN,
and MAN with GOD;
One in – JESUS CHRIST our Lord.
By Mr. Erbury Minister of the Word.
LONDON, Printed by M.P. for Rob. Milbourne,
at the Unicorne neere Fleet-Bridge. 1639.

THE GREAT MYSTERY OF GODLINESS:
JESUS CHRIST our Lord
GOD and MAN, and
MAN with GOD;
One in JESUS CHRIST our LORD.
By Mr. ERBURY Minister of the Word.
LONDON, Printed by M.P. for ROB. MILBOURNE,
in little Britain, at the signe of the Holy Lamb. 1640.

ERBERY SERVED AS curate at St Woolos at Newport from 1630 to 1633, when he became vicar of St Mary's in Cardiff. Instituted on the 7th August, 1633, he immediately expressed his Puritan convictions. *The Declaration of Sports* was issued on October 18th, 1633 and all clergy were instructed to read the King's commands in Sunday worship. One of the aims of the Act was to root out 'Puritans and precise people' who would object to the playing of games and sports on the Sabbath. Erbery refused to announce the King's injunction, and as a result he was summoned to appear before William Murray, Bishop of Llandaff and subsequently before the Court of High Commission at Lambeth. After a long process, he resigned his living in 1638.

At the same time he was holding conventicles (meetings of the faithful, those of a similar Puritan view) in Cardiff and as such was laying the foundation for an Independent cause which he began within two years of his resignation from the ministry of the Church of England. Evidence of his views and of his methods of teaching while in Cardiff came to light as a result of an extraordinary piece of good fortune.

In October 1963, I submitted the title of my research, 'The Life and Work of William Erbery, 1604–1654' for the Oxford degree of B.Litt. During the following year, books were being re-bound in Queen's College Library in Oxford. Originally the books had been bound with redundant letters, and one mentioning the name of Erbery caught the eagle-eye of Mr Paul Morgan of the Bodleian Library. When he checked the list of potential Oxford theses, he contacted my supervisor, Dr Stanley Greenslade of Christchurch. The consequence was the discovery of critical evidence suggesting the popularity of Erbery in Cardiff.

Dated August 1637, the letter was from Francis Harvey of Bristol to Webb, the Oxford bookseller and refers to the possible printing of a book by William Erbery. Harvey claims, 'I doe thinke that I shall sell 600 in his own towne of card/iff... If the book cannot be printed unless his name bee too it his name is william erberie.' It almost certainly refers to *The Great Mystery of Godlinesse* which was published in London in 1639, with a reprint in 1640. Probably the book could not be published earlier because Erbery's case was still continuing at the Court of High Commission. There is an entry for 24 January, 1638/9 in the Stationers' Register:

> Master Milbourne Entred for his Copie under the handes of Master Wykes and Master Mead warden a book called "The Misticall union of Christ and his Church" by Master Earbury.

This is the subtitle for *The Great Mystery of Godlinesse.*

It is a particularly significant tract. Carefully structured and well written, this 40-page treatise takes the form of a carefully prepared catechism. Erbery teaches a traditional Puritan approach to the Christian life. It reflects orthodox Calvinism and emphasizes the place of the Word and Sacraments. The tract would have been completely acceptable to his one-time curate at Cardiff, Walter Cradock, who was now developing his views as a leading Independent and was associated with the founding of Llanfaches in 1639. It would speak the same theological language as that of Christopher Love, converted under Erbery's ministry and soon to become a leading Presbyterian.

The treatise is of particular significance when compared with the radical changes which are expressed in Erbery's second work, published in 1647.

THIS CORRUPT AND CURSED CONDITION WITHOUT CHRIST!

O how miserable and wretched is that man or woman that lives and dies (as many doe, Mat. 7.13.) in this corrupt and cursed condition without Christ!... Hee hath for my sin in my stead suffered the whole wrath of the Lord, the curse of the Law which I could never suffer, Isa. 53.4, 5.2; Cor. 5.21; Gal. 3.13; I Pet. 2.24 (p.6ff.)

I AM OF HIS BODY, OF HIS FLESH, AND OF HIS BONES, NAY, BY FAITH I EATE HIS FLESH AND DRINK HIS BLOOD.

Q. What union then is this that is betweene Christ and you?

4 Mysticall, thus Christ and his Church are one by a nearer union then all the three; for Christ is not onely, first, partaker of flesh and blood with us, Heb. 2.14. Secondly, We are his friends, John 15.14. Thirdly, he is our husband also, Isay 54.5. Fourthly, But also he is our head, and we are members of his body, of his flesh, and of his bone; and this union is called Mysticall, because it is more then any, unconceivable in thought, and unutterable by tongue; kinsmen, friends, and married ones must die, and then their union ends. But Christ hath so taken my flesh as never to be divided from it; such a friend as not life nor death can divide me from him, whose love passeth all knowledge and time, loving me unto the end, and after all; and not onely beloved, but I am betrothed and married to him for ever, and not onely betrothed, but I am of his body, of his flesh, and of his bones, nay, by faith I eate his flesh and drink his blood, what nearer union can be? (p.10ff.)

HE HATH SATISFIED GODS JUSTICE IN SUFFERING IN MY STEAD

He hath satisfied Gods justice in suffering in my stead, being made a curse for me, and in his own self bearing my sins in his own body upon the tree… I see my self shut out of Paradise, I have no hope of heaven in my selfe, a dead dog, a damned creature, an heir of hell; but God which is rich in mercy, for his great love wherewith hee hath loved me when I was dead in sin, hath quickned me together with Christ, and raised mee up with him, and made me sit together in heavenly places with Christ Jesus. So then in Christ I rose, and in Christ now I raign in heaven being now on earth, (i.e.) I see by faith my own nature in Christ sitting at the right hand of God, who is my good and great high Priest. (pp.16–17)

WHAT MUST YOU DOE... TO CONTINUE YOUR COMMUNION WITH GOD?

Q. VVhat must you doe on your part to continue your communion with God the Father in Christ Jesus by the Spirit?

A. 1. Generally.

1 Fly for my life every sin open or secret...

2 Follow after holinesse, and in all holy occasions, company and courses, commanded by God and commended by good men, continue and increase in all goodnesse & all good duties, cleansing my selfe continually from all filthinesse of flesh and spirit, perfecting holinesse in his feare, 2 Cor. 7.1.

2 Particularly.

1 I give all diligence alwayes to make my calling and election sure...

2 Walke humbly with my God hourely...

3 Renew my repentance daily...

4 I humble my selfe weekly in fasting...

5 Remember to covenant monthly with my Lord in the Sacrament of the Body and Bloud of Christ Jesus, or as oft as it is administred, 1 Cor. 11.26.

6 Once in the yeare cast up all my accounts, see how my Communion is increased, and my corruptions lessened, and how far I am gone and grown in grace, and in the knowledge of Christ...

7 The Christian Sabbaths and Saints must be my delight...

8 The Word of God must abide & dwell in me richly...

9 Take heed of omitting any occasion of doing good...

10 Beware of carelesse and customary performance of any holy duty, but do it in love of Communion with my God...

11 Weane my selfe from the world...

12 Watch my heart with all diligence...

13. Worke out my salvation with feare and trembling, striving harder, running faster, and pressing on to the prize of the high calling of God in Christ Jesus, Phil. 2.12 and 3.14.

14. Observe still my present estate, the tempter of my soule, my spiritual decayes, deadnesse...

15 Goe forward in good duties, fruitfull in good works...

16 Stir up my faith continually, seek to the Lord…

17 In my nearest approaches, and dearest imbraces by him, I am not too bold…

18 Feare the Lord my God all my dayes… a feare not to drive me from God, but to draw mee to him…

19 Continue constant in prayer, watching thereunto with all perseverance, present my selfe oft before the Lord upon my knees, in my Closet, or some corner, if it bee but a word or two, 'twill increase my acquaintance and my communion with him; have my heart ever upward, heavenly and humble, sending up sometimes strong groanes, sudden sighs, short ejaculations, petitions or prayses in the midst of worldly affairs, callings and company, &c. when they think not of it, steale a secret thought to the throne of grace, and my Father which seeth in secret, &c. Luk. 18.1; Eph. 6.18; Col. 4.2; 1 Pet. 4.7; Neh. 2. 4. (pp.21–27)

BY THE SOUND OF A TRUMP, AT THE SECOND COMMING OF CHRIST

God with us: In calling us all up by the sound of a Trump, at the second comming of Christ, changing our bodies and carrying us up both body and soule to meet the Lord Jesus in the aire, where and when the whole Church militant and triumphant, the family in heaven and earth, both Jew and Gentile, and all the Israel of God shall meet at once, and so wee shall ever bee with the Lord. (p.36)

THE WICKED SHALL BE TURNED INTO HELL

The wicked shall be turned into hell, and all the nations that forget God, upon the sinners, he will raine snares, fire, and brimstone, storme and tempest; this shall bee their portion for ever, Psal. 9.17 and 11.6…

Hee that yeelds any one of his members to Sinne, is no member of Christ Jesus, but a limbe of the Devill, of the mystery of iniquity, and has no part in the Mysticall union of Christ and his Church, Rom. 6.13, 14. (pp.40–43)

2

PETITIONS TO THE HOUSE OF COMMONS 1640

ERBERY'S FIRST PUBLISHED work, *The Great Mystery of Godlinesse*, was printed in 1639 and reprinted in 1640. By the time of the second printing, the nation was on the cusp of great change. After many years of personal rule, Charles was obliged to recall parliament. Almost as soon as parliament formally opened in November 1640, petitions for reform were being prepared and delivered from many parts of the country. Among the first petitioners was William Erbery.

Dr Lloyd Bowen discovered in the British Library, three

manuscripts containing two early petitions and a supporting document. His article[1] explores the significance and relationship between the two petitions and the third document. He suggests that the lobbying of parliament was the consequence of a relationship between a small group of Welsh Puritan ministers and larger lay support, reflected by more than 300 signatories of the second petition. The petitions reflect the existence of a group of Puritans cooperating to reform the Church of England.

The three documents are presented in modernised spelling below. The petitions are of particular interest because they reveal Erbery at the forefront of these initiatives. Erbery was certainly the author of the first petition, and it is Dr Bowen's view that he had a hand in drafting the second, 'The petition itself reiterated Erbery's lament about the number of worthy ministers in Wales, once more employing the formula of there being fewer than thirteen preachers in the thirteen [*sic*] shires of Wales, suggesting perhaps that Erbery was again the principal author.'[2]

The First Petition was delivered to the House of Commons in December 1640 and was granted on the 12th January, 1640/1:

> The humble petition of Mr Erbury & the whole Principality of Wales, especiall of Glamorgan shire, Decemb. 1640... This petition was granted... Januar 12th 1640 [1641].

The Second Petition was delivered to the House of Commons on February 16th, 1641:

> To The honourable the Knights & Burgesses of the House of commons assembled in Parliament: The humble petition of many of the subjects in the Principality of Wales, in the names of themselves and many others.

It was presented by seven preachers of the word of God: Wm Wroth,[3] Henry Walter,[4] Wm Erbery, Richard Symonds,[5] Walter Cradock,[6] Ambrose Moston,[7] Robert Hart.[8]

Dr Bowen has also discovered a third document, *The scarcity of preachers in Wales 1640*, which includes material from the First Petition, and from the Second Petition.

Possibly the document was attached to the First Petition which refers to a 'particular declaracon here annexed'. However it could equally have served as supporting material for Petition Two.

The documents reflect a Puritan picture of the state of religion in Wales at the time of the outbreak of the Civil War. The First Petition reminds parliament that there are 13 shires in Wales, 1,000 parishes but only 13 preachers approved by this group of Puritans. Erbery pays special attention to his own county of Glamorgan with its five approved preachers. He states that the blame for this condition lies with 'Lord Bishopps, curats and common praisers', and suggests two solutions: permission for preachers 'to preach in any parish where there is want of preaching', and permission that 'people may have liberty to come to heere where preaching is'. Erbery concludes with the names of five preachers who are 'here present to offere their service for this worke': himself, Walter Cradock, Richard Seamans [Symonds], Ambrose Mostyn, and Henry Walter.

Both the Second Petition of February 1640/1 and the additional document, *The scarcity of preachers in Wales 1640*, present similar statistics to those of Petition 1, but are more detailed in describing the failings of curates and parsons, or vicars. The blame is laid firmly with the bishops: 'The true causes of all these miseries doth arise chiefly from Lord bishops.' Having described the problems, the Petition presented the solution: 'that there may be a freedome without any molestation for any whom the lord hath fitted with gifts and graces, to imploy their paines amongst them: and the whole countrey shal have cause to praise the Lord for you.'

The Petition is presented in the name of seven preachers of the word of God. It includes the five mentioned in the first petition with the addition of William Wroth and Robert Hart. There then follows a list of three hundred subscriptions.

The Petitions reveal that Erbery was at the forefront of the Puritan movement in Wales. He was one of a group associated both with the formation of the first Independent cause at

Llanfaches and probably with the supportive work of laymen like Sir Robert Harley of Brampton Bryan in Herefordshire.[9] These were the men who were at the forefront of the Propagation Act of February 1649 (1650), the attempt initiated by parliament 'for the Better Propagation and preaching of the Gospel in Wales.'[10]

By this time Erbery's life and theology had moved in a very different direction, as expressed in his next tract, *Nor Truth nor Errour* (1646). However, he seems to have remained on good terms with them, as reflected in his letters in *A Call to the Churches* (1652) and *The North Star* (1653).

B.L. HARLEIAN MS. 4931, f. 90. Petition of Erbury to Commons, Dec. 1640.

To the Honourable the House of Commons now assembled in Parliament· The humble petition of Mr Erbury & the whole Principality of Wales, especiall of Glamorgan shire, Decemb. 1640.

Sheweth That in ye whole dominion of Wales, conteining 13 shires, & that in above a 1000 parishes (as farre as by diligent search we could be any meanes find) there are not to be found 13 constant preachers, that preach morning & evening, or expound the catechisme every Lords day in the Welch tongue.

And that in our County of Glamorgan (counted the chiefest for preaching) conteining about an 115 parishes, there are not to be found 5 constant preachers that preach twice, or expound the catchitisme every Lords day in their owne charge, but for the rest they are all either pluralists, non-residents, slothfull, or scandalous psons, preaching somtimes some of them, some never, though taking but charge of many parishes, as may appeare in a particular declaracon here annexed.

So that there is no truth, or mercy, or knowledge in the land, but gross ignorance, idolatry, supstition, and all manner of sins abound every where; the people led by blind guides, & the sheepe having dumb doggs to be their sheepheards; so that the blood of soules, which hath long cried up to heaven, call now aloud to this Honourable House that in your godly wisdome, & zeale to gods glory, & the eternall good of man you wold be pleased timely [?] *to remove the causes of these grave evills, which we conceive to be in truth these three. Lord Bishopps, curats & common praisers, the last being the maintenance of an unlawfull ministry, when every silly reader ordered to by a bp may in a surplice & with a service booke take the cure of soules, & so the people perish & preaching also, if ye B*^p^ *& the Book be but removed then all or blind curats* [?] *will be also dumb in a day, & our reading priests being all silenced at once of themselves (as preachers before have beene by others) the people wold seeke out for a preaching ministry the meanes of their salvacon. To justify whose desires & for a present supply of the greate want of preaching till a seconde reformacon (which we hope & pray for).*

We most humbly pray the most Honourable House, that taking into your grave consideracon the estate of the country, & county aforesaid, you will be pleased to give Order for the redress thereof, And to give liberty to chose who are willing & honest (of which some are here psent to offere their service for this worke) to preach in any parish where there is want of preaching, And that the people may have liberty to come to heere where preaching is; for so many have beene vexatiously molested for going out of their parishes to heere the word of God.

And your petition's shall our humbly pray &c.

This petition was granted, & liberty given to William Erbury, Walter Cradock, Richard Seamans, Ambrose Mostyn, & Henry Walter to preach in Wales where it was wanting.

Januar. 12t1640 [1641]

B.L. Add. MS. 70, 109, no. 69.

***Petition from many in ye Principality of Wales. Also a Petition of South Wales: 1640/1641?* (copy thereof)**

To The honourable the Knights & Burgesses of the House of commons assembled in Parliamt:

The humble petition of many of the subjects in the Principality of Wales, in the names of themselves and many others.

Sheweth that

1. Ffirst if it please you to understand that in the Principalitie of Wales containing Thirteene shires and therin about a thousand parishes, there are not (as farre as uppon diligent search wee can find, or heare of) neither have there beene in our time thirteene constant preachers at one tyme which preach twice, or preach and expound the catechisme every lords day in the Welch tongue in their owne cure and that for the want of vision & teaching of gods word the people perish and the ignorance & superstition & the excesse of all sin is verie lamentable: and this is the more to bee bee wailed because the people are ingenious, devout, & as ready to receive the gospell soundly preached with all alacritie & zeale as any nation (wee have heard off) in Christendome.

2. Secondly that those few are both willing & able in some measure to preach profitably to them, are either suspended, or excommunicated, or exiled, all debarred utterly from the exercise of their ministry though most of them offer to doeit freely.

3. Thirdly, That Those That desire to live honestly in a religious course, are in diverse places excommunicated to the consuminge of their estates, & undoeing of their families: & many driven out of the land, for hearing of sermons out of their parishes, godly meetings, which are only for the good of their soules, and that indeed there is more safety & quietnes by farre for Papists, then earnest & faithfull Protestants.

4. ffourthly as for the ministers in wales those of them who are called curates, they are for the most parte dumbe, drunken fellowes & the very scumme & refuse of the countrey, good for noe trade or occupation, serving cures & some for fiftie shillings a peece, usually for foure pounds or five pounds p. annum, many of them keepe alehouses, may games[11] *& see all disorders: some are common relators,*[12] *some live by a practise of clandestine marriages to the undoing of well estated youth: divers of them runne begging from house to house: others goe like rogues from doore to doore readinge the gospell for bread & cheese, oatmeal & candels, & usually they serve divers parishes, some two, some three, some foure, & some being but very boyes.*

The other sort of ministers, commonly called parsons & vicars, as they are in their lives a great part of them full of deboistness [sic] *drunknes & contention, soe in their ministry they are either unlearned, or unacquainted with gods word: yet verie idle & soe consequentlie unable to preach or els if learned for the most part preach little to the capacity of the people & usuallie in English: & of those very many are pluralities & non-residents which allow some smal stipends to the aforesaid poore & drunken curates, & are for the most part the chiefe leaders & instigators of all trouble &*

persecution against those that live godlie being. some of them surrogates, & all of them men of place & power by reason other of their justice ships, greatnes & multitude of benefices, or speciall relation to the spiritual courts or prelates.

5. The true causes of all these miseries doth arise chiefly from Lord bishops (as wee conceive) their courts, canons, & who by their practises & administration are & have beene the causes & upholders of all those evils, by ordering & upholding all the foresaid unlearned & ungodly preists as they call them, by suppressing all godlines as farre as they bee able by suspensions, excommunications, delivering to the terrible Court of high commission: soe banishing out of the land both ministers & people which sought the welfare of the countrey & the salvation of their owne & other soules: many or most of them being conformable to the canons by severe urgeing of the service booke, soe slighting & labouring thereby to shoulder out all sound & sincere preaching by boulstering & abetting the fore said domineering clergie & upholding them in all their cruelty & persecutions of poore christians and their neighbour godly ministers. By exacting alsoe a more strict observing of their owne ceremonies then of gods ordinances, though they themselves doe account them but indifferent; multiplying their popish canons & articles, soe making voyde the commandements of god: To say nothinge of the wretched conversation of their families & followers, nor yet of their commendams,[13] *altars, pictures, croutching, excessive fees, with all those superstitious & popish abhominations of their cathedrals, choristers, & spiritual courts which above all the rest are growen odious to all the countrey, by their basenes, hypocrisie, tyranny, & lamentable oppression of poore people: together with that miserable compulsion of all sorts from sixteen yeares upwards, bee they never soe prophane & ignorant, to receive the lords supper once a yeare att the least. Wherfre the most humble desire of us whose names are subscribed that after this soe long misery with a great deale more, endured, to the dishonouring of god the undoeing of soules & bodies of our poore countreymen there may att last be found through your clemency & grave consideration, some comfortable redresse for the removal of al the greevances aforesaid, and of like nature: and that there may be a freedome without any molestation for any whom the lord hath fitted with gifts and graces, to imploy their paines amongst them: and the whole countrey shal have cause to praise the Lord for you.*

Seven Wm WrothHenry Walter
preachers of Wm ErberyRichard Symonds
the word of Walter Cradock Ambrose Moston
God Robert Hart

B.L. Add. MS. 70,002, fl. 367. [Endorsed]

The scarcity of preachers in Wales 1640

1. That in the 13 shires of Wales which containe above one thousand parishes, there are not to be found 13 preachers which preach constantly in the Welsh tongue in their owne chardges once every Lords day, and chatechize constantly in the afternoone.

2. That many which have good livings never preach at all and those which doe preach yet preach but seldome, few once a weeke or fortnight, the rest once in three weeks or a moneth or five weekes, and of these many if not halfe are English preachers in Welch chardges yea and of these all very many are pluralists having two or three parishes, very many are non residents.

3. There are many places which have no preaching at all and since the reformation have scarce ever heard any sermons, unlesse it were by some preachers which have collections after sermon.

4. The curates are for the most part illiterate, of very evill & scandalous conversation and many of them doe reade in two or three churches in a forenoone receiving some three pounds, some four, some five pounds for each place 'p. annum.'

Soe that by reason of these things, the people which are naturally devout and ingenuous and as ready to receive Christ duely preached unto them, as any nation in Christendome, yet lye in great ignorance, spirituall death and supersitition.

3

Nor Truth Nor Errour 1647

Nor Truth, nor Errour,
Nor Day, nor Night;
But in the Evening
Thereſhall be Light.
Zech. 14. 6,7.
Being the Relation of a Publike
DISCOURSE
In Maries Church at Oxford,
BETWEEN
Maſter CHEYNEL and Maſter ERBURY,
January 11. 1646.

Printed in the yeer 1647.

Nor Truth, nor Errour,
nor Day, nor Night;
But in the Evening
There shall be Light.
Zech 14. 6, 7.
Being, the Relation of a Publike
DISCOURSE In Maries Church at
OXFORD, BETWEEN Master Cheynel
and Master Erbury, January 11. 1646.
Printed in the yeer 1647.
(Received on August 26, 1647 into the
Thomason Collection)

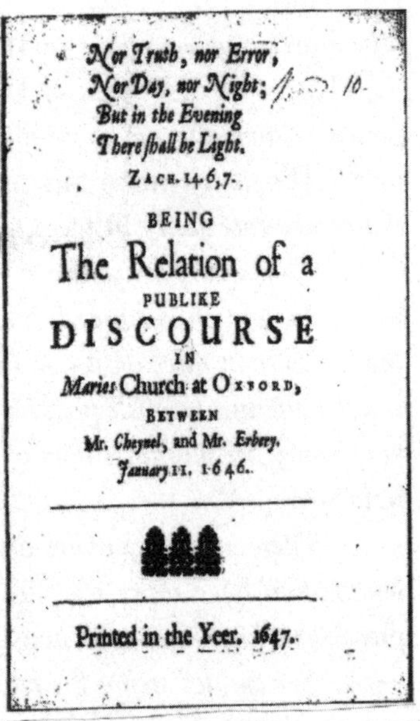

Nor Truth, nor Error,
Nor Day, nor Night;
But in the Evening
There ſhall be Light.
ZACH. 14.6,7.
BEING
The Relation of a
PUBLIKE
DISCOURSE
IN
Maries Church at OXFORD,
BETWEEN
Mr. Cheynel, and Mr. Erbery.
January 11. 1646.

Printed in the Yeer. 1647.

Nor Truth, nor Error,
Nor Day, nor Night;
But in the Evening
There shall be light.
Zach. 14.6, 7.
BEING
The Relation of a
PUBLIKE
DISCOURSE
IN
Maries Church at OXFORD,
BETWEEN
Mr. *Cheynel*, and Mr. *Erbery*.
January 11, 1646.
Printed in the Yeer. 1647

ERBERY'S THEOLOGY CHANGED dramatically during the seven years since *The Great Mystery of Godlinesse*. His life changed equally dramatically. In 1633 he was vicar of St Mary's in Cardiff but because of his opposition to the *Book of Sports*, he appeared before the Bishop of Llandaf, and his case was tried by the Court of High Commission. This was when he wrote his first tract. Forced to resign his living in 1638, he formed in 1640, the first Independent Church in Cardiff. Presumably this Independent Church, based on the New England pattern, and similar to the Llanfaches Church, was made up of parishioners who had belonged to the conventicles Erbery had been encouraging in Cardiff. At the outbreak of the Civil War, he was the first Plundered Minister in Wales and consequently lost his home. An Army chaplain from 1643 onwards, he was associated with radical movements in the parliamentary Army and in the London congregations. These formative factors created the new theology expressed at the Oxford Disputations. By this time, the foundation of Erbery's faith and theology had been firmly laid. This served as the springboard for further explorations during the following eight years of his life.

Erbery played a key role in the Oxford Disputations. He was a prime cause of the growth of sectarianism amongst students and soldiers (a heady mix!) in the city. Oxford had fallen to the parliamentary Army in the summer of 1646, and Erbery was there soon after the city's liberation/capture. His lectures and preaching created such a ferment in the city that parliament sent six Presbyterian ministers to maintain the orthodox line. The visitors reported to parliament that 'they found the University and City much corrupted'. Five separate accounts have survived of the debates between the Presbyterians and Erbery. They make fascinating reading and provide a contemporary picture of a critical struggle between those, like Erbery, who were 'enquiring only, and seeking the Lord our God', and those, like Francis Cheynell, who feared that 'a licentious spreading of damnable doctrines would be disturbing the civill peace and power'.

1. A PUBLIKE CONFERENCE Betwixt the Six Presbyterian Ministers And Some Independent Commanders: *Held at* OXFORD, On Thursday *Novemb. 12.* 1646.

The first report is anonymous. The writer was sympathetic neither to Erbery nor to the Presbyterian visitors. Was he a Royalist revelling in the chaos which he believed was an inevitable consequence of the removal of the King from Oxford? He reports little of the substance, but much of the flavour of the debate.

> 'Twas after three of the clock... the crowd divides, and gives way, as Jordan to the Arke, or rather a cloud to a flash of Lightning, his name ask'd, whisper'd aloud, Yerbery, What is he?
>
> Yerbery, The Champion of the Seekers, the Chaplain Errant, that makes not onely Sermons at all houres, but his Divinity too, like the first Artists, that found out the trade they profess'd. This, was hee ready to oppose, and to hold any thing. (p.2–3)

Supporting Erbery were 'Grimes, a Carpenter, the Deputy-Governour... Hewson, a Shoomaker, and Colonell... Under the Colonell many other Guifted Officers. A Major... A Captaine, and a Captaine.'[1]

The Chairman pro tempere was Wilkinson[2] and opposing Erbery and the Seekers were the Presbyterian Six:[3]

> Reynolds, the Oracle, with the hoarse and obscure voice... Harris, like Aaron and Hur on both sides Moses, to support his hands... Dr. Temple... that brought more Lungs and volubility, not much more Logick then the other. To back these, the other stood behind. Cornish, that help'd to disturbe the Disputation once or twice... Langley, the Mute... Cheynel. Cheynel is now cal'd for; he is much miss'd, no confidence of victory without him, the onely man that could oppose frenzy to frenzy, and outvie their zeale with greater heate, fling about Texts, cast wildly, but in Moode and figure. (p.4)

The substance of the debate according to our reporter was 'Whether the esteemed Ministers of the Church of England had more Authority from Jesus Christ to preach in publike, then ordinary Guifted Christians.' (p.5) The result of the debate was that 'Those that have no Calling, to be lawfull Preachers, and those that have a Calling to be no Preachers at all.' (p.12)

A postscript adds that 'The six Presbyterian Divines have beene much worsted by the Independent Commanders, in a late publike Disputation, who asserted, That they had no Commission from God to be Ministers; in the presence of two or three hundred Schollars, and others, which much blanked those Worthies, who were sent thither to reforme that University, and to resolve all Quaeries, Doubts, and Scruples of Conscience.' (p.13)

2. AN ACCOUNT Given to the PARLIAMENT BY THE *Ministers* sent by them to OXFORD.

In which you have the most remarkable passages which have fallen out in the six Moneths service there, divers Questions concerning the Covenant of Grace, Justification, &c. are briefly stated. Particularly, there is presented two Conferences, in which the Ministers together with the truth, have suffered by reproaches and falshoods in print and otherwise.

The chief points insisted on in those Conferences are,

1. Whether private men might lawfully Preach.

2. Whether the Ministers of the Church of England were Antichristian.

Both which Questions were disputed, objections answered, and the Truth confirmed.

3. And lastly, Divers of M. Erbury's dangerous errours which he broached and maintained, are recited and refuted.

The most complete account of the turbulent events of the winter of discontent, 1646/7 is provided by Francis Cheynell in his official report to parliament. He describes the condition of Oxford when the visitors arrived:

The truth is, they found the University and City much corrupted, and divers hopefull men in both, very much unsettled. (p.3)

The first time that Mr. Earbury was observed to come to our

> meeting, he brought with him a company of Soldiers… he told us that he did not acknowledge that Christ had any Church on earth, and therefore denied Independent Congregations to be Churches, and the Ministers of those (as well as of Presbyteriall) congregations, were by him denied to be true Ministers of Christ, and hath himself renounced the title, though not the pay and salary of a Minister… This Gentleman, we know not how else to stile him, professing that he exercises neither as a gifted man nor Minister… undertook to prove demonstratively, that the Ministers of Independent as well as Presbyterian Congregations are unchristian, and so by consequence Antichristian. (p.13)

Cheynell records that because a debate held on October 21st, 1646 had concluded with such fierce dispute, it was agreed to adjourn and convene at a later date. It proved impossible to convene earlier than three weeks later because of the monthly fast and remembering the fifth of November. At the next meeting, the debate focused on the nature of Christian ministry. The visitors proposed that 'They who were qualified, approved, called, ordained, according to the mind of Christ, are the ministers of Christ.' (p.22)

Erbery opposed this position by claiming that the six visiting ministers, and all ministers of the Church of England were strikers and not authorized ministers.

> But it was said by M. Earbury that we had no Gospel faith because no rivers of living water, nor gifts of the Spirit flowing out of us… It was added by Master Earbury, that the Ministers of the Church of England allow parish Churches, therefore they destroy the communion of Saints… that the Ministers of England did set up societies, viz. Presbyteries, which did destroy the communion of Saints… Master Earbury said also that they did allow of an Ordinance of Parliament for the punishment of errors and heresies, and therefore they did destroy the communion of Saints… they who take other mens goods from them by fraud and circumvention under pretence of giving *them* something for it which was worth nothing, are covetous; but so do all the Ministers of England by receiving Tythes, ergo all are covetous. (p.23f.)

A further public meeting was held on the eleventh of December when Erbery endeavoured to prove the following proposition:

> That the fulnesse of the Godhead, the same fulnesse of the Godhead which is in Christ, dwels bodily in the Saints, in the same measure, though not in the same manifestation as it dwelt in Christ whilest he was here below in the flesh. (p.30)

Cheynell and his colleagues had no doubt that this was 'damnable doctrine... blasphemous errours'. Erbery retorted that 'he did not deliver any thing dogmatically, for he did only enquire into the Truth of things as one that was to seek.' (p.31). After further attempts had been made to engage Erbery in debate, the visitors were at their wits' end and were determined to end Erbery's malign influence over students and soldiers.

> It was as we conceived high time to call Mr. Earbury to an account, after so many fair warnings given him, and so many foul errors preached by him, both to Scholars and Citizens; but because Master Earbury his followers were as confident as he was, that no man was able to disprove or refute him; one of our company undertook that Task, and offered to do it in the publick Schools, the fittest place for Scholars to dispute in, but Master Earbury desired that the meeting might be at the University Church upon Monday the 11 of January at two of the clock in the afternoon, because some of his followers were unwilling to meet at Schools: They met accordingly; Mr Earbury desired leave to explain himself; and began much after this manner: (p.38)

For Cheynell and his colleagues, the heart of the dispute was that dangerous heretics were undermining both the orthodox faith and the government of the state. His accusation is that Erbery said 'that it was not his custome to speak any thing dogmatically, for he did proceed in all his Lectures by way of enquiry'. This makes Erbery:

> ...a meer Sceptique, and the ready way to teach his Auditors to question all things, and hold nothing. But Master Earbury was not ashamed to own this deceit, for he presently added that he spake not as a Minister to them, for he had renounced his Ministry long since in the presence of the Bishops, nor did he speak as a gifted man knowing the mystery of Christ, but as one that was to seeke, and therefore (said he) we are now upon a way of enquiry... I find that Christ is a mystery hidden, not manifested by the Prophets or the Apostles, for the Apostles, saith he, did but see Christ in a glasse darkly; but we, saith he, behold the glory of Christ, shining in the man Christ... and we have Christ in us the hope of glory, and that is indeed The mystery, Coloss. 1.27. (p.39)

Erbery is labelled an anti-Trinitarian, a heretic, a Socinian, a Unitarian:

> Our brother desired them who were acquainted with the Socinian controversies, to observe that M. Earbury had not his revelation from Heaven, but Poland (p.42)... M. Cheynell told him that the interpretation smelt too strong of Poland (p.43)... M. Earbury held correspondence with the Socinians in their hereticall opinions. (p.45)

Finally, Cheynell attacks Erbery as a revolutionary, undermining secular authority and overthrowing the State:

> ...the Magistracy and Ministry of this Kingdome are both aimed at, because godly Ministers preach up the power of Magistrates, and prudent Magistrates countenance pious Ministers who were ordained (by a Colledge of Ministers separated from Rome and Antichrist, by a professed subjection to Jesus Christ) and set apart to preach the Gospel of Christ... it is clear that all well-grounded policy for the affairs of this life is grounded upon Religion; for God, and so godlinesse under God by his ordinance heaps all blessings upon the wisest, and wel-built State, it doth uphold and maintain all Common-weals in an happy order, and makes a Land to become the land of Immanuel; now the Christian religion cannot be upheld without a Christian Ministry... they then that are enemies to the Ministry, are enemies to the welfare of States and Churches. (p.50)

Erbery is tarred with heresy and blasphemy, a sceptic undermining the orthodox religion. He is a revolutionary, dangerous to the well-being of the state. The report was sent to General Fairfax[4] before its official presentation to parliament.

May it please your Excellency,
To take these few lines into your saddest thoughts: We are commanded to give an account to the Parliament of the state of this University, and City. M. Earbury doth publickly deliver divers blasphemous errours in this City… he was publickly refuted in the University Church. Colonel Ingolsby[5] hath been made so sensible of his intolerable insolence, that he hath (as we are assured) casheered him, and yet he continues in the Garrison; we make our addresse to your Excellency before we make any complaint, or give up our account to the Parliament (which must be done within this moneth) that your Excellency and we that are so deeply entrusted, may both give up our account with joy. The rest of our brethren are of our judgement, but are not now present with us. Nay, it is granted by all in our Assembly, that none are to be tolerated, whose errours are contrary to the common principles of Christianity, and we do thankefully remember when we received such noble entertainment at your Quarters, that you did zealously declare your judgement against a licentious spreading of damnable doctrines: We recommend this weighty businesse to your care and you, and your Army to God, as it becommeth
Your Excellencies humble servants,
H. Wilkinson. F. Cheynell. Hen. Langly. H. Cornish. (p.51)

Fairfax's response to Cheynell was written at Northampton on January 30th, 1646/7. He ordered Erbery to leave Oxford.

Gentlemen,
I cannot but acknowledge this as a very good respect to me, and this Army to give me Cognizance of what you apprehend touching M. Erbury… I hope I shall take care to prevent your further trouble in this matter; and therefore have sent to him to appear before me; I should be unwilling to be found one, who should either countenance any member of this Army, disturbing the civill peace

> and power (under whose protection we all are) or maintaining such Errours as impeach a greater power and soverainty, to which all men (who professe themselves Christians) must acknowledge themselves subject... (p.52)

After receiving Fairfax's letter, Cheynell and the other visitors sent this official report to the Houses of Parliament. Cheynell emphasized that the way the Oxford affair was handled should be seen as a precedent.

> And now we hope that the premises may present both advantage of opportunity to both Houses of Parliament to consider seriously of some expedient, for the speedy preventing of the more spreading dangerous errours, and the promoting of our covenanted reformation, as in all parts of the Kingdome, so especially in this University. (p.53)

3. TRUTH TRIUMPHING OVER Errour and Heresie. OR, A Relation of a Publike Disputation at Oxford in S. *Maries* Church, on Munday last, *Jan.* 11.1646. between Master *Cheynell* a Member of the Assembly, and Master *Erbury* the Seeker and Socinian. Wherein the Socinian Tenents maintained by Master *Erbury* are laid down, and Master *Cheynels* clear Confutation of them, to the joy and satisfaction of many hundreds there present, is declared.

The third tract was written on January 14th, 1646/7 by James Cranford,[6] three days after the disputation at St Mary's. Cranford, had no sympathy with Erbery's heresies. 'God hath left the Independents and Sectaries (this man being within these few yeers a famous Independent) and to what a height they advance, both for damnable Errours, and of confidence to maintain openly in one of the Universities, *i*n the most publike place, before many hundreds, such damnable Heresies, (p.4) ... (Erbery's) Revelation was not from heaven, but Poland... and the Socinian Chatechisme.' (p.6).

Cranford records that the dispute had lasted for four hours and, at its conclusion, Cheynell had 'generall approbation: and the truth was readily embraced with shouting and acclamations. Parliament should now proceed effectually against him [Erbery], and make him an example to all other Sectaries, both for his damnable errours, and unparallel'd boldnesse.' (p.7)

4. Thomas Edwards, The third Part of Gangraena, (1646)

It is no surprise that Thomas Edwards,[7] another staunch Presbyterian, received news of the Oxford Disputes and recorded his views in *Gangraena*.

> Some Letters written from Oxford by some of the Assembly to persons of worth in London, mention how M. Erbury (the same who is spoken of in my first part of Gangraena, and in this third Part, pag. 89, 90.) came attended with divers souldiers to a meeting that the Ministers sent downe to Oxford had weekly, for the satisfaction of the scruples of some in these times, and there started that Question, that there was no such Office upon earth now as Ministers, that none were now to be Select Officers, but every man might preach; that is, speak his thoughts (as one Letter expressed it) and propounded it, with divers of the Souldiers backing him, to dispute that point with them: what the carriage of the Sectaries was at the meeting to dispute it, and the issue of the disputation, I cannot speake certainly nor particularly, as having not spoken with any of our Ministers there present, onely I shall desire the Reader to observe this, That this Erbury who now comes on purpose to Oxford for such a disputation, and challenges our Ministers, when as he hath so many armed men to back him and to domineere, never could all the while he was in the Earle of Essexe's Army Chaplaine there, be drawne by the Ministers to any Conference or Dispute about the points he then held and often vented. [Mr. Bifield[8] and divers other Chaplains then in the Earl of Essex his Army are ready to testifie and prove this.] He was often moved to it, desired, but still declined, could never be brought to it, for then he knew he could not have those to backe him in his Dispute, who were Commanders of many men, and had the power of the Sword in their hands. (Part 3, p.250)

5. Nor Truth, nor Errour, nor Day, nor Night; But in the Evening There shall be Light. Zech 14. 6, 7. Being, the Relation of a Publike DISCOURSE In *Maries* Church at *OXFORD,* BETWEEN Master *Cheynel* and Master *Erbury, January* 11. 1646. Printed in the yeer 1647.

(Received by Thomason[9] on August 26. He states the tract was printed in London.)

The final report, published twice in 1647, is Erbery's own account of the Oxford debates. The tract is very different from Cheynell's report to parliament which gave a blow by blow account of the events leading to the disputation at St Mary's. Erbery's treatise feels like a sermon prepared carefully for the occasion. Erbery seems at ease with the audience and knew how to convince them of the rightness of his theological position.

At the outset, he shares his view of Christian Ministry. He has served twice, and resigned twice from ordained ministry. No longer a vicar of the Church of England, nor an Independent minister, he is now speaking as a seeker, an enquirer, a searcher for the truth. Saints are to 'sit still in submission and silence, waiting for the Lord himself to come and reveal himself to them.'

His theological foundation is completely at odds with his stance expressed in *The Great Mystery of Godlinesse* (1639 and 1640). His experience as an Army Chaplain and the views explored with the circle of radicals in the Army and in London changed his experience of God and its consequent theological expression.

The heart of the Gospel is the 'mystery of Christ, in us the hope of glory'. This mystery, revealed to the Early Church had been lost during the Apostasy which had begun in the Second Century and continued to the present day: 'the Knowledge and Worship of Christ was taught by mens Traditions, Forms framed by old Creeds and Councels, new Catechisms and Confessions of Churches (as if the Scriptures and Spirit, were not sufficient to teach men all the knowledge of God and Christ clear enough).'

Erbery's service as an Army Chaplain gave him a new experience of the living Christ. The intensity of Christ's presence assured him of the immanence of Christ in him, the saints and the whole of humankind. Coupled with this experience of the inner Christ, was his assurance that the revolutionary political period of the Civil War was a precursor of the end of the Apostasy and the imminence of the Third or Final Dispensation. The Last Age was at hand.

The dominating themes of the immanent and imminent Christ resulted in Erbery's breaking loose from the shackles of contemporary orthodoxy. God shares his being or essence not only with Christ, but also with all God's people and the whole of creation. The universe participates in the same divine nature, and this participation will be manifested at the Third Dispensation. Erbery's personal experience of the 'inwardness of God coupled with his conviction that God was providentially guiding the nation towards the Third Dispensation', were Erbery's core values.

Erbery was reflecting the millenarian vision of many fellow Puritans. These were halcyon days. England (or Scotland or Wales, or Britain) served as the ensign of God's final great act of providence. During the revolutionary decade following 1640, Puritans tried to clarify their certainty that everyday events were being shaped by the expected Last Day. These were the final battles of Christ in which the saints would fulfil a specific and critical role. The saints had suffered great persecution but had remained faithful. Erbery drew a golden line of martyrs from those who had been persecuted during the reign of Mary to those who, like himself were now tarred with the brush of being 'Sectaries, Hereticks, and Blasphemers'.

THE CHARGE... OF HERESIE AND BLASPHEMY AGAINST ME

Christian friends, and fellow-Souldiers, and worthy Schollars also, I am your servant: I am called this day to come here in publick from my private walkings; not by my desire or seeking, but as sought out and drawn forth by a twofold cord; a publick Charge, and a private Challenge: The Charge was publickly given out in a Pulpit, of Heresie and Blasphemy against me; the Challenge was privately sent unto me, by word, and writing also, in a Letter from Master Cheynel, that I should give him a meeting in the Schools, or some meeting-place in the University. The place appointed is Maries Church, where I now present my self to wait on you all, and to answer what shall be objected, or to desire a satisfactory answer to this my Querie I am questioned for. (p.3)

THE SAINTS SHALL BE ALL SET IN A SEEKING WAY

What ever I spake was not spoken as a Minister by outward Call, though twice I was made one: nor as a gifted man, knowing Christ, though once I was accounted somebody by others, and by my self also; but now I am nothing, know nothing; and let all men know so of me that I can neither see nor speak (as Ministers or gifted men should) with any clearness in my self, or conviction to others: but enquiring only, and seeking the Lord our God, and David our King. This is that condition the Church shall be brought unto, into a Wilderness, where no path nor company shall be to talk with; but being left alone, the Saints shall be all set in a seeking way… (p.3)

CHRIST IN US, THE HOPE OF GLORY

…by seeking I find in the Scriptures these seven things taught by the Spirit…

First, That Christ is a mystery, Col. 4.3.

Secondly, That the mystery is Christ, in us the hope of glory, Col. 1.27.

Thirdly, That the riches of the glory of this mystery was kept secret since the world began … Rom. 16.25.

Fourthly, That this mystery of Christ in us, the hope of glory, was manifested by revelation to the Apostles, and Prophets, and primitive Saints by the Spirit, Eph. 3.3, 4; Col. 1.26.

Fifthly, That what was manifested to them of the mystery of Christ, was only made known in part then to the Saints…

Sixthly, This mystery of Christ in us the hope of glory, of God manifest in mans flesh, which was manifest and in part made known to the Apostles and Primitive Saints before, hath been hid again from ages and generations, ever since the Apostacy…

Seventhly, That Book which was sealed before, shall be open again, and so it is, Rev. 10.1, 2 there the little Book is open… the mystery of God shall be more gloriously revealed in the last times, after Antichrist's destruction, and deliverance of the Saint… (pp.4–7)

THE SON AND THE SAINTS MAKE ONE PERFECT MAN

This is all I know of this yet, if yet I know any thing,

First, That the Son and the Saints make one perfect man, and that the fulness of the Godhead dwells in both in the same measure, though not in the same manifestation.

Secondly, That the fulness of the Godhead shall be manifested in the flesh of the Saints, as in the flesh of the Son.

These two things, which others see as Heresie and Blasphemy, seem to me as Truths, both in Scriptures, and by that Spirit which speaks in me… That the fulnesse of the Godhead dwels in the Saints, as in the Son, in the same measure, though not in the same manifestation, he being in this last sense anointed above his fellows, and God manifest in the flesh: But seeing we are his Brethren, we have the same Divine nature, our Fathers nature as full in us as he: and we being his body and fulnesse also, though the oyl first appear poured forth on the Head, yet it runneth down to his hem, all his Members are annointed with him… (p.8)

THE FULLEST MEASURE… BUT NOT IN THAT FULLEST MANIFESTATION

Christ received the Spirit before in the fullest measure: yea, but not in that fullest manifestation: He was the Son before, but not declared so to be the Son of God, but by the resurrection: God was in his flesh at his first conception, but God was not so manifest in flesh, till he was received up to glory, and received the promise of the Spirit, to shed it forth also on every believer to bring them to God also: …that glory which God gave the Son, the same is given the Saints: The glory is given already to them, though they injoy it not, nor that glory revealed in them, nor the Godhead yet manifested in their flesh: Therefore Christ prays there, not for the matter of Glory, as if that were not yet; but for the manifestation of that glory. What's the glory? First, perfect union... That's the second part of glory; The same love God bears to the Saints, as to his beloved Son, as hearty and as high a love, as intense and eternal: for extension also, as full expressions of love go forth from God to the Saints as to the Son... This again is a third story of that glory; The Saints are taken up with the Son, not only in perfect union with the Father, and fulnesse of love, but living for ever also with the Son in God. (p.9f.)

A GREAT WORD AND WONDERFUL GLORY

Here's a great word and wonderful Glory, a Mystery that hath all dimensions in it; such a height, that no carnal man can reach unto; a depth that none can dive into; a length that none can compasse the end thereof; and such a breadth, that none can comprehend with all their vast understandings: yet he prays that they, with all Saints of the lowest size, the least capacity may comprehend and know the love of Christ that passeth all knowledge: that is, the love of God in Christ, (as the Geneva notes well) that we may be filled with all the fulness of God, that is, that all the fulness of the Godhead may be manifest to them and others also: that he prays for; for they were already filled with all the fulness of God. (p.11)

AFTER THE APOSTACY AND FALLING AWAY, BEING FULL; THE DAY OF CHRIST FOLLOWS IMMEDIATELY

For as it pleased the Father, that all fulness should dwell in the Son, so it's his pleasure the same fulness and measure should dwell in the Saints, though the Son hath in all things the preh[e]*minence in manifestation, yet the fulnesses of the Godhead shall be also manifested in the Saints; which is my second to prove, That the fulness of the Godhead shall be also manifest in the flesh of the Saints, as in the Son... When he shall appear, that is, in us; when that glory shall be revealed in us: Then we shall be like him, that is, appear with him in glory, in the same glory of the Son, we shall be like him; for we shall see him as he is... But after the Apostacy and falling away, being full; the day of Christ follows immediately, and then we shall see him as he is; How is that? We shall see him in God even the Father, & in us also, and our selves in him, & with him living in God.* (p.11f.)

WHO WOULD THINK THAT POOR SAINTS SHOULD HAVE SUCH POWER?

Who would think that poor Saints should have such power? Yea, such honour have all the Saints, as to bind Kings with chains, and Nobles with links of iron, and to execute the judgment written of the Son, Psal. 149.8, 9. Who believes that all the blood-shed, and slaughters this day in the world, the dashings of Kings and Kingdoms one against another, is done by the Saints, though they stir not, but are quiet in the Land? Yet the Lord goes forth of them, working all, and wasting all by them, by the weakest Saints. (p.14)

NEW NAMES ON THE SAINTS: PROTESTANTS, PROFESSORS, PURITANS, SEPARATISTS, SECTARIES, HERETICKS, AND BLASPHEMERS

...when we shall see God only manifest in our flesh, & the flesh nothing, profiting nothing having no power nor wisdom; when thus we deny our selves, follow me, saith Christ; follow him who is our forerunner, and gone before into the Holiest, into the fulness of the Godhead with him; then we are said to overcome and inherit all things. God is our God, and we are his sons, then this shall be manifest; for Rev. 22.3 we shall see his face, and his name shall be in our foreheads: As the Father's name with Christ, Rev. 14 1 so the name of Christ also shall be read in our foreheads. Men shall see the Saints as the Son, that's his new name which he will write on us; and we shall be called by another name, by a new name, which the mouth of the Lord shall name. Mens mouths have still formed new names on the Saints, as from the beginning so of late. In Queen Maries daies, the Saints suffered as Protestants; in Queen Elizabeths, as Professors; in King James's, as Puritans: in King Charles's, as Separatists; in our days, as Sectaries, Hereticks, and Blasphemers: But the Lord God will give us a new name shortly himself... (p.16)

NOT YET CARRIED OUT OF THE WAY OF FURTHER ENQUIRY... THAT WAYFARING MAN

This is all he hath now to say. That as he first professed he knew nothing, nor maintained any thing as dogmatical, but only delivering his mind, drawn out to speak, because he should not be silent, so he confesseth himself not yet carried out of the way of further enquiry and seeking the Truth that God shall teach him, and not men; wishing all the Saints were in that way... there is a way, a high-way, that way-faring men, though fools, shall not err therein. If any man would be wise still, he dares not call him fool: But as for him who hath found himself a fool already, and sees himself be-wildernessed as a way-faring man, seeing no way of man on earth, or beaten path to lead him, let him look upward and within at once, and a high-way, the Way is found, Christ in us, God in our flesh. Wait here a while for that Spirit and Power from on high to appear in us, walking in the Spirit of holiness, love, and peace; and at last, yea within a little, we shall be led forth out of this confusion and Babylon, wherein we yet are not clearly knowing Truth nor Errour, Day nor Night; but in the evening there shall be light. (p.18)

4

The Lord of Hosts / The Armies Defence 1648

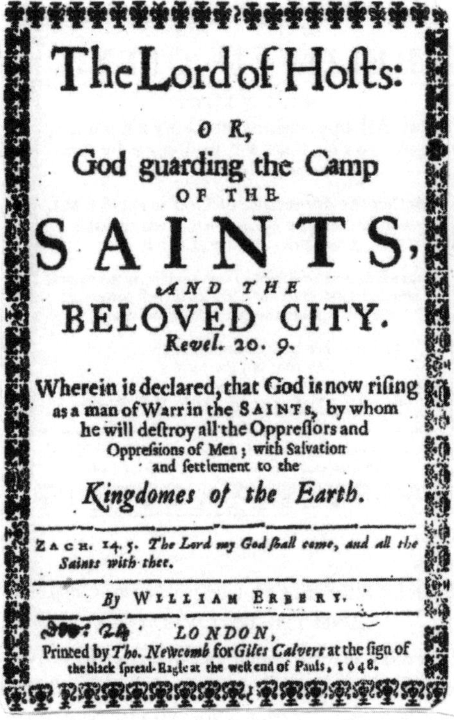

The Lord of Hoſts:
OR,
God guarding the Camp
OF THE
SAINTS,
AND THE
BELOVED CITY.
Revel. 20. 9.

Wherein is declared, that God is now riſing as a man of Warr in the SAINTS, by whom he will deſtroy all the Oppreſſors and Oppreſsions of Men; with Salvation and ſettlement to the
Kingdomes of the Earth.

ZACH. 14. 5. *The Lord my God ſhall come, and all the Saints with thee.*

By WILLIAM ERBERY.

LONDON,
Printed by *Tho. Newcomb* for *Giles Calvert* at the ſign of the black ſpread-Eagle at the weſt end of Pauls, 1648.

The Lord of Hosts: OR, God guarding the Camp of the SAINTS, and the BELOVED CITY. Revel. 20. 9.

Wherein is declared, that God is now rising as a man of Warr in the SAINTS, by whom he will destroy all the Oppressors and Oppressions of Men; with Salvation and settlement to the Kingdomes of the Earth.

By WILLIAM ERBERY.

LONDON, Printed by Tho. Newcomb for Giles Calvert at the sign of the black spread-Eagle at the west end of Pauls, 1648.

(Received into the Thomason Collection on Dec 24th, 1648).

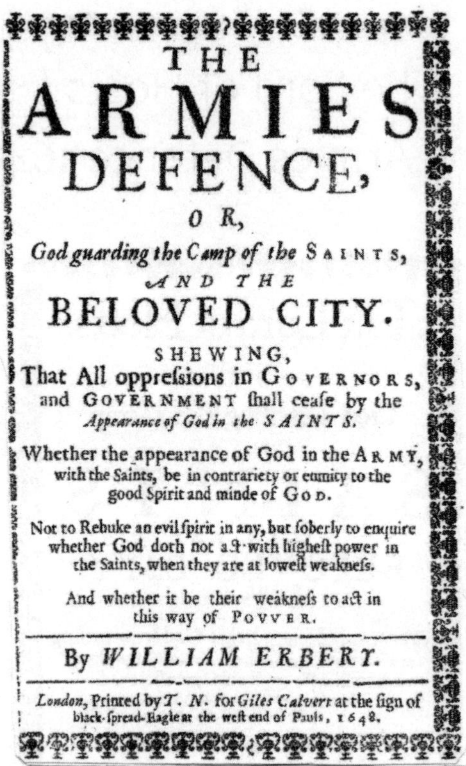

THE
ARMIES
DEFENCE,
OR,
God guarding the Camp of the SAINTS,
AND THE
BELOVED CITY.
SHEWING,
That All oppreſsions in GOVERNORS,
and GOVERNMENT ſhall ceaſe by the
Appearance of God in the SAINTS.
Whether the appearance of God in the ARMY,
with the Saints, be in contrariety or enmity to the
good Spirit and minde of GOD.
Not to Rebuke an evil ſpirit in any, but ſoberly to enquire
whether God doth not act with higheſt power in
the Saints, when they are at loweſt weakneſs.
And whether it be their weakneſs to act in
this way of POVVER.

By *WILLIAM ERBERY.*

London, Printed by *T. N.* for *Giles Calvert* at the ſign of
black-ſpread-Eagle at the weſt end of Pauls, 1648.

The ARMIES DEFENCE, *OR, God guarding the Camp of the* SAINTS,
AND THE BELOVED CITY.

SHEWING, that All oppressions in GOVERNORS, and GOVERNMENT shall cease by the Appearance of God in the SAINTS.

Whether the appearance of God in the ARMY, with the Saints, be in contrariety or enmity to the good Spirit and minde of GOD.

Not to Rebuke an evil spirit in any, but soberly to enquire whether God doth not act with highest power in the Saints, when they are at lowest weakness.

And whether it be their weakness to act in this way of POWER.

By WILLIAM ERBERY.

London, Printed by *T. N.* for *Giles Calvert* at the sign of black spread-Eagle at the west end of Pauls, 1648

Erbery's theological revolution had been fully expressed in *Nor Truth nor Errour.* His radical change marched alongside the radical changes in the nation. His experience of Christ in you, the hope of glory and his conviction that the Final Age was at hand were the two principles which helped him interpret the shifting context of the turbulent years between 1647 and his death in 1654. These were the years of the execution of the King and the rise of parliament to power. The Anglican establishment was replaced by the Presbyterian party. In turn parliament and Presbyterians gave way to the rise of the Independents and their allies in the New Model Army. The Long Parliament (the Rump) was dissolved in April 1653 and replaced by the ill-fated experiment of the Saints' or Barebone's or Nominated Parliament (July to December 1653). Finally Erbery witnessed John Lambert's Instrument of Government[1] and Cromwell's installation as Lord Protector.

After his removal from Oxford early in 1647, Erbery continued to serve as chaplain to Colonel Lambert's New Model regiment of foot, and was later chaplain to Fairfax's regiment of horse for which he received payment in arrears in 1650.[2] The fact that Erbery had served as a chaplain to Lambert may help explain his support for Cromwell when the Fifth Monarchists bitterly opposed Cromwell for his apostasy.[3]

Towards the end of 1648 Erbery published a tract which appeared under two titles: *The Lord of Hosts* and *The Armies Defence.* Both were published in London by Thomas Newcomb for Giles Calvert at the sign of the Black Spread-Eagle at the west end of Pauls. Erbery's third tract is far more political than either of his previous writings. This is conveyed by the title and frontispiece of both editions.

The Lord of Hosts begins with a powerful theological statement of the way God is at work in contemporary history. This reminds us of Erbery's assertion of God's immanence and imminence. The fullness of the Godhead, always dwelling in the saints will be fully manifested at the Third Dispensation. This is the period of the death throes of the Apostasy before the arrival of the fullness of the Kingdom of Christ.

Erbery spells out clearly his belief in universal salvation. This was anathema to most of his contemporaries who believed salvation was reserved only for the predestined, the elect, the saints, God's chosen.

This was expressed clearly in:

> ***The Thirty-Nine Articles of the Church of England***
> Predestination to Life is the everlasting purpose of God, whereby (before the foundations of the world were laid) he hath constantly decreed by his counsel secret to us, to deliver from curse and damnation those whom he hath chosen in Christ out of mankind, and to bring them by Christ to everlasting salvation, as vessels made to honour (Article XVII).

It was even more forcefully part of *The Westminster Confession of Faith* (1647), which the Presbyterian visitors to Oxford had helped draft:

> Those of mankind that are predestinated unto life, God, before the foundation of the world was laid, according to His eternal and immutable purpose, and the secret counsel and good pleasure of His will, hath chosen, in Christ, unto everlasting glory… The rest of mankind God was pleased, according to the unsearchable counsel of his own will… to ordain them to dishonour and wrath for their sin, to the praise of His glorious justice. (Chapter III, articles V and VII)

Erbery was undermining the foundations of this theological system – one he had held himself before the Civil War – and was consequently vilified as a dangerous subversive. Erbery's view of God and humankind was diametrically opposite to the views of the Church of England, Presbyterians and Independents. For Erbery, the saints were pioneers of an inheritance which would be gifted to the whole of God's creation. The present role of the saints was to serve as the spearhead of the new community. They would overthrow oppressions and oppressors until at the Third Dispensation, the promised world of righteousness would arrive.

How are the saints recognised? Are they parliament, or

in parliament? Are they the Army, or in the Army? Saints are replacing oppressive powers with a righteous society. The social fabric will be revolutionized by God's way of shalom. History is reaching its climax and the new world is on its way.

Erbery spells out the steps by which God is bringing the Age of Apostasy to a close. His theological foundation, his grasp of contemporary politics and his understanding of history are all intertwined. In powerful passages, he describes how oppressive powers, both religious and secular are being overthrown by God's work through the saints. The foundations of society were being shaken by the arm of the Lord. Oppressive powers in King, parliament and Army were all being overthrown by the humble life and work of the saints. Whenever authority develops a policy of persecution, God replaces that authority. In the recent history of England, the King was replaced by parliament, and in turn, parliament replaced by the Army.

These revolutionary changes reflected the culmination of God's process of fulfilling his purposes. Many Puritans were imbued with this hope of the new world. Erbery, like many of his fellow chaplains, divided history into three dispensations. Erbery's theory was that there had been a Dispensation of the Law, revealed in the Old Testament. When Israel was a theocracy, God acted in 'great deliverances' and Israel exercised gifts of 'prophesies, signs, miracles, healings'. This period was followed by the Dispensation of the Gospel when there were 'glorious discoveries of God in Men'. Theocracy was replaced by the Apostolic Church, which because of the gifts endowed by the Spirit of Pentecost, preached the Gospel of 'Christ in you the hope of glory'.

Although Erbery spoke of three dispensations, he divided history into four periods. Between the Second and Third Dispensations came the long period of Apostasy which had begun when Church and State failed to exercise their separate responsibilities. The State interfered in the role of the Church, and the Church attempted to dominate the State. The gifts of the Spirit were lost, and the 'mystery of Christ in you' once revealed to the saints, was once more hidden.

However Erbery was convinced that the Age of Apostasy was drawing to a close and would be replaced by the Third and Final Dispensation. This Final Age would combine 'deliverances and discoveries', and God in the Spirit would reconcile and fulfil the secular and the spiritual. All would be All in God.

History was reaching its conclusion and the saints were experiencing the first glimpses of the new world. Erbery rejected the popular literalist belief that God would return carnally from the clouds. On the contrary, the indwelling Spirit would emerge from within the life of men and women, and at the same time the Kingdom would be established in an outward, historical and political form.

GOD... DEFENDING AND SAVING HIMSELF IN THE SAINTS

This is not to defend an Army, or Arm of flesh; but God dwelling in flesh, defending and saving himself in the Saints from the power of flesh in the world, oppressing his Glorious Appearance in them; the Oppressor shall cease. This, in short is, the sense and sum of that Scripture, I will encamp about mine House, &c. (Zach 12.8) What is the House of God, but God dwelling in the flesh of the Saints, or the Saints filled with all the fulness of God? the fullness of the Godhead dwelling in them bodily, or the Godhead em-bodyed in their flesh. This house of God, God defends, encamping it about, with himself dwelling in the midst of them, though not yet manifest in All of them through weakness; yet all of them, though in weakest flesh & lowest forms, the Lord of Hosts owns as his Army... (p.19)

THOUGH GOD SHALL BE SO REVEALED TO ALL... YET THE SAINTS SHALL FIRST APPEAR IN GLORY

For as the whole Creation is a clear Image of God, Mankind a clearer Image then that, of the Godhead: but the Saints (that's the Son), are the clearest, the express Image of his substance or Godhead. God in his spiritual being, and blessedness, his grace, goodness, holiness, love, light, wisdom, power, and all, appearing most visibly to the world in them, whom the world of Mankind therefore hates, because they know them not, nor God even the Father dwelling in them, and their flesh full of God: so the whole Creation is called the House of God, yea, his holy Temple, Psa. 29.3 to the end… But as God yet dwels only in the Saints, or is manifest in their flesh only; the Saints in a special manner being called the House of God, his holy Temple, and habitation of his Holiness, the Holy of Holyes wherein all his glory appears, and to whom all his secrets are revealed, & made known: therefore though God shall be so revealed to all, that all flesh shall see his glory together; yet the Saints shall first appear in Glory, and Gods appearance be first manifested in them… (p.20)

GOD HATH CHOSEN A COMPANY OF MEN, TO WHOM HE WILL FIRST MANIFEST ALL HIS LOVE, LIGHT, LIFE, GLORY, SALVATION, AND HIMSELF TO THEM

…so the Saints are called the Elect and beloved of God; not but that God loves every man, as the Scriptures speak of the kindness and love of God to All Men; but All men having not God manifest In them, nor his love made Known to them, are said to be hated, condemned, and damn'd, because that his love, their life and salvation is not yet manifest to them; so they are said to be under wrath, under the power of death, darkness, and of the Devil, the Devil dwelling in them, working in them; not as if all men were not of God, and God the Father of all, and all men the off-spring of God, God dwelling in them, and they, being in God, as living in him, moving and having their very being in God, Acts 17.27, 28, 29. But, these being yet left under the power of death, and dark appearing of God, that is, the Devil; God hath chosen a company of men, to whom he will first manifest all his love, light, life, glory, salvation, and himself to them, dwelling in them: These are therefore called the Holy, the Elect, and the House of God. (p.21)

AT LAST THE SAINTS MAY BE THEIR SAVIOURS, SAVE THEM AND THEIR NATION AND KINGDOM

…all the Saints closing in love and peace together in God, shall cease their present divisions, and first fall to destroy the powers of the world

opposing God in them; and then they shall save the world and be the saviours of men… if righteous men never were saved without suffering, but must first die before they live, and suffer before they reign: surely the world of ungodly men who have hitherto lived merrily, and reigned as Kings, must be content to suffer and die, not in their persons, but in their power and glory at least, in that power opposing, persecuting and oppressing the appearance of God in the Saints; they must die to that, and have that destroyed by the Saints, or by God in them, that at last the Saints may be their saviours, save them and their Nation and Kingdom from all their oppressors and oppressions. (p.22)

THINE OFFICERS SHALL BE RIGHTEOUSNESS, AND THINE EXECTORS PEACE

God has been reigning in Kings, and judging the people by Parliaments or Judges of the earth: but this Government of Men has been to the grief and sufferings of the Saints, and of the world also, oppressed by worldly powers, who are therefore called Babylon the oppressing City; which when it falls, see how the world will sing… the world shall be at rest and peace, when violence shall be no more heard in the Land, but thine Officers shall be righteousness, and thine Exectors peace. (p.23)

GOD COMES REIGNING… IN THE BASEST OF MEN… DESPISED & DULL FELLOWS

And he rides upon an Asse, not as earthly Kings on stately horses; but God comes reigning and riding on an Asse, that is, Revealing himself in majesty and glory in the basest of men, men counted so of the Kingdom, despised & dull fellows… lest they might be markt as Rebels by men, God stampt them with the authority of a Parliament, at first, to break the beginning of their bondage; and when Parliament could go no further, the Army (for the Saints sake among them) had the Call of the Kingdom, petitioning by several Counties, and the common cry of all the oppressed in the Land, that the Oppressor might cease… All this to me is a manifest token of the hand of God lifted up, not only for the liberty of the Saints, but for the deliverance of the Land at last from all Oppressions and Oppressors. (p.24f.)

GOD IN THE SAINTS SHALL APPEAR AS THE SAVIOUR OF ALL MEN

The more glorious any deliverance is, which God will manifest in & by his appearance in the Saints, the more general and publick the deliverance will be not of a King or a Parliament, but of the Kingdom and People, yea, of all people also at last: for as Christ is the Saviour of the world, and of all men: so the Saints shall be Saviours in like manner, that is, God in the Saints shall appear as the Saviour of all Men... Therefore the saving of a particular person of a King or Parliament, is but a false Christ. (p.26)

GOD RAISED UP THE SAINTS TO AN ARMY

The Woman is the weaker vessel, and the Saints in this Land were the weakest party for power, the fewest for number, two or three in a Parish persecuted by King, Lords, and all the Commons, by Church and Common-wealth: God comes forth and makes a war with both, dividing the Kingdom against it self, and dividing the Church against it self: Thus God by dividing these waters, makes a way for the ransomed ones to passe over, Esay 51.10, that is, by dividing King and Parliament, and by dividing Prelats and Presbyters, the Saints have got liberty and freedom in their states and spirits to serve God, and Men also to their good. For this was the second step of the Kings coming, and Gods appearing in the Saints, when the Saints (who would and could not live in peace) were raised up in Arms, and strengthened to an Army. Now, though the Parliament and power of man raised the Army; yet it was God raised up the Saints to an Army. Alas, they were men most quiet in the Land, or Lambs in the midst of Wolves, they would not hurt, they could not hate those who hated them and abhorred them, and God in them; the Saints were silly sheepish men, harmless, or hornless, as Doves, they had no horns to push, nor hoofs to tread men under, not a sword to strike, nor a spirit to slay, but all to lye down and suffer: Who but God above could raise up the spirit of a Saint to be a man of war like Himself? (p.26f.)

GOD IN THE SAINTS THERE HATH JUDGED... THE CHURCH OF ENGLAND, THE PRESBYTERIAN AND INDEPENDENT CHURCHES

God in the Saints hath ruined in this Land, raising up the sons of Zion, and the spirits of Saints in the Army, to that height, that every high thing is fallen before them, both King, Countries, Councellors; His Statesmen, Souldiers, Scholars, Lords, Nobles, Gentlemen, with all the gallantry of men in the Kingdom, yea, the Churches also, for the first and last Churches of Christ, the seven Churches of Asia were all, and most of the rest in Greece; now All the Churches in the Kingdom, the Church of England, the Presbyterian and Independent Churches had a sword of the Spirit come forth from the Saints abroad, which hath slain their flesh, and forms of Doctrine and Worship, which God in the Saints there hath judged, discovered, and destroyed, by the appearance of a greater glory in them ready to be revealed. And indeed, the greatest destruction in the Land hath been by the appearance of God in the Saints, even at home, and in battel; for nothing but his appearance, and the mighty power of God in men could in so short a time cast down so many strong Holds, conquer so many Royal Armies, rout such multituds with so few a number, as the Nation of the Scots can witness, and the Cities of England, one of them able to encounter a Kingdom, yet fell twice in their Spirits before a small party... I speak not now of our Army of Souldiers, but of the Army of Saints; not only abroad in battel, but those also at home have had a hand in the destruction of Kingdoms... (p.27f.)

THE ETERNAL GOD DWELLS GLORIOUSLY IN THE LOWEST, WEAKEST STATE OF A SAINT

...for as Gods strength is perfected in weakness... 'tis the lowest, weakest state of a Saint to be so humble, broken, contrite, ground to powder... yet there the eternal, unchangeable God dwells as gloriously as in his holy place, and highest Heavens. (p.29)

AN OPPRESSING KING, PARLIAMENT AND ARMY

Look in that last particular of publick transaction, wherein the Army, that is, all the Saints, acted, in God, or God in them; for as we cannot divide

God from the Saints, so the Saints cannot be divided one from another: though some are in the Countrey, some in the City, some in the field, yet all make but one Army or Arm of God; for in them his mighty power appears, and is made bare before the world: now see when and why God made the Saints, the Army so weak as to passe by and return back again from their former principles of liberty and promises to free the Land from bondage and burthens… there was the power of an oppressing King, the power of an oppressing Parliament, the power of an oppressed people, yea, the power of an oppressing Army as a guard to the oppressor in all, all these stumbling blocks were then before God in his way with the Saints, therefore they returned in weakness, but the power of God appeared in it, that the oppressor might appear the more in King, Parliament, and People; in secret English so discovered, in open Scots since defeated, yea in the Saints own Divisions now united; all these stumbling blocks being taken out of the way, and the way, made plain for God to bring in settlement, salvation, freedom, righteousness, not only to the Saints, but to the world. (p.30f.)

SILENT TRUTH AND THESE SPEAKING TIMES

…the Saints shall no more act for themselves, but for the world also, to see how liberty may be setled on the whole earth; and foundations of Justice, of Righteousness, and Peace may be established in the Nations… The Saints shall first enjoy their glorious liberty inward and outward, and by them the world afterward, as we shall shew at another time, and Treatise… Let silent Truth, and these Speaking times interpret these Scriptures, and the reall experiments of Gods providences in this present Age, be a living Commentary to future Generations of the Saints, who shall Know clearly (what the Saints now but confusedly apprehend) that the Anointing, or Godhead filling their flesh, hath taken away the burdens of Egypt from off their shoulders, and destroyed the Assyrians or Babylons yoak from off their neck, that now the Oppressor ceaseth, yea the Golden City, that Church-state; and Saints rule over their oppressors: not the Saints, as exalting themselves, or exalted over men, but as exalting God alone in the midst of them, and in all Men also, This is the Lords land, the flesh of man, in whom God inhabits; &

these are the Lords mountains, Men and Women in whom God only is exalted... (pp.32–4)

ONE PERFECT MAN IN WHOM THE GODHEAD IS EMBODYED FULLY

What is this Man, but God manifest in flesh: For the Saints, though they be never so many millions of men in multiplyed flesh, yet they make but One perfect Man in whom the Godhead is embodyed fully, or One spirit, that is, God manifest in flesh... for as in God we live, and move, and have our being: so God has appointed our bounds and habitations; that's one Land therefore in truth, where God has brought us forth, appointing us to live in & inhabit, (though in spirit we inherit the whole earth, and are Princes in all Lands)... (p.34)

WE LAY CLAIM TO NOTHING BUT TO THIS PIECE OF EARTH WHICH IS OURS, WITH AS MUCH OR MORE RIGHT THEN PRINCES LANDS TO THEM

...yet we lay claim to nothing but to this piece of earth which is ours, with as much or more right then Princes Lands to them: Now if the Assyrian shall come into our Land, and tread in our Palaces, that is, if poor or rich among us shall have our propriety and peace invaded, by a Kingly Prerogative, or Parliamentary priviledge (that's the oppressing Assyrian) We shall raise against them seven Shepherds and eight principal Men: 'twas not the King that called a Parliament, but the Saints called a Parliament to oppose an oppressing King: so 'twas not the Parliament raised an Army against him, but we raised an Army against an oppressing Parliament: And if God raiseth not up the Army to act immediately in the immediate power of God, but to give that power back again to a Parliament, as the Parliament gave it up to the King, God will raise up a living power from the dust of King, Parliament, and Army, which shall appear in the Saints, who shall yet raise seven Shepherds, and eight principal men, a perfect and a sufficient strength to oppose all oppressing powers, and to establish righteousness, peace, and liberty in the Land, Mic. 5.7, 8. For as there is no power but of God, so there is no power of God executed but in & by the Saints among men. (p.34f.)

THE POWER OF GOD IN THE SAINTS, ONCE POSSESSED THE SPIRIT OF THE KING... SEATS IT SELF IN PARLIAMENT... (TO) THE POWER OF GOD IN THE ARMY

Thus the power of God in the Saints, once possessed the spirit of the King, and all men in the Kingdom were subject to the power of God in him. The Saints of all men would not stir, but suffer in silence what ever oppressions & persecutions he should burthen them with: But God who will not abide for ever in any form but in the flesh of Saints... therefore his power departs from that form where it was before in the King, and seats it self in that of a Parliament, to whom all the Saints are afterwards subject as to their King; yea, their Spirits who were before still in sufferings, now begin to stir, and to be raised up, shaking off all that Royal dust which stuck upon them, and seeing that the power of God departed from that first, and dwelleth now in other powers, they fly to this, and fight also for it as for God: but when the power of God departs from a Parliament also, led aside to selfish Principles, and oppressing practices not only toward the Saints, but to the whole Kingdom, then the Kingdom and all the Saints look upon the power of God in the Army: and though the Army, being in a fleshly posture, had well nigh forfeited the appearance of Gods power amongst them; yet the most of their Shepherds and principal men being Saints in truth though they passed by, yet they returned again to their first faith, their former principles, yea to higher actions of Honor then before. (p.35f.)

THE DISPENSATIONS OF LAW AND GOSPEL

This third dispensation is of a differing constitution from Law or Gospel; that of the Law appeared most in an outward policy of the Church, and Kingdom of Israel, that Church being National, the Kingdom was the Church of God, and the Kings were Ministers therein, as the Lords anointed, being types of Christ in spirit: but the Gospel state was most in the Spirit, and of a spiritual appearance in the Churches of Saints, with manifold gifts of the Spirit manifested among them: whereby they were differenced from Kingdoms and Nations without: and as Kings then, and the civil Magistrates medled not with Church or Gospel Mysteries, to order any thing in Doctrine or Worship, or stamp their authority on it: so the Churches of Saints, medled not with matters of state in Kings or Kingdoms, having nothing to do to judg them that are without, only in obedience to the Magistrate in Civil commands: the Saints were then taken up wholly with things within, in spiritual enjoyments, and expectations of a greater Glory to be revealed in them... But now as the glory of the Law was in great deliverances of God: so that of the Gospel was in Glorious discoveries of God in Men, the revealing of mysteries, and of the deep things of God by the Spirit in the Saints, who then enjoyed no great deliverances from outward powers, and persecutions, but laid as dead under all the sufferings of Men. (p.36f.)

GOD NOW AWAKES AS IN THE ANCIENT DAYS

The third dispensation of God in and to the Saints, is mixt therefore with both the glory of the Law and Gospel also; wherein the Saints do begin to see, (as if faith were failing) they see God manifest in flesh fully; they see God in great deliverances from men, and in glorious discoveries of God himself in the midst of them... sure God hath seemed to men to be asleep in all these sufferings of the Saints, in these latter ages; but God now awakes as in the Ancient days. (p.37)

THE PRINCE MUST BE, NOT ABOVE, BUT IN THE MIDST OF HIS BRETHREN

In this third dispensation, God in the Saints restores all things, Heaven and Earth, things spiritual and civil also, renews the forms of Kingdoms, of outward Governments and Order, as well as things in the Spirit, in and by the Saints; who as they have been in the hand of God to break Nations and destroy Kingdoms: so they are hid in the shadow of his hand, that he may plant the Heavens, and lay the foundation of the Earth again, Isay 51.16... First, the glory of God returns into his Temple, that is, all spiritual things are restored, &c. Ezek. 43.7, 8, 9, 10, 11 and then there follows restitution of civil power... the Prince here is not above, but in the midst of his brethren, not as our Princes and Parliaments have been, as if civil Magistrates, must have power in spiritual things, and the worship of God, to force or conform all to a form of godliness; nor the Prince now (if any power of Magistrate be when God shall appear): the Prince must be, not above, but in the midst of his brethren, in the knowledg and worship of God, waiting on God with them, to enlighten and lead them in and out together, out of one truth, into another, or into a higher light in the same truth of God. (p.39)

THE DAY OF GOD HAS BEGUN

...there has been a waiting in all Saints, not only for liberty, but for the Spirit to come again, for a second coming of Christ, which is called, the coming of God with all the Saints; now God comes not by changing his place, as Christians carnally conceive Christ to come in the clouds: but as the coming of Christ, is the coming of God; so the appearing of Christ is the appearing of the great God & Saviour in the Saints & as God comes, so the Saints must be said to come; God comes when he appears in glory in us, & the Saints therefore come when they appear with him in glory, when the glory of God comes & clothes the Saints, that men can see nothing but God in them... thus the day of God has begun, though the Saints have been and are still in confusion; neither day nor night, but in the evening, (when a man would think that light is even going away) all then shall be light, and a full glory flaming forth in the Saints, which shall darken all the glory of man, and dash in pieces the oppressing powers on earth... those high ones, Kings of the earth, who have invaded the Kingdom of God, and set themselves on high to rule in the Church, to determin of Doctrines and Divine worships, to order all things in the spiritual affairs of men by a temporal sword, by Parliaments or civil power, imprisoning and punishing all Saints who would not conform to their formal Religions... the Kings of the earth shall be punished with the spirit and strength of the sword: and those who imprisoned and captivated the Saints by their earthly power, or temporal sword, enslaving their spirits also, shall be led into captivity, shut up in Prison, and slain by the sword. (p.40f.)

IF GOD NOW APPEAR IN MEN FOR THEIR RELIEF AND RELEASE

There be many of these in this Land, like the Assyrian, many oppressing Laws, and Courts; but Clergy-men and Common Lawyers are the chiefest oppressors therein; the one by their legal tyths and teachings: the other by their tedious Suits and tricks of the Law, oppress and plague the Souls and states of Men: besides, the Prisoners, and the Poor have heavy oppressors, and are Chief among the oppressed. If God now appear in men for their relief and Release, that poor Families may have food, and the Prisoner go free: and if the Lord God shall now appear in the Saints to waste the land of Assyria with the sword, and the land of Nimrod in the entrances thereof, That no Oppressor nor Oppression enter in again into the Government of this Kingdom; I shall praise God that all Men shall have joy and Peace. (p.42)

5

Army Council: Whitehall Debates 1648/9

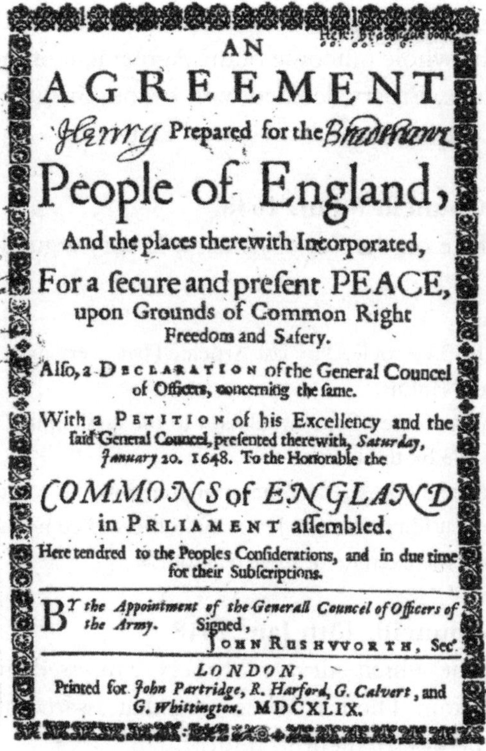

AN

AGREEMENT

Prepared for the

People of England,

And the places therewith Incorporated,

For a ſecure and preſent PEACE,

upon Grounds of Common Right Freedom and Safety.

Alſo, a DECLARATION of the General Councel of Officers, concerning the ſame.

With a PETITION of his Excellency and the ſaid General Councel, preſented therewith, *Saturday, January* 20. 1648. To the Honorable the

COMMONS of *ENGLAND*

in PRLIAMENT aſſembled.

Here tendred to the Peoples Conſiderations, and in due time for their Subſcriptions.

BY *the Appointment of the Generall Councel of Officers of the Army.* Signed,

JOHN RUSHWORTH, Sec.

LONDON,

Printed for *John Partridge, R. Harford, G. Calvert*, and *G. Whittington.* MDCXLIX.

THE DEBATES WERE recorded by Sir William Clarke,[1] Secretary to the Council of the Army and can be read either in the Clarke Papers or in *Puritanism and Liberty* by A.S.P. Woodhouse.[2]

Sir William Clarke, The Clarke Papers. Selections from the Papers of William Clarke, Secretary to the Council of the Army, 1647–1649, and to General Monck and the Commanders of the Army in Scotland, 1651–1660, ed. C. H. Firth (Camden Society, 1894). 4 Vols.

Both the Putney and Whitehall debates centred on the discussion of *The Agreement of the People,* in which the Levellers embodied their constitutional theories.[3] Erbery appeared at the Whitehall debates, on the 8th, 10th and 11th of January, 1649. Discussion centred on the issue of religious toleration, and in the fragments of the notes that remain, Erbery debated with Ireton,[4] leader of the conservative party in the Council, Captain William Butler and Captain Spencer. In the final debate on the 13th of January, in which the whole outcome of the Agreement of the People was on the agenda, Erbery debated with Ireton, Spencer, Sir Hardres Waller,[5] Captain Joyce[6] and General Harrison.[7]

Generall Council. 8 Jan. 1648.

On the debate on the 8th of January, Erbery argued for religious toleration:

> Mr. Erbury.
>
> Uppon the 3d Article, The last Article, That every man beleives his God of all Nations.
>
> If any man doe offend in relation to the civill injury of others, hee is punishable by the lawes.
>
> Uppon the 4th Article concerning religion. To what purpose will you give that libertie to the Jewes and others to come in unlesse you grant them the exercise of their religion?

Generall Councill. 13th Jan. 1648

In a fragment which survives, Erbery expressed his opposition to state religion. There is also a note that asserts that 'a sense of calling' is the key element in ministry:

> Question uppon the matter concerning Religion. Whether they doe by that goe about to sett uppe a State Religion?
>
> Men should bee call'd before they can teach publiquely.

A fuller report reflected Erbery's concern that 'all oppressive principles' be removed. This is more important than the creation of a new constitution.

> Mr. Erbury.
> Made a longe speech declaring his dissent to the Agreement; setting forth that whilest wee were in a way of putting downe of aucthority wee had the power of God going alonge with us: but as itt was with the Parliament in [imposing] the Covenant, that which they look't for to bee for agreement proved to bee a great disagreement amongst the Nation, soe [with us] this [agreement would prove] to be an Hellish thinge, and altogether tending to disagreement; and though hee likes the greatest parte of that Agreement, yett the last [article] as in relation to religion, is that which will doe much hurt.

The Whitehall debates were taking place only weeks before the trial and subsequent execution of the King. Charles was executed on January 29th, 1648/9. Erbery spoke on the 13th of January before the Army Council:

> Mr Erbury.
> One word, that I might nott bee mistaken [as to] the destruction that I speake of. Itt is nott minded or thought in my heart to destroy any mans person, noe nott to destroy the person of the Kinge, soe his power bee downe. I doe nott looke upon mens persons or destroying of that power of the Magistrate that is now. The Parliament are a power by whome men may act according to the appearance of God in them. I doe nott looke upon itt [as a power to be destroyed], neither doe I speake any thinge of that kinde; butt [I speak of] the destroying of those oppressive principalls both in powers and persons, and in courts and lawes. Those [are] thinges that have bin complained of and petitioned [against] by the poore country to the Parliament. The Parliament would never heare them. Many thousand Petitioners have petitioned [first] the Parliament, then the Lord Generall, that they would please to rectifie them; cries against unjust lawes, against tythes [against] many unrighteous thinges crept uppe amongst us heere, amonge Committees, Receivours of monies. God was with you to take away the oppressions of men, and nott the powers of men – nott to take away Magistracie, butt to take away those oppressions that lay before you and in your view, to remove them in the power of God.
>
> I conceive the settlement of the Nation is properly to remove

those thinges that are [the causes the nation is] unsettled. The thinges that trouble the Nation are these. I doe nott finde they are any wayes unsetled about Government, but they are unsetled about those oppressions that lie uppon them. I conceive the removing of these is a setling of them; butt I conceive this [agreement] will bee a meanes to unsettle them, acting the Nation that should bee settled by the worde of God. Now if God would soe worke and act by his people of this Army as to remove those thinges that unsettle them, they would agree, butt this would unsettle them to see all thinges putt into this frame. For my parte I doe thinke that a dozen or 24 may in a short time doe the kingdome as much good as 400 [the leveller suggestion] that sitt in the Parliament in 7 yeares may doe, and therfore that which I would have is to [remove those thinges that] unsettle them.

Mr. Erbury.
There is as just a power now [in this Army] by which you may act in appearance, as in other following Representatives. This [Army] is call'd now from a just power to remove oppressions. I doe nott speake of Armies and such thinges, butt there are oppressions hidden in and corrupt thinges that may bee removed [by] the power of God if itt appeare in them.

Sir Charles Firth's comments accurately reflect Erbery's opinions.

Erbury wants to have an immediate removal of the grievances of the nation effected by means of a committee of a few officers and 'faithful persons.'

Erbury, to use a modern phrase, demanded social reforms, and refused to be satisfied with improvements in the machinery of government. The Agreement had specified 400 as the number of members to sit in future parliaments. The proposal to entrust power to a small body appears again in 1653. Cromwell and his fellow officers urged the Rump 'to devolve their trust over to some well-affected men such as had an interest in the nation and were known to be of good affection to the Commonwealth, which we told them was no new thing when this land was under the like hurlyburlies.' (Carlyle's

Cromwell, Speech I.) So too Lambert, after the expulsion of the Rump, "moved that a few persons not exceeding the number of ten or twelve might be trusted with the supreme power."

Erbury's argument is that the Army is as lawful an authority as any of the Parliaments to be called under the Agreement.

6

The Grand Oppressor or The Terror of Tithes 1652

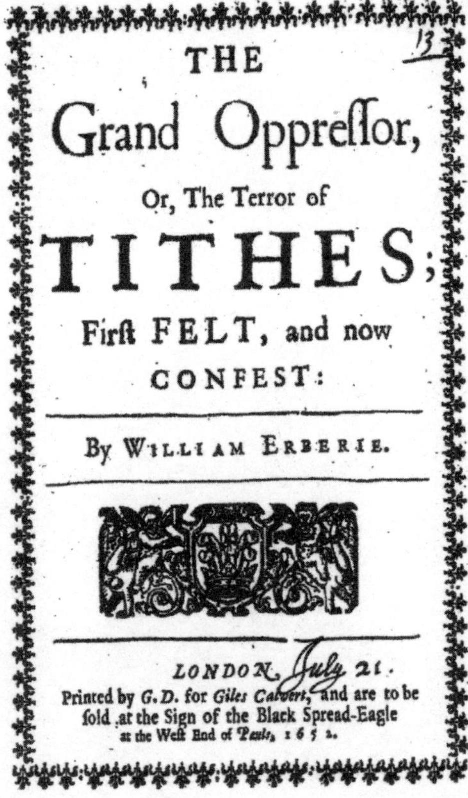

THE

Grand Oppreſſor,

Or, The Terror of

TITHES;

Firſt FELT, and now CONFEST:

By WILLIAM ERBERIE.

LONDON, July 21.

Printed by G.D. for Giles Calvert, and are to be ſold at the Sign of the Black Spread-Eagle at the Weſt End of Pauls, 1652.

THE Grand Oppressor, Or, The Terror of TITHES; First FELT, and now CONFEST: By William Erberie. LONDON. Printed by G.D. for Giles Calvert, and are to be sold at the Sign of the Black Spread-Eagle at the West End of Pauls, 1652.
(Received into the Thomason Collection on July 21st, 1652)

PARALLEL TO ERBERY'S theological movement from orthodox Calvinism towards a personal, spiritualist emphasis, was a rejection of traditional church structures, to be replaced by his sense of the indwelling Christ. For the first forty years of his life, he had been a member, and then a priest of the Church of England. After renouncing the priesthood, he became an Independent minister in Cardiff, but his experience of the Civil War and his service as an Army chaplain, resulted in the rejection of ecclesiastical formalism. Erbery had been ordained twice – to the ministry of the Church of England, and then as a minister of an Independent Church – and had resigned twice from ministry. This is the background to his struggle with the questions of the validity of ministry, and the maintenance of ministry.

Erbery typified many radical Puritans who were appalled by the long, bitter, intolerant controversies over ministry and ordinances. The hatred which divided Episcopalians, Presbyterians and Independents was anathema to many like Erbery. The period of Apostasy and the absence of the Spirit created an invalid ministry, and if there was no legitimate ministry, there could be no payment of ministerial stipends. The historic method of church finance through tithing was completely unacceptable. Should tithing be replaced by governmental taxation? Should ministers be supported by the voluntary contributions of their congregations? Should ministers live by the labour of their own hands?

The Grand Oppressor, or *The Terror of Tithes* gives a personal insight of Erbery wrestling with these issues, and how he rejected tithing. It was published in July 1652. Later that year, probably in February 1652/3, it was republished along with *A Scourge for the Assyrian* under the title, *The Sword Doubled* (entered Thomason's collection on February 14th).

The Grand Oppressor is 'the sum of a Letter written to one of the Commissioners in South Wales, Aprill 19th 1652.' It is one of Erbery's most personal tracts, sharing how he thought, deliberated, came to decisions and then acted on his decisions.

The particular reason for the letter was Erbery's decision to reject £100 promised him for his service as an itinerant preacher.

In February 1649/50, parliament had passed An Act for the Better Propagation and Preaching of the Gospel in Wales. Commissioners were appointed to eject clergymen from their livings for 'pluralism, delinquency, scandal, ignorance, drunkenness, swearing, assisting the King in the war.' They were replaced by itinerant preachers, one of whom was Erbery. One of the Commissioners was Henry Walter[1] who served in Glamorgan and Monmouth. Erbery's letter was probably written to Walter. Erbery had been paid £100 in 1650 and again in 1651, but at the beginning of 1652, he was convinced he should reject such payment.

It was no easy decision for Erbery personally. He approved of the work of the Commonwealth. For the first time in the history of Wales, the State had developed and paid for a programme enabling 'Pastors, Teachers, and Preachers of the Gospel in Wales' to fulfill their ministries. It was a bold attempt to provide a religious and educational policy for the whole nation. But, for Erbery, however well intentioned the programme, it betrayed principles these Independent ministers had once advocated.

Even more remarkable is Erbery's self-analysis, and the way he reveals the struggle by which he came to reject payment by tithes. Professor M. Wynn Thomas describes the tract as historical in its expression of the Welsh Nonconformist conscience.[2]

THE SUM OF A LETTER, WRITTEN TO ONE OF THE COMMISSIONERS IN SOUTH-WALES, APRIL 19, 1652.

TITHES WHICH I TOOK AT FIRST FROM YOUR HANDS

Sir,

You willed me to write unto you concerning the hundred pounds which you were pleased to promise present payment of, if your Treasury were not empty… Tithes, which I took at first from your hands as a maintenance allowed me by the Lord, in you and the rest of the honourable

Commissioners, who in much love appointed this as a portion for my poor Family, and as a reward for my former services and sufferings, for the State, and the Saints in Wales. (p.49f.)

GOD IN CHRIST HAD GLAD TYDINGS TO SPEAK, AND GREAT THINGS TO DO... FOR THE POOR, FOR THE OPPRESSED, AND FOR THE PRISONER.

I told you Sir in private, that in my late publick Teachings I was carried forth contrary to the inclinations of my own Spirit, willing rather to sit still in silence, and spiritual retirements with my God, waiting for his glorious appearance with power in all his people.

But so it was, that by a special providence I came abroad to the people, whom I acquainted, that to my present apprehension, I was not certain that I had any call from God or man, or from my self, but meerly by a strong hand, I know not how, I was thrust forth into the Harvest, where I was immediatly met with the noise of Tythes in this manner:

The first Scripture I opened, not to preach, but only to expound, (according to the Teaching of God in me) was Isa. 61.1, 2.

There I saw and said, that God in Christ had glad tydings to speak, and great things to do (in these last dayes also) for three sorts of people; for the poor, for the oppressed, and for the Prisoner. (p.49)

GOD SO APPEARING IN THE PRESENT POWERS, THAT 'TWAS HOPED THIS WAS THE ACCEPTABLE YEAR OF THE LORD

This day (saith Christ) is this Scripture fulfilled in your ears: and this have we heard and seen in our dayes, God so appearing in the present powers, that 'twas hoped this was the acceptable year of the Lord, for the people of the Land to look for their long expected and promised libertie to the Captives, who, by an Act of Justice and Mercy from the Parliament of England,[3] *are set free from their several Prisons (yea, from forraign Captivity in part), as the first fruits of that following Redemption which the oppressed and the poor of the Nation do likewise hope for.*

But before I heard of that News, I had formed my matter in this

Method; the first moneth of the year (March 7) I began to speak for the poor from these Scriptures on several Sundayes…

With this last, I began the second moneth for the oppressed… I ended the third moneth with the Prisoner. (p.49)

GOD BEGAN TO ROAR IN MY SPIRIT… THE OPPRESSION OF TITHES CAME TO MY EARS

Upon this, God began (as I said before) to roar in my Spirit, and I to hear nothing within me but the cry of the oppressed, 'twas far (me-thought) from my temper to tread on a worm, or to oppress the poorest creature in the world; but still 'twas told me both waking and sleeping… Then the oppression of Tithes came to my ears, and the cry of the oppressed filled my heart, telling me, That I and my children fed on their flesh, that we drunk their blood, and lived softly on their hard labour and sweat (p.50)

IT WAS LIKE FIRE IN MY BONES, WHICH I BELIEVE IS THE ETERNAL SPIRIT… WHICH WILL SHORTLY BREAK FORTH

And truly Sir, 'twas so with me in this, though I have been afflicted from my youth, and suffered the terrors of the Lord to distraction; yet (for the time) I was never so distracted, confounded, and filled with fears in all my former temptations, as in this of Tithes.

And yet this trouble was not like those legal terrors I suffered of old; but it was like fire in my bones, which I believe is the eternal Spirit, and everlasting burnings, which will shortly break forth upon all the oppressors of the land, to burn up their flesh, fulness, and those fair buildings which they have raised on the ruines of others; enrichings themselves in the Nation's poverty. (p.50f.)

BUT THERE WAS A BOOK WITHIN ME

These and many other Scriptures came not in by way of a Concordance, nor yet as sought out by me, but they found me out, so that I once feared to open the Book any more.

But there was a Book within me, which though I would shut, and be willingly deaf to what was written therein, yet I was made to hear with a witness, Isaiah 33.14. (p.51)

RELIEVE POOR FAMILIES WITH BREAD BY A PUBLICK STOCK

Thus many Ministers also are unsensibly fallen into a new light, which themselves condemned in others; for my part I follow the old, and profess, that I can see yet nothing in Tithes but the gain of oppression, continued and kept up meerly by Ministers, and Church-Members, who being men of power this day, might easily prevaile to remove this and many other oppressions, at least, with the people of the Land to petition the present Governours, to ease the oppressed of their burthens, as to release the prisoners from their bonds, and to relieve poor Families with bread by a publick stock. (p.53)

THEY ARE MORE OPPRESSIVE THAN POPISH TITHES IN FORRAIN PARTS

Secondly, they are more oppressive than Popish Tithes in forrain parts: France, the Kingdom of Asses (as 'tis called) hath not such an oppression in Tithes for their Priests, as our Protestant Teachers and Preachers of the Gospel do burthen this free Nation; for as 'tis credibly reported by some, who have long liv'd in France, that there and in Spain also, only Tithe of hard corn is paid, that is, of Wheat and Rye, but no Tithe of Barley, Oates, Pease, Beans, Fitches, Tills, much lesse Tithe of Hops, Hemp, Flax, Saffron, or of garden Hearbs.

Secondly, 'tis not the tenth sheaf as ours, but only the twentieth sheaf of Wheat and Rye is paid to them... They take no Tithe of Calves, Hay, Hay-grasse, or Justments, much lesse Tithe of Pigs, Geese, Apples, Egs, and of every thing almost the poor live on, our Gospel Ministers must have their Tithes. (p.53f.)

MORE OFFICERS IN THE CHURCH THAN EVER CHRIST COMMANDED

...since the Independent Pastors are turn'd Parsons and Preachers of the Gospel, Parish-Priests; the burthen of Tithes hath been more oppressive

in them, than in the Prelats and Presbyters heretofore. For first, These were National Ministers, and did service to every Parish in the Nation, therefore the National maintenance was more of right proper for them; but the Independent Churches, separating from the Nation, and professing a Gospel-practise, cannot for shame deny their own Principles, as to keep up Tithes, but rather to look for a maintenance from their own Churches, or to live of the Gospel, if they preach to the World... as Tithes under this oppressive Form was first established by the Churches of Wales, who have given example for the English to follow the pattern and oppression; so consider what the Churches there have gained by this, even more Officers in the Church than ever Christ commanded, as Commissioners, Treasurers, Sequestrators and Collectors for Tithes, a thing which neither Law nor Gospel, nor former Ages ever heard of. (p.54)

THE LORD'S ORDINANCE... THE BAPTISM OF THE SPIRIT AND OF FIRE

It is not Ordinances, but thine Ordinance, the Lord's Ordinance (as I shall shew another time) is the Spirits presence and power from on high; this was the first Gospel-Ordinance, the Baptism of the Spirit and of Fire: for the appearance of the Spirit, was on every Ordinance of the Gospel; in water-Baptism... in breaking of bread... all outward Ordinances of the Gospel were but the Ordinances of man, though appointed by God, the appearance and power of the Spirit was the Ordinance of God. (p.55)

SAINTS IN WALES WERE SIMPLE-HEARTED, SINCERE, SELF-DENYING, AND DYING TO THE WORLD

Truly, The Spirit's presence was more waited on, and the Saints [in] *Wales were far more spiritual before their Church-fellowship, more simple-hearted, sincere, self-denying, and dying to the world; yea, though they walkt in Ordinances, there was no talk of Ordinances, they were dead unto them (it being the worlds Religion) the Saints were all drawn up to the Spirit, which made them to be scoft of the world, which now they follow in their principles, practice, and desire of profit?* (p.55)

THEIR GOODNESS IS QUITE GONE, AND CARRIED AWAY INTO CAPTIVITY

Where many Nations, yea, strange and savage people, are brought into the House of God, who (I believe) in his due time will gather these three Nations into one Church, (as the first fruits of his glory and fame to the world)… As [God with us] *is the Nations Motto, so God in the Nation, or the whole Nation, is the offering or people of God… Oh how secretly and suddenly is the day of the Lord, or the Lords day stollen upon the Churches of Wales, Christ being come as a thief in the night to spoil them of all their glory and honour; yea, their goodness is quite gone, and carried away into captivity.* (p.56f.)

I THEN LABOURED TO BE RICH, I NOW LEARN TO BE POOR

Oh to live in the Lord alone, to look for maintenance from him only, no other maintenance but himself… Thus 'twas with the Apostles and Primitive Preachers of the Gospel… Others preach for a hundred pound a year, I have now preached to lose it, in which indeed I have found my life, and a better livelihood in the Lord: who hath promised that he will not leave me, nor forsake me, Heb. 13. And truely you may believe me, I have more content, quietness, comfort in my present losse, and low estate, then in all my gainful Tithes.

I then laboured to be rich, I now learn to be poor, to be Independent indeed… my children are now fatherless, and my wife a widdow, but God will be a father to them, and a husband to her; yea, her Physician also according to promise… (p.57f.)

GOD WILL FIND A WAY TO FEED THE POOR OUT OF THE BELLIES OF THE RICH

But all men are my flesh also, and because I would not hide my self from them, I had it once in my thoughts to take this hundred pound at present, and to give it as a publick stock for the poor of Cardiff.

It was presently answered unto me, I hate robbery for burnt offerings &c. God will shortly provide for the poor, though man will not… Lastly, In the day of wrath, when they shall cast their silver in the Streets, then

God will find a way to feed the poor out of the bellies of the rich, who shall not only make restitution according to their substance, but shall vomit up all that they have swallowed... I am waiting for the fulfilling of this Word, which God will hasten in his due time; in mean while, I can but pity the poor and the rich also, even the great Oppressor, whose plague is coming. (p.58)

7

The Sword Doubled: A Scourge for the Assyrian 1652

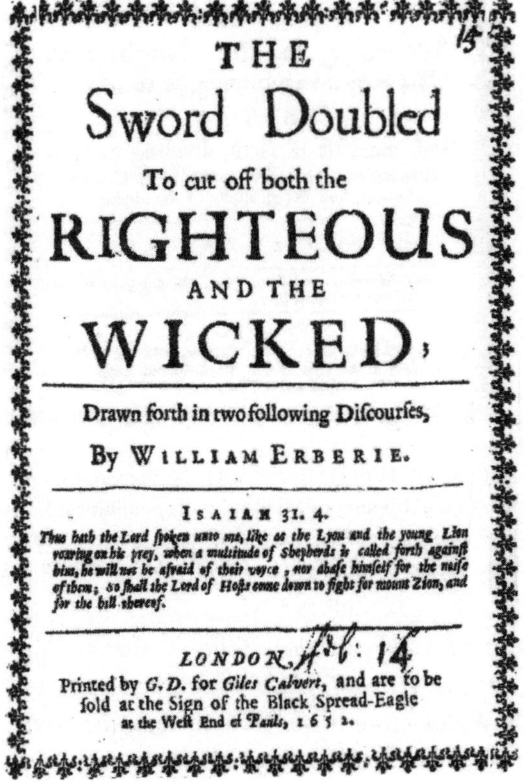

THE

Sword Doubled

To cut off both the

RIGHTEOUS

AND THE

WICKED;

Drawn forth in two following Discourses,

By WILLIAM ERBERIE.

ISAIAH 31. 4.

Thus hath the Lord spoken unto me, like as the Lyon and the young Lion roaring on his prey, when a multitude of Shepherds is called forth against him, he will not be afraid of their voyce, nor abase himself for the noise of them; so shall the Lord of Hosts come down to fight for mount Zion, and for the hill thereof.

LONDON, Feb: 14

Printed by *G. D.* for *Giles Calvert*, and are to be sold at the Sign of the Black Spread-Eagle at the West End of *Pauls*, 1652.

THE Sword Doubled To cut off both the RIGHTEOUS AND THE WICKED; Drawn forth in two following Discourses, By WILLIAM ERBERIE. (Received into the Thomason Collection on February 14th, 1652/3)

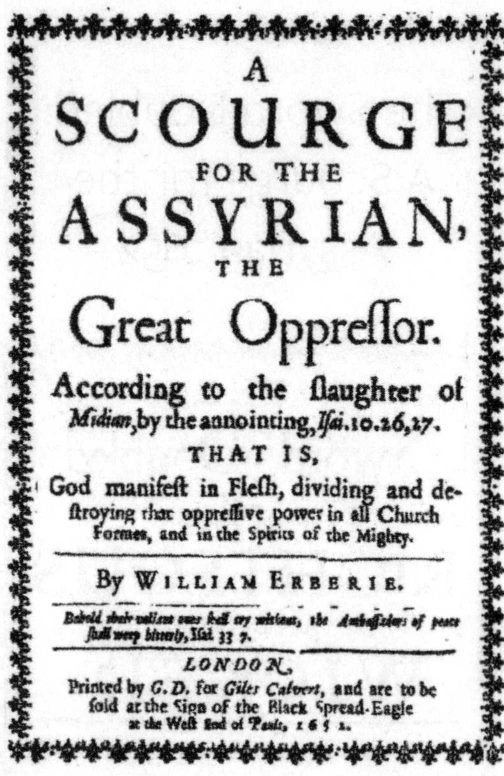

A
SCOURGE
FOR THE
ASSYRIAN,
THE
Great Oppressor.
According to the slaughter of *Midian*, by the annointing, *Isai*. 10. 26, 27.
THAT IS,
God manifest in Flesh, dividing and destroying that oppressive power in all Church Formes, and in the Spirits of the Mighty.

By WILLIAM ERBERIE.

Behold their valiant ones shall cry without, the Ambassadors of peace shall weep bitterly, Isai 33 7.

LONDON,
Printed by *G. D.* for *Giles Calvert*, and are to be sold at the Sign of the Black Spread-Eagle at the West End of *Pauls*, 1652.

A SCOURGE FOR THE ASSYRIAN, the Great Oppressor. According to the slaughter of Midian, by the annointing, Isa 10.26, 27. THAT IS, God manifest in Flesh, dividing and destroying that oppressive power in all Church Formes, and in the Spirits of the Mighty. By WILLIAM ERBERIE.

A Scourge for the Assyrian follows the earlier *The Grand Oppressor, or The Terror of Tithes* which had appeared as a Letter to a south Wales commissioner. The commissioners had been appointed to implement an Act for the Better Propagation and Preaching of the Gospel in Wales (February 22nd, 1649). The former tract, published early in 1652 appeared in Thomason's collection on July 21st, 1652.

The Sword Doubled including both *The Grand Oppressor* and *A Scourge for the Assyrian* was published later that year, entering the Thomason Collection on February 14th, 1652/3.

A Scourge for the Assyrian, addressed 'to the Independent Pastors and Teachers in Wales, and in England also', is much longer and less personal than *The Grand Oppressor.* Erbery carefully presents his interpretation of theology, history and social action. It is the only writing by Erbery to be re-published after *The Testimony of William Erbery* appeared in 1658. It was published in Salop in 1770 by Thomas Meredith.[1]

The Assyrian, or the Babylonian is an image representing an oppressive power which must be eliminated from Church and Commonwealth. Erbery's use of this Biblical metaphor reflected the same abusive style as that of the historic denominations. The Church of England branded the Papacy as the whore of Babylon; Presbyterians used the same image for Anglicans; and Independents for Presbyterians. Erbery took the image a stage further by describing all oppressive powers as Babylon. Babylon was both the civil government of monarchy, aristocracy and democracy, and the ecclesiological government of Prelate, Presbyterian and Independent.

In the introduction, Erbery explored different forms of church government. The main thrust of the treatise was however to explore the nature of Christ, and the relationship of Christ with God and the saints. In *The Great Mystery of Godliness* Erbery had adhered to the contemporary orthodox view of the substitutionary theory of the atonement, by which the death of Christ appeased a God, whose justice needed to be satisfied. Now Erbery speaks of God in Trinity, fully at work in creation, reconciliation and sanctification. The divine essence of the Father, is in the Son and in the saints.

What led Erbery to follow this path? As a student of theology, he was conversant with historic exploration of doctrine. His studies in Oxford and Cambridge led to his ordination and serving for a decade in the Church of England. *The Great Mystery of Godliness* was a catechism which pleased orthodox thinkers. Erbery was changed by the Civil War which gave him a fresh experience of the indwelling Christ and a conviction that God was guiding history to its climax in the Third Dispensation.

What determines Erbery's theological interpretation is his experience that God who brought all things into being, is incarnate in Christ and is eternally present in the saints. Christ in you, the hope of glory, is the Spirit to be manifested in fullness in the imminent Third Dispensation.

For most of Erbery's generation, the Gospel was salvation from sin, repentance, a holy life, deliverance from hell and a reward in heaven. Erbery saw that this might prove good news for a minority of saved saints, but it was dreadful news for the majority of humankind. Different churches might be convinced that they alone provided the secure path to the saintly life, but its consequence was intolerance, persecution and religious wars, including the English Civil War.

Was it Erbery's experience of the disasters of the war that led him to yearn for a tolerant society? This was an era when churches used history to justify their own position. Erbery interpreted history differently. He explored the theological changes within the puritanism of the previous 100 years, and argued that although interpretations of faith changed, the substance of the Gospel remained. He described four steps within English puritanism as a pilgrims' progress:

> Though I am but a child in understanding, and in years also to some of our Elders; yet here I observed four great steps of Gods glorious appearance in mens preaching… First, how low and legal were their teachings, as they learnt the way of preaching from Mr Perkins, Bolton, Byfield, Dod and Dike[2] … Next the Doctrine of free Grace came forth, but with lesse successe or fruit of conversion, by Doctor Preston, Sibs, Crispe[3]… Thirdly, the Letter of Scripture, and the flesh of Christ hath been highly set up by both the famous Goodwins[4]… this is the fourth step which some have attained to, holding forth Christ in the Spirit, as Mr William Sedgwick, Mr Sterrie, Mr Sprig, and others.[5]

God spoke through generations of preachers, all of whom were preparing for holding forth Christ in the Spirit. This would mark the climax of history. Even more startling was Erbery's claim that the fulfilment of God's purposes would be accompanied by the end of religion. What would replace religion? A world of righteousness!

> God will so appear in men, that instead of speakings, they shall go forth in actings of love to mankind, and to the miserable part thereof, to the poor, to the oppressed, to the fatherlesse, and the widow, and to all that want that which we abound in.

The recent history of these islands was proof that the Age of Apostasy was drawing to a close. Like many fellow Puritans, Erbery believed the saints had been raised to power by God's direct intervention in the history of seventeenth-century England. Saints had been persecuted, been forced to flee to Holland and New England, but by the late 1640s, they had been raised to political and religious power. This was the handiwork of the Lord! Erbery's chief premise was not that God was giving power to parliament or the Army, but that God was replacing oppressive regimes by those strengthening religious freedom, and propagating social righteousness.

How was God at work in the world? Erbery had discarded his orthodox emphasis upon God's action being centred on the Word and sacraments. His emphasis was on God at work through political and military instruments. Oppressions were being removed. Religious formalism was being replaced by potent, secular structures establishing national righteousness. Erbery castigated the churches for their blindness to society's needs. Because of their obsessive concern for forms of church government, ministries and ordinances, the churches were proving themselves to be irrelevant to the issues of the day.

Erbery was motivated by the dynamic of hope. In his prophetic vision of a world modelled by righteousness and peace, the three nations, particularly Wales, played a key role in the fulfilment of the divine purpose.

A Scourge for the Assyrian is a significant work. It holds together

Erbery's experience of Christ in you, the hope of glory, and his assurance that God's purposes will be fulfilled at the Third Dispensation. This sense of God's immanence and imminence gives consistency and intelligibility to the whole work. Erbery presents an alternative to a theological system and ecclesiological structures which had lost the life-giving spirit. Erbery had moved on. Although by 1647, Erbery had twice been accused of heresy, he was still prepared to continue his journey in the company of the suffering saints. Life ahead was likely to be even more uncomfortable.

TO THE INDEPENDENT PASTORS AND TEACHER IN WALES, AND IN ENGLAND ALSO

THE SWORD BEING DOUBLED

As King and Lords had an end, and twice the Sword hath been against the Prelatick and Presbyterian party; so the Sword being doubled the third time, will smite that prophane and wicked Prince, whatever he be, who is the Oppressor, who is imperious, proud, peevish, covetous, cruel, and cunning, for bloud; oh the Sword of the Lord will find him out. (p.60)

THE PEOPLE OF GOD ARE SILENT, & SIT STILL, SEEKING ONLY SELF

Art thou become like unto us, as one of the Kings of England, or the Princes of Wales? What man would think, that the Church or people of God should ever come to this, to oppress both God & man, good and bad at once?… the great things and Conquests here attained by the people of God was, when they were nothing; now being something they are overcome by all, and by themselves… But when the people of God are silent, & sit still, seeking only self, not sensible of the burthens of the oppressed, of the Prisoners bands, nor of poor families who cry for bread, how dwelleth the love of God in them, saith John?

Well, want of love, besides worldliness, wrath, & that oppressive power in the Churches, is the cause why they are so divided among themselves… (p.61f.)

THERE IS A THREEFOLD GOVERNMENT... MONARCHY, ARISTOCRACY, AND DEMOCRACY... ARCHBISHOP, PRESBYTERIAN, INDEPENDENT OR BAPTIZED

Now there is a threefold kind of Government among men, Monarchy, Aristocracy, and Democracy; the first is as of the King, the second is like that of the Parliament, the present Government some compare to the third, though it appears not yet; but Parliament and Army have voted the Supream power to be in the people.

Well, the Churches must have power and rule also, the Prelatick Church was Monarchical, all were ruled by one, by an Archbishop, the Kingly Power or Prerogative fell by that: The Presbyterian Church is an Aristocracy, the Elders or chief of these govern as 'twere in a Parliament, and Parliamentary Priviledges was like to fall by them, if not fallen already. The Independent or baptized Churches (both is one) are a pure Democracy, for not the ruling Men or Ministers, but all the Members, have equal power to order and ordain as they professe; and therefore called Independent. I wish they were so, but if they have a dependance on the Civil or Martial power, 'twill be worse for both, if both be not wiser than former times.

A word to the wise, 'tis my folly to use so many to understanding men as the Ministers are, especiall Independents, being men of parts, power, policy, and of piety also many; I shall fear none of them, because I love them all, and they me, though wrath at present may appear in both, as it doth among themselves. (p.63)

A SCOURGE FOR THE ASSYRIAN, THE GREAT OPPRESSOR... CHRIST IN US THE HOPE OF GLORY

As Christ is the glory of the Father, the appearance of God, or God manifest in flesh; so God in Christ, the Father in him, was that which was most hated by the Church of the Jewes, and Christ in us; Christ in the Church is abhorred by the Christian Churches; who not knowing the Deity nor the humanity of Christ indeed, will not acknowledg the Father to be the Godhead of Christ, nor his brethren to be his humanity, in whom the fulness of the Godhead is so embodyed, that he being the head, and they the members, they and he make one perfect man, in whom God appears to be all in all, I Cor. 15.28.

This Mystery of God, even the Father, and of Christ, is therefore abhorred by the Shepherds, or Pastors of Churches, because they knew not the Father in the Son, nor the Son in the Saints, nor the Spirit in both, which would reveal this glory in them, God in their F[l]esh, that is, Christ in us the hope of glory, which now they hate and abhor, not having higher discoveries of God, then what they have read in traditional forms of doctrine received and invented by men. (p.64)

THE FATHER IS THE INVISIBLE GOD INHABITING ETERNITY, SO CHRIST IS GOD VISIBLE

For as the Father is the invisible God inhabiting eternity, so Christ is God visible, the image or out-goings of God, the glory of the Father (in flesh) the appearance of God (as I said) or God manifest in flesh, who in the Spirit was from the beginning, and will be to the end, though this mystery of Christ was not manifested to men till the fulness of time, when the mighty God the everlasting Father, appeared in flesh, taken of a Virgin, then the Son was born; for God was brought forth in flesh, and was manifest in flesh, by mighty works and words which he spake and did, while he lived in the dayes of his flesh, but in his death God crucified that flesh to himself, which afterward he raised to glory, God rising or revealing himself gloriously therein; then God ascended up on high, that is, God in flesh did ascend not only to heaven, but far above all heavens, into his own eternal abysse, and incomprehensible Being, and unaccessible light, whence the brightness of his glory proceeded, and came forth in flesh in the fulness of time, as we said before. (p.64f.)

THE SAME SPIRIT AND POWER OF GOD, DWELLING IN THE FLESH OF CHRIST, APPEARED IN THE CHURCH WHICH IS CALLED CHRIST

But this Mystery was not made known nor manifested to the Sons of men, till God, who ascended up in flesh, sent down the Spirit from on high… the same Spirit and power of God, dwelling in the flesh of Christ, appeared in the Church which is called Christ, I Cor. 12.12 because the Son was revealed, or known in the Saints, and they in the Son, and both in the Father, all perfect in one… It is the promise of the Father, the power of God from on high, which the Saints received from and with the Son, they being Sons and Co-heirs with him, Joh. 15.26. This Mystery of Christ, though once manifested to the Apostles and Primitive Saints by the Spirit, and since then shut up as a sealed Book by the apostasie or spirit of Antichrist in the Churches; yet the book will be open, the mystery will be manifest again, for the mystery of God shall be finished, and fully known at last, Rev. 10.7. But as Christ is the first and the last, he who was, is, and is to come, so Christ was vailed in the Law and is revealed in the Gospel, (though but in part) the full Revelation of Christ Jesus is to come, Jesus Christ the same yesterday, and today, and for ever, not Christ after the flesh for that was not till the fulness of time, but Christ in the Spirit, God manifest in flesh, was both yesterday under the Law, and in the day of Gospel-dispensation; and in the third dispensation now approaching, he will abide for ever…

There was a change indeed from Law to Gospel, when the Spirit of Christ first came into the Church; the state of the Gospel changed also, when the Spirit of Antichrist came in power, and the Churches fell by the Apostasie; when Christ shall come the second time in Spirit and glory, time shall be no more, no more change of things shall be, for all things and times shall appear in eternity, which is the third dispensation: as the first was yesterday, the second to day, so the third is to be for ever. (p.65)

THERE WILL BE A FULL HARVEST, FLOUDS, AND RIVERS OF WATERS OF LIFE

…there will be a full harvest, flouds, and Rivers of waters of life which no man can passe over, when the earth shall be full of the knowledg of the Lord… There the Lord God Almighty and the Lamb, God even the Father, and Christ the Father's glory shall be fully known by men; For as Christ is the appearance of God, so when God shall appear in men, they shall know how Christ was under the Law, and as he is in the Gospel, and will be the same for ever.

All that I know at present of Christ is this. He was under the Law in Forms: In the Gospel he appeared in Flesh, he will appear wholly in Spirit, in Spirit only the appearance of the great GOD and Saviour shall be, and yet manifest in the flesh of men, that is, all the transactions of God, or all that God did in the flesh of Christ, shall visibly appear in the flesh of men; the birth of Christ, his life, death, resurrection, and ascension shall be seen in us, men shall see us ascend in a cloud, to sit in Heaven to judg the world and Angels, and to be Saviours of men in mount Zion at last. (p.66)

THIS GLORIOUS APPEARING OF THE GREAT GOD... IS THAT WHICH HATH BEEN EVER MOST OPPOSED AND PERSECUTED

This glorious appearing of the great God, rising up in higher discoveries of himself in men, is that which hath been ever most opposed and persecuted; I speak not now of the times under the Law, nor Gospel, nor yet of former appearances, since the Apostasie. But to go no further then our own age, what we have heard and seen: How was the appearance of God in the First Reformers, yea, in our Prelats and Bishops persecuted as Heresie by the Popish Hierarchy! Next the honest Presbyters or Puritans, how were they opposed by the same Prelats, who suffered before? Thirdly these Presbyterians, formerly themselves in a suffering condition, persecuted the appearance of God in those of higher forms and fellowships, as the Independent Churches; and these likewise are ready to oppose and persecute the spirits of the Saints, who in worship and doctrine are of higher discoveries then themselves. (p.67)

FOUR GREAT STEPS OF GOD'S GLORIOUS APPEARANCE IN MENS PREACHING

The doctrine of God and of Christ for substance is the same in all the Saints, though their apprehensions differ, or are divers rather. And who is ignorant of this, that the appearances of God in one man, hath not been the same as it was formerly in himself? and yet all have been going on from strength to strength, at least in their desires and aims toward Zion.

Though I am but a child in understanding, and in years also to some of our Elders; yet here I observed four great steps of Gods glorious appearance in mens preaching.

First, how low and legal were their teachings, as they learnt the way of preaching from M. Perkins, Bolton, Byfield, Dod and Dike, most blessed in their generation; by whom, and such conforming Ministers, more men were converted to God, then ever since in any period of time.

Next the Doctrine of free Grace came forth, but with lesse successe or fruit of conversion, by Doctor Preston, Sibs, Crispe; yet many before converted were confirmed and comforted by their words.

Thirdly, the Letter of Scripture, and the flesh of Christ hath been highly set up by both the famous Goodwins: the one, Mr. John Goodwin, like Apollos being mighty in Scriptures and strength of reason; the other excels in spiritual discourses of Christ's death, resurrection, ascension, and intercession, yet much according to the flesh; for he meddles not with the Mystery of Christ in us, or his dying in us (as Mr Dell[6] *in part discovers) but all of Christ without us, which though a truth, yet not the whole truth, nor that spirit and truth which Christ spake of... so Christ was sent, or God even the Father was manifest in his flesh, that we might see God in us, as he was in him, and our life with him in God: Lastly, thus Christ is the life, and thus he that hath the Son hath life; that is, the Son being once revealed in us, reveals the Father in us also, God in our flesh as in his, and we living with him in God alone...*

This is the knowledg of Christ in the Spirit, and this is the fourth step which some have attained to, holding forth Christ in the Spirit, as Mr. William Sedgwick, Mr. Sterrie, Mr. Sprig, and others, these with their fellows are nearest Zion, yet they are not come into it... it is not Zion, when there shall be such a glorious appearance of God in men, that all shall see and hear him in them... Then man shall be nothing and God shall be all in all; yet man shall be all in God, and nothing but God shall appear in man. (pp.67–69)

THESE ARE DIVIDED, NOT ONLY IN WORSHIP AND DISCIPLINE, BUT IN DOCTRINE ALSO

These are divided, not only in Worship and Discipline, but in Doctrine also, especially in three things. 1. In the free grace of God, which some call Antinomianism. 2. In the free-will of man, which others call Pelagianism. 3. In the death of Christ, or universal Redemption of mankind thereby, which both Presbyters and Independents abhor as Paganism, though nearest the Gospel indeed... [They] *follow the childish Dictates of Fathers, the Decrees of Councels, being a company of Bishops, with such Creeds, Confessions, and Catechisms formed by them, (and reformed Churches) whose conformities and fooleries in forms of worship, though our Churches cannot chuse but see, yet with a blind devotion they follow all their forms of doctrine, not suffering a doubt or the least debate to passe upon their reason and judgment therein…* [They are captivated] *by vain Philosophy, and metaphysical speculations of the Deity by the traditions and inventions of men, the rudiments of the world, the rudiments, that is, the A.B.C. or common Catechisms, which is the Religion of the world, and of little Children… Arminians and Socinians go no farther than Christ after the flesh, and the last especially, though religious and most learned men, yet look no higher than flesh; yea, the eternal Spirit and infinite God they confine to a place in Heaven, where, say they, his essential presence is, though his power be every where; a very carnal conceit of God and of Christ.* (p.70f.)

IS IT NOT BETTER FOR US TO WAIT IN PEACE AND PATIENCE?

What a madness is it then for men to war and wrangle about that they know not? Is it not better for us to wait in peace and patience, forbearing one another, and embracing one another in love, till the Lord God appear in all?… You think you know Christ, and can preach him well enough: we shall be all silent, and God himself shall speak at last, and speak himself, and manifest himself unto men: Oh that men could watch and wait in love together to that day. (p.72f.)

ALL RELIGIOUS FORMS SHALL FALL, THAT THE POWER OF RIGHTEOUSNESS MAY RISE AND APPEAR IN ALL

That which I conclude from this, is, that God is going out, and departing from all the preachings of men, that men may give themselves wholly to publick acts of love one to another, and to all mankind; therefore all religious forms shall fall, that the power of righteousness may rise and appear in all: The new Heaven and new Earth, where dwelleth righteousness, hath no form of Religion there. (2 Pet. 3.11; Rev. 21.22)

I see 'tis hastening by many things, and this to me is not the least prophetick providence and experience in the present powers of the Nation: When the Parliament of England first began, Oh what speakings were there? What Speeches of several Members of the House of Commons were printed every week? But now the Common-wealth comes on, there is more of Action done every day: and though the Parliament many times say more than they do; yet they do more than they say, which is best of all. (p.73)

PARLIAMENTS ORDINANCES ARE NOW TURNED INTO ACTS

...so 'tis remarkable, that all the Parliaments Ordinances are now turned into Acts; for Acts indeed are better than Ordinances, these are of form, those of power. The Army was best indeed when they were about their Ordnances, their Guns, going forth for common freedom, those were their Acts, and God did blesse them therein in all their publick actings, and in their publick Spirits; but as for their publick speakings, their Declarations, Protestations, Remonstrances, 'tis not worth a rush: So are their Councells of War, when judging the Consciences of men in the Mysterie of Christ, (a most high presumption:) yea, all their fasting and prayer before God is not worth a pins head, till they repent and return to their first principles, to the power of [of] *Righteousnesse, to Justice, and Mercy to the Nation without all self-seeking, striving for the universal good of mankind, even for Papists and Jewes themselves to live with freedom and comfort among us.*

This is the glorious appearance of the great God, not to talk and prate of things, but to be working and acting, to be ever doing good, as Christ did alwaies to all; and though there was a Ministry of men once to speak also glad tydings and good things to men, yet since the Apostacy, that Apostolick Ministery being silenced. (p.73f.)

WHY NOT A TREASURY FOR THE POOR?

Alas, what is it to send Preachers abroad before the burthens and oppressions of the people be eased?... I say, not all burthens taken off, because the charge of the Common-wealth encreaseth; but why may not rich Citizens, racking Landlords in the Country, and mighty moneyed men, be made immediatly to rise in their payments, that poor Farmers, Labourers, and honest Tradesmen may be spared? Why not oppression be presently eased, at least of Lawyers and Tithes? Why not a Treasury for the poor, when so many thousands a year, can be found out to give to the rich? would that hinder the publick more than this? It is the goodness of the State indeed, to honour and confer gifts on high deserving men; but it is dishonourable and base for such to receive it, who neglecting the publick good, seek their private gain; who would seem to be Saints, and self-denying men, yet forgetting their Vowes to God and men care not though the poor and the oppressed sink, starve, and dye, so they may live fat, and full, and free from those evils.

Gifts are as bad as bribes, when Justice and great things are to be done in a Nation, for as a bribe blinds the eyes… so a gift destroys the heart, that the most publick spirited man dares not think a good thought, much lesse to speak or act for common freedom and the good of mankind, while money stops the mouth, choaks and destroys the heart. (p.75)

IN PUBLICK ACTINGS, THE EVERLASTING GOSPEL SHALL GO FORTH IN THE LAST TIMES

This would be Gospel indeed and glad tydings to the poor, and make all the oppressed in the Land to sing; for this is the everlasting Gospel, which shall be preached, not in word but in power, not as the Gospel at first in speaking, or preachings; but in publick actings, the everlasting Gospel shall go forth in the last times… the Angel of the Covenant Christ in us, God in our flesh, that is, God fully manifest in us shall minister himself to us, God shall minister himself to men; a pure ministery of the Spirit shall be, the Spirit shall only minister both light and love among men, salvation, and strength, sufficiency, and fulness of all good things to the whole Creation at last. (p.76)

NOR YET CHRIST WERE HE AMONG THEM WOULD THEY CALL BROTHER

True, it is but flesh and fleshly forms that Churches fight and contend for, the cause of all the contention is in the Shepherds or the Ministers, the Church-members poor souls would be quiet, and come up again to walk in the Spirit; but because the Members will follow, not the Head, but their fellows, Members and Ministers, God gives them up their King, ver.6. Who is that? Sure some chief Pastor who commands in Church and Common-wealth...

The Independent Church was built once on a Covenant; now being ashamed of that they call it a Confession, others an Agreement, God breaks all in pieces, even the Covenant...

How clear doth this appear in the present Churches, who by a Law cal none brothers but such of their own societies: no Saint whatsoever, nor yet Christ were he among them would they call brother, unlesse he were of a Church-way, and of theirs also; therefore the brotherhood between Judah and Israel, (the Independent and baptized Churches) is broken... those fellow-Members who were more moderate and peacable minded men, not given to common division, are yet destroyed and die in their spirits, by being in Church-fellowship... All the people of God this day are a dead divided people; not only gathered Churches, but scattered Saints; these in their flesh, those in their forms and fellowships... yea, they are not so lowly and loving, as once they were, so humble and tenderly minded, so self-denying and dying to the world. (p.76f.)

BABYLON IS YET DIVIDED INTO THREE PARTS

But Babylon is yet divided into three parts; for since the Apostacy the Churches have been still divided into three parts, as the Greek and Latine Churches of old, and the Affrican Church that made the third, there was the Eastern, Western, and Southern Churches: So in the North at the first Reformation, the Calvinist, Lutheran, and Anabaptist in Germany. Thus it is in England, the Prelatick, Presbyterian, and Independent Churches, are Babylon divided into three parts. (p.78)

THE CHURCHES ARE BECOME THREE BODIES, AND THESE HAVE THREE BAPTISMS

The Apostolick Churches or Churches of Christ were but one Body, had but one Baptism, as there was but one Spirit leading all the Saints in one Church-way, one way of worship, one Church-government was among all the Saints, though there were differences between brother and brother; yea, between one Apostle and another, yet never was there a difference between Church and Church, as in Babylon this day; for the Spirit being then but one, kept the body in one Baptism. But now the Churches are become three bodies, and these have three Baptisms; Presbyterians baptize the whole Nation; Independents the children of believers only; the baptized Churches believers themselves: Here is Babylon in three parts: Again, the baptized Churches are subdivided into three parts, one Church is for Free-will, a second for universal Redemption, a third count themselves more Orthodox in Doctrine, as the Church of England: Neither of these three baptized Churches dare communicate one with another. (p.78)

PRELATICK, PRESBYTERIAN, AND INDEPENDENT CHURCHES

Thus it was with the Prelatick, Presbyterian, and Independent Churches: these two last stood up, utterly to slay and destroy the first both Root and Branch, and now they help to destroy one another, as Independent and baptized Churches both against Presbytery, and now these two against each other: Yea, the baptized Churches themselves are divided into three parts, are now in destruction by their own divisions…

I will not speak of the Popish Church which continued so many hundreds of years, look but into our own Land in these last daies, wherein the mystery of Iniquity, hath been most manifest, not only by the Spirit, but by sensible experience, and the event of things in a very little time.

Prelacy upheld by Kingly power, continued about seventy years, inslaving the people of God…

Presbytery reigned but three years and a half (the time of the Beast) by Parliamentary Authority…

Independency is down in a month… the whole Army cannot help them up again…

Thus it was with the Churches; The Prelats thought themselves Preachers of the Gospel: how high did they hold their heads…

It was just so with the Presbyters, when in power with the Parliament…

Well, the Independent Pastors and Teachers their month comes…

Oh, when will their moneth be? Whence can their sufferings arise, seeing the whole State, and the highest Souldiery is for them? For all this they must suffer, all the world cannot save them… (pp.79–81)

KINGLY PREROGATIVE… PARLIAMENTARY PRIVILEDGES… ARMY… THE COMMON-WEALTH

Oh, there is an Ensign set up in the Saints, ver 9 [Isaiah 31.9], *the glorious appearance of God in the scattered Saints makes the gathered Churches quake and fear; but where is the fire?… a third overturn will be: The first was of Kingly prerogative by the Parliament, then the Prelats fell; the second was of Parliamentary Priviledges, when the Army came up to purge it, then Presbyters fell: there will be a third overturn, whether for better or worse I know not, yet I hope well of the Common-wealth, and Rulers thereof; but down go the ruling Elders with all their Churches, the very next month, when a change of things will be.* (p.81f.)

THAT IMMORTALL SEED OF THE WORD

…the pure word is… that immortall seed of the Word, when it is sincere, spiritual, and pure, how precious and how powerful is it?… What lean, low, and legal teachings do our Preachers of the Gospel set forth and tell? it is but the refuse of all, that which good Mr. Perkins, Doctor Preston, and the rest of those pious men left behind; it is not their spirit these men speak with, it is but their words, or the language of old writers in a new dresse.

Nay, most of these Pastors or Preachers of the Gospel can go no farther than the flesh of Christ, and the Letter of Scripture. As for that eternal Spirit which dwelt in the one, and which spake in the other, they know not. (A chief one of the Army would once usually say, that the flesh of Christ, and Letter of Scripture, were the two great Idols of Antichrist.) (p.84)

FOR GOVERNMENT AND GAUDIES, OR EATING GOOD CHEER

But now see what Marchants we have in the world… an old Sermon, that is even mouldy with lying by, they will not part with without a price; yea, they sell it them at a dear rate, none will preach now under a hundred pound a year: teaching is turned to a meer Trade, he that will give most, shall have most Gospel. Under the Law, all the Priests had but the like allowance. Gospel-Ministers preached freely, yet wanted nothing: now men will not trust God, but must have before-hand, some twenty shillings for every Sermon they make, some forty shillings for every Sermon; yea, there are Pastors and Teachers in England, who have four pound for every Sunday Sermon, besides four pound every week, for government and gaudies, or eating good cheer.

I pray consider, is it according to the order of the Gospel, that Pastors should leave their own Church-fellowships, and turn fellows of Colledges? Is it according to the Gospel, that Pastors should become Princes and Presidents, Deans and Doctors? Is not this a secular employment? and this in the hands of spiritual men, is but the Instruments of a foolish Shepherd, as the Lord General Cromwel excellently words it.[7] (p.85)

MAMMON IS NOT ONLY THE GOD OF THE WORLD, BUT THE GOD OF CHURCHES ALSO

...if there be a righteous poor man that seeks the publick good of the Common-wealth, or the good of mankind, they will either keep him poor, or make him rich, they will stop his mouth with a piece of silver, or send him away in a pair of shooes. What's that? set him in a good office, or gainful imployment, that's a pair of shooes that many an honest heart is bought and sold for... I fear that Mammon is not only the god of the world, but the god of Churches also; yea, many good Christians make Mammon and mony their God. (p.86.)

THE MAGISTRATE IS THE MINISTER OF GOD

...these three Nations I believe will be the first saved ones in the world, from Monarchy, & Tyranny, and Babylons captivity from all Oppression and Bondage on mens States and Spirits... That Spirit which appeared in the Ministers of Christ preaching the Gospel at first, will now appear in the Christian Magistrate much more at last... As the Magistrate is the Minister of God, and the only true Minister now (there being none in the

Church); so God in the last dayes will first appear with power and glory, not in the Church but in the Common-wealth, not in Ministers at all, but in the Magistrate both Civil and Martial. (p.89f.)

THE FOOTSTEPS OF THE ALMIGHTY THIS DAY... HATH BEEN MOST VISIBLE TO, AND BY THE MAGISTRATE CIVIL AND MARTIAL

Indeed, if any man doth but observe and follow the foot-steps of the Almighty this day, in his waies and wonders among men; his glorious Appearance, and his Power, and Goodness in this Land hath been most visible to, and by the Magistrate Civil and Martial, at home and abroad, both by Land and Sea &c.

Alas, what have the Ministers done, but undone themselves and others? and still like to undo the whole Nation, as the Prelats in the first war, the Presbyters in the second war: and though a third war will not be; yet the prosperity, peace, and happy proceedings of the present Powers, how had the Independent and Baptized Churches like to hinder? How saucy and insolent were they about a new Representative? yea, no Parliament men, but Church-members, or chosen by them, was once in print: it is more observable, those Churches who could never communicate, nor come together before, became as one Congregation, to divide and undo the Common-wealth if possibly they could.

Well said noble General again We pray you own his people more and more, for they are the Chariots and Horsemen of Israel, disown your selves, but own your Authority and Power to curb the proud and the insolent, such as would disturb the tranquillity of England, under what specious pretences forever; relieve the oppressed, hear the groans of the Prisoners in England (when? Lord God holy and true, and a Treasury for the poor?) Be pleased to reform the abuses of all Professions and if there be any one that makes many poor to make a few rich, that suits not a Common-wealth: very well said indeed. The Lord General Cromwel's Letter from Dunbar. (p.90.)

IN WALES... IT IS BUT TO CHURCH THAT MULTITUDES RUN

That which you hear of so many called in Wales, is not so true as the report; it is but to Church that multitudes run, and most to the waters; but alas poor souls, they are still as simple and earthly as ever they were, as ignorant, carnal, and covetous, as little power of godliness, or knowledge in the Mystery of Christ, self denyal, sincerity, and singleness of heart: oh they are more double and divided, that light and love which was formerly in Wales in good Mr. Wroth's daies, is dead with him, and quite darkened. (p.91)

THE PRESENT GOVERNMENT WILL RIDE ON PROSPEROUSLY THROUGH THE THREE NATIONS

Again, I do not judge the Governours of our State, nor State-Ministers, sent forth by the power of man, to civilize and teach the people, to instruct the Nation in peace and holiness, and in (State Ministers will never do good till they gain the hearts of the people to the present Powers, in whom God hath so visibly appeared, that men cannot chuse but see and be convinced; that there is yet more good to be done by them, and for us, in Gods due time) honourable thoughts of the present Government, which (though yet clouded under particular corruptions, and crouching under its own greatness) will ride on prosperously through the three Nations, and rise above all the Nations round about, in spight of all their threats or attempts; yea, (though there be many a black month) yet the glory of the Lord shall cover it, till the glorious liberty of the Sons of God (and of men also) shall arise as the Sun in this Land as last, as the first fruits of freedom, and healing to the world. (p.91f.)

8

The Bishop of London 1652

THE
Bishop of London,
The Welsh Curate,
AND
Common Prayers,
WITH
Apocrypha
In the End.

By Will. Erbery.

Isai.24.1. to the end. *Behold, the Lord maketh the earth empty, and turneth it upside down.*
Acts 17.6. *These that have turned the world upside down, are come hither also.*

8th January

Printed at *London*, 1652.

THE Bishop of London, The Welsh Curate, AND
Common Prayers, WITH Apocrypha In the End.
By Will. Erbery.
Isai 24.1 to the end. *Behold, the Lord maketh the earth empty, and turneth it upside down.*
Acts 17.6. *These that have turned the world upside down, are come hither also.*
Printed at London, 1652.
(Received into the Thomason Collection on January 8th, 1652/3)

AT THE SAME time as he was writing *A Scourge for the Assyrian*, Erbery composed four short tracts, all appearing separately before being collected and published together in January 1652/3. *The Bishop of London* was the only one to be collected in *The Testimony*. The 1652 collection of the four tracts was published with the following titles: *The Bishop of London, The Welsh Curate, And Common Prayers with Apocrypha In the End, Printed at London, 1652.*

There are no publishing details, either for the works when they first appeared, or when they were later collected. There is also uncertainty about the titles. They were received by Thomason on January 8th, 1652. Four tracts are together in the same publication. They are *The Bishop of London*, *The Welsh Curate*, *Apocrypha* and *The General Epistle to the Hebrews*. Erbery's two previous works, *The Lord of Hosts* (December 1648) and *The Grand Oppressor* (July 1652) and his next tract, *The Sword Doubled* (February 1652/3), were all published by Giles Calvert, who was also responsible for *The Testimony* of 1658.

The Bishop of London and *The General Epistle to the Hebrews* respond to debates which had taken place at London House. Erbery had participated in the first debate on November 22nd, 1652. This was the period of the final months of the Long (Rump) Parliament which Cromwell dissolved on April 20th, 1653.

Political power in the House of Commons was slipping from the Presbyterians to the Independents who were supported by the New Model Army. One of the London congregations, consisting of Independents and Baptists and influenced by military men, had been meeting at Great All-Hallows[1] to pray for a new Representative. For some reason they moved from All-Hallows to London House. There is reference to both London House and Bishopsgate. Was London House the erstwhile residence of the Bishop of London? John Simpson[2] had been appointed to the rectory of St Botolph without Bishopsgate. Erbery attended several meetings of the congregation, listening impatiently to Captain Spencer, an Independent, and Mr Knight, a Baptist.

When Erbery returned the following week, he discovered that the major speakers were Christopher Feake[3] and John Simpson, leaders of the Fifth Monarchist movement. *The Bishop of London* makes no reference to their political intrigues,[4] but is confined to issues of prayer. After Feake had finished preaching, John Simpson stood to disagree with Feake's views. At this point Erbery interrupts the proceedings.

Did this outburst have a serious consequence? Was it the source of his reputation of being ill of his whimsies?[5] Was Erbery aware at the time of the possible consequence of his interruption? He seems to have felt the need to record that 'men said there, I was mad'.

What is certain is that the effect of Erbery's interruption was confusion at London House. Informality gave way to chaos. The Monday meetings at London House were more like a debating chamber without rules, than an act of liturgical worship. At this point Major William Packer[6] slandered Erbery for his 'Ranting Spirit', and Erbery in turn answered robustly before walking away. His final advice was to advise the saints to wait patiently and silently for the coming of the Third Dispensation. Erbery did not always take his own advice.

FROM GREAT ALL-HALLOWS TO LONDON HOUSE

The Churches of London, both Independent and Baptized ones, having formerly associated and girt themselves with a Sword, or Martial power, I mean, some Army-preaching men, joyned in a Body at Great Alhallows, to pray for a new Representative, and to preach somewhat against the old; for which they received no Countenance, but rather a Check from the State, and some highest of the Army. Having there laboured in vain, and spent their strength for nought; not finding the Spirit in a Presbyterial or Parochial Church, they changed their quarters, and came to seek it in the Episcopal Sea at London-house. (p.43)

A STRUCTURE OF TWO STORIES... TO PREACH AND PRAY

...they founded a Structure of two Stories high; not a Pulpit and Reading-Pue, but a stately frame of wood to preach and pray, in two distinct Forms.

The one, being the highest, I conceive is for the Independent Fellowship, (for such only I saw sitting there) the lower is the Baptized's Foot-stool.

The Lord brought me there, at first, to behold their Order; but seeing their Confusion, I yet heard one praying below, afterwards another above, Captain Spencer; at whose loud and long Prayer, my spirit was so stirred, I could scarce contain from crying out, Vox, & praeterea nihil.[7]

Mr Knight was next: but hoping to find no better from him, I departed in peace and silence. (p.43f.)

MR FEAK SPAKE TO THE PURPOSE CONCERNING PRAYER

The first man that I heard preaching, was Mr. Feak, who (methought) spake to the purpose concerning Prayer, That the Saints should now return to their old Spirit of Prayer in Gospel times, which was not in loose requests, and long confessions of sins, but in short breathings out their present desires to God, with abundance of fervency and faith to obtain... whereas Mr. Feak had truly declared what was said before concerning Prayer, Mr. Simpson doth presently censure, and publicly condemn, in preaching, what his brother had spoken in truth and peace, with much submission. (p.44f.)

THOUGH MEN SAID THERE, I WAS MAD

Though men said there, I was mad; yet truely I spake nothing but words of Soberness and Truth to me, with peace and love to all.

My Spirit indeed was exceedingly stirred; and though I came thither to hear in silence, yet my heart being hot, I spake at last with my tongue;

Mr. Simpson, you have preached long; will you suffer another fool to speak a little concerning Prayer? (p.45)

PRAYERS WERE PECULIAR AND PROPER ONLY TO SAINTS

Prelats had their Common-prayers, and your Prayers are common also; Presbyters had their Directory, so have you this day, teaching one another how to pray… but as Common Prayers, because quite contrary to the Practise of Primitive Churches, wherein Prayers were peculiar and proper only to Saints, and among Saints alone, as fellowship and breaking of bread: And Prayers was a Private exercise of Saints together in the Church, not with the world. (p.46)

9

The Welsh Curate 1652

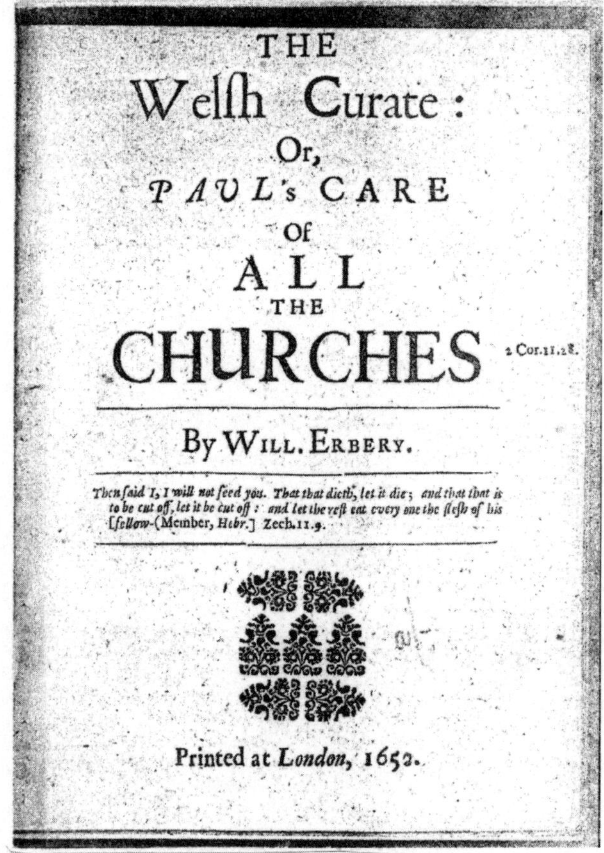

THE

Welſh Curate:

Or,

PAUL's CARE

Of

ALL

THE

CHURCHES 2 Cor.11.28.

By WILL. ERBERY.

Then ſaid I, I will not feed you. That that dieth, let it die; and that that is to be cut off, let it be cut off: and let the reſt eat every one the fleſh of his [*fellow*-(Member, *Hebr.*] Zech.11.9.

Printed at *London*, 1652.

THE Welsh Curate:
Or, PAUL's CARE of ALL THE CHURCHES
Printed at London, 1652.

FIRST PUBLISHED IN 1652, *The Welsh Curate* was the second of the four tracts in the collection of January 1652/3. Its theme is the nature of the church and the place of ordinances. Erbery's thinking about the life of the church was dominated by his theory of Three Dispensations. The Second, or Gospel Dispensation had ended with the arrival of the Age of Apostasy. Even during the Apostolic Age, the ordinances of Baptism and the Lord's Supper were of value only for the weak disciples, but when the Church fell into Apostasy, ordinances became mere forms. The saint should wait patiently for the Third Dispensation and live as a 'Free company, with an inward spirit, a voluntary joyning, a readiness of minde'. Erbery's language parallels that of the emerging Quaker movement, although there is no evidence that he joined such a Society of Friends. After his death, his widow and children all became Quakers.

THE BAPTISM OF THE SPIRIT... YET WAS IT FOR THE WORLD

But the first Ordinance, the Baptism of the Spirit, though on the Church, yet was it for the world; the rest were for the weak in the Church... the strong, who were spiritual and perfect, had the Anointing in them, that they needed not any man to teach them. So the Baptism of water was for a time, because of the weak disciples of John called to Christ... so breaking of bread was to shew forth the Lords death till he come, that is, till the same should be revealed fully in them all, and All be gathered up unto Christ... for even Gospel-Ordinances, in themselves, were but a Legal Dispensation, and gifts of the Spirit likewise, for the Church under the Law had the same... (p.3f.)

'TIS THE WISDOM OF GOD THIS WAY TO BEFOOL THE WORLD, AND THE WISEST OF THE CHURCHES

Therefore the present Churches are far belowe the Legal or Jewish Church under the Law: which proves the Apostacie or falling away to be already, and long since, though not revealed till now the Churches are come up to purest forms, where yet the Ordinances are defiled, and fail in spirit and form from the first.

Thus the Spirit not appearing in them, 'tis the wisdom of God this way to befool the world, and the wisest of the Churches, who coming neerest to Gospel-order in form, they must be the first in whom the spirit of Antichrist must come forth with power to appear in them and to All. (p.4)

THE CHURCH IS A FREE COMPANY, OR SOCIETY OF FRIENDS

Hark how the Apostle roars, and chides the Churches. Is this the Order I set you in? To creep together six or seven in a corner; then to close in a Covenant: thirdly, to cause the rest of the Saints to wait at your Church-doors for admission?... Admission of members manifests some Authority and Power in the fellow-members made up into a Body before: But was this ever among visible Saints, that some should be left behinde out of the Church? Must any of the members be out of the Body?

Again, Admission intimates the Church of Christ to be a Corporation, as if there were a Common Councel among them: whereas the Church is a Free company, or Society of Friends; who come together, not as called by an outward power, but freely closing by the inward spirit.

Therefore the adding of those to the Church, was nothing but a voluntary joyning of them whom the Lord did call.

Neither was there need of a confession of sins, or of their faith (as John's disciples did) to be received; but a readiness of minde to walk with the Saints.

Neither did poor Saints wait a yeer or two, as 'tis with the New English Churches in England and Wales (though the Rich are sooner received), but they did joyn, without being judg'd or questioned at all...

Were it not better for you (Brethren) to abide at Jerusalem? that is, the indwellings of God in you; this might content you for a time, to wait in your spiritual weakness, and bewildernessed state, till power come from on high, to carry ye forth to the world. (pp.7–9)

THEIR MAINTENANCE COMES IN THROUGH THE BOWELS OF THE POOR

Oh! how Pauls care for the Churches, doth tear the Pastors and Teachers in pieces, who run from Parish to Parish, from place to place, from Lectures and Livings, where they can get the best; not considering how their maintenance comes in through the bowels of the poor, from the empty bellies and sweat of hard-labouring men… Oh how doth this now plague our young lusty Scholars, and Souldiers, and Trades men, who would go forth as preachers of the Gospel, yet dare not live of the Gospel, nor trust God, till they have a command, and setled maintenance from men. (p.12f.)

THOU HAST MADE ME A MAN OF CONTENTION TO ALL THE EARTH

Truly, Brethren, for my part, I am no Prophet, nor the son of a Prophet, but am trembling at the word of God; and 'tis not my content or temper, to contend with men, and torment them: Onely I must say one word with the Prophet, Wo is me, my mother, that thou hast made me a man of contention to all the earth; (Jeremiah 15.10)… First to Prelates, then to Presbyters, now again to Independent and Baptized Churches: Alas! that I must fall upon them in their owne City and quarters, that a naked man must rush upon their swords points, upon all pikes, their powers, and places of strength.

Wo is me, it is my misery, that contrary to my owne principles of light and love to the Saints, I must be made a man of war and wrath to the Churches; (p.13f.)

NOT THAT I DO PROFESSE MY SELF ABOVE ALL ORDINANCES, BUT FAR BELOW THEM

…not that I do professe my self above all Ordinances, but far below them, not seeing that Spirit of life which once appeared with them, nor any Gospel-Ordinance at present according to the letter of Scriptures, neither the baptisme of the Spirit which was the first, nor fellowship, nor breaking of Bread, nor Prayers, as they were: And yet I am in a lower form then any of the Churches: theirs are for edification, mine for destruction; they

edifie one another, and build in Babylon, and I break down or destroy both it and them, and my self in it with them: their forms and my flesh suffer together, not onely in my outward comforts, but my inward also, my peace and joy, for this and all, is but the goodliness of flesh, which must wither, when the Glory is to be revealed in it, Isa. 40.5, 6. (p.14f.)

AS IF THE WORLD WERE RUNNING INTO ITS FIRST CHAOS

...the National Churches, and gathered ones, all must be scatterd, and snared, and broken... The Earth reels to and fro like a drunken man, verse 20. [Isaiah 24] *It reeled from Popery to Prelacy, from Prelacy to Presbytery, from Presbytery to Independency, and now the whole Earth, in England, Scotland, and Ireland, is reeling from Independency, to Anabaptisme; as if the world were running into its first Chaos, and to be covered againe with waters, verse 23.* (p.14)

WHAT'S THE GLORY? BUT GOD HIMSELF IN THE MIDST OF HIS PEOPLE

What's the Glory? but God himself in the midst of his people: what's this? but the new Jerusalem: what's that? but when God shall dwell with men, or discover himself with glory in them: when this glory is brought forth in the Saints, Jerusalem is said to come down from God out of heaven; in whom, because all our life is hid or wrapt up, as in the womb of eternity, Jerusalem is called the mother of us all. This my Mother hath made me a wretched man, before my Brethren be brought forth with me, and gathered up together into our God & Father; then we are out of Babylon, out of bondage from earth, and from things below; for Jerusalem that is above, is free, free from formes and flesh... (p.15)

GOD WILL BRING FORTH PERFECT GOVERNMENT

God will bring forth perfect Government, and glory on earth, wherein righteousness shall dwell; when no form of religion shall appear. (p.16)

10

Apocrypha 1652

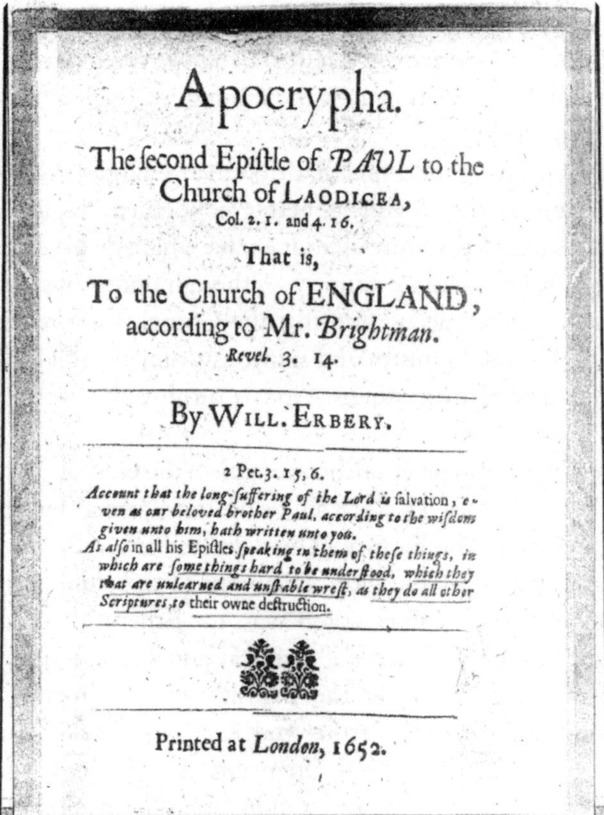
Apocrypha.

The ſecond Epiſtle of PAUL to the Church of LAODICEA, Col. 2. 1. and 4. 16.

That is,

To the Church of ENGLAND, according to Mr. Brightman. Revel. 3. 14.

By WILL. ERBERY.

2 Pet. 3. 15, 6.

Account that the long-ſuffering of the Lord is ſalvation, *even as our beloved brother Paul, according to the wiſdom given unto him, hath written unto you.*

As alſo in all his Epiſtles *ſpeaking in them of theſe things, in which are ſome things hard to be underſtood, which they that are unlearned and unſtable wreſt, as they do all other Scriptures, to* their owne deſtruction.

Printed at *London*, 1652.

APOCRYPHA. The second Epistle of PAUL to the Church of LAODICEA,
Col. 2.1. and 4.16. That is,
To the Church of ENGLAND, according to Mr Brightman. Revel. 3.14.
By WILL. ERBERY.
Printed at London, 1652.

THE *APOCRYPHA* WAS the third treatise to be printed in London in 1652 without details of printer or bookseller. It was later collected into the quartet of tracts under the general title of *The Bishop of London*. *Apocrypha*'s light touch combines humour with love for his fellow Welsh men and women. Erbery's reference to the tract being the second epistle to the Church of Laodicea is a reminder that the first epistle to the Laodiceans was a lost letter of Paul. This is the rediscovered letter. Laodicea (the church neither cold or hot in Revelation 3) is the Church of England described by Mr Brightman.[1]

Erbery makes gentle fun of Brightman's English chauvinism by referring to the Welsh as better gentlemen. Lightness and seriousness interweave throughout a tract which deserved popular reading in Erbery's home country. Although humorous, Erbery is making the serious accusation that the Gospel is not reflected in the Church's false ministry and spurious ordinances. The Gospel will be entrusted to heathens. God is turning the world upside down.

Erbery presents a profound expression of the Gospel. The saints, humankind, the universe are all being transformed by an inner divine presence. The Earth will be delivered from its bondage to decay and will enjoy the glorious liberty of the children of God (Romans 8). The Pauline vision was, for Erbery, the manifesto under-girding God's universal political and social action which was coming into being in the British nations. Erbery and his fellow radicals were dangerous and exciting as they translated their vision of the Gospel into the reality of today and this place.

Erbery seeks to prove the validity of this manifesto in his interpretation of Scripture, history and contemporary events. Erbery revolutionized the contemporary view of history. Historians, like Thomas Brightman, proved the validity of their church tradition by claiming precedents in the New Testament Church and in national historical traditions. Erbery reversed the argument by claiming that because Wales was the first nation to receive the Gospel, it was the first to fall into Apostasy, and would be the first to welcome the Third Dispensation.

In the *Apocrypha* Erbery provides accurate descriptions of contemporary Welsh religious life. He defines the ideal period of Welsh puritanism as a time when the saints lived faithfully within the Church of England, and had not separated into Independent congregations. When conventicles (the faithful worshipping within the church) became separatist, they became embondaged to forms.

However the poverty of the contemporary church signifies that God is about to do something surprising. The poverty of the Welsh saints reflects that the Third Dispensation is imminent. Episcopacy no longer exists; Presbyterianism has lost its power; Independents and Baptists are being transformed. Future hope is revealed in the teacher of north Wales, the chiefest of pastors in south Wales, and those going from the Waters to the Air.

What was taking place in Wales was not so much another religious movement, as the signs of the arrival of a world of righteousness, peace and joy. The Third Dispensation will arrive first in Wales and will soon include Great Britain and the whole of humankind. Erbery's vision is neither limited nor limiting.

THE WELSH BE THE BETTER GENTLEMEN

Why Paul should be call'd a Welshman, is no disparagement to the English, though the Welsh be the better Gentlemen, being pure Britaines, but the English are of kin to the Dutch, that dull and muddy people, designed to destruction or subjection, as Esau was to his younger brother.

Besides 'tis the opinion of some, that the Britaines are of the Jewes, but the old Dutch and Germanes are meer Gentiles, and so are the English still, as in their linage and language like unto them, so in their love to the earth, that's pure Gentilisme; and in love to the waters also, as the purest Churches in England and Wales. (p.2)

THE HEATHENS ARE AT HAND TO CONVERT US CHRISTIANS

But as the Lord is turning the earth… This is the Earth turned upside down: for the Church was once the Heaven, and Heavenly being, now but Earth, and the Earthly power, in their Ordinances, Designes, Desires, and Delights; but God is now turning mens upside down…

We think of converting the Heathens, and the Heathens are at hand to convert us Christians and Churches, from our forms of Religion to the power of righteousness. (p.2)

ALL MEN ARE IN GOD, GOD IN THEM, AND THEY HIS OFF-SPRING

Therefore leaving the Churches, let us Go to the Heathens to propagate the Gospel among us, to tell the world that all men are in God, God in them, and they his off-spring… that to think evil of no man, is the best religion, to do good to all, and do to every one, as we would that men do to us; that sooner the Sun should be turned from his course, then an honest man or Magistrate from the way of Justice, or works of Mercy; that God is the soul of the world, that the soul in Man (or Spirit) is nothing but God dwelling in the humane body. This and many more that is Gospel and glad tydings to all, every Scholar will tell you, that Heathens can teach. (p.2f.)

THE WHOLE CREATION OF MANKIND WAITS FOR IT ALSO, NOT TO THE SAINTS ONELY

But Church-pastors, Teachers, and Preachers of the Gospel now, know not the glad tydings, they know neither God nor Man, nor the mystery of either, nor the mystery of the God-man Christ Jesus; how God is in Christ, and Christ in Man: for Paul could present every man in Christ… the Gospel was preached by Paul, warning every man, teaching every man, that we might present every man in Christ, Col. 1.28.

Although 'tis true in a sense, that in Christ every man in the world is perfect, Christ being the Saviour of the world, taking away the sin of the world, a propitiation for the sins of the world, giving himself a ransome for all, and tasting death for every man…

This glory Paul (with all the Creation) waited for, not a glory without, (as Christians dream of God) but a glory to be revealed in us, and that in this life: for, 'tis in us, not about us, as men think the glory of heaven to be; besides, the whole creation of mankind waits for it also, not to the Saints onely, verse 21. [Romans 8] *but in themselves, to be delivered from the bondage of corruption, to the glorious liberty of the sons of God.* (p.3f.)

MY SPIRIT IS SILENT UNTO GOD

For my part, I am wholly silent; for though I speak sometimes unto men in the flesh, yet my Spirit is silent unto God; thus I am wholly silent, waiting as one of the dry bones in the dust, when the Lord will raise me with all his people out of our Graves, by revealing his glory in us. (p.4)

THE GLORY SHALL FIRST ARISE, AND BE REVEALED IN WALES

This glorious liberty is hinted and held forth in the Armes of the Commonwealth of England, but 'twill first arise in the Christians and Churches in Wales; Where Paul also will first appear, not in a Pulpit, as Saint Augustine wisht to see him, and Rome in her glory; no, both shall be ruined, and the glory shall first arise, and be revealed in Wales, or (to take away all envies and animosities from the English) in great Britain, in the British Isles... So the everlasting Gospel and glad tydings to all men, shall first be made known to our British Isle. (p.4f.)

AND AS CHRIST, SO ANTICHRIST FIRST APPEARED WITH POWER IN WALES

This whirlwind comes out of the North... that is, Christ in us, God in our flesh will be fully manifest.

But this will be first in the North; for these Northern Isles were the first that acknowledged Christ; here the first King and Kingdom was.

Lucius the first Christian King, was a Britain; and Constantine the great, the first Christian Emperour in the world, was a Britain or Welshman.

And as Britain was the first National Church, the mother of

Christendom: (An. Dom. 185) so her old heathenish Priests, the Flamines and Arch-Flamines were, then converted into Arch-Bishops and Bishops: for as formerly there were three Arch-Flamines here; so three Arch-Bishops with us at first; at London, York, and the third at Caerleon in Wales. Sir H. Spelman's Antiq. Brit.[2]

And as Christ, so Antichrist first appeared with power in Wales: for when Kings and Kingdoms became Christian, then Antichrist began to be great; and as the National Church was Babylon the great, so were their great Councels and Synods in Wales: yea about two hundred years after Christ, the Apostacie so prevailed, both in Doctrine and Worship there, as in the midst of Popery. (p.6f.)

BABYLONS FALL SHALL BE FROM THE NORTH

But here's the glory again; Babylons fall shall be from the North, Jer. 50.3. Other Heresies had a blow by the Greek and Latine writers, the Easterne and Western worthies, yea the Southern and Affrican Fathers, as Augustine, &c. but the Popish Hierarchy in all its parts, from first to last, fell in these Northern Isles.

I will not speak of Popery, and the first reformers in Germany, England and Scotland; though our English Wickliff was long before Luther, Huss, or Jerome of Prague.

I say Prelacy fell first by the Scots, Presbytery by the English, Independents and Anabaptists will by the Welsh at last.

And 'tis a wonder, how all formes stand fast and abide as they were from the beginning in other Nations; but in this, one falls after another, as if nothing should stand on English earth, but pure Spirit, but the Lord himself.

Popery stands in Spain and France, Prelacy or Bishops among the Luther[a]*n Germans, Presbytery at Geneva, and Independency in New England and Holland; Anabaptisme for a time in England and Ireland, but very shortly all will fall, and first in Wales; unless our Scots, like Pharez*[3] *break forth out of the womb before us...*

For though separated Churches were before in England, yet the first Independent Church (according to the New-England pattern) was set up in Wales; where the Saints have out-lived their persecutors, as there they suffered and stood out all the times of persecution, when the proudest Pastors in England dared not to show their faces; but hid their heads in Holland. (p.7f.)

ALL WILL FALL AND FIRST, AS I SAID, IN WALES

Now publick liberty, and Peace, and Power and Pomp attends the Churches, what a company of them appear and multiply in England, and Ireland, and Scotland too, as they say! but all will fall, and first, as I said, in Wales.

For as there the first Independent Church, so the Baptized Churches last were there, unless there be some in Scotland since; 'tis onely of late the Baptized Churches came and increased in Wales; and yet 'tis but the weakest of the Christians there are fallen into the waters. (p.8)

SAINTS... CAME IN MULTITUDES WITH DELIGHT TO LANVAGHES

For I will speak the truth without partiality; there were not more spiritual and suffering Saints in any part of English ground, as were in Wales; so self-denying, and dying to the world, yea so wise-hearted and knowing Christians; let all the English Counties about them testifie, and will tell, how many Saints from Somerset, Gloucester-shire, Hereford-shire, Radnor, Glamorgan-shire came in multitudes with delight to Lanvaghes.

What light, and labour in the Spirit was then? how heavenly minded? what holy language among them? what watching? what prayers night and day, in the way they went, in the work they did at their plow; everywhere in private, that Spirit of prayer and pureness of heart appeared, nothing of Ordinances was then mentioned, but with fear in themselves, and forcing others by the Spirit, from living in them: all was Spirit and life; the Saints in Wales then lookt for. (p.8f.)

OH THERE'S A PLACE FOR CHRIST TO COME

And 'twould be so still, but that they are enbondaged to their Pastors and Teachers, and which is worse, to the world, in which they gaine much, by pleasing men.

Ah pity pitty poor Wales! how are thy mighty fallen? but they are rising againe. England is yet too high, too stately, too proud, too full of pomp, and profit, and pleasure, to come down in the flesh, and to rise in the Spirit; though they can speak fine words: but Wales is a poor oppressed people, and despised also: Gentlemen and all are down already; there's Frize & Flannen; there's Bread and Cheese, and an Oaten-cake, with runing water; Oh there's a place for Christ to come. (p.9)

FROM THE WATERS TO THE AIR, YEA TO FIRE, AND THE HEAVENLY SPIRIT

...not a Prelate or Presbyter appeares with power in all South-Wales to preach or pray.

Behold, O English, Scots, and Irish Churches, yee shall shortly see what gallant Spirits, and noble hearts we have in Wales, a man going into the inward world, and walking up to the eternal Spirit; not in word and in tongue, but in deed and in truth; as you shall shortly read in a Teacher of North-Wales.[4] *And in South-Wales also, the chiefest of the Pastors there,*[5] *forsakes not onely his Tithes, but his forms of Prayer before and after Sermon; I mean, his Lords prayer before and his Episcopal or Priestly benediction, and blessing after it; yea, what he told me himself in private, I must preach on the housetop to the world, that there is Antichrist in all their Ordinances, and all their Churches shall fall.*

Again, he has left his singing of Psalmes, though he said once it was an Ordinance of Christ, the onely Church musick...

Againe, my Independent Brother and Pastor cannot Baptize children of Believers any more, though he be no more Anabaptist then I.

Yea, all the Baptized Churches now in Wales, are going from the Waters to the Air, yea to Fire, and the heavenly Spirit: for all speak high things, of the raign of Christ on earth, at hand. (p.9f.)[6]

NEW JERUSALEM... WILL FIRST APPEAR ON THIS NO[R]*THERN BRITISH ISLE*

When the Spirit shall come, it will shew them the truth, and teach them their present mistakes in this... not that the Saints shall raigne as earthly Kings, in worldly power and plenty, but in righteousness, peace, and joy in the holy Spirit, joy unspeakable and full of glory; more glorious then ever was in the Apostles or Apostolick Churches…

Lastly, as New Jerusalem is coming downe from God out of Heaven: so it will first appear on this No[r]*thern British Isle; Therefore I look for all the Nations of the earth to gather against it, Gog and Magog, Dutch and Danes, with the rest, to arise like the sands of the Sea, to compass the camp of the Saints, and the beloved City; 'tis neither Fleets nor Armies, nor strength of man on earth or waters, can defend us; but fire shall come down from Heaven and destroy them; for 'tis not the King that is dead, but the King that lives among us, that makes the Nations about so angry with us. Rev. 11.17, 38.* [should be verse 18]

England is part of the Northern British Isle; but Wales is the sides of the North, being just the wing of great Britain, the greatest Isle of the world, where will be the City of the great King. (p.10f.)

11
The General Epistle to the Hebrews 1652

THE
General Epiſtle
To the
HEBREWS;
That is,
To the JEWS, the Miniſters of
LONDON-CHURCHES.

SHEWING,

1. That the Gathered Churches are the Jews to be called: when they are ſcattered, they ſhall know it, *Jer*.31.10. *Hoſ*.5.9. and 9.7. compare.
2. That for theſe 1400 yeers, ſince the Apoſtacie, the ſtate of the Church (fallen to a Jewiſh Conſtitution) has been far differing from ſpiritual Saints therein, who were the onely bleſſed, when the Church was accurſed, *Iſai*.56.5,8. *Iſai*.43.21,22,28. compare. with *Iſa*.65.5,8,
3. That ſpiritual Saints were ever hated and caſt out of the Church, in which they were as ſignes and wonders, men wondered at, or monſtrous men, as the *Geneva*-Tranſlation reads, *Zech*. 3. 8. *Iſai*.8.18. *Iſai*.66.5. compare.
4. That the Miniſters of Churches have been in all Ages the onely leaders of Churches and Chriſtians from one form to another, from mountain to hill; but not to the holy mount of the Lord at *Jeruſalem*, *Iſai*.65.7,11. *Jer*.50.6. *Iſai*.9.16. compare with *Iſai*.27.12,13.

By WIL. ERBERY.

Jer.12.10. *Many Paſtors have deſtroyed my vineyard, they have trodden my portion under foot, they have made my pleaſant portion a deſolate wilderneſs.*

Printed at *London*, 1652.

THE General Epistle to the HEBREWS; That is,
To the JEWS, the Ministers of LONDON-CHURCHES.
By Wil. Erbery. Printed at London, 1652.

THE LAST OF the four tracts contained in *The Bishop of London* had also been published earlier in 1652. This treatise is linked with *The Bishop of London* in which Erbery had described meetings taking place at London House in November 1652. Because of the confusion on that occasion, Erbery felt it necessary to express his position more clearly: 'Be not offended, for I was forced in spirit to what I spake unto you at London-house, and now on the house top to the world; that since the Apostacy God never bless'd the Churches.' (p.1)

During the Apostasy which had continued for 1,400 years, the Church's obsessive conformity had caused the persecution of all non-conformists. 'Spiritual Saints… have been hated and cast out of the Church.' Erbery interpreted church history as a relationship between authoritarianism, the demand for uniformity and the subsequent persecution of the non-conformist. English history was the story of the persecuted becoming the persecutor. Papists persecuted Protestants; Protestants persecuted Puritans or Presbyters; Presbyters persecuted Independents and sectaries; the. Independents of New England persecuted Baptists. There was an inevitable relationship between power, uniformity, arrogance and intolerance.

This was anathema to the way of God. The wheel of history was turning, and soon will come the destruction of the craving for power and the spirit of persecution.

HATED OF THEIR OWNE CHURCH… PAPISTS, PROTESTANTS, PRESBYTERS OR PURITANS, INDEPENDENTS, BAPTIZED BRETHREN

Observe from the beginning, these 1400 years, and more, how unclean, carnal, covetous, and cruel the Church has been, drunk with the blood of Saints that were in it; these in their spiritual Principles and practice being still contrary to those formes of godliness, and common Christianity of Churches, in their Members, & Ministers. I will not now mention the Popish Church, how Protestants were persecuted there, yea the honest Papist, and pious Saints of the same profession, hated of their owne Church!

Look back but into that which we have seen and felt, how sincere professors have fared in Protestant Churches, and honest Presbyters or Puritans by the Prelatick Church; yea the zealous Presbyters, when raised into Church Government, were the same to the Independent or godly party in England, as the Independent Churches in New England to the Baptized Brethren, or to the Saints above them in Spirit and truth. (p.2f.)

LET US ALL WAIT... TILL ALL THE SAINTS WITH US BE FILLED WITH THE SPIRIT FROM ON HIGH

Truly then 'tis neither honour nor safety to be in Church-fellowship this day, but a shame, and will be a suffering in the flesh, both to members and Ministers, as it has been to their fore-fathers; for the eternal Spirit (as I said) is coming forth, and visibly come already as Fire in the scattered Saints, to burn up all the gathered Churches.

Oh come then (my beloved brethren) let us be and abide for a while in the Wilderness; for there we have a place apointed by God...

I would not wake my Beloved till he please, nor bring you out of your Church-fellowship, till the Lord call you; nor call you forth to any particular form, to a Conventicle or secret Chamber, nor yet to a Desart, nor to any fellowship distinct from the rest of the Saints; for that's a false Christ, not only the false Churches now (for the true was Christ) but all separated fellowships of Christians, though true Saints, are false Christs, being far below that glorious appearance of his, as lightning from East to West, which will gather up all the Saints into himself, 2 Thes. 2.1.

Till this be, let us all wait as wise Virgins... till all the Saints with us be filled with the Spirit from on high...

If before the Spirit we go forth to any form, fellowship, or fleshly Ordinance or Office, the presence of the Lord goes not with us, but we are liable to Babylons plagues, death, mourning, famine and fire, Rev. 18.8.

This fire is the Spirits fulness, which in its first fruits set the Churches of Christ in Gospel order; but since the Churches are come to Babylon, building and abiding there in forms, without the Baptisme of the Spirit and of Fire, the Spirit comes forth in fulness as Fire, to confound and consume the Churches: See the Sword doubled. (pp.3–5)

BE AS THE GODLY OF OLD, THE HONEST PURITANS

'Tis safest then for you and me, to be alone, from all men, unto God, or to be as the godly of old, the honest Puritans were; to be self-denying, and strict in our life, sweet in love together, doing good to all, and suffering for well doing, to be true in our words, just in our dealings; to watch our owne hearts and this present evil world, to be preserved pure and spotless in it, to have our conversation in Heaven, and use all earthly things in a heavenly manner, to minde things that are above, not in place, but in affection and attainment, to see Christ sitting at the right hand of God in our hearts, and nothing raigning there but himself; thus walking humbly with our God, and waiting for his glorious appearance in us; we then were in all good duties, more in Spirit and less in form, thus 'twas with us formerly. (p.5f.)

MY RELIGION IS, TO BE OF NO RELIGION, WITH MAN; THAT IS, TO HAVE FELLOWSHIP WITH NONE, AND YET TO HAVE FELLOWSHIP WITH ALL IN GOD

...we are but the carcase of a Church and Christian conversation; let us then in love lye downe as dead together, or every bone alone by itself, every one like Doves on the mountaines, yea every man apart and his wife apart, those of neerest flesh and fellowship to be alone from all, waiting when the Spirit will come from on high, and take us up all into God, when God shall be all in all.

In a word, because you would know my Religion, 'tis thus. Next to my eternal being in God with Christ, and Christ in me, by the Spirit of holiness, coming forth in part, and carrying me out in all things to be an honest man, My Religion is, to be of no Religion, with man; that is, to have fellowship with none, and yet to have fellowship with all in God. Farewell. (p.5) [should be p.6]

12

William Erberry to the Lord General Cromwell 1652

ORIGINAL LETTERS

AND

PAPERS of STATE,

Addreffed to

OLIVER CROMWELL;

Concerning the Affairs of

GREAT BRITAIN.

From the Year MDCXLIX to MDCLVIII.

Found among the POLITICAL COLLECTIONS

OF

Mr. JOHN MILTON.

Now firft Publifhed from the ORIGINALS.

BY

JOHN NICKOLLS, *Jun.*

MEMBER of the SOCIETY of ANTIQUARIES, LONDON.

Mr. William Erberry, *to the Lord General* Cromwell.

Yours for ever in the Lord,
and in all Chriftian fervice,
WILLIAM ERBERRY

London the 19th of July, 1652.

ORIGINAL LETTERS AND PAPERS of STATE,
Addressed to OLIVER CROMWELL;
Concerning the Affairs of GREAT BRITAIN.
From the year MDCXLIX to MDCLVIII.
Found among the POLITICAL COLLECTIONS OF Mr. JOHN MILTON.
Now first Published from the ORIGINALS. By JOHN NICKOLLS, Jun
LONDON MDCCXLIII.

SOON AFTER THE four tracts were published in *The Bishop of London*, Erbery wrote a letter to Oliver Cromwell. The letter's survival is remarkable. Found in the political papers of John Milton, it was first published by John Nickolls[1] in his collection of Cromwell's letters and papers of state in 1743.

Mr. William Erberry, to the Lord General Cromwell.

SIR,

Greate thinges God has done by you in warr, and good things men expect from you in peace; to breake in pieces the oppressor, to ease the oppressed of their burdens, to release the prisoners of their bandes, and to relieve poore familys with bread, by raisinge a publique stocke out of the estates of the unrighteous rich ones, or parliamentary delinquents and from the ruines of most unjust courts, judicatures and judges, brought in by the conqueror, and embondaging the commonweale; as alsoe the tythes of the preists, the fees of the lawyers, whom the whole land has longe cry'd out and complain'd against, besides the many unnecessary clerks offices, with the attendants to law, who are more oppressive and numerous then the prelates and their clergicall cathedrall company, whom (from the highest to the lowest, and least Querister) God in judgment has rooted out; by whose fall, as some have bin raysed, and many enriched, so now the poare of the nation are waiting at your gates, beseeching your Excellency to move effectually our present Governors, to hasten a publique treasury for them, from those, that there be noe begger in Israel, nor base covetousness among Christians; but that it may be punished as double idolatry by the magistrate, as the primitive ministers of Christ did excommunicate the covetous (amonge the worst of men) out of the churches. If this virgin commonwealth could bee preserved chast and pure, if the oppressed, the prisoner, and the poore might bee speedily heard and helped, how would the most high God bee praysed, and men pray for you, and your most unworthy servant professe himselfe in truth, Sir,

Yours for ever in the Lord,
and in all Christian service,

WILLIAM ERBERRY
London, the 19th of July, 1652.

P.S. If your Excellency judge this petition fit and feasable, 'tis humble desired that your honour would please to present it to the parliament, in the behalfe of the inhabitants of Cardiffe, whose loynes shall bless you and yours; though they knowe not of this, nor mind theire owne good, nor any of theire governors move once for the prosperity of that poore nation.

Sir, I cannot waite longer to attend and prosecute this petition, because I am called by God and men to returne speedily to Wales; where my countrymen, and many Christian freinds in Cardiff and thereabout, longe for my service to them in the Lord Christ.

For his Excellency the Lord General Cromwell these.

13

A Call to the Churches 1652

A Call to the Churches;

OR,

A Packet of Letters

To the PASTORS of

WALES

Preſented

To the Baptized Teachers there.

WITH

A Poſtſcript of a Welſh Diſpute.

By WILL. ERBERY.

What ſhall one then anſwer the Meſſengers of the Nation? That the Lord hath founded Zion, *and the poor of his people ſhall repair unto it,* Iſa. 14. 32.
The firſt ſhall ſay to Zion, *Behold them, and I will give to* Jeruſalem *one that bringeth good tydings.*
For I beheld and there was no man amongſt them and there was no Counſellor, that when I asked of them, could anſwer me a word. Iſai. 41. 27, 28, 29.

Feb: 19 1652

Printed at *London*, 1653.

A Call to the Churches; OR, A Packet of Letters To the PASTORS of WALES Presented To the Baptized TEACHERS[1] there.
WITH A Postscript of a Welsh Dispute.
By Will. Erbery.
Printed at London, 1653.
(Received into the Thomason Collection on February 19th, 1652/3)

ERBERY PUBLISHED THREE collections of letters, *A Call to the Churches* in February 1652/3, *The Babe of Glory* in November 1653 and *The North Star,* also in November 1653. The first collection, addressed specifically to the 'Baptized Churches in South Wales' entered the Thomason Collection on the 19th of February 1652/3.

The collection begins with a letter from Morgan Llwyd[2] to Erbery. All the other letters were written by Erbery to leading Welsh Puritans. Each letter is quite distinct, written with the recipient in mind. The collection has a long introduction (as long as all the letters together) addressed specifically to the Baptized Churches in Wales. There is also a letter to David Walter with Erbery's account of a dispute at Cowbridge with Henry Nichols, an Independent minister. We shall look at that separately because Nichols wrote a riposte which gives his account of the encounter. *A Call to the Churches* presents a remarkable insight into the state of religion in Wales in the early 1650s.

The correspondence between Morgan Llwyd and William Erbery reflect their shared religious experience. The renewal of their relationship, after many years of silence, was initiated by Llwyd in a letter written at Wrexham in 1652, 29 of 4 month (presumably June 1652). Erbery received the letter at Roth, near Cardiff on 12th of August, and seems to have answered promptly. Erbery published Llwyd's letter (without permission) with his own response in *A Call to the Churches.* The correspondence continued for a year. The next letter from Llwyd was from M.L. from Wales to Erbery, to which Erbery responded with 'To an Afflicted woman, or Be-wildernessed Saint'. Both letters were published in *The Babe of Glory* (November 1653). The final series was published in *The North Star,* also published in November 1653. This contains four letters, two each from Llwyd and two from Erbery; the last written by Erbery in London in May 1653.

Erbery's correspondence with Llwyd is very different from his other letters: something new is stirring in north Wales. This stimulates Erbery to meditate on the inner spirit and presence of

Christ. Two Welsh scholars, M. Wynn Thomas[3] and Medwin Hughes[4] have drawn parallels between Erbery's writing and the creation of Llwyd's classic writings in the Welsh language.

Erbery delighted in Llwyd's mystical exploration and approved of Llwyd's rejection of formal ordinances, false and oppressive ministry, and barren ecclesiastical structures. He challenged the Baptist pastors in south Wales to follow Llwyd's example.

Erbery wrote in detail about his debate at Llantrisant with a Baptist minister, David Davies of Gelligaer, pastor to the Puritan Pritchard family of Llancaiach Hall. The controversy focussed on their understanding of the Gospel. It provides a fascinating insight into the content and method of debate.

Erbery shares his radical interpretation of the heart of the Gospel by focussing on words from the Gospel of John: 'why first, 'tis to know Christ in the Father and the Father in him, and he in us, and we in him, John 14.10. Secondly, to know Christ as the way to the Father for us… for Christ and we are perfect in one, one with the Father; thus he is the way to the Father, and thus by him (as the way) we believe on God…'

Erbery focuses on the mystery of the Trinity. The eternal Trinitarian relationship is revealed in history. The truth about God's purposes were revealed in part in the Dispensation of the Law (the Age of the Father), fully in the Dispensation of the Gospel (the Age of the Son), hidden during the age of Apostasy and will be fully revealed in the Third Dispensation, or the Age of the Spirit.

During the Dispensation of the Law, faith was trusting the promises of God. During the Dispensation of the Gospel, faith was the gift of the Spirit of Pentecost. The tragedy of history was the disappearance of this gift because of the coming of the Age of Apostasy. Replacing the Gospel community of faith came obsessive adherence to orthodoxy, accompanied by a search for absolutes in forms of ministry and ordinances. Erbery describes the consequences for the churches in Wales. Pastors created intolerant and insular communities. Saints walking the way of Christ were being persecuted. Erbery pleads for a compassion which would include not only brothers and sisters but also Sodomits and Sinners.

Saints should live in love with Papists, Prelates, Presbyters, Independents, Baptists. Baptists, to whom this letter is directed, restrict their love to those who accept their church covenant. They are intolerant towards other churches, let alone the wider community of sinners. There 'is lesse love among the Brethren then among Popish Churches.'

He accused the Baptists of neglecting the life of faith, hope and love. Their literal reading of the Bible created literal interpretations of baptism and the second coming of Christ. Many Baptists became Fifth Monarchists who were convinced Christ would soon return in physical form. Baptist congregations will rule over Commonwealths and Kingdoms. Erbery replaced that carnal view by inviting his fellow saints to come out of the graves of forms and flesh, and celebrate now the life, love and power of God. In the final days of the Apostasy, God is dashing, dividing, disquieting and destroying all comforts (ministries, ordinances and structures). This ministry of destruction will help the saint discover the Lord living within. Do not look into the skies for the return of Christ. Look internally. God dwells there, loving you as God loves his own Son.

TO THE BAPTIZED CHURCHES IN SOUTH WALES

ALL THIS YOU MAY BEHOLD IN THIS HONEST MAN

What I have written to the Independent Pastors in Wales, that I present to the Baptized Churches there, that in the first Letter of Mr. Floyd, you may see a man in the Clouds, come with me to his A.B.C. after all his teachings; not knowing what God is, where, when, or how he is above all, through all, in all, and all of him, &c. yet in this Cloud coming from the North, he begins to see the Lord in the Aire, and meets him there; yea in this confusion, he beholds Christ in him crucified in his flesh, whose inward flesh, and former spiritual attainments in life, light, knowledge, &c. being so slain, so dead, so dark, so confounded, that he knows not what he is, nor where he goes, and yet he is going into the internall eternall spirit, as a blind man not seeing any thing of Men, Saints, Offices, Ordinances, Spirits, Churches, &c. though there he be, and one of the best, yet now he is nothing, God appearing in him to be all in all. There you may find him following the intern spirit of the inward Heaven dropping down in the Nights, and in darknesse the Lord a light unto him; for that's the great mystery of Godlinesse, when God is so manifest in our flesh, that he makes our flesh and the goodliness thereof to wither unto nothing, that his glory may be revealed in us, and he to be All in All.

That being blind to self, we see all things in God, being deaf to men we hear God alone; in the death of pure flesh, we live perfectly in the Spirit: thus we live in death, have light in darknesse, &c. or the Lord onely is both life and light unto us, we nothing, God being All in All.

All this you may behold in this honest man, acquainted at last with the heavenly nature, walking up to the Angelicall world, and withdrawing himself into the inner world (the more spiritual chamber) to converse with the inhabitants there, &c. looking down on the son of man as a vanity, a glance, a branch, yea a shadow, yet an off-spring of the eternal root where the least child of God (like the little twig) co-saps with the other branches, of highest growth, in the most high God, or glory that is in us. (p.217f.)

THE APOSTACY IS COMPLEAT AND PERFECT, AND APPEARS MOST VISIBLE IN YOUR CHURCHES

...other Lords besides thee have had dominion over us, and that is, not only Lord Bishops, but other ruling Elders beside what the Lord ordained; other Ordinances in the Church, which never came to his minde, as I shall prove in particular (with God) another time; there being no Gospel-Order, nor Ordinance, nor Officer in any of your Churches this day.

Yea, I proved it plain at Bridg-end, that you are not in a capacity to baptize or be baptized, there being no true Administrator, nor a man sent of God, with power from on high to baptize: First, because you have not the faith of the Gospel. Secondly, you are fallen from your first love, therefore the Apostacy is compleat and perfect, and appears most visible in your Churches. (p.219)

SURE THIS WAS NOT GOSPEL AND GLAD TYDINGS TO ALL PEOPLE THAT SO FEW SHOULD BE SAVED

Yea one of your own Pastors or Teachers (Mr. Davis of Kelligare… coming purposely to oppose at Llantrishant, where I was speaking of the common salvation, as Jude calls it) tells the people that this was not Gospel. What then I pray you? why saith he, the Gospel is that written in the four Evangelists. Then said I, Our Father which art in Heaven is Gospel. No that's prayer; but the Gospel to be preached, saith he, is, Straight is the Gate, and narrow the way that leadeth to life, and few there be that find it; for so it's written in the Gospel of Saint Mathew. Sure this was not Gospel and glad tydings to all people that so few should be saved; and yet I could shew in the Spirit the Gospel of Salvation of Life, and Love in that Letter, though few find it, or the way to it, as Christ tells them. (p.219)

CHRIST CAME TO SAVE ONELY THE LOST, GIVING A WORD OF LIFE TO ALL MEN, THAT THEY MIGHT BELIEVE

Again, said the good Man, this is another part of the Gospel, As many as received him, to them he gave power to become the Sons of God, even to those that believed in his name. For so 'tis written in the Gospel of Saint John, saith he; as if all were Gospel which is written in the Evangelists; whereas Christ was a Minister of the Circumcision, or legal Teacher. Secondly, the Gospel that he taught was but in part, that which was proper onely to the Jewish Church, not that to be preached to the world. Thirdly, what Gospel or glad tydings is it to tell the world, that none should be saved but the Elect and Believers? whereas Christ came to save onely the lost, giving a word of life to all men, that they might believe, or shutting up all in unbelief, that he might have mercy upon all, Rom. 11.32.

But the man thought there was no Gospel, but what is written in the Gospels of Mathew, Mark, Luke, and John. (p.219f.)

THE INHABITANTS OF THE NEW JERUSALEM, THE ONELY THING I WAS ALWAYES UPON, TO MY DEAR COUNTRY

I promised to speak once more to my honest Country-men there in that place, a fortnight after; when he coming there again, stept up before me to preach in Welsh; whom yet I quietly heard all the time, till he had ended his Sermon, not contradicting him at all, though I could in many things, and in most.

Afterward I began to speak to the English (for many of the Welsh understood) declaring something concerning the glorious appearance of the great God in the last dayes; that he would so appear in man, that men should be made like him, that God would be both a Heaven and a Hell to men, that most men should be in a Hell upon earth, as that some should have a Heaven here; I mean the inhabitants of the new Jerusalem, the onely thing I was alwayes upon, to my dear Country. I also spake of Gods coming forth as Fire in the last times, &c. but had no sooner finished my discourse, but the Gentleman starts up again, and begins to contradict and withstand my words the second time, to the trouble and tumult of the company; who being strange to such open affronts, and publique contests in the Church, began to forget what they heard before, and to rise up on their seats, as if they were to see a shew.

Upon this, without answering a word, I went out of the place in silence, leaving the man to speake what he pleas'd to the people; but as I was going out of the Church, he turning about and crying after me, I answered no more, but this unto him; Mr. Davys, you will be shortly in the Fire (for the fire was that I then had spoken of) and so I departed to peace. (p.220f.)

THE GOSPEL WAS A MYSTERY, WHICH IN THE LIGHT OF GOD, THEY COULD MANIFEST TO MEN, AND MAKE ALL MEN SEE THEMSELVES, IN GOD, THAT'S IN CHRIST

But (as I said before) let all men judge from that aforesaid, whether such men are fit to be Ministers of the Gospel, who think the Gospel to be that, which is written in the four Evangelists, or in the Apostles Epistles;

whereas the one is but an Historical relation, or report of Christ in his life & death, &c. The Epistles are only particular Letters of some special concernment to the Churches, not that which the Apostles preached to the world; and as Christ was a Minister of the Circumcision in the days of his flesh, while he was alive on earth: so Christ never preached the Gospel indeed, till after he was dead; then he came forth in the Spirit preaching peace, &c. in the Apostles. (Eph. 2.17)

And the Gospel which the Apostles preached to the world,'twas not that which they wrote to the Churches, nor yet what they read in the Scriptures of the Prophets (for to what purpose was this to the Heathens, to tell them of Moses and the Psalmes?). But the Gospel was a Mystery, which in the light of God, they could manifest to men, and make all men see themselves, in God, that's in Christ. (p.221)

THERE MAY BE A SEED OF IT IN THEM, AS ALSO WAS IN LEGAL SAINTS

This I only speak, to shew the Ignorance, or inconsiderate proceeds of our Gospel-preachers, who know not what they say, nor the way they go, nor the work they do, nor the word they speak, nor the Gospel which they pretend to preach unto the world.

But because I now write to the baptized Churches, I would convince them also of this, that they are not the true, nor can baptize in truth, having not a Gospel yet manifest among them: I say not manifest; for there may be a seed of it in them, as also was in Legal Saints. (p.222)

TRUE FAITH WAS EVER THE SAME FOR SUBSTANCE, BUT NOT FOR MANIFESTATION

As for Gospel-faith, sutable to the present state of the Spirit, and spirituall Saints; it was (though not differing, yet) diverse from the legal faith of Gods people under the Law: true faith was ever the same for substance, but not for manifestation, as the Gospel is everlasting, and Christ the same to day, yesterday, and for ever.

But as Christ was only vayled in the Law, and revealed in the Gospel; so the Gospel and Christ Jesus were both Mysteries hid since the world began from the Sons of men, yea from the Sons of God under the Law, Rom. 16.25; Eph. 3.5; Col. 2.6 compare... [Should be Col. 1.26]

Besides, as the object of a Gospel-faith was a mystery, that's Christ in us the hope of glory, the Son of God revealed in us, living in us, and dying in us, and we crucified with Him (for both Christ and him crucified also was a mystery, as the Gospel the object of that faith) so this Gospel-faith was a mystery likewise; the Mystery of Faith in a pure conscience, I Tim. 3.9. (p.222f.)

CHRIST AND WE ARE PERFECT IN ONE, ONE WITH THE FATHER

...to believe on God by Christ, is that which believing Christians this day know not, nor consider. For what's this? why first, 'tis to know Christ in the Father, and the Father in him, and he in us, and we in him, John 14.10. Secondly, to know Christ as the way to the Father for us... for Christ and we are perfect in one, one with the Father; thus he is the way to the Father, and thus by him (as the way) we believe on God... So that in truth, to believe on Christ, is not to believe on Christ, but on the Father in him, God in his flesh, and in ours also; for our faith does tend, and end in God, yet through him and by him, as I said before. (p.223)

THERE HAS NOT BEEN A GOSPEL-FAITH IN THE SAINTS THESE 1400 YEARS

And by this it appears, there has not been in the Churches a Gospel faith, at least formally, for vertually there might be in some, but formally and effectually there has not been a Gospel-faith in the Saints these 1400 years... Gospel believers were all of one heart and one soul, because but one body, &c. ours are all divided: believers then had all things common, &c. our Churches and Christians are all for self-interests, and to seek their own. (p.224)

GOSPEL-FAITH PROPERLY WAS THIS, IN KNOWING OUR FELLOWSHIP WITH THE FATHER AND THE SON IN THE SPIRIT

Gospel-Faith properly was this, in knowing our fellowship with the Father and the Son in the Spirit, to know our union with God in Christ, and Christ so in us, that we are in one with the Father, as He, in the same love and life in God with him, John 14.19; John 17.1, 20, 21, 22, 23 now the mystery of God even the Father and of Christ was not manifest to any under the Law; not to Abraham himself, who though he saw the day of Christ, yet it was a far off, for so the Fathers saluted the promises, whose faith was on the promise or power of his God in performing the same, and so its justified, Rom.4.14 to 21. But the justifying faith of Christians was on Christ dying and raised up, vers. 24, 25... But as Christ was a Mystery, so his death and resurrection was a mystery also, that none but the Apostles could manifest it by the Spirit; which being not given to any one living, the Faith which comes by hearing is no higher then theirs under the Law, to justify and to save; yea we know by experience, the best Preachers when they would raise men to believe, pitch them on the promise, not on that power from on high, or promise of the Father, which they that believed on Christ did receive, and by which the first Preachers of the Gospel brought men to believe. (p.225f.)

THERE BEING NO LOVE, THERE IS NO BELIEVER AMONG YOU

...when there is no love among you, neither to other Churches or Saints differing from you, nor to your own Churches who differ in doctrine (as I have said before) much lesse love to all Saints, to those scattered ones, who cannot come to any of your Church-wayes: as for love to all men, its a thing you look not after, though this be a higher degree of love, then brotherly kindnesse, or love to the bretheren... But where's Faith or Love? for both are one. Faith works by Love, and love believeth also, believeth all things: therefore there being no love, there is no believer among you... all the world sees now there is no love in the Churches; how can they then be the Disciples of Christ, who are thus divided, and dash one against another? not onely brother against brother, but Church

against Church: Churches of Saints; Good-Lord, saith the world, what shall we do? whither shall we go, when Churches go this way and that way, one against another? (p.226f.)

OH! THAT GOD WOULD SEND MEN OF ONE MIND TO MINISTER A WORD TO WALES

Ah poor Wales, many Pastors have destroyed thee, and distract thee! How many have I heard crying out, where to find their Religion; their old Priests and Common-prayer are gone, and new Pastors and Preachers, are come in, who cannot agree together: Oh! that God would send men of one mind to minister a word to Wales, were it but to speak love, or to shew the Lord Christ that's love in practice, in purenesse, in power and peace, I John 4.7, 8 to the end. (p.227)

SODOM AND SAMARIA ARE THE CHURCHES SISTERS

Indeed brethren, there is much love among your Church-members, in word and tongue, calling one another Brother and Sister; but where's Lots love, to call Sodomits and Sinners, Ah my brethren no not so wickedly! But when ye shall remember your wayes and be ashamed then you shall receive your Sisters, your Elder and Younger, for God gives them unto you for Daughters, but not by your Covenant, Ezek 16.61. Sodom and Samaria are the Churches sisters, vers. 46. (p.227)

BY YOUR COVENANT, NONE ARE CALLED BRETHEREN SAVE THOSE OF YOUR OWN CHURCH

For your love shall be so dear unto them, not onely love to one another, but toward all men: thus 'twas in Gospel-Churches, this will be again, and more also, but not by thy Covenant saith, God not by your Church-covenant (never known in Gospel-Churches): by your Covenant, none are called Bretheren save those of your own Church; not visible Saints, much lesse sinners.

Truly this want of love to all men, shewes, you have no true love among yourselves, no love unfeigned, out of a pure heart, fervently one to another. You speak much of the command of Christ for baptisme, but let me ask you one question, why do ye not obey all the commands of

Christ in his Apostles, yea what he commanded himself? …Greet ye one another with a holy Kisse, 2 Cor. 13.12. Greet ye one another with a kisse of love, I Pet. 5.14. The Papists have a Pax to represent this, for all must kisse the Pax when they come to Masse, in remembrance of this kisse of love: but ye (brethren) have not so much as a shew of this; lesse love among the Brethren then among Popish Churches. (p.228)

LOVE… BELIEVES THE BEST OF ALL, AND HOPES THEY WILL BE BETTER

…for love believes all things, and hopes all things; believes the best of all, and hopes they will be better.

But yet there is one mark of love I have not mentioned, that's Christs love, not in word and in tongue, but in deed and in truth; pray what's that? 'Tis I John 3.16. Hereby perceive we the love of God, because he laid down his life for us, and we ought to lay down our life for our brethren. Here's first a Mystery that men know not, how God did lay down his life: for the death of the man Christ all conceive; but how that man was nothing but God manifest in flesh, and how God shed his blood, crucifying that flesh to himself, is the Mystery of Christ and him crucified, not known to the Churches; but because God laid down his life for us, we ought to lay our life for our brethren. (p.229)

WE YOUR BRETHREN ARE NOT ALIVE, BUT DEAD IN BABYLON

So many scattered Saints, are weeping and full of sorrow, in their bewildernessed state, in the want of the solemn Assembly, because it cannot be; yea, by the waters of Babylon they sit down and weep, while you are dipping in them; and while others are merry with singing of Psalmes, your brethrens Harps are hanged upon the Willowes (on fruitless trees) because they cannot sing one of the songs of Zion, they being in a strange land, not in the life of God alone, but living still in Babylon, in flesh, and self, in which they feel themselves imbondaged. We your brethren are not alive, but dead in Babylon, as dry bones there we lye, even your brethren. (p.230)

WE HAVE NO HOPES TO ENJOY IT, OR IN THIS LIFE TO BE RAISED OUT OF OUR GRAVES

...we with our Churches must bear rule in Common-wealths and Kingdomes, yea though Christs Kingdom was not of this world, yet the best of us fancy a reign of Christ on earth for a thousand years, and the Saints to reign with him in an earthly manner, and outward observation, with rest and peace, and power, and plenty; this was not the flesh of Christ.

...Yea we are so dead and dry, we have neither Faith nor Love, nor yet any lively hope by the resurrection of Jesus Christ from the dead; the fruit of whose resurrection we look not for, till many hundred years hence at the last day, when we are dead and gone, and turned to dust, or dry bones; whereas we consider not we are dry bones already, and dwell in the dust this day.

I do not condemn you (brethren) for this, that your hope is not lively, that you look not for your resurrection from Babylon... it may be other generations may see the glory talked to be in the last times, but we are cut off, for our parts; our children may possesse it, but for our parts we have no hopes to enjoy it, or in this life to be raised out of our graves. (p.232)

THE GREATEST WORK THAT GOD HATH TO DO WITH YOU THIS DAY, IS TO MAKE YOU SEE YOU ARE DEAD

Pray (brethren) consider, God will not only open your graves, that you may know you are dead and dry bones, but he will cause you (whether you will or no) to come out of your graves (of forms and flesh) and bring you to the land of Israel, to live in the Spirit, to see your life in the Lord alone, that your life may be no more hid with Christ in God, but that Christ who is your life shall appear in you, and your life may appear to be in God.

The greatest work that God hath to do with you this day, is to make you see you are dead; that's the end why he does dash and divide you, disquiet and destroy all your comforts; for I know you are shaking already, and 'tis a mercy to you, that God will disquiet the Inhabitants of Babylon, that you shall have no rest, till you return to his land, even to the Lord that lives within you, and loves you as his own Son, though the Body be dead; for then (when dead) the beloved of your Father was in perfect union with him, as well as when he as living in the flesh, and doing wonders in the Spirit. (p.233)

SEE YOUR SELVES AT LAST THE DEAD BODY OF THE LORD, FOR THEN YOU SHALL ARISE AND LIVE

Oh brethren, see your selves at last the dead body of the Lord, for then you shall arise and live; Thy dead men shall live, together with my dead body they shall arise; awake, and sing ye that dwell in the dust (that's dry bones) Isa. 26.19. This cannot be meant of the last resurrection when all shall rise; for here some shall not rise, vers. 14. but you brethren shall rise; when? as soon as you are become the dead body of the Lord, for so the words are read, Thy dead men shall live, my dead body they shall arise; that is, when we see ourselves the dead body of the Lord, we rise and live immediately in the midst of death, and sing in the dust; yea, though dry bones, and in the lowest estate of flesh, we can comfortably wait for the Spirit, and for the comming of the Lord in us, that by the same Spirit which raised his dead body, we the dead body of the Lord may be raised up together with him.

Truly brethren, the living God knows, that all I have written, or shall, is not intended by me to trouble your walkings, but to give you rest in the Lord alone at last; not meerly to throw down your Churches, or for your fall, but to raise you up, that we all may live together with Christ in God. Farewell. (p.233)

The introduction to *The Call to the Churches* was written to the 'Baptized Churches in South Wales'. It is followed by Erbery's letters to six Church leaders in Wales. The letters differ considerably as Erbery writes to men with different theological and ecclesiological stances. Erbery refers to several letters which he had received previously, but only Morgan Llwyd's letter survives. Llwyd had written it at Wrexham on the 29th of the 4th month (June?) 1652. He wishes to renew contact with Erbery after a long absence. The letter suggests that Llwyd was exploring his inner life and needs to anchor himself securely in the substance of faith. He questions Erbery on the being or essence of God. Llwyd is asking philosophical or mystical questions, outside orthodox Calvinism. These dangerous questions might invoke perilous answers.

MORGAN LLWYD'S LETTER TO WILLIAM ERBERY

FOR MR. WILLIAM ERBERY

IF MY ONCE-DEAR SCHOOL-MASTER ERBERY CAN TEACH IT ME

The Milk and Honey (ever-remembred friend) which formerly I sucked in your Ministration, makes me apt to conclude that your pit is not dryed up, nor your root withered, but that the intern Spirit of the inward heaven doth raign in you in the night. It's many years since I looked on you as an Image; I never heard (nor had a line) from you (as some hereabout had.) It may be you thought me lesse teachable, and more uncapable of understanding then some others; indeed I am so. I knew not where to direct a line to find you, by reason of your private life, which to some is safe and serene, and to others tempestuous and dangerous.

The Hermite is not very useful to man or beast (nor the Christ to him) because Talents will rust and rot the living creature, unlesse they be thrown out of your private chest and ship... The more you be in the heavenly action (which is publick also to millions every day in the year) the more like the God of all beings and inhabitant of eternity. I do but long and professe to become a little child again, willing to learn my A.B.C. anew, if my once-dear School-master Erbery can teach it me. (p.234)

WHAT, WHERE, WHEN, AND HOW, GOD IS?

I desire you (according to your attainment) to help me (I mean to scribble a few lines to me) in answering these things. How is God above all, through all, and in all his people? How all things are of him, through, and to him? How do we live, move, and have our being in him? what is that heresie of perdition the holy One (in Peter) mentions? and chiefly what, where, when, and how, God is?

I am not ashamed to enquire, or wait of a meer post near the gate of the wisdom of God, about these matters; neither do I disown you (as some strange notionist, or sceptick gnostick) in what you in the light of the Father, can or will hold forth, for satisfaction by the Spirit; for since I knew you, or tasted the wine in you, I ever lodged respectful thoughts of you, I fear neither truth nor its enemies; I would try all things (all spirits, bodies, and beings in the light, liberty, rest and power of the Spirit of Jesus)... I only beg of you a sound about your grounds in Scripture-nature, and in the internal eternal Spirit concerning Men, Saints, Officers, Ordinances, Churches, and Societies of men. (p.234f.)

1. ERBERY'S LETTER TO MORGAN LLWYD

Erbery received Llwyd's letter on the 12th of August. He was at Roth near Cardiff, Erbery's address as a Brasenose College student in 1619. He has no doubt that Llwyd would understand his theological response, however abstruse it might have seemed to his contemporaries – and to later readers! His response is rooted in Scripture and he avoids philosophical abstractions. The letter which answers Llwyd's questions seems to be that of a teacher to a pupil. Erbery writes to Llwyd about two resurrections: that last and general of the world, and the former resurrection... the third estate of the saints now approaching. The saints are to wait in solitariness and silence, forerunners of the fulfilment of God's purposes for humankind.

FOR MR. MORGAN LLOYD

WE ARE BOTH IN THE ETERNAL SPIRIT

Yours of the twenty ninth of the fourth month, I received at Roth near Cardiff this 12 of August; and I return an Answer in silence, seeing we are both in the Eternal Spirit, with the spirits of just men made perfect, where there is no need of speech to communicate our thoughts or attainments to each other; being taken up into him who is our All, and all in All. (p.235f.)

THE THIRD ESTATE OF THE SAINTS NOW APPROACHING

There the Mystery of the Resurrection begins, and the Apostle goes on in that height from I Cor.14.28 [should be 15.28] *to the end; that this is the Resurrection, not that last and general of the world, but the first Resurrection; the rising of the Saints, or of the dead in Christ, who shall rise first: I say, That this is the Resurrection only of the just, and not of the unjust, nor of All; any man (even without the Spirit of Revelation) may judge by reason, and reading of that Chapter; where the rising of the spiritual body to incorruption, immortality, power and glory, is the glorious appearing of the second Man, the quicking Spirit, the Lord from Heaven (in us) to the heavenly Image; which is the third estate of the Saints now approaching, and the latter part of your Letter points at.*

This I call the third dispensation, or last discovery of God unto and in men, differing from Law and Gospel-order; yet comprehending both, and above both, yea above all: for here all men and things are nothing, but God is all and alone, yea God is All in all.

This third dispensation, as all the Prophets and Apostles did write and wait for; so in this I wait in silence, with God (though I speak sometimes to men) for a full discovery of him in me, and to all the Saints with me; for when the Lord my God shall come or appear, all the Saints shall come with thee, Zach.14.5. (p.236)

THE FALL OF THIS FORM OF CHURCH-FELLOWSHIP

The Earth-quake there spoken of is at hand… the third or last fall of Babylon, will be in the fall of this form of Church-fellowship (so called) you may see in your spirit, and in some printed scriblings of mine: therefore for Order, Ordinances, Officers, Churches, Societies of men, all are in Babylon, in confusion of Tongues; that's out of order, &c. though many of the Saints conceive they are come to Sion already. (p.236)

ALL THINGS BOTH IN HEAVEN AND EARTH SHALL BE GATHERED UP INTO ONE

Then the dead bones shall rise out of Babylon, and God will open the graves of his people, who shall all come forth out of their forms and flesh, when the glory of the Lord shall cover them, and they live in the Eternal Spirit together: then the two sticks also, the divided societies of Saints shall become one, &c. for that's the third dispensation, called the dispensation of the fulnesse of time, when all things both in heaven and earth shall be gathered up into one, all the Saints of highest appearances, and of lowest performances, both those of Legal tempers and Gospel attainments, shall be gathered up into one, into that glory, into God himself. (p.237)

EVERY MAN... TO LIVE SOLITARY AND ALONE IN HIS OWN LIGHT, THAT LIGHT WHICH SHINES IN EVERY MAN, AND EVERY MAN IN HIS GOD

...there's no more Sea (saith John), no more of that dividing and destroying Principle in man; for that's the Sea, which has made the Saints not only to dash one against another, but every one to be as an Isle by himself, and so indeed it must be in Babylons fall, not a man to be found, Isai. 13.12, but every man flyes to his own Land, vers. 14. (to live solitary and alone in his own light, that light which shines in every man, and every man in his God)... (p.237)

RETIRE ALONE INTO OUR SELVES, OR THE SPIRIT RATHER IN US

There's no building of Temples in Babylon, nor joyning there in Church-fellowship; for that will fall, and we with it, till we retire alone into our selves, or the Spirit rather in us; and this we must be, every man apart by himself; every Family apart, and their wives apart; man and his wife, though nearest and dearest flesh, must be separated, when the Spirit of Grace and Supplication (or favours) begins to appear to take us up into glory. (p.237)

ALL THE PEOPLE OF GOD SHALL BECOME ONE LAND, ONE CONTINENT

Then the multitude of the Isles shall rejoyce, when the Lord comes to Raign, Psal. 97.1... all the people of God shall become one Land, one Continent, wherein the Lord alone shall live; this is the Land so much spoken of by the Prophets... he that scattered Israel, will gather him; and the Saints who are now scattered in and by their gathered Churches, yea all the scattered Saints with them shall be gathered up into God, who indeed is he who scatters as well as gathers; we do nothing, we can do nothing, but in him who is All in all. (p.238)

WE SHALL NOT ONLY SEE GOD, BUT MEN SHALL SEE GOD IN US

In this Mystery of the Resurrection, all your Questions in the Letter will be answered, your doubts satisfied, your darkness cleared, your Captivity ended; for 'tis the glorious liberty of the children of God, the manifestation of the sons of God, the appearing of the great God in us, when we shall be like him, see him as he is, know him as we are known, see him eye to eye; as he sees us, we shall see him, see his Face, and his Name on our foreheads; that is, we shall not only see God, but men shall see God in us; for all that see us shall acknowledge that we are the seed which the Lord hath blessed: the blessed seed is Christ the Son of God, so all the Saints shall be in the glory of the Father, when the Son shall be subject, and God be All in all.

This is the Adoption and Redemption of the body, the Resurrection of the body when the body, now natural or soule-ly (as the Greek reads it) shall be raised spiritual, the Eternal Spirit appearing to be all in all. (p.238)

WHEN WE ARE NOTHING, WE ARE ALL IN GOD, AND GOD IS ALL IN ALL, AND IN THIS WE MAY SING TOGETHER

This will be in every one of us in particular (for we must be gathered one by one) and this will be in all the Saints in general… we must all dye, come down to the dust, lye there, as the dry bones… yet we shall live, though now dead, yea the dead shall live: that is, as none see God but the blind, none hear him but the deaf (deaf to man and to self) so the dead alone can live, and they live in death, who find themselves the dead body of the Lord: my dead body they shall arise: Awake and sing ye that dwell in the dust, &c. in the lowest estate of flesh, when the first man Adam is turned to dust; when we are nothing, we are all in God, and

God is all in all, and in this we may sing together: For the second man bears the Image of the heavenly, which is the third dispensation typified in the third daies Resurrection of Christ, as I shall tell you another time, with God. (p.238f.)

2. ERBERY'S LETTER TO HENRY WALTER

Erbery's second letter was to Henry Walter,[5] a member of the Puritan establishment. Erbery's letter is a clear, unequivocal statement of the centrality of his faith in the indwelling Christ and imminence of the Third Dispensation. This faith distinguishes him from his fellow Welsh Puritans.

FOR MR. HENRY WALTER

THAT LIFE AND GLORY WHICH WE HAVE WITH CHRIST IN GOD (THOUGH NOW HID FROM US), SHALL BE REVEALED IN US AND UPON US ALSO

Dear Brother,

I am bold thus to salute you; because we are both in the Father, and in Jerusalem that is above, which is free, and the mother of us all, though all the Saints see not, nor the glory in which they are already; but when the glory shall be revealed in them, they shall then see the new Jerusalem coming down from God out of heaven, and him alone dwelling in them; that is, the state of all the Saints that ever were or shall be, their being was and is in God, and there they were from the beginning and before the worlds: and this we wait for to appear in us all in these last times, when the mystery of God shall be finished and fully known, when that life and glory which we have with Christ in God (though now hid from us), shall be revealed in us and upon us also; so that not only we shall see God in us, but men shall see and say, that surely God is in you of a truth, as my Letter to Mr. Cradock will tell you at large: this is the new Jerusalem; and then we see that holy City coming down from God out of Heaven; when that which was hid with God as 'twere in Heaven, shall be manifested to us & in us on earth; and our life (as I said) which was hid with Christ in God, shall so visibly or clearly appear in us, and to men, that it shall be seen a tree of life in the midst of us, not only yielding fruit every month to our selves to strengthen us; but holding forth leaves, such an outward appearance of glory in us to men, that it shall heal and satisfie them, Rev. 22.2 this is that pure River of life, clear as Crystal, proceeding out of the throne of God, and out of the Lamb, that is in us, when all that glory of God in Christ shall be so clearly manifest on us, that this River of life which is in us, shall run forth and stream abundantly among the sons of men, who are as the sea spoken of, Ezek. 47.8. (p.239f.)

HOW MANY CHURCHES DIVIDED IN SPIRIT AND IN FORM?

Oh! how many streets are in the great city Babylon? how many streets in our Cities below? how many Societies? how many Churches divided in Spirit and in Form also, one from another, and in themselves? Surely the Saints are in Babylon, when their Societies and gathered Churches are become not only the scattered bones, dead; but as the two sticks, divided and dry too; for 'tis but sticks, not living branches. I call the Churches so, not the Saints therein: for the life of grace is in them, though truly it be much hid from others, and hid to themselves this day. (p.241)

3. ERBERY'S LETTER TO AMBROSE MOSTYN

Erbery's third letter was written to Ambrose Mostyn[6] from Brecknock on the 23rd of August 1652. The present letter was the second of a series. Erbery's first letter seems to have miscarried, but Erbery regards it as unimportant because it was concerned about outward things. This letter presents his familiar arguments that ministry and ordinances are invalid because there is no longer any 'Baptisme of the Spirit'.

FOR MR. AMBROSE MOSTYN

I TEACH NOTHING NOW TO MAN, BUT THE NEW JERUSALEM

These were the things I then enlarged to you, in the Letter that was lost; and truly I intended not now to speak a word of this, when I first put pen to paper; there is a providence, and the hand of God in it, which led mine thus far that you might lay it to heart.

Indeed (Sir), these are but outward things; there are more inward, [s]*piritual, and eternal truths, I purposed to present to your serious thoughts, that is, the new Jerusalem coming down from God out of Heaven: What the Lord has taught me therin, I cannot now expresse, only to tell you, that I teach nothing now to man, but the new Jerusalem, in which the Saints shall be gathered, as they shall all be one... the divided forms of Church-worship (being fallen with Babylon) shall appear no more; but God will be seen to dwell in his people, with that light and love, that many Nations shall be joyned to the Lord (in them, 'tis not said joyned to them now) for God shall be all in all.*

This I call the third Dispensation, differing from Law and Gospel order, yet comprehending both and above both; for Jerusalem is above; and that which was above to the highest Apostle, will come down and appear to the least and lowest of Gods people, for 'tis the mother of us all; yea the child shall dye a hundred years old, for the least child of God shall come to a perfect man, to the fulnesse of the stature of Christ; that is, shall see himself filled with all the fulness of God, as the most perfect man on earth. Eph. 4.13. (p.243)

GOD DWELLING IN MEN, IMMANUEL, GOD WITH US, THAT'S CHRIST, GOD IN US

But this is the comfort to me and many with me, that as the eares of the deaf shall hear the words of the book; so the eyes of the blind shall see out of obscurity, and out of darkness, Isa. 29.18, 19.

This Scripture I spake of at Brecknock, the last first day. The Book, I shewed, was God dwelling in men, Immanuel, God with us, that's Christ, God in us; God manifest in our flesh, as in his, is Christ in us the hope of glory; for all the Saints shall be taken up into the same glory with himself, and the Nations by this called, and joyned to the Lord. (p.244)

YOUR DEAR DECEASED WIFE, WHO LIVES WITH ME AND IN ME

I shall repeat no more; only the remembrance of the Lord, and his love to me, in your dear deceased Wife, who lives with me and in me: for there's the Lord in whom she is, and in whom we both are, though we know not: but we shall, when the book shall be opened. My dearest salutes to all the Saints with you. Farewell. (p.244)

4. ERBERY'S LETTER TO VAVASOR POWELL

The next letter, written three days later (August 26th, 1652), from Brecknock was to Vavasor Powell.[7] This letter responds to an earlier lost one by Powell. Erbery opposed Powell's literal interpretation of Scripture, including his expectation of a physical Kingdom. Powell's views were carnal and earthly. Erbery's fears were expressed even more clearly in two tracts written in 1654, after the collapse of the Nominated Parliament, which Powell and other Fifth Monarchists anticipated would usher in the reign of Christ. When Cromwell dissolved parliament, Powell depicted Cromwell as the Antichrist. Erbery forewarned Powell that his misinterpretation of Scripture would have dangerous repercussions for church and state.

FOR MR. VAVASOR POWEL

YOUR SECOND THOUGHTS [ON] ***THE PERSONAL REIGN OF CHRIST***

This is not to direct you in preaching, but to desire your second thoughts in the things you spake of, the personal reign of Christ: which with confidence you declare to be in that fleshly presence of his, with which he ascended, and shall so descend to reign a thousand years on earth, and the Saints with him.

This hath some shew in the Letter of Scripture: but if the Spirit hid in your flesh, and mine, shall be suffered to come forth, and truly to interpret, without the Tradition and Teaching of men, God may shew you another sense, than what is commonly revealed by Christians and Churches. (p.245)

WHAT FLESHLY THOUGHTS AND INTERPRETATIONS HAVE PASSED OVER THESE WORDS, BY THE MILLENARIES OF OLD, AND BY MANY GRACIOUS SAINTS OF LATE?

This, my dear Brother, shall be made known to you and me, that the Kingdom of God comes not by outward observation; but seeing the Spirit shall again be poured forth from on high, Isa. 32.15. let us wait for this together, though our Palaces be forsaken, vers. 14. though our Church-fellowships and flesh fall; for so 'twill be before the Spirit come, verse 9. to 13. for Christs pure flesh was crucified through weakenesse, before he was raised in power, or received the Spirits fulnesse.

Then shall we know the reign of Christ, and of the Saints with him, for a thousand years, Rev. 20.4, 6 [should be 20.3, 6]. *But, as yet, what fleshly thoughts and interpretations have passed over these words, by the Millenaries of old, and by many gracious Saints of late? what, Is all the book of the Revelation a Mystery? and must these one thousand years? and will not the Saints be more spirituall, but still to think of a fleshly reign, a reign of Christ after the flesh, and of Saints after the flesh? whereas, no man nor Christ is to be known so any more.*

And may not the one thousand years be but one day, and that one day, the day of God? (when God shall appear) for that day is called one day, Zach. 14.7. known to the Lord, to the Lord, alone in us. (p.247)

DOTH NOT THAT PREACHING OF YOURS, CAUSE MANY SAINTS TO BE MORE CARNALL, EARTHLY, LOOKING FOR A KINGDOM HERE BELOW

...doth not the Reign of Christ, which you hold forth in a fleshly presence, hinder the Saints from looking for the Spirit? that fulnesse of the Spirit, promised by all the Prophets to be poured forth in the last dayes? when he comes the second time without sin to salvation, with fulnesse of the Spirit in us.

Lastly, doth not that preaching of yours, cause many Saints to be more carnall, earthly, looking for a kingdom here below; for they begin to reign already as Kings, but not with Christ, not in righteousnesse, which is that alone (and not in forms of Religion) that shall dwell in the new Heaven and new Earth, now waited for. (p.248)

5. ERBERY'S LETTER TO WALTER CRADOCK

Erbery's fifth letter, written in Cardiff on August 31st, 1652, was to Walter Cradock,[8] his erstwhile curate at St Mary's in Cardiff.

FOR MR. WALTER CRADOCK

THE SAINTS... ARE FALLEN FROM THEIR FIRST LOVE

...the Churches of Saints being this day divided in both, and defiled also in their worships and walkings, shew, that they are fallen from their first love, and from that Gospel-Faith which wrought by love unfained to all Saints, and to all men; besides, that pure conscience, peaceable converse, with holinesse and heavenly mindednesse, self-denial, and zeal, once appearing among the Saints in Wales, being so far from their present profession. (p.249)

NOT ADMITTED, OR NOT INVITED TO... YOUR CONGREGATIONS

I could not but write, and print, because not admitted, or not invited to confer in your Congregations. What I have said and done in publique, I am not sorry for; though sorrow and sufferings are in my flesh, being forced in Spirit to make my self bare first, and then my brethrens nakednesse. (p.249)

I AM COME IN THE SPIRIT OF LOVE... TO GIVE AN ACCOUNT OF THE HOPE THAT IS IN ME, TO MY OWN COUNTRY FIRST, WHERE I HOLD FORTH NOTHING BUT THE NEW JERUSALEM

For my part, I am willing to bear my shame, and his wrath with you, and thus to suffer with all the Saints, yea to dye, and lye down in the open valley with the dry bones, till God raise us up together from Babylon, and bring us out of our graves of Forms and Flesh, which do even bury, and hide from the sight of men, the glorious appearance of the great God in us, now ready to be revealed in these last times, when God shall appear; when he shall rise, and his glory be revealed in us, the Saints in Wales will not onely walk in the same light they formerly did, but in higher discoveries of God, and of Christ; yea in more holy and righteous wayes with men. This is the new Jerusalem, and new Earth, wherein dwells righteousnesse: and because I hear a sound of the new Jerusalem coming down from God out of Heaven among you; and one of you saying, that one Form should knock out another till that come, &c. I am come in the Spirit of Love, with meeknesse and fear, to give an account of the hope that is in me, to my own Country first, where I hold forth nothing but the new Jerusalem, in which God shall gather all the Saints first, even those who look for his coming; in whom he will so appear in power and glory, dwelling in the midst of them, that many Nations shall joyn to the Lord in that day; and these Northern Nations, I believe will be the first fruits of the world; for the Nations of them that are saved, shall walk in the light of the new Jerusalem, and men shall dwell in it, and there shall be no more utter destruction, but Jerusalem shall be safely inhabited, Zach 14.11; Rev. 21.24. (p.249f.)

THE ABUNDANCE OF SAVAGE PEOPLE SHALL COME IN

What multitude of men shall inhabit that City, the Prophets shew; not onely that Jerusalem shall be without Walls, and that a Nation shall be born in one day, but many shall flow in like the Sea; that our hearts shall fear and be inlarged for the abundance of Savage people shall come in and cover us, &c. Isa. 60.5, 6, 8, 9. I say, we shall fear at first, whether such may be received by us; but again our hearts shall be enlarged to accept those whom God doth, causing them to come up to his Altar, and to beautifie the house of his glory, verse 7.13 and though but little of this appear at present, and it appears but to a few, yet a little one shall become a thousand, and a small one, a strong Nation. I the Lord will hasten it, in his time, verse 22. (p.250)

YOU ARE THE SEED WHICH THE LORD HATH BLESSED

This health and happinesse, and a heaven upon earth (as well as hereafter), I wish unto you, and wait for in my flesh, with all the Apostles and Prophets, that the throne of God and the Lamb may be in you, that you may not onely serve him (waiting on him and for him) but see his face, and his name on your foreheads, verse 4. [Revelation 22] *that yourselves may not onely see the Lord fully in you, but that all who see you, may say, Surely the Lord is in you of a truth, and so joyn to the Lord with you; then he shall be named the Priests of the Lord, men shall call you the Ministers of our God, (that's the glory of the Law and Gospel in you) Isa. 51.6, yea all that see you, shall acknowledge that you are the seed which the Lord hath blessed, verse 2.* [Isaiah 51]

That's more then many will yet say of you; but I can, knowing not onely the grace, but the glory that is in you; and when that glory shall be seen on you (as it shall, Isa. 60.1) then men shall see, and you will say that I am in the truth. (p.251)

14
A Call to the Churches; A Dispute at Cowbridge 1652

A Call to the Churches;

OR,

A Packet of Letters

To the PASTORS of

WALES

Presented

To the Baptized Teachers there.

WITH

A Postscript of a Welsh Dispute.

By WILL. ERBERY.

What shall one then answer the Messengers of the Nation? That the Lord hath founded Zion, *and the poor of his people shall repair unto it,* Isa. 14.32.

The first shall say to Zion*, Behold them, and I will give to* Jerusalem *one that bringeth good tydings.*

For I beheld and there was no man amongst them and there was no Counsellor, that when I asked of them, could answer me a word. Isai. 41.27,28,29.

Feb: 19 1652

Printed at *London*, 1653.

18

The Shield Single

AGAINST

The Sword Doubled.

To defend the *Righteous* againſt the Wicked.

Whereby are waved thoſe cuts and blows, which Mr *Erbury* deals to the Righteous;

And wherein alſo is ſhewed, That *His now-New-Light is No-Light,* BUT *Blackneſs of Darkneſs.*

By HENRY NICCOLS, Miniſter of the Word in *South-Wales.*

Thou O Lord art a Shield for me, Pſal. 3.3.

Deliver my ſoul from the wicked, which is a ſword of thine, Pſal. 17.13.

My ſoul is among Lions, and I lie even among them that are ſet on fire, even the Sons of men, whoſe teeth are ſpears, and arrows, and their tongue a ſharp ſword, Pſal. 57.4.

Ignem fatuum qui ſequuntur in avia abducuntur, & in præcipitia ſæpenumero ruunt. *Keckerm. Syſtem. Phyſ.*

LONDON. Printed by *J. M.* for *H. Cripps,* and *L. Lloyd,* and are to be ſold at their Shop in *Popes-head* Alley. 1653. Aug. 15.

The Shield Single AGAINST The Sword Doubled. To defend the Righteous against the Wicked. Whereby are waved those cuts and blows, which Mr. Erbury deals to the Righteous; And wherein also is shewed, That His now-New-Light is No-Light, But Blackness of Darkness.
By HENRY NICCOLS, Minister of the Word In South-Wales.
LONDON, Printed by J.M. for H. Cripps and L. Lloyd, and are to be sold at their Shop in Popes-head Alley, 1653.
(Received into the Thomason Collection on August 15th, 1653)

THE FINAL LETTER in *A Call to the Churches* has similarities with the opening section written to the 'Baptized Teachers of South Wales', when Erbery wrote about his dispute at Llantrisant with David Davies, the Baptist minister of Gelligaer. This letter, addressed to David Walter,[1] reports on a dispute between Erbery and Henry Nichols[2] at Cowbridge. This is of particular interest because both Nichols and Erbery produced versions of the same encounter.

The letter was written from London on January 13th, 1652/3, nearly five months after the letters written in Cardiff and Brecon. Erbery had returned to London where *A Call to the Churches* was published. Thomason received it into his collection on February 19th, 1652/3. The treatise is entitled:

> ***A Dispute at Cowbridge, with Mr.* Henry Nichols, *Pastor of an Independent Church, and Parson of a Parish-Church:* Ergo, *None of the best (though a new-modeled Minister) Nor one of the old Welsh Saints, who minded* Godlinesse more then Gain, *I Tim. 6.6. For Mr. Davy Walter.***

Another public dispute ending in disorder! Erbery had tried to persuade Mr Nichols to discuss certain issues privately, but Nichols insisted on a public debate. Erbery believed David Walter would listen sympathetically.

At the close of the Cowbridge disputation, Erbery recorded that they 'both departed in Peace, as Friends'. However, neither Erbery nor Nichols were prepared to let the matter rest. Erbery wrote to Davy Walter, and Nichols published his treatise. Both had an argument to win! During this age of controversial debates, Erbery seemed to enjoy the struggle of wits despite his advice to fellow saints to remain silent and withdraw from controversy!

FOR MR. DAVY WALTER WAITING FOR A HIGHER POWER, AND SPIRIT, TO APPEAR IN THE SAINTS

Sir, I know your sincerity and singlenesse of heart, yea your unsetlednesse and loosnesse of spirit from all Church-forms, and empty forms of godlinesse, waiting for a higher Power, and Spirit, to appear in the Saints which will gather up not themselves only, but many Nations with them into God.

This is all I have taught my dear Country-men in Wales... (p.252)

MR NICHOLS... HAD RUMOURED ABROAD TO BE ERROUR AND HERESIE

But it was agreed upon at last, that Mr. Nichols should be Respondent, because I was by Argument to maintain the truth that I taught; which he had rumoured abroad to be Errour and Heresie.

The things were these:

First, That the new Jerusalem is a State of the Saints in this life.

This he denied.

Secondly, That the Saints this day have not a Gospel-faith.

This he affirmed.

Thirdly, That God is in union with mankind. This he was negative to.

But I was to maintain all three, in these following Arguments. (p.253)

IN THE THIRD DISPENSATION... NOT... RELIGION, BUT IN THE POWER OF RIGHTEOUSNESSE

But in the third dispensation, many Nations shall be saved, or joyned to the Lord: not to a Church, but to the Lord; not in any particular form of Religion, but in the power of righteousnesse. (p.253)

SAINTS... BEGIN TO WALK NOT BY FAITH, BUT BY SIGHT (THAT'S THE THIRD DISPENSATION)

I say, the weakest of scattered Saints this day do greater works then Christ did in the dayes of his flesh; though the Spirit appear not in them nor they as doing those works... the weakest, even worms do this day thresh mountaines, throw down hills, tear the rocks, and whole armies in peices, break kingdomes, bind kings, nobles, and judges, yea, judge the world and Angels of Churches...

All this we see done by the Saints this day, and the Saints thus to be, though they believe not: for now they begin to walk not by faith, but by sight (that's the third dispensation), which being full faith shall be swallowed up into vision, hope into possession of that glory, wherein we shall see God as he is, see his face, and the Father's Name on our foreheads; yea, his Name is visible and clear upon us, that all men shall see God the Father in us; and whole Nations joyn to the Lord with us in that day. (p.256)

Later in 1653 (the tract entered the Thomason Collection on August 15th) Henry Niccols published his answer to Erbery's *The Sword Doubled* and also reported on the Cowbridge debates. Niccols shares first-hand evidence about Erbery's past ministry. He is saddened that Erbery has fallen from orthodoxy to blasphemy. Erbery should now be tried for heresy, in accordance with the Act against Blasphemy, passed in September 1650.

HIS DANGEROUS, AND ERRONEOUS PRINCIPLES

Before ever I read any of Master Erburies books, I had read in other mens works of his dangerous, and erroneous principles, not of, but against Religion; whereupon hearing of a Book of his come forth, bearing the Title of the Sword doubled, &c. I earnestly desired the sight of it... And seeing that too great a portion of the professing part of our dear Native Country, are ever ready to be slain, and drawn to a worse death, then that of the Sword, I have (by way of Answer to some particulars in that Book) endeavoured the composure of an Antidote against that spreading canker, and infection, that may endanger the souls of such as shall embrace the things delivered in it. (p.1)

MR. WILLIAM ERBERY... NOW A PROFESSED OPPOSER OF ALL THE SAINTS, BOTH WELSH, AND ENGLISH

Mr William Erbery, Pastor of no Church; Sometimes Vicar of a Parish Church; None of the best (though a Minister of the newest Model that ever any knew). Once an old English professed Saint, though now a professed Opposer of all the Saints, both Welsh, and English. (p.5)

MASTER ERBERY WAS TO PREACH AT NEWCASTLE

Hearing that Master Erbery was to preach at Newcastle in Glamorganshire, I was perswaded by some friends to go, and hear him; Thither I came, being not sorry to close with that opportunity... All this while I was dumb with silence, and held my peace, but my heart was hot within me, and while I was thus musing, the fire kindled, and at the last (after he had ended) I spake with my tongue; and that in a fair peacable way; that I humbly conceived, he had delivered such things as my Spirit could not bear, & therefore I desired him to clear them up, for the further satisfaction both of my self & the hearers... (p.5f.)

HE CAME TO COWBRIDG

And on the twenty eighth day of the seventh month he came to Cowbridg, where he began to speak from Revel. 20.12 but very little to that Scripture; but after the needless repetition of many things out of his printed Book (Sword doubled), he takes occasion to fasten all the reproaches he could on the Presbyterians, Independants, and Anabaptists... which did not a little please the many Royalists... present... (p.8)

MASTER ERBURY, THOUGH A WELSH MAN BORN CANNOT DELIVER HIMSELF IN THE WELSH TONGUE

...he himself received two hundred pound Tythes in Wales, for the years 1650. and 1651 and (for ought I perceive) he had not cryed them down yet... This is the main of what passed at that dispute, to which Master Erbury is pleased to give the Epithite of Welsh, in which (I

profess seriously) I do not remember, that there past one Welsh word (for indeed 'tis no small mercy to poor Wales, that Master Erbury, though a Welsh man born,) cannot deliver himself in the Welsh tongue; and I wonder he gives it the undervaluing title of Welsh, especially in a book entituled the Welsh Curate (which, as I am informed, was first presented to, and then caused to be burned by an eminent hand,) he makes the Welsh men to be better born then his own father; for, saith he, they are descended from the Jews, and so himself is the better Gentleman by the mothers side; and yet to fasten a reproach upon the dispute, he doth in an opprobrious way give it the name of a Welsh One… In the mean time I wish him a sight of his errours, and a conversion to the Truths of God. (pp.10, 12)

THE LORD DID WITNESS WITH HIS MINISTRY

I will not derogate so much from Master Erburies worth, and merit; as to conclude him sterril, and barren of testimony in this way, while he used the Ordinances of the Gospel, Prayer, Preaching, &c. While he did follow Christ in his own way fully, the Lord did witness with his Ministry, even to the awaking of many sleepy souls in his own, and other Countries; there are not a few godly people, that yet bless the Lord for him, who made him instrumental to deliver them from the power of darkness, and so to translate them into the Kingdom of his dear Son, Col. 1.13 and therefore have there been many prayers and tears poured forth before the Lord on his behalf; and that by many godly people, whose souls weep in secret for him, by reason of his wofull fall, and apostacy… (p.32f.)

I PRAY FOR HIS CONVICTION, AND CONVERSION

The late Act of Parliament against Ranting, Heresie, and Blasphemy, hath bespoke that Magistracy, honourable, and precious, in the eyes of Gods people, and yet do not I stir up the Christian Magistrate against Master Erbury, but if he hath not sinned the sin unto death, I pray for his conviction, and conversion, if God peradventure will give him repentance to the acknowledging of the Truth. I contend with him with no other weapon, but the Sword of the Spirit, which… may grate upon his Conscience, and cause him to remember from whence he is fallen, and do his first works, and come up to his first Love. (p.74)

15

The Honest Heretique 1652

A Collection of the Writings of the aforesaid Authour, for the benefit of Posterity.

Whereunto is added, *The Honest Heretick*. Being his Tryal at *Westminster*, a piece never Printed before.

TOWARDS THE END of his life, Erbery wrote two tracts which express his faith systematically. *The Great Earthquake* was published in July 1654, three months after Erbery's death, but *The Honest Heretique* remained unpublished until John Webster's collection of 1658. *The Great Earthquake* seems to have been completed just before Erbery's sudden death, but *The Honest Heretique* was written a year earlier, immediately after the trial of 1653.

Until comparatively recently, the only known report of Erbery's trial at Westminster was his own account, but a semi-official account of the Erbery trial has been discovered in the Clarke Papers.[1] Because Clarke's report was catalogued incorrectly under the name 'John Erbury', it has been largely ignored. It presents a fascinating first-hand account of the events of February 1652/3. Erbery faced serious charges, which could possibly have incurred the death penalty. The Blasphemy Acts had been passed in 1648 and 1650, and James Nayler was later to be tried, convicted and punished for blasphemy in 1656. Erbery's widow Mary, and daughter Dorcas, were close followers of James Nayler.[2]

The trial of Mr. John Erbury.

Sir William Clarke, The Clarke Papers. Selections from the Papers of William Clarke, vol. 2 [1894]

Sir William Clarke, The Clarke Papers. Selections from the Papers of William Clarke, Secretary to the Council of the Army, 1647-1649, and to General Monck and the Commanders of the Army in Scotland, 1651-1660, ed. C. H. Firth (Camden Society, 1894). 4 Vols. Chapter: [The trial of Mr. John Erbury.]

Checquer Chamber, 8th Febr. (52)

The trial of Erbery, held in the Chequer Chamber at Westminster (the scene of the trial of the King), was a major event in the calendar of February 1652/3. Erbery appeared before the Committee of Plundered Ministers, chaired by Gilbert Millington.[3] The Clerk to the Committee was John Phelps.[4]

William Clarke presents a fascinating picture of the trial: 'Neere the Barr on the Right hand Capt. Chillenden[5] & witnesses against Erbery.' Were the charges against Erbery initiated by Captain Chillenden? Later that year (October 31st, 1653), Erbery attacked Chillenden for his Baptist and Fifth Monarchist ideas. Spectators included 'Cobbett, myself, & about 4 or 500 more, 2 or 3 files Musqteers & 2 Officers.' This was no friendly theological discussion in a backstairs room. There was a very large audience. This was the third time for Erbery to defend his radical views: as a priest of the Church of England when he appeared at Lambeth Palace in the 1630s; before the Presbyterian Commissioners at St Mary's, Oxford in January 1646/7; and now before a Parliamentary Committee at Westminster.

Clarke records the proceedings in summary fashion: 'Prisoner call'd. Then Phelps reade how farr they proceeded last time.'

> Captn Chillenden
> I heard Mr. Erbery say, That these saints are much against the sinnes of Adultery outwardly, but comitt them wholly inwardly; also a poore Ranter hes but one night in a moneth with a whore, but these

saints this wel-favor'd harlott can lye with twenty betweene this and Westminster.

Maj. Gen. Skippon[6]
I think hee said Christ was a Beast.

Chillenden
Hee said. Don't we see a morall man hee continues in his morality still, but your Church Members & holy men continue in sin, & the Ranters were the holyest in the nacion but their knowledge came to nothing, & that Christ was a Beast, the apostles & prophetts were Beasts & knew nothing, the Saints or Church Members knew nothing, nor hee knew nothing. God in us knew all, but wee nothing, 65 Isaiah 20 etc. 'There shalbe noe more an infant of daies' etc. That hee knew God was coming to destroy the knowledge of all the Saints as they call themselves.

Mr Millington invited Mr Grey[7] to speak. He also reported on Erbery's blasphemies:

Grey
1. Mr. Erbery called the bread of the Lords Supper uncleane bread, & hee said because it was the bread of mourners, & will yee sitt downe att the Table of whores; yee cannot discerne the Lords body lyes in Babilon.
2. Concerning Baptisme, 9 Proverbs, 17, 'Stolen waters are sweete.' The waters of Babilon are stolen, they are wordes of the whore. 18 Rev. 22, And the voice of Harpers musick, etc. Yee shall have Baptisme noe more, Lords Supper noe more, preaching noe more.
3. 30 Isaiah. By removing there into Corners is ment pulpitt preachers, such yee shall have noe more; every object shall teach you, your food & rayement shall teach you.
4. That prayer was a work of God, & when the Spiritt of Christ came in the flesh it did consume, 66 Isa. Christ as a worme will consume, corode, & destroy the flesh, faith etc.
5. When Christ was neerest dissolucion of his flesh then the Spiritt of prayer forsook him, hee prayed onely these few words, 'Father lett this Cupp pass,' etc. I tell you this came from the darkness of his Spiritt.

At this point the clerk, Mr Phelps read the second charge against Erbery: 'That hee blasphemously preached downe the Godhead of Christ.'

Mr. Gray
That Christ would consume our faith. I wonder what evill men see in the Turkish Alcheron. When Christ comes into your flesh, hee will make you in love with all Religions, yea Papists & all. Hee dyed the just for the unjust is mistaken, for Christ in the Spiritt will destroy your flesh that hee may bring you to God.

Luke saith hee was Crucified in the 9th houre, & John who was onely present att his death the 6th.

That Christ dyed not for pardon of sin, or [to] satisfy the Father, but [to] declare the Father's love.

Those Churches call'd Anabaptists etc. & State governments, all those formes, saith hee, God will destroy.

After Grey had finished speaking, the Chairman invited Mr Pemberton[8] to speak:

Mr. Pemberton
I was att Somersett House & heard Mr. Erbury on the 8th Revelacon 1st, uppon opening the 7th seale, 'and there was silence in heaven for ye space of half an howre.' Hee said Christ was going out of all formes. 12 Rev: 1st, concerning the woeman clothed with the Sun & the Moone under her feete, [those] were the Ordinances which shold now cease. 18 Rev: [22nd], when the noise of the Harpers shalbe noe more, which was the comon preaching & singing wee now have. This noise was hee said the musick of Babilon, & further as hee said, as God was going out of all formes soe that there was a more glorious manifestacon of God coming out this day, viz. a 3d dispensacon never knowne to the Saints of old, diffring from the law & gospell Order. What saies God, remember nor former things, I will doe a new thing saith God, soe are wee, as hee was perfectly one with God soe are wee. When Christ came to suffrings the Spiritt of prayer dyed in him, shewing the feebleness & confusion of his Spiritt hereby. It pleased the Lord to bruise him, his understanding was confounded, hee was afraid & knew not what hee said. Hee tooke Peter & James with him

> because hee was afraid to goe alone; that the darkness then was the confusion of his understanding.
>
> And the Vaile of the Temple was rent fro topp to bottome, hee was onely amased, for what was the Vaile but our pure flesh, our guifts, our graces, our performances. This is the flesh of Christ, all of them shalbe torne from highest attainements to lowest performances.

Having heard the evidence against the defendant, the chairman invited Erbery to respond. Although Clarke was still the recorder, there seems to be a different dimension to the debate. Erbery had prepared his brief well, and spoke with eloquence, honesty, and humour – the humour must have riled his persecutors, but probably pleased the audience. This appears to have been the second day of the trial:

> Mr. Erbery
> I humbly thank this Honorable Committee for having liberty once more to speak heere before you. It is thus, I told you the first time the power of the Lord uppon my Spiritt. I came to London to preach onely the new Jerusalem. I confess most what the last evidence said is true; but because I am charg'd by Capt: Chillington [with saying] that Christ is a Beast, & that the Saints & all men knew nothing, I knew nothing. But had I now withheld my coming Capt. Chillington had slided his necke out of the collar; and for mee to say that hee was worse than a Beast, I onely said hee was worse then a goose.

Erbery was defending himself against familiar charges. He had arrived at this theological position as early as the Oxford Disputations in 1646/7, and had spoken and written about these issues on innumerable occasions.

> Erbery
> True I said the Churches were a welfavor'd harlott, Ezek. 30. I told the old prelatick Churches they were an old rotten whore, but these a fayre whore, but the Presbytereans call the Independent Churches whore, & the Independent call them whore againe, & I say they are all whores together. Isa. 47, that whore said, I am a Queene, but

the Scripture saith shee is a whore, her knowledge hath deceived her. I speake as in the presence of God, I meane nothing against the Saints, but [against] Apostates; nay it hath been preacht publiquely in Blackfryers, if men would have good places they must goe into the Independent Churches.

11 Job. 12. Vaine man would bee wise, though born an Asses Colt. 49 Psal. 12, man being in honor abideth not, but becomes as a Beast that perisheth, & wisest men have proved the greatest fooles.

Moses a Minister of the law, some say his face shined, but the originall renders it horned, beastlike.

As Christ to the theife on the Cross – This day shalt thou bee with mee in Paradice. God onely is wise, & that any man account himself soe Ile say hee is as the wild Asses Colt. Every man is a Beast. The prophett speaking of Christ, 30 Pro: saith. 'I am more brutish then any man.' Christ is the Glory of the Father. The word wisedome & power of God in the Father. Christ was in God from Eternity, but became man. The words in Hebrew, Adam signifies weakness or dust of the Earth, 2d Ish: man also but signifies heat. 31 Jer: A woman shall compass a man. All that appeared to Christ was in the power of the Father.

Baptisme & Lords Supper, as in the Anabaptists & Independent Churches, were not Gospell Ordinances. Baptisme of the Spiritt was by power from on high, but the apostles could not goe forth till it came, though comaunded.

They delude their hearers with this word teach & baptize etc. But they mince & cutt the word in halfs.

As breaking of bread among the Churches is uncleane to them it is the bread of mourners.

There was in Gospell times noe breaking of bread but by a spirituall breaking; there ws formerly but one body, one bread, one Church, one Baptisme, but heere all is in a confusion; therefore Christs body is in Babilon, & one clashing against another, & now I waite when the spiritt will appeare to make us all one & convince us of our being yet in Babilon.

Clarke's notes are substantially what Erbery wrote in his formal defence in *The Honest Heretique*. Because darkness was falling, Millington decided to defer the trial until the following

Tuesday. At this point Chillenden interrupted with 'He said that Christ in flesh was a Beast, & that I was worse than Balaams ass, for that spoke truth, but I a lye; consider it.' The chairman ignored the interruption and the day's proceedings drew to a close. One wishes that Clarke had been present on previous and later occasions. Fortunately, we have Erbery's defence.

The Honest Heretique; OR *Orthodox Blasphemer*

Accused of *Heresie* and *Blasphemie;* but cleared of both, by the Judgment of God, and of good men, at a Committee for Plundered Ministers of the *Parliament*, *MARCH* 9th. 1652.

With a double answer to Articles charged against him; whereupon he was freed from his Prison, and liberty granted by the Lord to preach again, which he hath as a *private Christian*, in all subjection to God in the present Powers, with love to Truth and Peace.

By *WILL. ERBERY*

The Answer of* Mr. William Erbery, *to the Charge exhibited by him, before the Honourable Committee of Plundered Ministers, March the 9th. 1652.

The trial continued until March the 9th, 1652/3, when Erbery was eventually cleared of heresy and blasphemy. Erbery presented his defence in two forms: a brief summary, followed by careful answers to each accusation.

Erbery defended himself against the charge of being a minister who preached heresy, by simply pointing out that he was no longer an ordained minister. He had resigned from the ministry of the Church of England, and later from the ministry of an Independent congregation. He defends his position as one whose ministry is common to every Christian.

Liberty of conscience is now part of the Constitution of the State which afffirms that 'Light and Truth might more break forth'. Is he reminding the Committee of the words of Pastor John Robinson to the Pilgrims as they left for America?[9] Erbery accuses Captain Chillenden for undermining freedom of speech. He concludes by asserting his allegiance to the church:

> It is not necessary the Church should be always visible: So this Defendant confesseth, That he holdeth no Fellowship with any Church, but the Invisible Catholique Church, of the first-born, whose Names are written in Heaven. (p.312)

A FREE-BORN SUBJECT OF ENGLAND AND WALES

The Defendant reserving to himself all the liberty to a free-born Subject of England and Wales:

In obedience to your Honours Commands, humbly saith, That he renounceth, and did, before he was upon the Articles called before your Honours, any other pretence to the Ministry, then that which is common to every Christian. And denyeth, that he hath preached, as by the Articles is suggested.

And therefore the Defendant humbly conceives, that the power granted to this Honourable Committee, to inquire into, and report all matters concerning scandalous or sequestred Ministers, concerns him not. (p.310f.)

AS TO THE MATTER CALLED BLASPHEMY AND HERESIE, HE DOTH DETEST AND ABHOR

The Defendant further saith, That as to the matter called Blasphemy and Heresie, he doth detest and abhor; but humbly conceives himself not bound to answer, except some person did charge him therewith. Besides, the Defendant hath already not onely denied what was charged against him as Blasphemy; but given an Account to your Honours, that he said not any such thing, but openly asserted the Deity of Christ, and that Christ was not a Beast, nor his flesh rotted in the Grave: Shewing, by sundry Reasons (justifying the perfection of his Humane Nature), that your Defendant could not speak so unworthily against the Son of God;

but was misunderstood in what he had said, which he hopes he hath cleared to your Honours. (p.310f.)

LIGHT AND TRUTH MIGHT MORE BREAK FORTH

...there is no Supream Head nor Governour Ecclesiastical declared, as in the days of King Henry the 8th, and Queen Elizabeth, with their Successors Royal. And that there is no Church setled by the Law of this Nation, but the National Church, which is the Episcopal Body, though the Heads be removed; which though the Presbyters are supposed to supply, as they did in Scotland, yet their Churches here do consist of voluntary Members, as in France and Holland: And withall, the Presbyterian, Independent, and Anabaptist-Churches, so called: As also, the Erastians, and Assembling-Seekers, do preach, write, and speak, more against her, and one another, then he hath spoken against any of them; And that they are likewise in greater Contests concerning the Sacraments, than as the Defendant conceives he is charged withall: And the reason of this liberty taken by them is, their conceiving there is no Law against them, but what is either Repealed, or Antiquated: And that they have countenance from the Civil-Authority, that so Light and Truth might more break forth. And this Defendant humbly conceives, that it is the freedom intended to all persons of this Nation, to search and try all things, and all persons were as free, as the Defendant, to speak where he spake; and Captain Chillinden doth confess to have spoken, where he spake, in contradiction. (p.311)

Following the summary, Erbery presented a carefully prepared defence against every charge. He reminded this government committee that he had supported and suffered for the cause for more than twenty years. In fact he remains a persecuted man under house arrest and forbidden to speak or write. Erbery applauds the present government as a foretaste of the coming Kingdom. This, he reminds the Committee, has always been the substance of his ministry.

Erbery was familiar with the charges made against him. He had been accused of denying the divinity of Christ by Thomas

Edwards in the 1640s, and by Francis Cheynell in the Oxford debates of 1646/7. He passionately and eloquently rejected all their accusations and shared his vision of the infinite mystery and glory of God. At the centre of Erbery's theology was his conviction that Christ revealed God's eternal intention for humankind. The Third Dispensation would present the fulfilment of God's mysterious, powerful compassion. The divine essence, eternally dwelling in the Son would soon be revealed in the saints, humankind and the whole of created life.

Because humankind was united in God, individuals belonged to one community. Humanity is corporate, united by God's love in Christ. Here and now, saints lived with the assurance of the indwelling Spirit, and in the coming Third Age, the whole universe would reflect the fullness of God's purposes.

Although Erbery believed that humankind could not be permanently separated from God, there was always the temptation to replace God as the centre of life. There was an inner struggle between 'the two mysteries of Christ and Antichrist, godliness and iniquity; God in us, and Man in us'.

During the Second Dispensation, the Age of the Son, the true nature of being human was revealed, but because of the Apostasy, there was no longer any sense of God's presence. The Third Dispensation will reveal the destiny of humankind. Erbery uses three Hebrew words for 'Man: Adam, Ish and Geber'. Quoting the prophet Jeremiah, Erbery calls Jesus, 'geber, the man who encompasses a woman.' Humankind is more than male and female. Geber is the prototype of the new humanity, the destiny of being human.

At the heart of the controversy between Erbery and his detractors was the interpretation of Scripture. Erbery's theology was anchored in Scriptural reference. Although advocating scholarly tools for understanding the Bible, he also called for Scripture to be interpreted by the leading of the Spirit. Many Army chaplains shared this approach. They insisted that the written word was not enough. Only by revelation could the message within Scripture be revealed. Reason and human knowledge were means of discovering the history or letter, but only through the Spirit could the inner mystery be discerned.

For Erbery, scholarship was a proper tool for the exegesis of Scripture. Christ's earthly life was limited by the conventions of the first century. The Gospels were but an historical relation and the Epistles only particular letters of some special concernment to the Churches. He disputed the canonicity of I John 5.7, suggested that the text of the English Bible might not be complete, and that portions of Scripture were incorrectly translated.

Erbery advocated toleration for the three chief religions in the world, the Christians, Jews and Turks. He also believed that some truth and much good has been brought forth by men in a false Ministry, as our old conformists, and honest non-conformists. Intolerance was dangerous for both persecuted and persecutor. His openness of mind and spirit was the result of his personal experience of the immanent Christ, and his conviction that with the imminence of the Third Dispensation, humankind would discover its unity as God's children. That day was dawning, and he had no doubt that God is setting up his 'Ensign in this Land, and his glory to arise in this Nation first.'

A SUFFERER FROM THE BEGINNING

Having been a Sufferer from the beginning; first, by the Prelates, in the High-Commission: next, by the Royall-Party for my affection to the Parliament, being the first Plundered Minister in Wales: I hope the favour of this Honourable Committee will so look upon a man (though no Minister now), as to grant, this freedom, at least to Preface a few things to his following Answer. First, I do humbly, and thankfully acknowledge the goodness of the Lord, in your Honours, who have had those tender respects to my low condition, as to appoint my hired house for my Prison, and to afford that liberty of speech, and now of writing, to a Man, made a Monster by men, not worthy to live. (p.313)

IN THE LAND OF APPROACHING LIGHT, AND PROMISED LIBERTY

But being brought forth in the Land of the Living, in the Lord himself, 'Tis a blessing to me, and to many with me, who are born at this time, not onely into Eternity above, but here below, in the Land of approaching light, and promised liberty, where the Dead are looking out of their Graves to rise, and the Captives be redeemed at last from all that Bondage on their Spirits and States.

God with Us, being the Nations Motto, and the Liberty of the Common-wealth of England published, speaks to me the spirit of Cyrus, and of Christ rising in our present Governours, Civil and Martial, proclaiming Liberty to all the People of God, to go out of Babylon, and to build Jerusalem anew.

The New Jerusalem is that I have all in my heart (as I have hinted to my own Countrey first) and being called to London, to visit my poor Family, 'twas my onely thought to speak of that more fully in this City, even the glory of the New Jerusalem. (p.313)

A BROTHERHOOD OF BLACKNESS AND DARKNESS

I said then, that since the World began, there was not such a thing acted, nor heard among men, that men and women, formerly professing godliness, many of them in the power of it, precise, spiritual, and knowing people, some of them Church-members also, should fall so low, below the worst of men; yea, below the nature of Beasts, from Heaven to Earth, yea to Hell it self, in Blasphemy, Swearing, Cursing, Whoring, &c. not onely to drink, but to dance, and be merry in their madness, and these mad-folks to be yet sometimes (as they say) so sober, to speak so highly of God, and his glory, and then again to fall, not in a fit (as the best of Saints have done in the hour of temptation) but to go on boldly, not in single small Companies, but in great Fellowships; not in one place of the Land, but in many; not in secret, but openly to rejoyce and glory in their wickedness. Yea, whereas they would by this break all Church-fellowship, they enter into Church-fellowship themselves, into a Brotherhood of blackness and darkness, being not afraid, nor ashamed, for the light of the Sun to see them. (p.314)

I AM A MAN IN BABYLON, WITH ALL THE GATHERED CHURCHES, AND SCATTERED SAINTS

But now the truth of my Answer, to all that is charged against me, I humbly present, with myself, at your Honours feet; professing, first, that I am a man in Babylon, with all the gathered Churches, and scattered Saints; my own continued Confessions, both in Print, and Publique Speakings, shew the same. Besides, my acknowledged Confusion in my apprehensions, and present attainments, may be a just Apologie, at least a Motive, to your Honours Indulgence over all my weaknesses.

Secondly, as God did bring forth Light out of Darkness: so Love will arise out of our Divisions; and perfect Order, at last, out of this Confusion. Yet seeing there is a Call from Heaven to all the people of God to come out of Babylon: and the judgment of good men is, that we are about the seventh Vial: If this bring forth Voyces, and Thunderings, and Lightings, and a great Earth-quake, such as was not, since men were upon the Earth… (p.315)

CALLED A BLASPHEMER, AN APOSTATE… I DESIRE TO BE MORE IN THE TRUTH AND POWER OF GODLINESS

And now I come to answer the Articles, First, in generall, Whereas I am therein accused, and called a Blasphemer, an Apostate, profane, scandalous, wicked, and of Hellish Designs (being untruly charged upon me) all these, and a thousand reproaches I take up as a Crown on my Head, and go on in the Name of the Lord, with love to Truth and Peace. And I trust it will appear, in time, that I am no Apostate: for, as in the strength of God I have stood to my ground, and not shrunk for fear or favour from any principle of Christ, or Christian practise: so, though I am not so much in the observation of some outward Forms of Religion as formerly I have been, and as some now apprehend it their duty to be; yet I desire to be more in the truth and power of godliness (i.e.) in the knowledge of my union with God, walking in the light thereof in spiritual communion, and converse with him, and in works of Righteousness, Judgment, and Mercy, among men: and if this be Apostasie, I shall be contented to be accounted so, and to be yet more vile then thus; my Conscience bearing me Witness in the Holy Spirit, that I do aim at the most Spiritual Discoveries of God in Christ Jesus, which are prophesied by the Holy Prophets, to be brought forth in the last days. (p.316)

THE GODHEAD, DWELLING IN THE SON, DWELS ALSO IN THE SAINTS

1. To the first particular in my Charge, I answer, That I preached not at Somerset-house, nor said, that Jesus Christ was no more then another man; nor that every one who had God manifest to him, was as perfect: for God, in Christ, is manifest to many, in whom God is not yet manifest, nor Christ revealed in them, but they still resist the Spirit. Neither said I, that we are perfect with God, as Christ was; but perfect with Christ, in God, we are, I asserted; and that the Godhead, dwelling in the Son, dwels also in the Saints, as the Apostle prays, That ye might be filled with all the fulness of God Eph. 3.19. that is, that the fulness of God, even all the fulness of God, of the God-head, might be manifested in them, and to the World also, as Christ prayeth, That they all may be one... Joh. 17.22, 23. That glory of Union, which Christ had with the Father, the glory of love which God has to his Beloved, and the life also that Christ has with God, even the Father, all that have we, with Christ, in God, Col. 3.1, 2, 3. (p.316f.)

MEN LOOKT UPON THE FLESH TOO MUCH

And as the life of Christ, was the glory of the Father, and the life of Christ, in the Father, was not so manifest to men, while he lived in flesh; and because men lookt upon the flesh too much, and not on the Father in him (men still hearing and beholding the gracious words that he spake, and the glorious works that he did), therefore God, even the Father, did crucifie his flesh to himself, and Christ willingly offered that pure flesh, as a Sacrifice to God, to be made weak, as ever man was, even a Worm, and no man; that God, in him, might appear to be All in All. (p.317)

THAT SPIRIT OR POWER OF THE GOD-HEAD WAS IN HIS FLESH, SHOULD APPEAR IN THEIRS

For this cause Christ said, the Comforter shall not come, except I depart and go away, Joh. 16.7 that is, till Christ did disappear in flesh, the

Spirit or Power of God in his flesh could not appear in theirs, but when that power from on High came upon them, and in them, then the works that he did in the flesh, they did also, and greater also; which was not the undervaluing of Christ (as I am charged) but he being the Quickning Spirit in Truth, and the Spirit appearing now so gloriously in the Saints, was for the glory of the Son, who was therefore said not to be glorified, till that Spirit or Power of the God-head that was in his flesh, should appear in theirs, Joh. 6.63; Joh. 7.39. That the world may know (saith he) that thou hast sent me, and hast loved them, as thou hast loved me, Joh. 17, as if the sending of the Son was for the sake of the Saints, that the Son should be revealed in them, and that the Saints, in the Spirit, might appear in the love of the Father, in the same love that the Father has to his Beloved, Eph. 3.19. (p.318)

THOSE GLORIOUS MANIFESTATIONS OF HIS WISDOM AND POWER IN THEM

This is the glory that the Saints of the most High have with Christ, even to judge and raign with Him on Earth, not in an Earthly and outward manner, but in those glorious manifestations o[f] *his wisdom and power in them, that by overcoming all that is of Man within them, their flesh being crucified to God, they overcome by the bloud of the Lamb, by which they are raised up to that glory, as to sit with him in his Fathers Throne, to judge the World, and Angels of Churches; yea, to rule the Nations with a Rod of Iron, dashing them in pieces like a Potters Vessel. This glory of the Son shall be manifest in the Saints, Psal. 2.3, 9; Rev. 2.27; Rev. 3.21; I Cor. 6.2, 3.* (p.318f.)

CHRIST... BEING RISEN... THAT HE MIGHT FILL ALL THINGS

But those were Deluders, who taught Christ sitting at the right hand of God in a fleshly manner (as one man sits by another) whereas God is a Spirit infinite, and incomprehensible, whose right hand is in the Rivers, and in Hell also his right hand finds us out; and Christ who is a Quickning Spirit, being risen, a Spiritual Body is ascended, not onely into Heaven, but far above all Heavens, that he might fill all things; that is, he sate down at the right hand of God, in highest Majesty and Glory of the God-head, executing Judgment, and all that power given him in Heaven and in Earth, having the Keys of Death and Hell, farre above all Principalities and Powers, Men and Devils; all being subject to him. (p.319)

'TIS NOT SATISFACTION ONELY, BUT THE FELLOWSHIP OF CHRIST'S SUFFERINGS IS HERE INTENDED

3. To the third, he said not, That Christ dyed not for sinners, to save that of sinners; but that of I Pet. 3.18 was much mistaken by most Ministers, who hold forth Christ, as dying for Saints onely, not for sinners; nor for the ungodly, for the unjust, as Paul and Peter both do witness, Rom. 5.6, 8.

Secondly, 'tis not satisfaction onely, but the fellowship of Christ's sufferings is here intended; and our conformity to his Death, to follow him, in suffering all reproaches and revilings from men, I Pet. 2.21, 22. Yea, to suffer as evil-doers for well-doing, I Pet. 3.17 and to suffer not onely in our outward flesh, in our credit and repute, and worldly comforts; but in our inward flesh also, to lay down our own Reason, to deny our own Will, and to dye to our own Wisdom, I Pet. 4.1, 2. Yea, to dye, not onely to our inward flesh, or natural inclinations, but to our spiritual excellencies (for as there is a fleshly spirit, so spiritual flesh.) To this Christ dyed, even to all his created excellency of Wisdom and Knowledge, to his highest Comprehensions of Divine Mysteries, to his strongest confidence, and sweet contents: his joy, and peace, and all his spiritual strength was so weakned and wasted, that he became a Worm, and no Man… (p.319f.)

HIS SPIRIT WAS WILLING, YET HIS FLESH WAS SO WEAK

For Christ being made sinne for us, who knew no sinne, stood as a sinner, in the similitude of sinful flesh, bearing in his Body and Soul all those sufferings, sorrows, temptations, troubles, terrours, those fears of Death, and pangs of Hell, which take hold on sinners; that sinners being brought to the lowest state of flesh, might this way be brought to God. How? By beholding God in Christ one with them, though seemingly forsaken of God, and his love to them, as to his Beloved, and their life in God with Christ, though their Soul be sorrowful to the death; for never was a sinner so afraid to be damned, as the Son of God was afraid to dye; so amazed, that he knew not what to say, or do: My Soul (saith he) is sore troubled, and what shall I say? Father, save me from this hour; yea, praying over and over the same words; Abba Father, let this Cup pass from me: and though he knew it was the Will of God, and for the salvation of Man, yet He would fain have his own Will (so weak he was in suffering), though again he submitted, and his Spirit was willing, yet his flesh was so weak, that he cryes out as a man forsaken of God; My God my God, why hast thou so forsaken me? Yea, he so strangled with despair, that Mr. Calvin saith, he uttered the voyce of a despairing man; not onely crying out, but he roars in his cry; Lord, why art thou so far from the voice of my roaring? (Psal. 22.2) Yet for all this, in this lowest estate of flesh, Christ was as high in the glory of the Father, as ever; yea, in his apprehensions of wrath, and pangs of Hell, was as perfect in the Divine Love, as when he lay in his Fathers Bosome: and when his spiritual pure flesh was dying within him, and sweetest comforts almost dead; yet he lay down in the life of God, and lived in God alone.

Thus men, yea the best of men may be brought to God, not onely in their spiritual desertions, but in their sinful Falls they may be brought to God, being now themselves become unjust and ungodly; as not onely Ranters, but some Religious men this day may be brought to God this way by Christ, suffering for sins the just for the unjust, &c in their greatest infirmities, fears, temptations, troubles, terrours of Death, and horrors of Hell (which are at hand) they may hold up their heads, and behold their union with God in Christ, God's love to them, as to his Beloved, and their life with Christ in God. (p.320)

THE SPIRIT (SAITH HE) IS READY, BUT THE FLESH IS WEAK

Besides, that he was afraid to be alone in prayer, is plain to me by both the Evangelists: for being soire amazed, and distracted with fears; he desired his three Disciples to stay with him a little... The spirit (saith he) is ready, but the flesh is weak; this was not applied by him to their sleepy bodies onely, but to his sinking soul, so exceeding sorrowful to the Death, as those three Greek words well Englished, and understood do witnesse, for ekthambeisthai, ademonein, perilupos, hold forth to me the perfect weaknesse and wasting of his spiritual strength, the first word signifies the astonishment of all his inward senses, the second shews the sinking down or heavynesse of his soul, the third notes his soul encompassed about, or besieged with sorrow... (p.321)

GOD IS NOT TO BE RECONCILED TO MAN, BUT MAN TO GOD

And here follows the Merit of Christs death and satisfaction for us, neither of which do I deny (though the word merit and satisfaction of Divine justice be not written in the Letter of Scripture) but the substance of both in the spirit and according to Scripture, I assert... his death was the manifestation of Gods love, and the love of God brought forth Christ to live, and to die for us.

But thus the death of Christ is meritorious, in that 'tis a work of infinite worth and price for the pardon and purging of sin, that men in the spirit may have peace with God, and purenesse of converse. Again, as merit properly presupposeth not love; so satisfaction supposeth wrath to be pacified, and he who is offended to be reconciled: so God is not (for fury is not in me), and as Gods wrath to be pacified is not written in Scripture, so God is not to be reconciled to Man, but Man to God, 2 Cor. 5.19. (p.321f.)

GOD IS UNCHANGEABLE IN HIS ESSENCE

...yet in truth God is unchangeable in his Essence, not being (as men conceive) first in love, then in wrath, then in love again, first pleased, then offended, then reconciled; but as the Attonement was not made to God, but received by men, in the Ministry of the Gospel; so it was manifested then that God was not to be reconciled to men, but men to be reconciled to God... wrath is not of Gods part, but of Mans, men being by nature Children of wrath, not that God hath wrath to any man (as man to

another) but men naturally apprehending wrath in God do fear and fly from him, as fallen Adam did (though God fled not from him, but sought him out)… (though God be no enemy to man). But when the grace of God bringing Salvation to all men appeareth, then the kindness & love of God our Saviour toward man so appeareth in the death of Christ given for all, for the ungodly, and for the unjust, that all enmity is slain thereby: for if being Enemies we were reconciled to God by the death of his Son, much more being reconciled we shall be saved by his life; and so 'tis not the death of Christ only, but the life of Christ in God, revealed in us by the Spirit, that must save us. (p.322)

IN THIS 2D DISPENSATION MAN WAS BROUGHT BY CHRIST… BUT TO THE STATE OF THE FIRST ADAM… THE HEAVENLY IMAGE… WAS RESERVED TILL THE 3D DISPENSATION

4. To the fourth; he said not, that Christ was a Beast, or that he knew nothing, &c. onely he shewed, in what sense man was a Beast… He stood not in his integrity for a Night, but fell the same day of his Creation. Man indeed was made in the Image, and likenesse of God, nothing but God appeared then in Man; he knew nothing, but as God knew in him, for he knew not of himself that he was naked; not that man was made blind, but God was his knowledge, light and sight: for as upon his fall his eyes were opened to see, and he saw himself naked… (p.323)

This fall of man to a Beast, to live by sight, and sense, and outward observance, was held forth in the dispensation of the Law, where all was outward, the sacrifices were Beasts… but Christ in the dispensation of the Gospel brings Man to God again, and man is brought to Paradise, (to Paradise in spirit and truth) so Christ told the thief on the Crosse, this day shall thou be with me in Paradise (to live in the Father alone, and no more in the flesh). For as Christ the 2d Adam lived so, even while he was in the flesh he lived in the Father, (and so the first Adam did as I said, he lived in God alone) so the Apostles life was in Christ onely. Paul lived not, but Christ in him: and he knew not, but was rather known of God: yet in this 2d dispensation man was brought by Christ, but to the state of the first Adam, to the Image of the Earthly, and living soul, (for all that which the Apostle had, his gifts and graces were but the Image of the Earthly) the Heavenly Image or substance, the Quickening spirit was reserved till the 3d dispensation, as (with God) I shall shew hereafter: for the Tree of life was not fully tasted, nor toucht by the Apostles themselves, whilst in the outward dispensation; but it shall be by them, who overcome, and are citizens of the new Jerusalem. (p.323f.)

ADAM, ISH, GEBER THE LORD HATH CREATED A NEW THING ON THE EARTH

But as the Man Christ Jesus was the Lamb of God, not onely full of love, but far from blood: so he was not as the Beast, or naturall man, but the Quickning spirit, not onely the son of man, but the Son of God, and this man, God blessed for ever.

Therefore there are three names of Man in the Hebrew, Adam, Ish, and Geber: Adam and Ish we translate high and low, Psal. 49.2. but 'tis Ben Adam gam Ben Ish: filii hominis, etiam filii viri, as Ar. Montanus; or as Ainsworth[10] *reads, base Man, and Noble man. Adam is low man, not onely of the Earth, but of Dust, yea not made of the dust, (as we render) but made dust of the Earth, as the Hebrew reads, and as Abraham saith, I am dust and ashes, &c. Adam then is Man fallen in weaknesse to dust and death; Ish is man rising in power to life and glory: But Geber is the mighty power, or quickning spirit it self, the life of all men, so Christ is called the wisdom of God, and power of God, that's Geber, Jer. 31.22. The Lord hath created a new thing on the Earth, a Woman shall compasse a Man; or Geber, that is, Christ Jesus our Lord.*

Now as the woman is the weaker vessel: so holy men of God, (when having the high discoveries of God in them) saw themselves not onely in lowest weaknesse, but as Beasts. (p.325)

THE BAPTISME OF THE SPIRIT BEING NOT IN THE CHURCHES

First the Baptisme of the Spirit being not in the Churches, there could not be water-Baptisme in a Gospel-way. Secondly, there is no man sent of God, with power from on high to Teach all Nations and Baptize (for so is the Commission). Thirdly, nor can any this day Baptize with a promise of the spirit, or gift of the spirit to be given thereby. For grace believers had before they were baptized: Likewise in Breaking of Bread, the present Churches cannot drink into one Spirit, having not one Baptisme.

Presbyterian Churches baptize all children of the Nation, Independents, children of Believers onely; Anabap[t]*ists, onely believers. Secondly, as there is not one Spirit, one Baptisme: so neither one Body: And the body being divided, how can there be a Communion, where there is no union? as in the Churches appears, where there is not only division between brother and brother (as in the Apostles and Apostolique Churches might be), but the division this day is between Church and Church, between Body and Body: which was never in the Churches of Christ, when all the Saints were in Church-fellowship, and all walked in one Church-way, had one way of worship: One Baptisme, One Spirit, One Body. Thirdly the Churches this day do not discern the Lords Body...* (p.325f.)

THE PRESENT CHURCHES, HARLOTS AND WHORES

Therefore I called the present Churches, Harlots and Whores, Prelatique and Presbty[yt]*erian Churches, I called the old Rotten Whores, being in fellowship with the whole Nation, with every man in the Parish; but Independent and Baptized Churches being in fellowship with Saints so called, I compared to the well-favoured harlot, Nahum 3.4; Ezek. 23. 41, 42.*

And why should any take offence at my words? Seeing each Church calls the other whore. Prelates called the Popish Church the great Whore, Presbyters call Prelates Whore, Independents call Presbyters Whore, Anabaptists call Independents Whore. I call Anabaptists Whore. And to me they are all Whores.

For though Rome be the Mother of Harlots, yet reformed; and most refined Churches may be her Daughters... so there is one whorish spirit, the mother of all the present Churches: and as one of those was called the old Adulteresse, Ezek. 23.43 so Prelacy was much elder than Presbytery, this being born of Mr. Calvin at Geneva, as Independent Churches of Mr. Cotton and others in New-England. I mean not onely their Church-Covenant, but that forme of Ministry and Magistracy made up in one Church-state. (p.326f.)

GOSPEL SAINTS DID CALL ON THE FATHER IN CHRIST OR IN HIS NAME

As for Praying to God by his Attributes I denyed not, only showed a difference between Legal and Gospel prayers, for as the people of God under the Law, did know God in Covenant: so they commonly prayed to him in his Attributes, as O Lord God, great and terrible, &c. but Gospel-Saints knowing God in Christ, did by the spirit of the Son call God Father. Therefore Christ in his prayers, did not cry Oh Lord! Oh God! save once in his spirituall desertion on the Crosse but usually called God Father, and so prayed, O Father, holy Father, Abba Father &c. Again, the people of God under the Law (though looking for the Messiah) not knowing the Mystery of God, not of Christ in us, nor Messiah the Anoynted in themselves), did look upon God and Christ at a distance from them; and therefore in praying, called upon God for the Lords sake, Dan. 9.17 but Gospel Saints did call on the Father in Christ or in his name; not that they did alwayes name Christ in the end of their prayers, (as we do), Act 1.24 nor yet for Christ Jesus sake, at all, Act. 4.30 but onely in Christ, or through Christ Jesus, that is in that union they had with Christ in God, and love that God had to them in his beloved; and as his beloved Son, Gospel-Saints in the spirit of life with him did go to the Father, and therefore that Scripture, Eph.4.32 as God for Christs sake hath forgiven us &c. is falsely translated: or 'tis in the Greek, as God in Christ hath forgiven vers. [?] *Theosen Christo.* (p.328f.)

BAPTISME... IS THE ANSWER OF A GOOD CONSCIENCE TOWARD GOD

Lastly, as Paul calls it the washing of Regeneration: so Peter tells us what baptisme is in truth, not the putting away or washing the filth of the flesh, but the answer of a good Conscience toward God, by the Resurrection of Jesus Christ. All that the Anabaptists have besides this, is, but stollen waters, and because I honour their persons, and those precious Saints among them, therefore I would call them to arise, not out of the water; but into those waters waited for, which no man can passe over, Ezek. 47.5 yea their dipping too (though a false form) is to me a type or figure of this Truth, our Plunging into the spirit. (p.331)

THESE I CALL WORSE THEN RANTERS

I never said that Ranters as they are now though Ranters, are the best of Saints &c. but that spiritual Ranters, who see not their wickednesse and whoredoms within, walking in the secret of their souls before God in manifold sins, and false worships without, these I call worse then Ranters in as much as spiritual wickednesses are worse then carnal; These, it may be lye with a woman once a month, but those men having eyes full of Adultery (or full of the Adulteresse as the Greek reads) do lye with 20 women between Pauls and Westminster, as I said; not with whores, as the charge speaks, but with women, as Christ saith Math. 5.28. Whosoever looketh on a woman to lust after her hath committed adultery with her &c. (p.331)

AS FOR THE DARKNESSE OF THE SUNNE AFORESAID

But as for the darknesse of the sunne aforesaid, as it were that spiritual darknesse onely on the Son of God, I did not positively resolve, only put it to the Question, not to question the Authority of Scriptures, but to set the spirits of men on work, to wait on the spirit of God, to teach us all things, yet as Paul speaking of Sarai and Hagar, saith, it was an Allegory, though the History be plain, that such persons were: so though that darknesse of the same was truly visible, in the letter; yet the spirit might teach us a mystery therein, first that darknesse which was on the flesh of Christ, as I said before. Secondly, that the Church then was in utter darknesse, who had cast away Christ, crying away with him who yet prayed for them the ninth hour, Father forgive them; then the Sun began to shine again. Thirdly, John, who spake more in the mystery of Christ, doth not mention that visible darknesse at all. Fourthly, Luke saith that Christ being present on the Crosse, darknesse was on the earth from the sixth hour to the ninth; but John being present there saith, that Christ stood before Pilate at the sixth hour. Fifthly, no Historian nor Chronologer that I know, doth mention this three houres darknesse over the whole Earth, 'tis enough that the holy Scriptures mention it. 6, 'twas much then to me, that seeing the Egyptians in that gross darkness stirred not, nor spake a word, how in this horrible darknesse of the Sun, the Church of the Jewes with the Priests should be so merry, as to mock and scoff at Christ &c. But this I can answer, the Church was wonderfully hardned. (p.332f.)

THIS CHRISTIAN COMMON-WEALTH APPEARING SO FAVOURABLE TO THE JEWS, WHY NOT TO THE TURKS?

To the 10th, That I saw no evil in the Turkish Alkaron, and wished liberty to the Popish Religion, &c. Truly the Turkish Alkaron I never saw, therefore knew not the evil of it: but (not to repeat what I spake last to your Honours) I shall onely add, That as the three chief Religions in the World, are the Christians, Jews and Turks; so this Christian Common-wealth appearing so favourable to the Jews, why not to the Turks?

Who more honour Christ Jesus, than the Jews do, who curse and blaspheme him, yet Liberty of Conscience was once highly moved in a Councel of War by the General Officers, to Petition the Parliament for Liberty of Conscience to the Jews: And if for unbelieving Jews, why not for misbelieving Christians, who to their utmost knowledge love the Truth and Peace? Secondly, as the Calling of the Jews is a Mystery which most Christians understand not, (Rom. 11.26) (for Mr. Calvin interprets that Israel of God, in the Spirit which our Divines do of the Jews in the letter) so, though the Turks are turned away from the Son to the Father, because the Spirit of Christ did not commonly appear in Christians; yet the Teutonick Theosopher[11] *saith, That the Turks do (in their righteous ways) worship the Son in the Father, though not naming Christ as Christians do. The same Author adds, That the Turks shal yet turn to be true Christians, and that Christians shall all know the Truth as it is in Jesus. Thirdly, What if God should so appear among men, that the Turks on the East-side of Christendom; and this Nation, on the North, should in the Spirit, besiege all the Superstitious Christians, and Western Churches: for when the Lord shall roar, the Children shall tremble from the West, Hos. 11.12.* (p.333)

IF CHRISTIANS, WITH US, TURN TO BE TURKS, WHY MAY NOT TURKS TURN TO BE CHRISTIANS?

If Christians, with us, turn to be Turks, why may not Turks turn to be Christians? Jacob Behme compares Christians to that Son who said, He would go to the Vineyard, but went not. And the Turks, to the second Son, who told his Father, He would not go, but afterwards repented, and went, Mat. 21.28, 29.

Again, as the Turks are Ishmaelites in their Original: so the Angel came to Ishmael (being yet in the Wombe), when his Mother fled from Sarah, and did enrich him with a Blessing and Worldly Dominion, end bad the Mother with the Child return to Sarah. Likewise, when the Eastern Countries entred again into the Mother's womb with their Knowledge of Religion, God gave unto them the Kingdom of Nature, Power, and Authority, over the Princely Dominions, of the World for to posses and rule them under the Light of Nature in its time. Then they shall come in again with great joy and humility to Abraham, viz. to Christ; and not in the form of the Babylonical, Formal, Literal, Christendom, in their invented and contrived Orders, &c Mercurius Teutonicus, Pag. 27. (p.333f.)

MEN SHALL WORSHIP HIM EVERY ONE FROM HIS PLACE

Seventhly, What saith the Lord to the Churches? Are ye not as the Children of Ethiopians to me? O ye Children of Israel, Amos 9.7.

Ethiopians are worse then Turks, and farthest from God: But when God shall arise with power and peace in his People, Princes shall come out of Aegypt, and Ethiopia shall soon stretch out her hands unto God, Psa. 68.24, 31. Eightly, When God shall famish all the gods of the Earth, men shall worship him every one from his place, even all the Isles of the Sea, Zeph. 2.11.

Lastly, as Christ was terrible to the Church of the Jews, to Pharisees and Hypocrites, but tender to Publicans and Sinners; so the Apostles, (though persecuted by the Jews contradicting and blaspheming the Gospel) were never harsh to the Heathens, acknowledging themselves to be men of like passion with the worst, and confessing those to worship the true God, though in a false form, or ignorantly (as we may be): yea he (calling their Idolatries, Devotions) declares no rigidness of spirit to their Heathenish Religion, nor yet refuseth the testimony of a profane Poet to prove the true God, Act. 17.28. (p.334)

WHY MAY NOT HONEST PAPISTS HAVE THE LIKE LIBERTY OF CONSCIENCE?

It follows not from this, that the Apostles were in love with all Religions, but with men of all Religions; and that was my meaning, as the close of the charge confesseth, and with Papists also. As for these, I'le say no more, till they can give assurance to the State of their peaceable subjection. Protestant Churches (though counted Hereticks) have free and publique exercise of their Religion in Popish States, as France; and why may not honest Papists have the like liberty of Conscience, in due time, amongst Protestants in England, when our Governours see good. (p.334)

I DENY THAT I LAUGHED AT THEM, THOUGH I MIGHT SMILE

Again, I deny that I laughed at them, though I might smile if the Lord had made my face to shine, and guard my heart from fear: but if that were an Errour in me, might it not be just with God by my Errour to reprove theirs, who being Independent Ministers, could mock and jear at the honest Prebyters?... I did not encourage the People against their Ministers, nor scoff at the Saints indeed. What? Saints who are the Sons of God? Coheirs with Christ's Temples of the Spirit? the High born of Heaven? the most excellent of the Earth? God forbid, that ever I should be so wicked, so base and vile? but are not the Saints Princes in all Land! (p.335)

I WAS FIRST A GENTLEMAN OF WALES

And as for that objected against me, saying, I was first a Gentleman of Wales, then a Master of Arts of both Universities, then Pastor of a Church, a Presbyterian, Independent, Anabaptist, Chaplain to the Earl of Essex, and the Lord Fairfax his Army, Surveyor, and so John of all Trades.

That which I spake, was but a sober Sarcasme to some of the Churches, shewing us the unsetled state of the Saints, who run from Mountain to Hill, from one form to another: so to tell the Ministers what Marchants they are, and what a Trade they drive in the World, as those who have been first pure Prelates, then Presbyters, then Independents, then Anabaptists. And again, first Parson of a Parish, then of the Royal party, then Parliament-Convert, then Preacher in the City, then Pastor of a Church, then Chaplain to a Regiment of Foot, then Captain of a Troop of Horse, then Pastour and Chaplain again? Are there not then some John of all Trades, who turn from one thing to another, meerly for worldly gain. (p.336)

PROPHECIES CONCERNING THE LAST TIMES

The sense of the State, in the Act for Liberty to tender Consciences, makes a clear difference between Preaching, Expounding, and Conference. Mine were but plain Expositions of some Prophecies concerning the last Times. Besides, the aforesaid Order expounds Preaching by officiating: now I did not officiate, as Parson, Vicar, Curate, or any such Creature.

And thus I say, that in my own sense, I did not preach at all, Preaching is for edification; mine was for destruction; I did not preach then, but by a mighty power (I knew not how) was carried up above my natural strength (and first purpose) not to Preach, but to pour out a Vial, full of the wrath of God, even a Plague upon all the Churches, who say, they are in Gospel-order; and are not, but do lye in Babylon. (p.337)

I HAVE BEEN EVER INTIRE TO THE INTEREST OF THIS COMMON-WEALTH

And there not they onely, but all the scattered Saints this day do dwell, and I also with them waiting for deliverance.

To conclude, as I have been ever intire to the Interest of this Commonwealth, to my utmost knowledge, and with my earnest endeavour; so I desire alway to continue in all things that becometh a Christian man. (p.338)

16

Ministers for Tythes 1653

MINISTERS
FOR
TYTHES,
BEING
A manifeſt proof
That theſe Men are
No MINISTERS of the GOSPEL,
Who follow the Magiſtrate for a worldly
maintenance, and Fee the Lawyers
to plead for Tythes.

By WILLAM ERBERY.

But they ſhall proceed no farther, for their folly ſhall be mani-ſeſt unto All men, 2 Tim. 3. 9.

London, Printed by *J. C.* For *Giles Calvet*, at the Signe of the Black ſpread-Eagle, at the Weſt end of *Pauls*, 1653.

MINISTERS FOR TYTHES,
BEING A manifest proof, that these Men are No MINISTERS of the GOSPEL, Who follow the Magistrate for a worldly maintenance, and Fee the Lawyers to plead for Tythes.
By WILLIAM ERBERY.
London, Printed by J.C. For Giles Calvet, at the Signe of the Black spread-Eagle, at the West end of Pauls, 1653.
(Received into the Thomason Collection on October 18th, 1653)

ON MARCH 9TH, 1652/3, Erbery was released from house arrest, found not guilty of the charges of heresy and blasphemy. Free to speak and write, he took advantage of his newly-gained liberty, and during the final year of his life, he produced a large number of tracts, many dealing with specific events in London. He was obviously a well-recognized, if not always a well-respected character. He had friends, like Webster and Calvert, but he had also made many enemies. On September 2nd, 1653 he attended a meeting of the Committee for Tithes. He had previously refused personal payment from tithes in Wales and he adopted the same attitude in London.

Lazarus Seaman[1] and Cornelius Burges[2] appeared before the Committee to ask for payment from the state to support their ministries. Tithing had been the norm during both the pre-Reformation and Reformation Church of England, and was perfectly acceptable to Presbyterians. Erbery rejected tithing for several reasons. The State had no responsibility for maintaining the Church. Payment should be either through the free will offering of the saints, or preachers should live of their own earnings. Tithing was a heavy burden on the poor. In *Ministers for Tythes*, he writes humorously, a humour not appreciated by the victims of his satire.

Erbery's treatise was printed by J.C. for Giles Calvet (should be Calvert) to be sold at his shop at the 'Black-spread Eagle, at the West end of Pauls'. This misprint (was it deliberate?) also occurs in *A Monstrous Dispute* and *The Babe of Glory*.

TO DOCTOR SEAMAN, DOCTOR BURGES, AND THE REST OF THE MINISTERS FOR TYTHES

I HAVE BEEN A MINISTER OF THE CHURCH OF ENGLAND

I have been a Minister of the Church of England, as you are; Master of Arts of both Universities, and might have been Dr. in Divinity as well as you, had I so Much mony, as the Ministers have in their purses. (p.198)

IT MADE MY WELSH BLOOD TO RISE AT YOUR ENGLISH RELIGION

But coming last Wednesday (Sept. 2. 1653) to the Committee for Tythes, I expected there the Ministers for Tyths, to hear what they could say for themselves. A Committee for Tyths is a proper name: Honourable and honest men being on a debate for Tythes on a civil account in point of Law: but Ministers for Tyths is such a thing! and Ministers of the Gospel to demand it as their spiritual due! its such a Monster, that it made my Welsh blood to rise at your English Religion. I heard that Dr. Seaman was that day to prove himself and his fellows, Ministers of the Gospel: but because he is a godly man, and may serve to make a Chaplain for the Navy at Sea, I shall rather deal with Dr. Burges because he is a landed man, and has a great deal of money, being the better Sailer, who can shift his sail and turn with the wind: for as the Ministers are Marchants; so they are those Ship-masters and Seamen, who have all the trade this day… I took him once for a poor Sir John, or Welsh Curate not for a Dr. or rich Divine he was so meanly clad. (p.198f.)

MASTER STRONG

What are you but Parliamentary converts? not like Master Strong,[3] *who was of the Kings Army, a cavalier Chaplain, now an Independent Pastor…* (p.200)

THE FREE-CONTRIBUTION OF THE PEOPLE

As your Mission, so your maintenance is not according to the Gospel, being meerly by custome, compulsion, or compact with the people, contrary to the express command of Christ, and practise of the Apostle who lived (next to God) on the Free-contribution of the people. (p.200)

LIBERTY TO PREACH THE GOSPEL FREELY

Lastly, let it appear to the Parliament and people of the Nation, that you are Ministers of the Gospel, that you have a Mission and Commission from Christ, and the maintenance of Christ also; you may have liberty to preach the Gospel freely and go where you will, which is more than ever your forefathers saw, and a greater favour than any Governors of England gave to the godly Preachers or people of God. (p.201)

PAPISTS, PRELATES AND PRESBYTERS

The man of sin, and Mystery of iniquity must be first manifest in the Saints (that's a Mystery indeed), I mean fully manifest: 'twas revealed in part before, in the Popish and prelatique Clergy. Again, 'twas no dispute, but their own discovery threw them down: That is, by their iniquity, the Mystery of iniquity came forth. 'Twas blood in the Papists, pride in the Prelates, persecution, covetousness, and cunning designs, in the Presbyter and others, makes it appear to All Men, they are no Ministers of the Gospel, but Ministers for Tythes.

I was forced in my spirit to write this to the world, to whom the Lord God will so speak good things, when all the Ministery of Man is silent. (p.201)

17

A Monstrous Dispute 1653

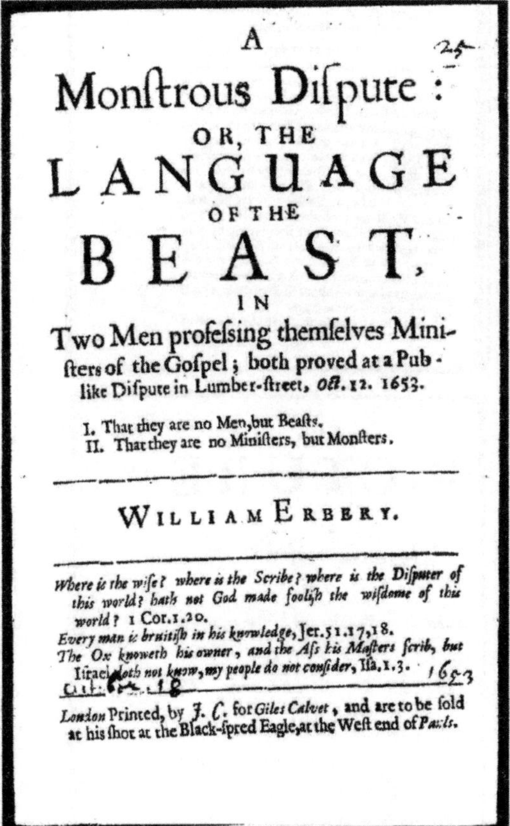

A

Monſtrous Diſpute:

OR, THE

LANGUAGE

OF THE

BEAST,

IN

Two Men profeſsing themſelves Miniſters of the Goſpel; both proved at a Publike Diſpute in Lumber-ſtreet, *Oct.* 12. 1653.

I. That they are no Men, but Beaſts.
II. That they are no Miniſters, but Monſters.

WILLIAM ERBERY.

Where is the wiſe? where is the Scribe? where is the Diſputer of this world? hath not God made fooliſh the wiſdome of this world? 1 Cor.1.20.
Every man is bruitiſh in his knowledge, Jer.51.17,18.
The Ox knoweth his owner, and the Aſs his Maſters ſcrib, but Iſrael *doth not know, my people do not conſider*, Iſa.1.3.

London Printed, by *J. C.* for *Giles Calvet*, and are to be ſold at his ſhop at the Black-ſpred Eagle, at the Weſt end of *Pauls.*

A Monstrous Dispute: OR, THE LANGUAGE OF THE BEAST, IN Two Men professing themselves Ministers of the Gospel; both proved at a Publike Dispute in Lumber-Street, Oct 12. 1653

I. That they are no Men, but Beasts.

II. That they are no Ministers, but Monsters.

London, Printed by J.C. for Giles Calvet, and are to be sold at his shop at the Black-spred Eagle, at the West end of Pauls.

(Received into the Thomason Collection on October 18th, 1653)

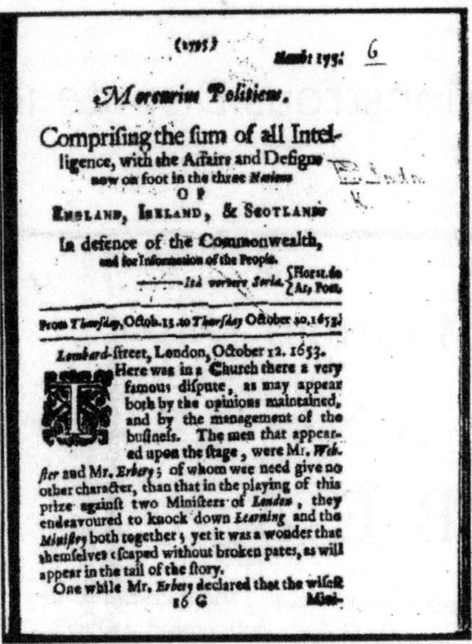

Mercurius Politicus.

Comprising the ſum of all Intelligence, with the Affairs and Deſigns now on foot in the three *Nations* OF ENGLAND, IRELAND, & SCOTLAND.

In defence of the Commonwealth, and for Information of the People.

——*Ità vertere Seria.* {Horat. de Ar. Poet.

From *Thurſday*, Octob. 13. to *Thurſday* October 20. 1653.

Lombard-ſtreet, London, October 12. 1653.

There was in a Church there a very famous diſpute, as may appear both by the opinions maintained, and by the management of the buſineſs. The men that appeared upon the ſtage, were Mr. *Webſter* and Mr. *Erbery*; of whom wee need give no other character, than that in the playing of this prize againſt two Miniſters of *London*, they endeavoured to knock down *Learning* and the *Miniſtry* both together; yet it was a wonder that themſelves eſcaped without broken pates, as will appear in the tail of the ſtory.

One while Mr. *Erbery* declared that the wiſeſt Mini-

16 G

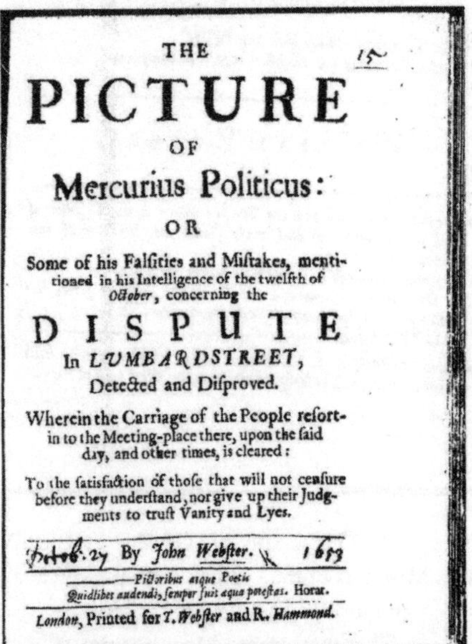

THE PICTURE OF Mercurius Politicus: OR Some of his Falſities and Miſtakes, mentioned in his Intelligence of the twelfth of *October*, concerning the DISPUTE In *LUMBARDSTREET*, Detected and Diſproved.

Wherein the Carriage of the People reſorting to the Meeting-place there, upon the ſaid day, and other times, is cleared:

To the ſatisfaction of thoſe that will not cenſure before they underſtand, nor give up their Judgments to truſt Vanity and Lyes.

Octob. 27 By *John Webſter*. 1653

——*Pictoribus atque Poetis Quidlibet audendi, ſemper fuit æqua poteſtas.* Horat.

London, Printed for *T. Webſter* and R. *Hammond*.

THE PICTURE OF Mercurius Politicus: OR Some of his Falsities and Mistakes, mentioned in his Intelligence of the twelfth of October, concerning the DISPUTE in Lumbard Street, Detected and Disproved.
(Received into the Thomason Collection on October 27th, 1653)

A MONTH AFTER the meeting of the Committee for Tithes, Erbery was again the centre of controversy. He attended the launch of a book by his friend, John Webster[1] at All-Hallows, Lumber Street (Lombard Street) on October 12th, 1653. Webster published Erbery's collected works in 1658.

The meeting at All-Hallows was reported in *Mercurius Politicus*, from Thursday, October 13 to Thursday, October 20, 1653.

> Lombard-street, London, October 12, 1653.
> There was in a Church there a very famous dispute, as may appear both by the opinions maintained, and by the management of the business. The men that appeared upon the stage, were Mr. Webster and Mr. Erbury; of whom wee need give no other character, than that in the playing of this prize against two Ministers of London, they endeavoured to knock down Learning and the Ministry both together; yet it was a wonder that themselves escaped without broken pates, as will appear in the tail of the story… While these things were babled to and fro, the multitude being of various opinions, began to mutter, and many to crie out, but immediately it came to a mutiny or tumult (call it which you please) wherein the women bore away the Bell but lost (some of them) their Kerchiefs, the dispute being hot… And so this worthy Convention ended.

It was inevitable that both Erbery and Webster should respond to the scurrilous report of the popular press. The dispute had taken place in Lumber Street on October 12th, 1653. *Mercurius Politicus* published their article within days. And by the 18th of that month, Thomason had catalogued his copy of Erbery's response. No time was lost.

The tract combined Erbery's description of the events at Lumber Street with his defence of Webster's position on ministry. Their view of ministry was very similar. There was no valid ministry during the Apostasy because there was no manifestation of the Spirit to validate ministry. Three ministers, a Presbyter, Independent and Anabaptist, all spoke against Webster, but Erbery accused them for being 'befooled, confounded, and defiled also with their natural Reason, and humane learning, that such things are as much set up by these Men, in the things of God, as by Papists or Prelats'.

One of the three ministers, a Mr. C. (Cradock, 'my worthy friend'?[2] or Edmund Chillenden, the Baptist?[3]) called for prayer before opening the meeting. Erbery's response was that prayer should not be debased by being offered in public meetings. Erbery writes humorously about how prayer can be invoked on the most trivial occasions.

Within a week (the tract was received by Thomason on October 27th), John Webster had published his own response to the Lombard Street affair. Theological debate was vigorous, no holds were barred and was all part of the mainstream of daily interest. No time was wasted before reports in the press and private responses were published.

Webster accuses *Mercurius Politicus'* reporter for presenting a totally prejudiced report. He assures his readers that:

> So that there was no tumult, nor I, nor Mr Erbery in any danger of broken pates, as the broken-brain'd, and broken-conscienced Politicus hath most falsly divulged to the World... I neither heard nor saw any such thing: and truly if the Women lost their Kerchiefs, they would be most useful to stop the mouths of all such lyars... For Mr Erbery, he is a godly conscientious man, and none but an Ishmael will deride, or hate him. (p.7)

CHRIST BEING THE ONLY ORDINANCE

The Dispute I call Monstrous, because it had neither head nor tail (as they say): the Opponent could not at first find the Question, nor form an Argument to the last; and the Defendant was faine to frame both for him.

Mr. Webster the Respondent had published a Book, and publickly preached for the exalting of God alone, and of Christ in the Spirit: Christ being the only Ordinance, or means to bring men to God; and the Spirit alone the Teacher of his people; Christ the way to the Father, and none knowing the Father but the Son (in us); neither any able to say that Jesus is the Lord, but by the Spirit &c. such spiritual Truths two professed

Ministers came publickly to oppose, though pretending some errours, I shall not name the opposing ministers, because they were sham'd enough at the Dispute, therefore I will not strip them bare before the world; because I honour them both, especially one of them my worthy friend; There was also a third, that is a Presbyter, Independent and Anabaptist, three against one; but one was too many for three. (p.193f.)

PRAYERS BEFORE A PIPE OF TOBACCO?

...why then do they not say grace before eating of Oysters or Apples? And why do they not say their prayers before a pipe of Tobacco? a good creature. The word and prayer is a more spiritual and secret thing in the Spirits of the Saints, then understood by common men or Ministers. (p.195)

SAINTS, WHO CAME TO CATCH, NOT TO FIND THE TRUTH

Truely, there was no fighting, nor blows at the Dispute (as 'twas reported at Westminster) but the Dispute was so confused without any form or order, without method, or matter indeed, that I never saw lesse Reason or Learning in rational men and Schollars, lesse Religion in Saints, who came to catch, not to find the truth, but to seek out errours, and set up snares in which themselves fell at last. (p.195)

RUN FROM ONE FAT PARSONAGE TO ANOTHER

Let their own conscience, and the experience of these times witness, if godly Ministers were ever more greedy of gain; none will preach under one hundred pound per an. who formerly were content with fifty pound for a Lecture, or a little in their own Church, who now must have five hundred pound, or seven hundred pounds per. an. in a Colledge, and run from one fat Parsonage to another in the Countrey, changing their quarters. (p.197)

THE GREAT DESIGN OF GOD THIS DAY

This fire is the Spirit of the Lord in our godly Magistrates, who are the most absolute men, both Civil and Martial, by Land and Sea, joyned together to manage the great design of God this day, in destroying all that is of man (or fleshly Ministery) and setting up God alone in the Land, that at last we may cease from man, and God may be All in All... (p.197f.)

NEW MODEL'D TYTHS IN WALES

Lastly, Let men know, that Independent Ministers were the first who new model'd Tyths in Wales: and are the last who establish Tyths in England; contrary to their old light, love, and spirit of Liberty. (p.198)

18

The Mad Mans Plea 1653

THE

Mad Mans PLEA:

OR, A

SOBER DEFENCE

OF

Captaine CHILLINTONS

CHURCH.

SHEWING

The Destruction and Derision ready to fall on all the Baptized Churches, not Baptized with Fire, whose forms of Religion shall be made ridiculous among men, when the power of righteousness and glorious appearance of God in his people shall come to the Nation.

By W. E.

Thus saith the Lord God, thou shalt drink of thy sisters cup deep and large; thou shalt be laught to scorn, and had in derision, it containeth much, Ezek. 23. 32.

London, Printed 1653.

THE Mad Mans PLEA: OR,
A SOBER DEFENCE OF Captaine CHILLINTONS CHURCH
SHEWING The Destruction and Derision ready to fall on all the Baptized Churches, not Baptized with Fire, whose forms of Religion shall be made ridiculous among men, when the power of righteousness and glorious appearance of God in his people shall come to the Nation.
By W.E. London, Printed 1653.
(Received into the Thomason Collection on October 28th, 1653)

THE AUTUMN OF 1653 was a particularly creative period for Erbery. On September 12th, he had attended the Committee for Tithes and written about the pleas by Seaman and Burgess for assistance. *Ministers for Tythes* was received by Thomason on October 18th. On October 12th he had participated at the debate at All-Hallows, Lombard Street and written *A Monstrous Dispute*, also received by Thomason on the 18th of that month. Four days later, on October the 16th, Erbery found himself at Captaine Chillintons Church. This Baptist congregation met in St Paul's Cathedral.

Chillenden was probably responsible for bringing the charges earlier that year against Erbery before the Committee for Plundered Ministers. After a vigorous defence, Erbery was released in March 1653. By the autumn of 1653, Chillenden was a leader of the Fifth Monarchists, a movement Erbery opposed for its political opposition to the Cromwellian government.

The Mad Mans Plea was received by Thomason on October 28th. For some reason it was neither collected by John Webster in *The Testimony*, nor printed by James Cottrell for the bookseller, Giles Calvert. A further puzzle is that the author is W.E. Were the title and substance of the treatise so controversial?

Chillenden and his colleagues failed in their accusation of blasphemy against Erbery. Did they then seek to undermine his credibility by slandering him as insane? When Anthony à Wood inserted his information about Erbery in *Alumni Oxoniensis*,[1] he stated his uncertainty about the place of Erbery's burial. Was it at Christchurch, Newgate? Or was it in the graveyard attached to the Old Bedlam (the hospital for the mentally ill)? Are these the hints which led the anonymous writer of *A Winding Sheet*[2] to state that Mr Erbery had been taken 'ill of his whimsies'? The repercussions of these hints and guesses affected Erbery's reputation for the next three centuries!

It seems certain that Erbery knew of the aspersions on his character and he met them head-on in this treatise. As is the case in several of his shorter treatises, Erbery used the weapon of humour.

TO THE LORDS FOOLS AND MAD FOLKS THE LORDS FOOLS AND MAD FOLKS

But because I would first comfort the Lords fools and mad folks, let me tell the wise, That fools are the wisest men, and mad men the most sober minded (as babes are the highest men) with God, Mat. 12.25; I Cor. 3.18, 2; Cor. 5.13…

And not onely Paul, but Christ was counted mad, and besides himself, by his own friends, or kinsmen, and by the Church of the Jews, Mark 3.21 the reason is, the wisdome of God is foolishness with men, I Cor. 1.18, Act. 26.25.

How Christ being the wisdom of God and power of God should appear to men as a fool and a madman, is the Mystery of God manifest in flesh, crucified through weakness, yet justified in spirit, I Tim. 3.16; 2 Cor. 13.4. (p.1f.)

I AM NEITHER PROPHET, NOR SPIRITUAL MAN, BUT HAVE THE FOLLY AND MADNESS OF BOTH

Well, the Prophet then is a fool, and the spiritual man is mad. Truely (friends) I am neither prophet, nor spiritual man, but have the folly and madness of both: 'tis God has made me so for the Churches sake. For if God makes natural innocents, why not spiritual fools? and mad men too? And if God had not made me a fool, surely I should never have made the Ministers mad.

That which I spake of Captaine Chillingtons Church or Horse-guard, was my folly and madness: but as the foolishness of God is wiser then man, so I cannot but observe the wisdome of God in bringing forth my words at such a time (a strange providence), when there was such a tumult and confusion in the Captaines Church, which truely I never heard of, till I had ended my publike afternoons discourse, which was far more peacable; as also our dispute with the Ministers the week before, though Politicus be pleased to present it to the world with manifest lies, as of a mutiny, and tearing womens Kerchiefs in the place, which is most false, as hundreds can witness. Therefore if Pragmaticus be turned Politicus, that's in plain English a turn-coat, or a man of the times; let him now as a Christian confess his mistake in the next weekly Mercury, else truly, I'll toss him in a Blanket (with the Ministers) in a sheet of paper; then blow him away as dust into the four windes: for the present powers are resolved, that their Ministers shall tell no more lies to the Nation. Politicus says that the Dispute had like to have thrown down the church with the ministers; that's false again, & not so true as that the Captaines Church might have confounded City and Army; but blessed be God who hath preserved both from fools and flatterers. Indeed folly and madness appeared to men in my proving the Captaines Church not to be of Christ, in these following reasons. (p.3)

I COULD BUT JEST OUT THESE ARGUMENTS

Truely as Elijah jeer'd at Baals priests; so though I am sad and serious at other times, yet now I could but jest out these Arguments, because they would not answer mine in earnest. (p.4)

IS IT NOT RIDICULOUS TO BUILD CHURCHES NOW, WHEN HEAVEN AND EARTH ARE SHAKING

...I scorn to speak of those who from Independants turn to be Anabaptists; there are some more spiritual and sincere Saints in Baptized Churches, who return, but not to the most high, they are content to lye below in the waters, not to ascend to the fire and spirit of burning that was, and must be againe, Isa. 4.4 they return, but not to the most high, to the highest discoveries of God, to the height of Zion Jer. 31.12 but sit down in their formal doctrines and dippings...

Truely, I spake not then, nor now, of the Captaines Church in private revenge, but in that publike spirit of vengeance, that is in ten thousand of Saints (though they speak not) against carnal Churches, and against ungodly ones, who separate themselves, not having the spirit, Jud. 19 for is it not ridiculous to build Churches now, when heaven and earth are shaking... for if the day of the Lord be against every high tower, Isa. 2.25 [should be 2.15] *the Towers fall will be on the Churches, as the Kingly power fell on the Prelats, the Parliamentary Tower fell on the Presbyters, and though the Independant and baptized Churches build a Babel Tower to heaven, 'twill fall on their heads at last.* (p.5f.)

IS IT NOT RIDICULOUS FOR ANABAPTISTS TO BUILD A CHURCH AT PAULS?

2. Is it not ridiculous for Anabaptists to build a Church at Pauls (in the highest place of the City) when Paul never owned a Church of Anabaptists or dippers?

3. Is it not ridiculous that they cannot see old Pauls in a new coat of Free stone, as a visible monument of the folly and madness of Bishops?

4. Is it not ridiculous that the Anabaptist Church should expend so much on sticks and seats in a Horse-guard, when living stones and members of Christ want the money?

5. How far is this Horse-guard from the order of Gospel-Churches, who never made a meeting place for themselves, to preach and pray in, but went forth to the world, to the Temple or Synagogues to preach, and to pray in their own houses.

6. Answer, ye Anabaptists, Was ever water-baptism in a Gospel-way without the baptisme of fire before? Did ever any baptize who was not first baptized with the spirit himself? was not the way of baptisme by washing the feet, or going down to the waters up to the anckles, and not by dipping?

...where could so many modest garments be had in a moment? surely all the Taylors and Semsters in Jerusalem could scarce make so many in a moneth. (p.6f.)

COME, LET'S ALL BE MAD TOGETHER

Therefore though men may say, that my reasons before were but ridiculous, it was because their religion is so, and God will make it a derision to all...

This land (though the house of bondage) shall one day break forth into singing, and smile at those empty forms of Religion, when the power of righteousness appears, and all their oppressors perish, Psal. 72.4, 7, 11 verses...

Neither is it by controversie (as before) nor by disputes (as now) but by derision and scorne, they shall all sink as a stone in the sea, or like a great milstone in mighty waters...

Lastly, If madness be in the heart of every man, Eccles. 9.3 then this is the Island of great Bedlam, and (as a great man of the Sea[3] *said, when he heard of the Parliament dissolved) Come, let's all be mad together.* (p.7f.)

THE CHURCH... WOULD NOT HAVE A GUARD OF HORSE TO DEFEND THEM

But, where's the Sober Defence of Captaine Chillingtons Church?

I answer, first, 'Twas well defended by souldiers. Again, there's now a Sober Defence of Citizens or Holderds...

Lastly, the Church coming out of Babylon, would not have a guard of Horse to defend them, as Captains Church or horse-guard had, Ezra 8.22. (p.9)

19

The Babe of Glory 1653

THE

BABE

OF

GLORY,

Breaking forth in the broken Fleſh

OF THE

SAINTS

Breathing out

The Life of God

(Hid in their Fleſh) now to be revealed and raiſed, *Iſa.* 40.5,6.

By WILLIAM ERBERY.

And ſhe brought forth a Man child who was to rule the Nations with a rod of Iron, and the child was caught up to God and to his throne. Rev. 12.2,5.

London, Printed by *J.C.* For *Giles Calvet*, at the Signe of the Black ſpread-Eagle, at the Weſt end of *Pauls*, 1653.

THE BABE OF GLORY,
Breaking forth in the broken Flesh OF THE SAINTS
Breathing out The Life of God (Hid in their Flesh) now to be revealed and raised, Isa. 40.5,6.
By WILLIAM ERBERY
London, Printed by J.C. For Giles Calvet, at the Signe of the Black spread-Eagle, at the West end of Pauls, 1653.
(Received into the Thomason Collection on November 11th, 1653)

THE BABE OF Glory was printed in November 1653 by J.C. for Giles Calvet (note *Ministers for Tythes*). Prepared with care, it did not report on any specific occasion, as did Erbery's three previous publications. It presents a theological stance very similar to that of *Nor Truth nor Errour* in 1647, revealing how remarkably consistent Erbery was throughout his eight years of prolific creativity.

The Babe of Glory contains a preface and a collection of letters. They are from M.L. of Wales, T.R. in Ireland, A.H. in England and E.W. in Scotland. Unfortunately it is only M.L. of whom we have any knowledge. W.E. responds to M.L. (Morgan Llwyd) in the letter addressed 'To an Afflicted Woman, or Be-wildernessed Saint'. The letters are part of that remarkable correspondence between Erbery and Llwyd.[1] All these saints share Erbery's dual convictions of the sense of the inner presence of Christ, and the imminence of the Third Dispensation.

The Mad Mans Plea, published in October 1653 was soon followed in November by *The Babe of Glory*. Two months later, in January 1653/4, they were attacked in the treatise, *Proh Tempora! Proh Mores!* by J.N. a Mechanick.[2]

A PREFACE TO THE FOLLOWING LETTERS

A TONGUE, INTERPRETATION, AND REVELATION

The Gospel is a mystery, the mystery of the Gospel is Christ in us the hope of glory, Col. 1.27. The manifestation of the Spirit in manifold gifts, was most necessary for those who should manifest the Mystery of God to men; three gifts especially, of a Tongue, Interpretation, and Revelation; a Tongue, to open the Original, as to utter it to all Nations. The gift of Interpretation, to interpret Scripture infallibly translated, and to transcribe the thoughts and writings even of heathen Poets to a holy sense of the Mystery of God. The Spirit of Revelation was not only that which was common to Saints, Eph. 1.17, but a special gift of the Spirit, to reveal both the Mystery of Christ, Eph. 3.3 and by that mighty power working in them, to present every man in Christ, Col. 1.27, 28, 29. (p.93)

THE MYSTERY OF GOD IN US

For as Christ was the brightness of his Father's glory, and this glory vailed in flesh while he lived in it: so in death his flesh being crucified and slain to God, God raised it up to glory the third day, and so the glory was revealed: This was to manifest the Mystery of God in us; The same God and Father being in our flesh as in his, will raise us up to the same glory of Christ risen... when Jesus shall descend from Heaven, from his hidden Di[e]*ity or Godhead, and come down in the Spirit, fully manifest in our flesh, we shall be changed and raised up to the same glory, even to the life of God himself; for as our life is now hid with Christ in God: so when Christ who is our life shall appear (fully in us) we shall appear with him in glory; but we must suffer first, and dye to flesh as he did, before we live and reign with him.* (p.94)

THE THIRD DISPENSATION

This Resurrection and reign of the Saints, I call often a third dispensation: for as Christ and the glory was revealed but in part, even in the Apostles themselves, who knew but in part and prophesied but in part, so all of that second dispensation went no further then death, they were baptized into Christs death, by breaking of bread shewed forth his death in them, they being in a dying and suffering condition; but in the third dispensation, typified by the third dayes resurrection, the Body of Christ the Saints shall so rise in the Spirit, and their life hid before shall be so fully manifest in their flesh, that nothing but God, nothing but glory shall appear in them: yea, they shall so rise and shine, that the glory shall rise upon them, and the glory shall be not only in them, but so on them, that both themselves and all those that see them shall acknowledge that they are the seed whom the Lord hath blessed. (p.94f.)

SAINTS IN PURE APPREHENSION

These are the Saints of the most high this day, who are above all forms, and flesh; not in attainment or present enjoyment, but in pure apprehension, perfect conviction, and patient waiting for it. (p.95)

TO AN AFFLICTED WOMAN, OR BE-WILDERNESSED SAINT

GOD LEADING US IN A WAY WE KNOW NOT OF

Christian Friend,

My best love salutes you in the Lord, with thanks for your loving lines. I understand by your Letter that you walk alone in the dark, which is indeed a solitary and sad condition... Communion of Saints and the company of men is sweet to flesh, sweet to man to walk with men, but that's no wilderness where company or path is before us; but when we can see none with us but God, and God leading us in a way we know not of, this is sweet to a Saint in Spirit... For truly in that Apostacy we now are, we cannot company with men, no, not with Saints in spiritual worships, but we shall commit spiritual whoredom with them... when we are be-wildernessed, and at a losse in all things, that we cannot look on any man, nor find God in any means, then we will seek the Lord our God, God dwelling in us, that's David our King, God in our flesh. (p.100f.)

GOD DWELLS AS GLORIOUS IN A SAINT WHEN HE IS IN THE DARK, AS WHEN HE IS IN LIGHT

God dwells in the dark as well as in the light, light and darknesse is all one with him, yea, Heaven and Hell also with God and with men also who live in God alone, 'tis all one with them however they be, or where they are, they are still in God, sit down in his will, his will is theirs, for they dwell in God, and God in them, even in their darkest condition. If I go up to Heaven thou art there; and if I go down to Hell also, thou art there, Lord. Heaven and Hell are things men much mistake in; for David was sometimes in Heaven, and in Hell also when he was in weaknesse; but then when he was in spirit and strength, and spiritual joy, he was in Heaven; he could go up and down, to Heaven or Hell and wherever he was, he was still in God, and God dwelt in him when he was in the darkest state, Psal. 139. This is a word full of comfort (if God speaks it in you), that God dwells as glorious in a Saint when he is in the dark, as when he is in light (yea, in darkness the Lord shall be my light, Mich.

7.8)… God retires to his secret chamber of presence when he brings a poor soul to the dark, there God dwells most gloriously, as you may read Isa. 57.15. the high and holy place there, is that heart which has the glorious injoyment of God, with exceeding joy and constant peace, the contrite and humble spirit, is that which is shaken and shivered to pieces, ground to powder, that's contrite; yet there God inhabits, even in the humble, in the lowest heart, as the words signifie, for the humble heart is not an excellency (as men interpret it to be humble) but a low poor dark spirit, that is even stark dead, that's the humble; therefore God is said there to revive it, and how is that? but by revealing himself to dwell there in glory. (p.101f.)

IN THE DARKEST NIGHT WE SHALL MERRILY FEAST ON GOD

…there's a night in man as well as a day, darkness as well as light: now in the night season, in the darkest state, God teacheth men most, that's my reins instruct me, not the reins of my back, but God dwelling in me, and revealing himself in me instructs me more than all the teachings of men, these cannot come to me nor counsel me in the dark, but God can do it, and doth: I will blesse the Lord who giveth me counsel. That's the meaning of Psal. 19.2. Day to day uttereth speech, and night unto night teacheth knowledge, that is, the glory of God revealed to us in the dark, in the night, gives more knowledge unto us, then men who speak with most light, and language.

The last thing that I would speak (but I must be silent) is this, that God will yet give you to see, not only the glory, and knowledge of God, but comfort also in the dark; ye shall have a song, as in the night, when a holy solemnity is kept, and gladness of heart, &c. Isa. 30.29. When's this joy, that song? in the Night; not only in the night of the Nation, as 'tis now, vers 27, 28. but in your darkest condition you shall have joy in God. Therefore 'tis said, ye shall have a song in the night, when the holy solemnity is kept: the solemn feasts of the Heathens, and holy feasts of Saints also under the Law were in the night, not only of Passeover, but the Lords Supper; 'tis a mystery, that in the darkest night we shall merrily Feast on God, and so farewell. (p.102)

20

The North Star 1653

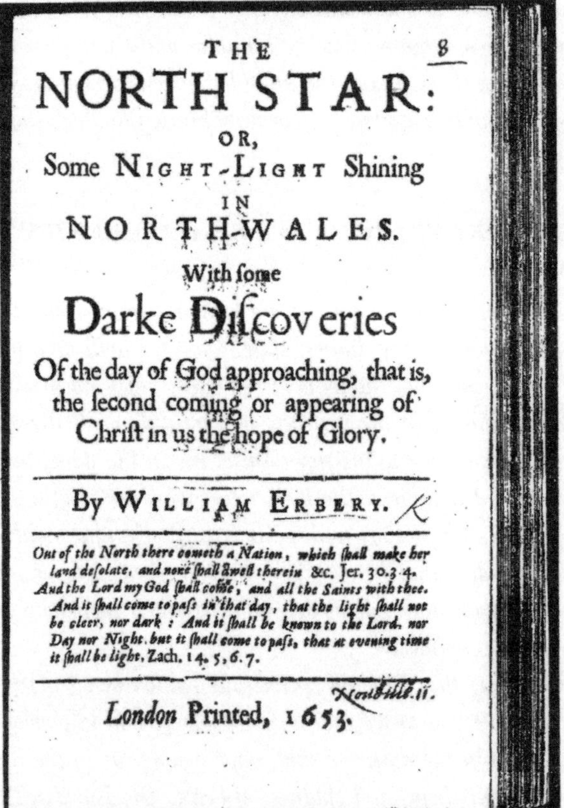

THE

NORTH STAR:

OR,

Some NIGHT-LIGHT Shining

IN

NORTH-WALES.

With ſome

Darke Diſcoveries

Of the day of God approaching, that is, the ſecond coming or appearing of Chriſt in us the hope of Glory.

By WILLIAM ERBERY.

Out of the North there cometh a Nation, which ſhall make her land deſolate, and none ſhall dwell therein &c. Jer. 30.3.4.
And the Lord my God ſhall come, and all the Saints with thee. And it ſhall come to paſs in that day, that the light ſhall not be cleer, nor dark: And it ſhall be known to the Lord, nor Day nor Night, but it ſhall come to paſs, that at evening time it ſhall be light, Zach. 14. 5, 6. 7.

London Printed, 1653.

The NORTH STAR: OR,
Some NIGHT-LIGHT Shining IN NORTH-WALES.
With some Darke Discoveries Of the day of God approaching, that is,
the second coming or appearing of Christ in us the hope of Glory.
By William Erbery.
London Printed, 1653.
(Received into the Thomason Collection on November 11th, 1653)

ON NOVEMBER 11TH, 1653, Thomason added two new Erbery publications to his collection: *The Babe of Glory,* and *The North Star.* The latter is the overarching title for seven pamphlets. Four have titles which include compass-points: *The North Star, A Whirlewind from the South, The Children of the West,* and *A Flash of Lightning from the East.* They are followed by *The Woman Preacher, The Idol Pastor* and *The Wretched People.* Unusually for Erbery's work, *The North Star* contains no information about printer or bookseller. Some of this material was prepared when Erbery was under house-arrest, which may explain why so many were published at one time, and possibly why there is no reference to a printer or bookseller. There are some slight typographical differences between the frontispiece of the original publication and as it appears in *The Testimony.* I have used the original publication.

The North Star contains five letters. The first is from Erbery 'To the gathered Church at Wrexham' where Morgan Llwyd served as minister. It is followed by an undated letter from Llwyd to Erbery, to which he responds, probably while under house arrest. His release came soon after March 9th, 1653. Llwyd writes again from 'Wrexham 3.m.52'. Probably this can be dated the 3rd March 1652/3. The final letter was Erbery's reply written from London in May 1653. This was their third exchange of letters, the earlier ones having been collected in *A Call to the Churches* (February 1652/3) and *The Babe of Glory* (November 1653). The letter of May 1653 was the last in this invaluable series between two radical Welsh Puritans. Llwyd, writing in Welsh, became posthumously a national hero. Erbery, his mentor, was to be neglected and castigated. History can be most unjust.[1]

The letters follow a pattern. Llwyd asks the questions and Erbery responds. Llwyd was eager to explore theological questions, particularly in light of the imminence of the End. He was exploring his Christian experience, and wanted help to put this experience into words. Both shared an experience of the indwelling Christ, and both were convinced that God's action in contemporary history was a foretaste of the coming of the Kingdom. God was internally motivating the saints, and externally shaping the destiny of humankind through his work of liberty and righteousness. Erbery believed that the divine essence was shared in Father, Son and saints. In the Second Dispensation, the Father revealed himself to be in the Son; in the Third Dispensation, the Father will reveal himself in the saints. Erbery's attempt to express his Trinitarian faith is a consequence of his experience of God in Christ in the saints.

TO THE GATHERED CHURCH AT WREXHAM

WE ARE IN THE DAY OF GOD ALREADY, THOUGH WE KNOW IT NOT

Beloved brethren.

The following Letters I call Night-light, for nothing else has shined forth to the world, or to Saints, since the Apostacie… more of the mystery of Babylon appears this day within us, which makes me believe, we are in the day of God already, though we know it not; for 'tis known to the Lord alone, whose day has not a certain constant shine, but is neither light nor darkness, 'tis neither Day nor Night, but in the evening… there shall be light, or God appears to all… (p.103f.)

FOR MR. WILLIAM ERBERY

I LONG TO KNOW THE TEACHINGS OF GOD WITHIN… WHAT MANNER OF PEOPLE WHOULD WE BE IN THIS AGE

SIR,

The sweetness of the Fathers love (for so I take it) in you is very pleasant to my taste. And though you have not particularly and clearly written to me, as I perceive you still do, concerning the things I desired to know of you in what I sent: yet your promise of more makes me now only mind you again… I dare not believe what I hear of you (and it's no matter what flesh without truth speaketh) yet love would be satisfied; I long to know the teachings of God within, more effectually, concerning the hypostasis of the Lord Jesus, and in what spirit you leave off publick teaching, and what the witnesses are, and the Olive-trees. If men and books, and letters were my teachers, I should little know my self in him who fashioned me; but the more spiritual any is, the more communicative, as the Angels of the Father; therefore I enquire what that morning-star is that is risen, what vial, or seal, or trumpet are we under, and what manner of people should we be in this age… My true love with my wives to your self and to Mistris Erbery, I add this truth, that I am

Yours in the love, light, and peace of the Comforter, though as nothing,

Mor. Lloyd. (p.104f.)

FOR MR. MORGAN LLOYD

ALL THAT HE KNOWS OF GOD AT PRESENT, IS THAT HE IS KNOWN OF GOD

SIR,

Your second Letter is exceeding welcome to a friend of yours, who is now the Lord's prisoner, and has been so indeed, these many daies, and years also, in the Spirit.

Truly, he would not know anything of man any more, and all that he knows of God at present, is that he is known of God, or God become his knowledge; this also, but in much confusion: therefore (Dear Sir) expect not clearness from a man that dwells in Babylon.

All my life at present, and liberty also, is, to serve the King of Babylon, and to be quietly subject to God in this captive state, wherein himself hath brought me, who is my life and glorious liberty. (p.105)

KNOWLEDGE OF GOD AND OF CHRIST COMES… BY THE SPIRIT OF REVELATION, THOUGH THE SCRIPTURE SPEAKS THE SAME

But the Son of God is he you enquire after, the hypostasis of the Lord Jesus, &c. I see by this, you are with me in Babylon; for who knows the Son but the Father? the Father in you may shew you the Son, and the Son revealed in you will shew you the Father. This knowledge of God and of Christ comes not by reading, nor yet by Scripture, but by the Spirit of Revelation, though the Scripture also speaks the same. (p.106)

NO PLAIN DISCOVERY… OF THE MYSTERY OF CHRIST CAN BE HAD FROM THE EPISTLES OR GOSPELS

And yet what the Apostle writes of himself in his highest knowledge of the Mystery of Christ, was but in part; (Eph. 3.4; I Cor. 13.9) what he knew, or what he prophesied (that is, preached or writ of Christ) was but in part, therefore his Epistles to us will give out but a partial discovery of God and of Christ; yea, all that Christ spake of himself in the Evangelists was but in parables : therefore no plain discovery or manifestation of the Mystery of Christ can be had from the Epistles or Gospels: Hitherto, saith he, I have spoken to you in parables, or proverbs, but I will shew you plainly of the Father, that is, when he should depart or disappear in flesh, then they should know him in the Father. And the promise of the Father or power from on high, even the power of the Godhead that was in his flesh, should appear in theirs, that's he in them, and they in him… (p.106f.)

THE SON… WAS NONE ELSE BUT THE MIGHTY GOD, THE EVERLASTING FATHER MANIFEST IN FLESH

To know then the hypostasis or substance of the Son, is to know the Son in your self, that is, God even the Father, in our flesh as in his, as you may see in my little Book, Neither Truth nor Error, nor light nor darkness, but in the evening there shall be light…

The hypostatical union of the Son then is this, that the Father is one and all with the man, the man Christ Jesus is one with the Father; for the Father in him was all in all, and he nothing, or could do nothing, but as he was in the Father, and the Father in him, doing all his works, and words. (Joh. 8.30, 33; Joh 14.9, 10)

And because God even the Father cannot be known in his own naked Being and Godhead, but as cloathed with flesh, therefore the Son that was born, and the child given to men, was none else but the mighty God, the everlasting Father manifest in flesh. (Joh. 5.37; Joh. 9.6 compared)

For no man hath seen God at any time, but the only begotten Son, who is in the bosome of the Father, he hath declared him, not in word only, but in works which the Father did in him, and by him; for the Son could do nothing of himself, &c. And because the Father spake all in the Son, God in the Man, therefore the Man Christ Jesus is called the Word of God (for God was that Word, as the Greek there reads, Joh. 1.1) that is, God even the Father, being manifest in wisdom and power in the Man, the Man Christ Jesus is called the Wisdom of God, and the Power of God. (p.107f.)

FOR AS ALL THINGS WERE OF THE FATHER, SO BY CHRIST ARE ALL THINGS MANIFEST

And as Christ the Divine wisdom and power was set up from everlasting, Prov. 8.21, that is, from the beginning, ver. 22. So Christ is called he that was from the beginning, Joh. 1.1; I Joh. 1.1; I Joh. 2.13 not begotten from eternity (as men say); but because the eternal God even the Father brought forth himself, with wisdom and power in the beginning, wisdom was said to be in the beginning brought forth, Prov. 8.24 or begotten, as the Geneva Translation hath it, or born, as another translation reads. And thus Christ is called the heir of all things, by whom all things were made, or made forth, that is, all things manifested from the beginning, were in that wisdom and power that was in Christ, called therefore the beginning of the Creation of God: For as all things were of the Father, so by Christ are all things manifest, and made forth in the Creation, and in man, I Cor. 8.6. (p.108)

OUT OF HIS FULNESS WE MIGHT RECEIVE GRACE FOR GRACE, SO GLORY FOR GLORY

...the fulness of the Godhead in Christ, that wisdom and power in him, was by the Father's pleasure and appointment; not natural to the Son (as Schollars speak without Book, for no Scripture says it) nor yet was it proper and peculiar to him only, but for us also, he being set up for this very purpose with all fulness of glory, that out of his fulness we might receive grace for grace, and to be filled with all the fulness of God: yea, as we receive grace for grace, so glory for glory; that glory or grace of union which the Son had with the Father, that have we perfect in one with the Son, Gods love to us being as to his beloved, and our life with Christ in God, Joh. 7.22, 23. (p.108)

A THREEFOLD DISCOVERY, OR MAKING FORTH OF THAT ONE GOD TO MAN

But if we knew the Mystery of God even the Father, and of Christ in the Spirit, it would shew Christ in us, that's God in our flesh as in his, Christ as God being onė with the Father, and Christ as man being one with his brethren, who are not only one flesh with him, but of his bone and of his flesh; though he be the elder brother, and above his fellows. (Eph. 5.30; Heb. 2.11)

Thus the Scripture (speaking of God, and Christ, and the Spirit) must be spiritually understood; not in a carnal sense, as three distinct persons, but as a threefold discovery, or making forth of that one God to Man. God in himself, of whom are all things, is the Father: the same God and Father manifest in flesh, is the Son; that mighty God powerfully acting and exerting himself in flesh, is the Spirit. Thus the Word being said to be God, and God sending his Son, and the Son sending forth the Spirit, are spiritually to be understood, Again, the Son giving himself, sending the Comforter from the Father, &c. all this (as Christ said before) is parabolically spoken, or in a figure: the Word was not with God, as one person with another, for God is the Divine Nature, and God sent not his Son, as a man sends his servant, a distinct person from himself, and from a distinct place, as men imagine: but as the glory of God is that which appears in all things; so God even the Father coming forth with glory in the Man Christ Jesus, is God giving or sending his Son, called also his servant. (p.109)

THE GLORY OF GOD THAT WAS IN CHRIST IS REVEALED IN US BY THE SPIRIT

Again, saith Christ, the glory which thou hast given me, I have given them: Observe first, The glory was given him, and he giving that glory to us, is nothing else, but as God is pleased to reveal his Son in us; then the glory of God that was in Christ is revealed in us by the Spirit; and by the Spirit, to the world. The Spirit (as I said) being called the power of God, or God powerfully exerting himself not only in the Creation (for so 'tis the Spirit simply) but this Spirit or power appearing in us also (even in the Saints) as in Christ, in our flesh, as in his, is called the holy Spirit. (p.109)

THE HYPOSTATICAL UNION

By all this it appears to me, that what you ask concerning the hypostasis of Christ, must be only answered by the Spirit, which will speak the Father in you to be the hypostasis of the Son. The Letter of Scripture shews this abundantly, but I must be brief.

1. The hypostatical union is this, viz, the man Christ Jesus one with the Father, that's the Son: for the Son the second person, is not said to be one with the man, (as men do say) but the man one with God even the Father is the Son.

2. The Spirit is given to the Son, and the Son is said to receive it from the Father, therefore called the promise of the Father.

3. The Son is said to send the Spirit from the Father.

4. The Spirit proceeds from the Father, not from the Son, though sent by him, Joh. 15.26. (p.110)

SEEK HIM AND ALL IN YOUR SELF; WHERE YOU MAY FIND HIM AND ALL

My dear friend, ask no more of man the things of God, but seek him and all in your self; where you may find him and all. There wait to see the morning Star, The sons of oyl, or two witnesses, with the seals opened, the Trumpets sounding, and the Vials full of wrath poured forth on all that is flesh within you, that nothing but pure spirit may appear, nothing of man, but God may be All in All. (p.110)

WHAT MANNER OF PERSONS OUGHT WE TO BE IN THIS AGE?

Your last question is, what manner of persons ought we to be in this age? Your own retired spirit will tell you, and the eternal spirit taking you up, first to the mount, to see Christ transfigured in glory, then into the Garden, to be not only an eye-witness, but a companion of his sufferings in you, will shew you. Those three Apostles who were witnesses of both, even Peter, James, and John call upon you, First, To be pure in heart. Secondly, Holy in conversation. Thirdly, To be patient, or (as the margin reads) long-patient, or suffering with long patience)[2] *to the coming of the Lord, Jam. 5.7. Farwel.* (p.110)

FOR MR WILLIAM ERBERY

HOW FEW SEE THAT THE VERY SAME SON… IS IN SAINTS

But, Oh! how few see that the very same Son, in whom the three is in one, is in Saints, though the Scripture be not afraid to say, that the Trinity is in all Saints… yet the eternal pleasure must be as infinite as the eternal father-like will, who moved all. How this is, if you can tell, send. (p.112)

FOR MR MOR. LLOYD

NONE BUT THE WOMEN, THE WEAKEST SAINTS, SEE THE RESURRECTION AT HAND

'Tis your love, and the Lord in you that gives you that liberty to write so oft to an abhorred man and in bondage, every way unworthy of this favour… the time is come, that he will have mercy on her, and raise her sons to wait for that glory to be revealed in them, Christ in us the hope of glory, God being in our flesh as in his: though our flesh as yet be the grave wherein the Lord is laid, and our life is also hid with him in God; yet God in us will rise, and his glory so be revealed on us, that we shall rise, and shine as surely, as the Son was raised to glory; the glory being the same, though not now manifest in us, as 'twas in him when risen. None but the Women, the weakest Saints, see the resurrection at hand, which the present Apostles and Ministers of the Gospel laugh at, and look upon as idle tales, Luke 24.11. (p.113)

I COUNT YOU AS ONE OF THE ANGELS OF GOD

Your Letter I printed for publick use, because I count you as one of the Angels of God, who are (as you said once) to millions every day, so is not that which we speak to a particular Congregation or company.

Again, I would not be a Hermite cloystered in a Church, but fly through the world that's more then publick preaching; though this I do also… The last part of the Letter I understand not, onely the last line, wherein I am learning to rest with you, and to remain yours in love. (p.114f.)

21

A Whirlewind from the South 1653

A

WHIRLEWIND

FROM THE

SOUTH;

OR,

An Anſwer to a Letter ſent from a Friend in Plymouth.

Wherein

Something of God and of Chriſt, and of Mans ſalvation in God is hinted.

By *Will. E.*

And the Lord God ſhall blow the Trumpet, and ſhall go with whirlewinds of the South, Zach. 9. 14.
Awake O thou North wind, come thou South blow upon my Garden, that the ſpices thereof may flow out. &c. Cant. 4. 16.

To the ſcattered Saints in *Plymouth.*

Chriſtian friends,

THough unknown to you by face or fleſh, yet in ſpirit I ſalute you in the Lord, who is raiſing up the ſons of *Sion* againſt

A WHIRLEWIND FROM THE SOUTH; OR,
An Answer to a Letter sent from a Friend in Plymouth. Wherein Something of God and of Christ, and of Mans salvation in God, is hinted.
By WILL. E.
To the scattered Saints in Plymouth

THE LETTERS PUBLISHED in *The North Star* were personal, reflecting the close relationship between Erbery and Morgan Llwyd. The second tract, *A Whirlewind from the South* contains Erbery's response to a letter sent from a friend in Plymouth, and is addressed to the scattered saints in Plymouth. Like Erbery, the saints in Plymouth no longer belong to gathered churches, and were waiting for the arrival of the Third Dispensation. Although Erbery had not met his correspondents, 'though unknown to you by face or flesh, yet in spirit I salute you in the Lord', there were obviously links between these like-minded saints. *The Babe of Glory* had given further evidence of a continuing contact with saints from all the British nations. Now, in *A Whirlewind*, Erbery specifically replies to a letter from Mr. N.C. of Plymouth.

N.C., like Llwyd, was seeking guidance. His questions related to the nature of God and the nature of being human. Erbery's response explores the mystery of God as Trinity, and humankind's relationship with God. Erbery rejects the orthodox division of humankind into saints and sinners, predestined by an almighty and inscrutable divinity.

Erbery's writings reveal a consistent theological approach. He struggles with the most challenging issues. At the heart of Erbery's experience is his conviction that God shares in, and empowers the life of all that exists. Nothing is outside God's grace and glory. The fulfilment of God's purposes will soon become manifest in the Third Dispensation. The days of the Apostasy are numbered! The Age of Spirit is dawning and the nations of Britain are the precursors of a world of righteousness.

TO THE SCATTERED SAINTS, IN PLYMOUTH.

'TWAS NOT IN WORSHIP, BUT IN DOCTRINE, THE APOSTASIE... FIRST APPEARED

Christian Friends...

'Twas not in worship, but in doctrine, the Apostasie and spirit of Antichrist first appeared, the doctrines of men or doctrines of devils (that's

of wise and knowing Christians)... nothing but carnal apprehensions of the mystery of Heaven are received by men in common this day; yea, those Philosophical notions, and Metaphysical speculations of the Deity with their Sophistical ratiocinations... are come to pass, and mightily prevail with the present Churches... (p.117)

FOR MR. N.C. OF PLYMOUTH

I RECEIVED YOUR LETTER IN THE MIDST OF MY TROUBLES

Sir,

I Received your Letter in the midst of my troubles, or rather in the end of my sufferings, when I was finishing my answer in writing to the Committee for plundred Ministers; who having done all they could against me, saw at last they could do nothing... One thing you queried, was, concerning Father, Son, and Spirit; which you understood not according to the Tradition and Doctrine of men, as three persons in God, but as God manifesting himself in a threefold discovery of himself, who yet would appear as one at last, and his name One: When one King and one Lord should reign over all the earth, then these words of Father, Son, and Spirit, should cease, as you think, from Zach. 14.9. (p.117f.)

BY THIS THEY MAKE A QUATERNITY

Truly, I am not superstitious, nor scrupulous about names; so the things of God be delivered in truth by men or Ministers, who as I conceive, are this day very carnal in comprehending and acknowledging the Mystery of God, and the Father, and of Christ, so they read, as if there was, First, God the Divine essence, then the Father; the Father the first person then Christ the second person in the Trinity; which by this they make a Quaternity, when the Spirit or third person comes in; for the Divine Essence (as I said) they set in a distinct notion, which is the fourth; for so common Christians cannot chuse but understand it, as delivered by their Divines. (p.118)

THE FATHER, THE DIVINE NATURE... THE SON, THE DIVINE PERSON... THE SPIRIT, THE DIVINE POWER

Whereas to me the Mystery is plain in the Letter of Scripture... As that one only true God is the Father of all, and of Christ also: so the man Christ Jesus is none else, but God manifest in flesh; the Spirit being that mighty Power of God, or the same God and Father powerfully acting and exerting himself in the flesh of Christ, and in the flesh of the Saints, called the holy Spirit, though the Spirit indeed being as 'twere the soul of the world, filling all things, is called the Spirit simply in man. So that me-thinks 'tis liker the language of Scripture or holy dialect, to call the Father the Divine Nature, the Essence, or Godhead itself. The Son, the Divine person, being God manifest in flesh or the man one with the Father. The Spirit, the Divine power, or promise of the Father; called so, because God even the Father powerfully appearing in the flesh of the Son, promised so to appear and act with power in the flesh of the Saints, which was performed in the Primitive Churches: but these this day being faln from that, the Apostacy or falling away is come almost to perfection: For more flesh than spirit appears not only in the gathered Churches, but generally in scattered Saints, whose walkings are as carnal & earthly as their Worship and Doctrine. John saith (I Joh. 5.7) There are three that bear record in Heaven, the Father, the Word, and Spirit; and these three are one. And there are three that bear record in earth, the Spirit, Water, and Blood, and the three agree in one.

I will not question this Scripture, as not canonical, though some do scruple at it, seeing many of the ancient Fathers both Greek and Latine, read not this verse in their Bibles, as Beza notes; yea, a Father who wrote many books for the Trinity, in all his Arguments against the Arians never quoted this of I John 5.7 which is the clearest Scripture for proof of this point.[1]

Again, the Syriack Translation, which is very ancient, and even parallel to the Apostolick times, reads not that verse at all. (p.118f.)

MEN LIVING IN LOW DISCOVERIES OF GOD

...so men living in low discoveries of God, as 'twere on earth, or (as the Apostle phraseth) living in the world, subject to Ordinances, duties, and

holy qualifications, and performances... their spiritual life was altogether in the death of Christ: from whose side as water and blood came forth; so the water-Baptism of Christ (with their breaking of bread, where was the communion of blood) also their justification and sanctification (that's water and blood too) this (as I said) was the life of Saints, who lived on earth, and taught by men...

And yet our sottish Doctors and silly Divines, would bring down this high Mystery of God, not only to their own carnal understandings, and to men in common; but think to manifest that by their childish Catechisms, and Systems of Divinity, which must be by revelation only. (p.119f.)

THOSE WHO LIVED IN THE INNER WORLD IN GOD HIMSELF

But those who lived in the inner world in God himself, who had the anointing in them, whereby they knew all things, and needed not that any man teach them, these knew the Mystery of God, even the Father, and of Christ, yea, had all the riches of the full assurance of understanding to the acknowledgment of it, leaving this record in themselves, of Father, Word, and Spirit... so these Babes are not children in understanding, but men who are become little children to God, not acquainted with the traditions and teachings of men, but are taught of God, and learn the truth as it is in Jesus: and know Christ Jesus only as revealed in them by the Spirit. (p.120)

BY THE REVELATION OF JESUS CHRIST, HIS DEITY, DEATH, AND RESURRECTION COMES TO BE KNOWN

So then, 'tis not by any humane learning, nor yet by divine labours, nor by study, nor by striving, nor yet by reading Scripture, or receiving any thing from man, but meerly by the Revelation of Jesus Christ; his Deity, Death, and Resurrection comes to be known: for no man can say, that Jesus is the Lord, but by the Spirit; that is, though he was the Son of God from his first conception in the Womb, yet he was not declared to be the Son of God with power, but by the resurrection from the dead, wch [which] *was the day he was begotten by the Spirit of holiness. So no man can say (confess) that Jesus is the Lord, but by the holy Spirit; that spirit of life or power of God that was in Jesus, raising up his flesh from death, must be manifest in our flesh before we can come to the knowledg of the Son of God, or the Godhead of Christ; then we shall see the three bearing record in heaven, the Father, the Word & Spirit, & these three one in us.* (p.121)

ALL MEN LIVE TO GOD, AND ALL LIVE IN HIM

Your second Query was, as I remember, Whether there should be ever to the end, that which was from the beginning, viz. a differing state of men with God, clean and unclean; some without God, and God in others.

I can answer you nothing in this, but according to letter of Scripture, and my own spirit telling me, that All men live to God, and all live in him, not as other Creatures, but as his Image and Off-spring live, move, and have their being in him: and though men are said to be without God in this world, because men mind not God, God being not in all their thoughts and far from their reins, yet God is not far from them, nor God without men in the world; only God doth manifest himself to some, and not to others, not to the world; there's the difference, Joh. 14.22. (p.122)

THE SEVENTH TRUMPET, OR LAST DISPENSATION, WHICH I CALL THE THIRD

...when the Mystery of God shall be finished at the sounding of the seventh Trumpet, or last dispensation, which I call the third, in respect of Law and Gospel-order... the glorious appearing of the great God and Saviour, the new Heaven and new Earth, the new Jerusalem where God shall dwell with men, even God himself: not God in Covenant only, as under the Law, nor God in Christ only, as under the Gospel-dispensation, but God in us, this Paul calls the Glory to be revealed in us, the manifestation of the Sons of God... not one Nation, as the Church of the Jews, nor believers of all Nations, as the Church of Christ, but many whole Nations shall joyn, not to the Church as at first; but to the Lord himself the Nations shall joyn at last... And because no Saint shall fully rise till all the Saints, the whole body, be redeemed; therefore the Apostle was waiting for the Adoption, the Redemption of the body,

not of his body, or theirs only then living with him; but the Redemption of the body, that is, of the whole church of all the people of God... (p.123f.)

GOD BEGINS TO APPEAR, AS ALL IN ALL IN SOME, THAT THEY CAN SEE NOTHING IN MEN BUT GOD

I will not enlarge unto you at present the grounds of this, and the goings forth of God this day, how he is staining the pride of all glory; we begin to see it already with our eyes, men who were most excellent in knowledge (I say not Ranters, but) even Religious men, and living in highest forms of godliness, as unrighteous in their government of the world; unrighteous in their judging of Saints above them; yea, as unrighteous in their words and walkings with men.

I will not speak now of their oppression, pride, cruelty, covetousness, their cunning designs, and covered desires of preferment, profit, pleasure, their earthly-mindedness all the day long, unless when they be at their prayers, and then (saith God) their heart goeth after their covetousness.

Those poor Saints whom God is pleased by his mighty power and mercy to preserve to himself pure and blameless without and within, are so crucified and slain by the Lord, not only in outward sufferings, but in their inmost pure flesh, their knowledge so confounded, their comforts so clouded, their strength so weakened, and all their spiritual glory so wasted, that nothing but the Lord alone appears to dwell there, and to live in them; and their life in him only, for they are dead to all besides.

To sum up all, these men can see no good in themselves, nor the evil in others, but God in all; not but that evils are to men, and the men godly who see not the good, but God begins so to appear, as All in all in some, that they can see nothing in men but God... (p.124f.)

EVERY MAN BEING MY BROTHER... EVERY MAN IS MY FLESH

Truly I have forgotten your other Queries, only the Talents you ask, what it is? I conceive it to be both our outward abilities or fulness, as well as our inward and spiritual sufficiency; both are to be improved for the glory of God, and the good of mankind, not only for our Christian brethren, but for the whole Creation our fellow-creatures, every man being my brother, as the Sodomites were to Lot. My neighbour is not only one of the next house, or of my own family, my friend; but every man is my flesh; if then I shut up my bowels from the needy, and draw not forth my soul to the hungry; if I hid my self from my own flesh my talent is then hid in the earth. Wo is me, if the Lord when he comes, find me so doing, though I speak like an angel. (p.125)

POST-SCRIPT

JOHN'S SPIRIT IN THE NORTH OF ENGLAND, AND THE SPIRIT OF JESUS RISING IN NORTH-WALES

If I may speak my experience, 'tis this, Babylons fall is from the North, Jer. 50.3. and the Northern Nations have been for the fall of spiritual Babylon; other Heresies fell by the Eastern and Western worthies, and Affrican Fathers of the South also, as Augustine and others; but the Antichristian Hierarchy, has fallen first in the North of the world, Popery in France, Germany, and in England also before by Wickliffe, &c. Prelacy by the Scots, the Scots Presbyters by the English, the new English Independency by the Welsh, or the Baptized Churches there; Baptized Churches have the greatest fall from the Northern Saints both in England and Wales; John's spirit in the North of England, and the Spirit of Jesus rising in North-wales, is for the fall of all the Churches in the South; for here and in South-wales, and in the Western parts of England and Ireland, the baptized Churches do most multiply. I will not say, 'tis the warmness of the Climate, but I believe the delicacy of the Countries, East, West, and South, doth much soften the spirits of men, who more tast the delicacies of the whore here, then in Northern parts, where such hardships and shakings appear in the Spirits of the Saints, that it terrifies the Churches to consider, that their heavenly and earthly excellency must dye, that their outward government and worldly glory must come down. This the Northern Saints shew, and a fire in their spirits enfolding itself, but the Southern Churches see it not, nor consider the work of the Lord this day: therefore terrible whirlewinds must needs rise in the South, either their own self-divisions, or some destruction from the Almighty; for nothing but confusion will convince the Churches. Then the whirlewind comes from the North, (as Ezekiel saw on the Church of Israel) 'tis from the North, as I said; but in the South the whirlewinds rage and rest. (p.126)

22
The Children of the West 1653

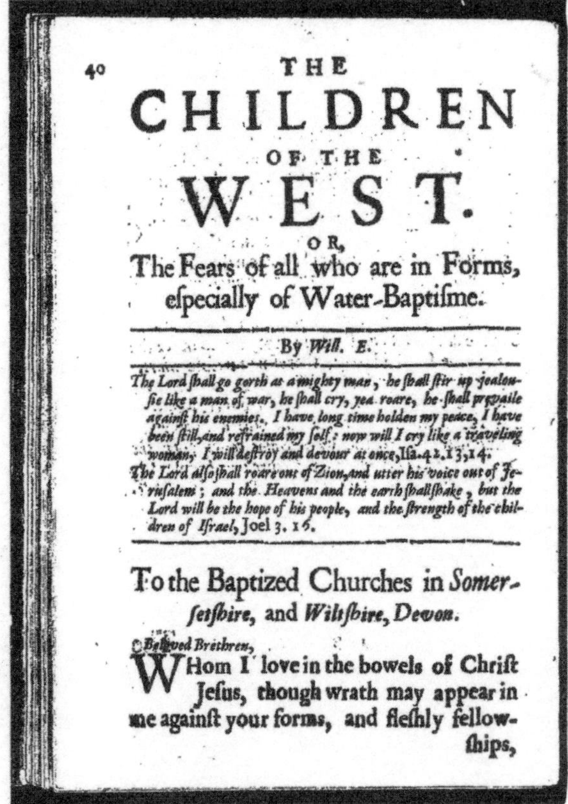

40

THE

CHILDREN

OF THE

WEST.

OR,

The Fears of all who are in Forms, especially of Water-Baptisme.

By *Will.* E.

The Lord shall go forth as a mighty man, he shall stir up jealousie like a man of war, he shall cry, yea roare, he shall prevaile against his enemies. I have long time holden my peace, I have been still, and refrained my self: now will I cry like a traveling woman, I will destroy and devour at once, Isa. 42. 13, 14.
The Lord also shall roare out of Zion, and utter his voice out of Jerusalem; and the Heavens and the earth shall shake, but the Lord will be the hope of his people, and the strength of the children of Israel, Joel 3. 16.

To the Baptized Churches in *Somersetshire,* and *Wiltshire, Devon.*

Beloved Brethren,

WHom I love in the bowels of Christ Jesus, though wrath may appear in me against your forms, and fleshly fellowships,

THE CHILDREN OF THE WEST. OR,
The Fears of all who are in Forms, especially of Water-Baptisme.
By WILL. E
To the Baptized Churches in Somersetshire, and Wiltshire, Devon.

THE CHILDREN OF *the West* is the third letter in *The North Star* collection. Erbery seems to have prepared the whole publication with care. *The North Star* encouraged his friend and kindred spirit, Morgan Llwyd. *A Whirelwind from the South* was directed to the scattered saints of Plymouth, friends unknown to Erbery but sharing similar convictions. *The Children of the West* was written for those trapped in formalism.

Although the treatise was written specifically for Baptist churches, it includes Erbery's interpretation of history. The Third Dispensation would soon replace the Age of Apostasy. The end of history was approaching. In *The Children of the West,* Erbery analysed the history of post-Reformation Britain. Three forms of secular government, monarchy, aristocracy and democracy were paralleled by three forms of ecclesiastical government: Episcopal, Presbyterian and Independent. While these still existed in different European nations, they were all being replaced in Britain as a result of the dramatic events of contemporary history. Each church pattern had fallen into the same error of believing that it alone was the true expression of God's will. The search for purity resulted in being captivated by Pharisaism.

An obsessive search for correct liturgical and sacramental forms eroded spiritual unity, and created zealotry which persecuted the less than orthodox. The ordinances of Baptism and the Lord's Supper stifled the direct relationship with God and proved obstacles to, rather than channels of, grace. An example of this was the recent arrival of Baptists to Wales which had destroyed the sense of unity within the communities of saints.[1]

THE PEOPLE OF GOD IN THIS LAND WERE AS A LITTLE CHILD

...a time was when the people of God in this Land were as a little child, so humble, so harmless, so teachable, so tender-hearted, so full of self-denyal and simplicity; and then, O what love did God manifest to them!

Truly for their sakes God came forth in this Nation, threw down mighty enemies before them, all their enemies both Civil and Spiritual, King, Parliament, Lords and Commons, yea Courtiers also: for the greatest in the Kingdom, both Temporal and Spiritual, were enemies against the appearance of God in his people. (p.129)

THE PEOPLE OF GOD WERE AS CHILDREN, THEY ARE NOW MEN

Now God hath thrown them all down, because the people of God were then but as little children, that is, they could go no where, but as God led them... Thus the people of God were as children, they are now men; they were then simple, now subtil; they were self-denying, now scrape up all to themselves; they were dying to the world, now living wholly to world, and worldly honours; they were content to be poor, now all must be rich; they were tender-hearted, would not tread upon a worm, now they can kill men: my people that call themselves by the most High, pretend high things for the liberties and freedom of a Nation, yet none exalts him, no, they exalt themselves, and not the pureness of Religion, which is to visit the widdow in affliction, and to keep themselves unspotted in the world. (p.129)

THE POWER OF RIGHTEOUSNESS APPEARS IN THE HEARTS OF ALL THE PEOPLE

The children of the Sea, or the children of the waters, who are they? why, they are the inhabitants of the Isles, these are the children of the West. I will show you but one place for it out of the Prophets Isa. 24.14 there was a great Jewish rabbi who saith it belongs to the Isle of great Britain... these uttermost parts of the earth, saith he, are the Isles of Great Britain, their songs shall be heard to the righteous; for no form of Religion can stand in this Land, only the power of righteousness appears in the hearts of all the people. No people under Heaven go forth for righteousness more, fight for it, speak for it; all are for righteousness, for justice, mercy, and common liberty; but the treacherous dealers have dealt treacherously; yea, the treacherous dealers have dealt very treacherously; that is, some both in Church and Common-wealth are treacherous to God and men; false in their Trust, fall from their promises, set up empty forms of Religion, instead of the power of righteousness... (p.131)

MONARCHY, ARISTOCRACY, DEMOCRACY

But to our business: The children of the West is to me in these three things. First, It is the new worldly Government, that is here meant by the children of the West. Government we know is divided into these three parts: First, Monarchy. Secondly, Aristocracy. Thirdly, Democracy.

First, Monarchy is by any one man, Aristocracy is by many or the best of the people, Democracy is the government of the people themselves in their Representatives. Monarchy is in France and Spain, Aristocracy in Venice and Holland. Democracy is in Switzerland, because their magistrates there every year give an account to the people of their Acts.

I call all this government a new worldly government, not in respect of men, but in respect of God, that is, of his reign, it is a new thing Psal. 74.12. God is my king of old working salvation in the midst of the earth, that is, the reign of God it is in working up the salvation of men in their estates and spirits; the reign of men, whether Monarchy, Aristocracy, or Democracy, or whatever else, hath been for the destruction of men. We have had all three in this Nation, and I call this new worldly government, the children of the West, because no part of the world do I know of a pure Democracy, but in the Western parts; in the Eastern parts they are Monarchs or Kings: therefore take the whole body of Civil government, it is in the West to be found. We have found all this in our Isle: Monarchy was that of the King; Aristocracy, Lords and Commons; Democracy, that of the Parliament; for both Parliament and Army did vote the Supreme Power to be in the People; Well, we see all these thrown down. The children of the West have trembled, the Lord hath roared: what the present government is, I will say nothing of, I do not know but leave it to God. (p.131f.)

THE CHRISTIAN RELIGION WAS IN BRITAIN BEFORE IT WAS IN ROME

Secondly, By the children of the West is meant, the old Christian Religion: I do not call it old in respect of God, but in respect of man;

for God sees that the new is the same with the old: but the old Religion with man is that Christian Religion which was first in Christendom. Where was that? Answer, it was in the West, the Western Romish Church was the first Christian Church in the world, I mean after Christ & the Apostles, or Apostolick Churches. So that Christendom was first called from the Popish Church, possessing this Western part of the world. Indeed the Christian religion was in Britain before it was in Rome, I mean the Christian Religion established by Civil Authority, was first confessed by this Nation; as Lucius the Britain, the first Christian king, and Constantine the great, the first Christian Emperour was a Britain, but both were of the Popish Religion, and the Christian here in Britain was mere popish, even before Austin the Monk came from the Pope, as you may read in Ecclesiastick Stories, in Sir Henry Spelman Antiquitates Britannicae,[2] *what Archbishops, Bishops, with their Councels and Canons, were set up in Wales, with as much superstition as ever was in Rome; therefore I call it the Romish Religion, or that of the West; yea, the Eastern Churches, were for this cause children of the West, not only because the Western Religion, with the Romish Empire, came from thence, but because all their forms of worship and religious exercises, were meerly superstitious and Popish, as you may see by their Patriarchs, Metropolitans, Prayers, their mouldy Manuscripts, and limping Liturgies shew the same.* (p.132)

THE DISCIPLES OF CHRIST, CHRIST'S ASSES

Therefore the old Christian Religion or Christendom came from Popery, who are for this cause the Children of the West; and all that Christian Religion among Protestants is the same, being called Christendom in common with that; both mistaking the name Christian, as if it were a word of honor, whereas the word Christian at first was a name of contempt: as honest professors with us were called Puritans: so the purest Disciples of Christ were in reproach called Christians, and first at Antioch; therefore Peter saith, If ye be reproach't for the name of Christ, happy are ye, &c. that is, if any man suffer as a Christian, let him not be ashamed, I Pet. 4.16 for this cause some old Copies in the Greek read not christianos, but christionos, that's Christs Asses; for so they called the Disciples of Christ,

Christ's Asses; because they were ready to bear his burden, to obey his commands, and to carry his Crosse. (p.132f.)

THEY ARE ALL FALN TO THOSE ALREADY WHO STAND IN GOD ALONE

But now, that Christian Religion, which we profess (as part of Christendom), is but a piece of Popery, and the best Protestants are but the children of the West; when the Lord shall roar, truly they shall tremble. Had I time, I could shew that the purest forms of Religion this day are but the old Religion in a new dress; their Churches, Ministers, Order, Ordinances, all, I say, are the children of the West, only the Lord roars more terribly against our Religion in this Nation, then in any besides in Christendom. It is a wonder Christian Religion stands so upright in all Nations but in this; Popery in France and Spain; Prelacy in Germany; Presbytery in Geneva, Independency in New England, Anabaptism in Ireland; but none of this Christian Religion stands still in England or Wales. Popery is faln, Prelacy faln, Presbytery and Independency are faln, likewise; nothing stands now but the last of Anabaptism, and that is falling too.

Thus they are all faln to those already who stand in God alone, who see God in Spirit: and to spiritual Saints in this Nation the Churches are nothing; therefore I say there is something in this Nation that God will do, which shall be as an Ensign to all Nations round about us, the children of the West shall tremble at it, when their old Christian Religion shall fall at once. (p.133)

THE ORDINATION... OF ROMISH PRIESTS, PRELATS, PRESBYTERIANS, INDEPENDENTS, BAPTIZED CHURCHES

Lastly, As the children of the West was the new worldly government: Secondly, the old Christian religion: So thirdly, the new Churches with their old Ministers, are the children of the West: for (as I told you before) the first visible Church since the Apostacy (since the two hundred years after Christ Jesus) was the Popish Romish church, and the reformed Churches; yea, the most refined Churches this day have but the old

Ministery still, even the Romish Priests among them. 'Tis plain in the Prelats and Presbyterian Ministers, who do officiate in their holy orders, as Priests and Deacons; but what's the ordination of Independents, and Baptized Churches? they lay on hands: but what gift of the Spirit follows by the laying on of hands of the Presbytery? I Tim. 4.14 or by the laying on hands of the Prophets? Acts 13.3, 4 or by the Apostles hands? for these were with the Presbytery or Eldership in Ordination, as Acts 20.17; I Tim. 4.14; 2 Tim. 1.6 the purest Ministery appearing this day is nothing but the old. You remember when Popery was cast out of England, What followed? the Prelats the new Churches came in, but the old Ministery stood, as Priests and Deacons. When the old Prelats were gone, then the new Presbyterian Churches followed, yet their Ministers do still officiate by their holy orders they received from the Bishop. Behold the next purest Independent Ministery, they comply with the the Presbyters, conform to all their National worships, or Parish-preaching, praying, singing of Psalms, sit in the Synodical chair, rise to Civil and Martial affairs, run after Tyths, and the Treasury of the State &c... The Papists and Prelats were the nearer in form to the true ordination of Ministers, then we are now; the Papist pretended to have the holy Spirit to be given to the Priest; and I, when made a Priest by the Bishops, had the same said to me, Receive the Holy Ghost; Here was the form they had; yea, some Bishops blowed on the Minister to be made, as Christ breathed the holy Spirit, Joh. 20.22. Indeed that of the Prelats was but a form, and a foolery too, yet was it wiser than that ordination of our English Presbyter, where no gift of the Spirit is pretended or expected; far foolisher then the Scots Presbytery, who lay no hands at all, because no gift follows. These make Ministers and ordain Elders without the laying on of hands. (p.134f.)

THE CHILDREN OF THE WATERS

Lastly, the children of the West, are the children of the waters, as the Hebrew reads, Ben Majim. You may say, What are the children of the waters? Truly to me the purest form of Churches this day, the baptized Churches are the children of the waters, they are the purest form of Church-fellowship this day, yet are they but the children of the waters, that's of the

West. I'le tell you, Popery, Prelacy, and Independency, I can find them all. In the East, 'tis plain Popery in the Eastern Churches; and Jerom tells us of a Presbytery in his time, for a Bishop and a Presbyter is the same, saith he: I find Independency (I mean separated Churches) in the South, that is, in Affrick. Those whom they formerly called Donatists, (though Augustine counts them Hereticks) were very good Christians,[3] *they were like the Independent or separate Churches; as for the Anabaptist, truly I do not reproach them in this; but I never found them in any part of the world save in the West, first Northwest in Germany, then in England, since in Wales, now in Ireland, all Westward still; these children of the West, when the Lord shall roar, shall surely tremble: the word is this, Those Churches that are in purest forms, that have not the appearance of the Spirit from on high, the Lord will roar in them, and make every one of them to tremble; yea, the time is come that the Lord shall roar, and they shall tremble, who pretend a Gospel-order, and Ordinances of Christ, which are meerly Antichristian, I mean that of Baptism or dipping, this day.* (p.135f.)

THE INDWELLING OF GOD, THE SPIRIT OF CHRIST IN US

First, Because therein they disobey the command of Christ; they tell their proselytes, You must be dipt, because you must obey the command of Christ. I say, going forth to baptize, or be baptized, without the baptism of the Spirit on the Church, is not the command of Christ, but against it… Jerusalem, to you and me, dear Christians, is the indwelling of God, the Spirit of Christ in us, though much clouded and confounded (we being in Babylon) therefore we should not go forth out of the indwelling of God, and holy walking with men, love to all Saints, and to the world also; We should not go forth of this to teach and baptize: yea, we cannot baptize, because not teach all Nations; not every teacher but he that could teach all Nations was to baptize: and this could not be without the baptism of the Spirit.

2. As they disobey the command of Christ, so they do deny the Spirit of Jesus… So for those to go forth to teach and baptize, who have not the baptism of the Spirit, is to deny the Spirit of Jesus. (p.136)

SINCE THE WATERS CAME OVER THE MOUNTAINS, THE SAINTS THERE HAVE BEEN WONDERFULLY DIVIDED

3. As the childen of the waters deny the Spirit of Jesus, so they divide the Saints themselves. I do not know how it was in England, but I know, in Wales all that feared God and professed Christ in truth, were once of one heart and one mind; but since the waters came over the mountains, the Saints there have been wonderfully divided; some of one Church call the others, devils; and indeed, no form of Church-fellowship doth more divide, then this of water-baptism: Presbyterians are all of one form, so Independent-Churches agree together, but God hath so roared among the baptized Churches, that they are divided like Babylon into three parts: some for Free-will, some for General Redemption; some for the Orthodox doctrine of the Church of England: these last are the worst; but neither of them can break bread with other, not with those of the same form: yea, there is a fourth divided part of Anabaptists, who are by themselves about laying on of hands: surely, the Lord hath roared like a Loyn [Lion] *among them, and they begin to tremble.* (p.137)

AS THEY DECEIVE THE WORLD IN BAPTIZING AND BELIEVING, SO BY DIPPING

Nay, rather the faith that the people of God have this day, is but a Legal faith (as I have proved in my Call to the Churches). It is not faith on Christ, no, the Mystery of Christ is not manifest to Christians; our faith goes no further then the flesh of Christ, it goes so far as to believe Christ born of a Virgin, and suffered at Jerusalem for us, 1653 years ago; and so think to be saved by him, not being revealed in us, and dying in us, and so rise the hope of glory. But who knows Christ in Spirit, the Father in the Son, and the Son in the Saints, so to dye with him, as to rise with him? This is a mystery they know not.

2. As they deceive the world in believing, so they deceive the world in Baptizing… The Apostles in the Primitive times they had the manifestation of the Spirit in manifold gifts: What manifestation of the Spirit have any of the Churches this day?…

Thirdly and lastly, As they deceive the world in baptizing and believing, so by dipping; a great deal of do, they make about dipping, whereas it may be proved that never any such thing was in all the Gospel-Churches: the way of Baptizing in the Primitive Churches was by way of washing the Disciples feet, or believers going down into the waters up to the ankels... What is in their Catechism? they say, He that is the Minister must have a modest garbe, or garment, and those that are to be dipt must have garments; when Peter baptized five thousand in one day, where could the Apostle have so many modest garments at once? (p.138)

THOSE HONEST MEN AND WOMEN IN THE NORTH

What is the meaning of those honest men and women in the North, that so many of them are taken with that power, that they can do nothing else but quake and tremble? For my part, I look upon it as a sign of something both to you and me; that when God shall roar in us, and speak forth himself with glory in us, God shall make our flesh to shake, quake, & tremble; that is, he will make our most heavenly enjoyments and attainments, peace and power, he will make it all to shake and tremble before him. (p.140)

A DAY IS COMING THAT THE LORD WILL ROAR IN THE MIDST OF YOU

In Joel 3.16. The Lord shall roar out of Sion, and utter his voice from Jerusalem, and the Heavens and the earth shall shake. O friends, there be many of the people of God that will call those that do apprehend things higher then they do, they will call them Notionists; Are not you a Notionist? What is this Scripture to you? When was this Scripture fulfilled in you? I profess you are Sion, God dwels in you; you are Jerusalem, the City of God, God dwells with you. I pray, when did the Lord utter his voice from you Jerusalem, and roar in you Sion? Well, he hath not yet, Why so? because the Lord is yet silent, and saith nothing, he is still; but a day is coming that the Lord will roar in the midst of you, then the Heavens and the earth shall shake, your heavenly apprehensions, and your earthy performances, your heavenly hopes, and your earthly affections, all shall shake in that day of the appearance of the great God in you. (p.140)

ALL THIS SHAKING IS FOR SETLING OF THAT WHICH ABIDES

Brethren, all my speaking cannot stir you, but when the Lord shall speak, when he roars in you, he'le shake your foundations, your Forms and Faith too; but this is the comfort, that this shaking of Heaven and earth is not threatned, but promised, Heb. 12.26 'tis the last and greatest promise, that God will yet once more shake, not only the earth, but the Heavens also; once more (saith he) for the earth of Legal-dispensation was shaken, when the Gospel came in; yea, their Heaven, or highest light of Sun or Moon, that's the light of the Law, was darkened, &c. Acts 2. 18, 20, 21. Then again, the heaven of that Gospel-dispensation was shaken, and sunk down into the Apostasie or falling away, when all that Gospel-glory in gifts, and a Ministery of the Spirit, with spiritual and heavenly Ordinances, were darkened, confounded, and filled with smoak of the bottomless pit, darkening the Sun and the Air, &c. all this, and more has come to pass upon us in Babylon, though we know it not. Now in Babylons fall, the heavens shall shake again, more terribly than ever: a greater Earth-quake also then was since man was upon the Earth; a most dreadful darkness shall fall upon Sun and Moon, and on all the lights of Heaven, &c. Isa.14.10, 13; Revel. 16.18.

This will be also when the Lord shall reign in mount Zion, Isa. 24.23. Therefore all this shaking is for setling of that which abides, that these things which cannot be shaken may remain, Heb. 12.27. What's that? the Lord himself, and man's life in God alone; all besides must shake and fall, and none stand upon the earth but God only, Zach. 14.5, 9. (p.143)

23

A Flash of Lightning from the East 1653

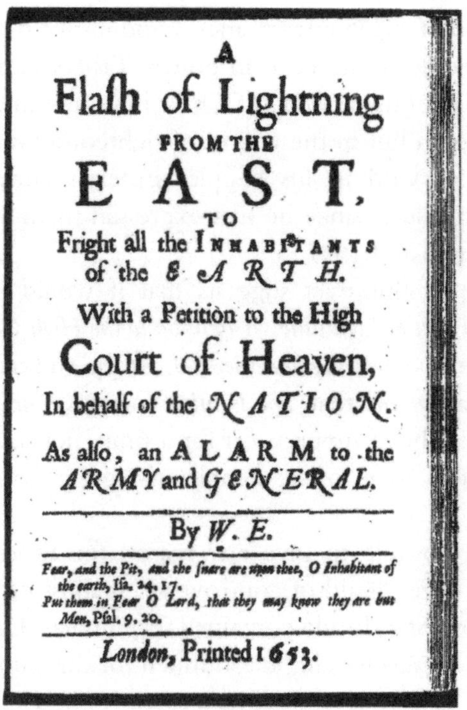

A
Flaſh of Lightning
FROM THE
EAST,
TO
Fright all the INHABITANTS
of the EARTH.
With a Petition to the High
Court of Heaven,
In behalf of the NATION.
As alſo, an ALARM to the
ARMY and GENERAL.

By W. E.

Fear, and the Pit, and the ſnare are upon thee, O Inhabitant of the earth, Iſa. 24. 17.
Put them in Fear O Lord, that they may know they are but Men, Pſal. 9. 20.

London, Printed 1653.

A Flash of Lightning FROM THE EAST,
TO fright all the INHABITANTS of the EARTH.
With a Petition to the High Court of Heaven, In behalf of the NATION.
As Also, an ALARM to the ARMY and GENERAL.
By W. E.
London, Printed 1653.

THE TITLES OF the four tracts have moved from north to south, and west to east. In the north, they were directed to the followers of Morgan Llwyd; in the south to the scattered saints of Plymouth, and in the west to the Baptists, the purest of the gathered churches. *A Flash of Lightning from the East* proclaims Erbery's confidence in God who acts in ways of righteousness, and not in forms of religion.

In this short, direct tract, Erbery proclaims the Christian hope. A new world of righteousness, mercy and justice is being ushered in by the people of the Lord in power. Erbery confidently lives in expectation of the coming of Christ in us, not in any particular form of religion but in the power of righteousness and universal appearance of God in his people. Erbery's convictions have remained consistent since he first expressed them at the Oxford debates in 1646 and 1647.

The title of this tract suggests that it would include three treatises: *A Flash of Lightning, A Petition to the High Court of Heaven* and *An Alarm to the Army and General.* At the end of *The Wretched People,* Erbery wrote that *The Petition* and the *Alarm* 'were ready for the Presse, but I suppress't if for a time, not only out of fear of man, but in love to the People of God (especially those in Power)'.

It is not possible to give any reason for Erbery's decision. Erbery was never afraid of controversy. It must be remembered that *The North Star* already contained seven tracts. Did he feel that a further two tracts would be too much for this publication?[1]

TO THE SONS OF PEACE AND QUIET IN THE LAND

THE COMING OF CHRIST... WILL NOT BE IN ANY PARTICULAR FORM OF RELIGION... BUT IN THE POWER OF RIGHTEOUSNESS AND UNIVERSAL APPEARANCE OF GOD IN HIS PEOPLE

Dear Hearts,

...The coming of Christ, and his second appearance in us, will not be

in any particular form of Religion, or private opinion of man, but in the power of righteousness and universal appearance of God in his people; 'tis not, Lo here is Christ, lo there; he's neither in the Chamber, nor in the Desart, ver.26. [Matthew 24] *that is, 'tis neither in gathered Churches, nor Conventicles of Seekers, nor yet in the Desart of Bewildernessed and scattered Saints: he'le come in none, yet comes in All at once, as Lightning shines from East to West...* (p.144f.)

IN RIGHTEOUSNESS ALL AGREE, THOUGH IN FORMS OF RELIGION AND OPINION THEY DIFFER

This Angel [Revelation 18.1] *(as the others) is no particular man or spirit, but the glorious appearance of God in his people; which is universal already, and in All in parts: for in righteousness All agree, though in forms of Religion and opinion they differ: therefore these particular forms of Religion, and private opinions must fall with Babylon, that the power of righteousness may appear to All.*

...the Righteousness of Saints, that's their righteous Actings among men, which would sooner convince, quiet, and call the world, then all their religious forms or shews of holiness. (p.145)

THERE IS AN UNIVERSALL LOOKING FOR OF RIGHTEOUSNESS, MERCY AND JUSTICE FROM THE PEOPLE OF THE LORD IN POWER

There is a little small remnant of the Sons of Peace, and the quiet in the Land, who are waiting for this to hasten on the Nation; in whom also there is an universall looking for of Righteousness, Mercy, and Justice from the people of the Lord in power, that nothing may appear in them but God only; and do to others, not only as we would that men should do unto us, but as God would do to men. This is the reign of God and of Christ, who shall judg the poor of the people, save the children of the needy, and break in pieces the oppressor. Psal. 72.4. (p.145)

THERE IS AN ENSIGN SET UP IN THE NATION

There is an Ensign set up in the Nation, and a Fire in the Saints of the most high, even the spirit of publick righteousness, which frights men of private interest, that's the mighty oppressor, who shall fall not by the sword of man, nor of a mean man, as former oppressors have done, but by the Lord God he shall fall, and burn as in a Furnace. Farewel. (p.145f.)

24

The Woman Preacher 1653

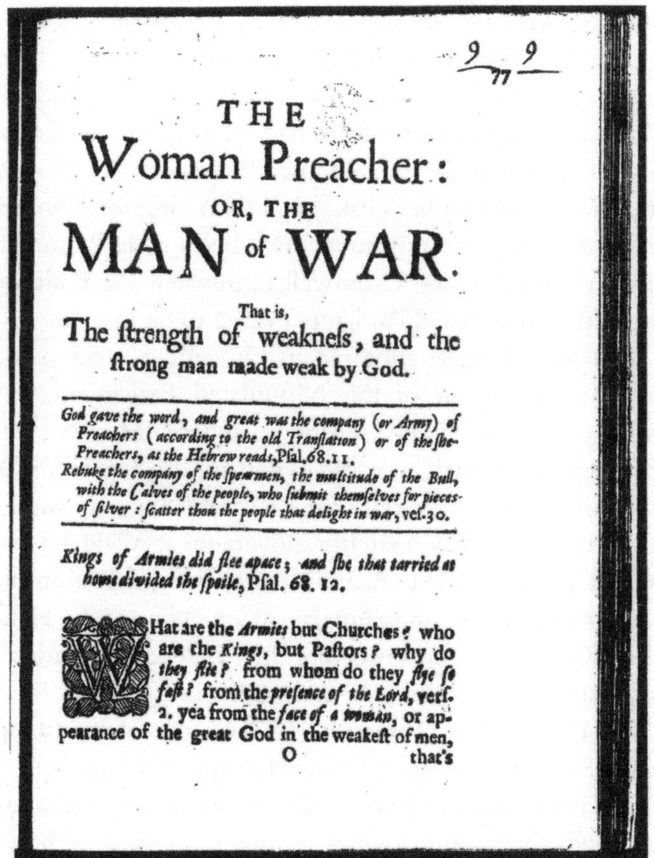

THE
Woman Preacher:
OR, THE
MAN of WAR.

That is,
The ſtrength of weakneſs, and the ſtrong man made weak by God.

God gave the word, and great was the company (or Army) of Preachers (according to the old Tranſlation) or of the ſhe-Preachers, as the Hebrew reads, Pſal. 68. 11.
Rebuke the company of the ſpearmen, the multitude of the Bull, with the Calves of the people, who ſubmit themſelves for pieces of ſilver: ſcatter thou the people that delight in war, veſ. 30.

Kings of Armies did flee apace; and ſhe that tarried at home divided the ſpoile, Pſal. 68. 12.

WHat are the *Armies* but Churches? who are the *Kings*, but Paſtors? why do *they flie?* from whom do they *flye ſo faſt?* from the *preſence of the Lord*, verſ. 2. yea from the *face of a woman*, or appearance of the great God in the weakeſt of men, O that's

THE Woman Preacher: OR,
THE MAN of WAR.
That is, the strength of weakness, and the strong man made weak by God.

ERBERY WROTE FOUR tracts which relate specifically to the religious and political issues of 1653 and early 1654. The Long Parliament (the Rump) was dissolved by Cromwell on April 20th, 1653 and replaced by the Nominated, or Barebone's Parliament which sat from July 4th to December 12th, 1653. That too was dissolved by Cromwell who was then installed as Lord Protector. The first of the four tracts was *The Bishop of London,*[1] published in January 1652/3 during the dying months of the Long Parliament. It described several meetings, one on November 22nd, 1652, of a London congregation which had recently moved from All-Hallows Church to London-House. Present at the November meeting were Christopher Feake[2] and John Simpson,[3] both Fifth Monarchists. This extremist movement became disillusioned and potentially violent when Cromwell terminated the Rule of the Saints, as the Nominated Parliament came to be known.

The Woman Preacher appeared in November 1653, a month before the dissolution of the Nominated Parliament. Erbery reported of a meeting in Cheapside, where 'Ministers of the Gospel appear in such a warlike posture, as Captain Kiffin[4], Captain Simpson and the rest of the Pastors'. Simpson and Feake had founded the Fifth Monarchist movement at All-Hallows-the-Great in December 1651. A month after the publication of *The Woman Preacher*, Feake and Simpson, at a meeting at All-Hallows, attacked Cromwell for dissolving the Barebone's Parliament. Erbery responded with two tracts, *An Olive Leaf* (January 1653/4)[5] and *The Man of Peace* (February 1653/4)[6] in a vain attempt to persuade Feake, Simpson and others to support Cromwell.

The Woman Preacher gives evidence that Kiffin and Simpson were already beginning to plot against Cromwell. Erbery had served under the Earl of Essex who was for Prelacy, and General Fairfax who supported the Presbyterian cause. Fairfax had sided with the six Presbyterian visitors against Erbery at the Oxford debates in 1646/7.[7] Erbery urged Simpson and the others to refrain from violence and to support the third General, Cromwell, who advocated a policy of toleration.

Erbery recognized the explosive consequences when

fundamentalist interpretations of the Bible are combined with political arrogance. In contrast, Erbery advocated non-violence and negotiation. Erbery had served as an Army chaplain, and had observed at first hand that change in government had not ended the oppression of the poor. Each new government became intolerant when it gained power. Erbery anticipates the theology behind much feminist and non-violent theology. God's purposes will be fulfilled through 'the common, the obscure and the feeblest'. This was anathema to the majority of his orthodox contemporaries. Erbery under-girded his argument with remarkable Bible allusions, surprising for the twenty-first, let alone the seventeenth century. If Erbery had written only this tract, he deserves to be remembered.

THE FEMALE DOVE GOES FORTH... THE FEEBLE, THE WEAKEST SAINTS

Who is this that lies among the pots? the woman that sits in the chimney corner: she stayes at home; 'tis also the scullion or common souldier, in field, who dresseth his meat between two stones, where this pot hangs over the fire, there he lies down to sleep with his head between the stones or pots, as Mr. Aynsworth[8] *well interprets, Psal. 68.13.*

Such common creatures and obscure fellows there are abroad, who are not taken notice of nor respected by men, but by God they are, who will send them forth out of their holes, and hidden retirements into publick view at last, with power and glory, like winged Doves covered with silver, and her feathers covered with yellow gold. Mark, 'tis not the black Raven, but the Dove; that brings an olive-branch in her mouth, a message of peace and gladness to men... 'tis not the Cock, but the Female Dove goes forth... The feeble, the weakest Saints God will most glorifie with power from on high, to bring forth the glorious appearance of himself to the world... the place it seems was a Northern part, where much snow fell, a cold cloudy Countrey, far from heat (as Scotland is) yet there the woman is white, as if the weakest Saints should there in the Spirit conquer first. (Revelation 19.18, 14) [should be 19.8, 14] (p.147)

SCOTLAND... THE WOMAN, THE WEAKEST OF ALL THE PEOPLE

Oh, Scotland, how my soul loves thee; because thou who wert the man, are now become the woman, the weakest of all the people, and of all the people of God, so thou appearest to most, therefore with most power and glory, thou appearest to me... thy Highlanders may be the first from whom the Saints of the most high shall come forth not in outward pomp and glory, not in the delights and delicacies of the Whore, but in the womans weakness of flesh the fulness of the Godhead shall so appear in thee, that in the midst of thy lowness, among thy high hills, where nothing but barrenness, Oaten bread and water is to be had, there the most high God shall dwell; yea, all the English and Welsh hills, even our mighty men shall leap before thee. This Island of Great Britain is that Land where the Jewish Rabbi tells us the Lord shall reign... Scotland is the uttermost part of this Northern Isle, though Wales be the wing (as the Hebrew read) or sides of the North, where will be the City of the great king, Psal. 42.2. But Scotland must have the chiefest part if not the first of the songs, even of the new song. (p.147f.)

POPISH PRIESTS, PRELATES, PRESBYTERS, INDEPENDENTS, BAPTIZED PASTORS... SAINTS IN SPIRIT

That the Kings of Armies flie a pace, is plainer yet: Popish Priests stood many hundred years; Prelats in power seventy years, or more; Presbyters three years and a half, Independents but one month, Baptized Pastors in one day fly away; yea, they all fly away in the day of God; they fly apace... those who worship God in spirit and truth, whose flesh is crucified to God (that's the Altar); and the Temple is the Saints in spirit, who dwell in their God, who stay at home; these are measured and have been so in all Ages since the Apostasie: spiritual Saints have been alwaies taken notice of by God, as men separated from the Churches in which they were. Yet have the Churches continually been spoiled by Saints in the spirit, even all the glory and fellowship of former Churches; not only their Common prayers and Ceremonies, &c. but their Covenant, Classes, Catechisms, Directory &c. yea scattered Saints are already upon the chase, and dividing the spoil of gathered Churches, confounding their order, and defiling their Ordinances, being found not of a Gospel state. (p.148)

MONARCHY, ARISTOCRACY, DEMOCRACIE

There is yet more in the Kings Armies, that's Civil and Martial powers; the Kings of both in our times have fled apace: first, Monarchy in the King is quickly gone; Aristocracy in the Lords and Commons followed swiftly after; Democracie or the Commons power in their Representatives fled away. For as Parliament and Army confessed the supreme power in the people: so the Parliament being faln, the Army must not think to stand for ever, when Kings of Armies fly apace. Kings of Armies are therefore Martial powers, also Grandees and Generals. (p.148)

THREE GENERALS

Two Generals I have served already, and observed the third, and the Churches to fall under all three. The first Captain General was for Prelacy, which fell with him. The second General was for Presbytery in part, which fled away likewise. The third is neither for Independency or Anabaptism, but for all the people of God, as he saith, I had rather Mahumetism should be tolerated among us, then any of the people of God should suffer.

The two first Generals or Kings of Armies fled or laid down while they lived. The third or last King will fly away when he is dead and gone… (p.149)

NEVER DID MINISTERS OF THE GOSPEL APPEAR IN SUCH A WARLIKE POSTURE

Never did Ministers of the Gospel appear in such a warlike posture, as Captain Kiffin, Captain Simpson and the rest of the Pastors did. I will not mention the French Waldenses,[9] *who were all wasted by war, excepting a small remnant that escaped, whose posterity at present (though Protestants) are called, Lutheran Fryers. Neither will I speak of the German Anabaptists, who rose up in Arms, and fell by the sword (as they say) many thousands in one day, and so were dipt in blood.*[10]

That of Zisca's drum all have heard who read Ecclesiastick stories, that's a drum-head made of the skin of a Minister called Zisca,[11] *to encourage his Disciples and followers to fight: but since the reformation we never read such a randevouz of Ministers and Churches, as was in London. Never did Prelats appear in such a warlike posture, much less Presbyterian Ministers, who though Chaplains in the Army; yet were not Captains, & Colonels, as the Pastors of Churches, Independent and Anabaptists, then did appear.*

I wonder how these last are faln of late to be men of war, whereas in former years Anabaptists would wear no weapons, yea nor carry Guns in their ships to defend themselves withal. (p.150)

ORDINANCES AND ORDNANCES

I had thought when the Prelats were gone, we should have no more the Instrumr[e]*nts of a foolish Shepherd; but the Presbyters followed as wise as they; and the Independent Pastors after both... the Instruments of the Prelats were Ceremonies and Common-Prayers; Those of the Presbyters were Classes, and the Covenant; but the foolish Instruments of Independent and Baptized churches, are a Sword and a pair of Pistols. The Churches still cry out of us, that we walk without Ordinances; truly the Churches then were without all Ordnances, for only small guns and spears I saw among them.* (p.150)

SCATTERED SAINTS... NOT LIVING BELOW IN FORMS OF RELIGION, BUT IN THE POWER OF RIGHTEOUSNESS

So are not the Sons of Peace, or scattered Saints who live alone in the Lord, who are the Armies of Heaven, not living below in forms of Religion, but in the power of righteousness, called there the righteousnesses of Saints, Rev. 19.8.

...though now they are in no fellowship with man, yet the Lord will free them from chains, and from their captive state at last, Psal. 68.5, 6. (p.150f.)

THE WEAKEST SAINTS MUST BE THE SHE-PREACHERS

For though the Apostles first preached the Gospel to the world, yet the women first preach'd the Gospel (Christ risen) to the Apostles; yea, when all the Apostles forsook Christ, the women followed him to his cross, waited for him at the grave, and were the first who both saw him risen, and preached his resurrection. The Apostles would not believe the Message nor Ministery of the women, but thought it no better than an old wives tale. Thus the Teachers and Preachers of the Gospel this day count no otherwise of Christ in us the hope of glory; yea, the glory of the resurrection, or Christ risen in us, the Pastors pish at, Luke 24.11. Oh 'tis the woman the weakest vessel, the weakest Saints must be the She-preachers, who go not forth visibly to men, but stay at home and abide in their God, waiting for the glory to be revealed in them. Then shall they publish, and preach the everlasting Gospel, not with the speech of men, but with the language of God, and light of an Angel which shall fill the earth with glory, Rev. 18.1. (p.151)

25
The Idol Pastor: or Foolish Shepherd 1653

THE 87

IDOL PASTOR:

OR,

Foolish Shepherd.

SHEWING,

How unlike these are to the Primitive Pastors of CHURCHES.

Preached at Newport in Munmouthshire, by *Will. Erbery.*

As for me, I have not hastened from being a Pastor to follow thee, (or, I have not thrust my self for a Pastor after thee, as the Geneva translate) neither have I desired the woful day, thou knowest. That which came out of my lips was right before thee, Jer. 17. 16.

TO THE

Gathered Churches at *Lanvaghes.*

Brethren,

BEing called by the Lord to preach at Newport, the town where I was a Preacher first; It was strong upon my spi-

P 2 rit

THE IDOL PASTOR: OR Foolish Shepherd.
SHEWING, How unlike these are to the Primitive Pastors of CHURCHES.
Preached at Newport in Munmouthshire, by Will. Erbery.

THE FIRST TRACT published under the general title of *The North Star,* was written to the gathered church at Wrexham and included letters between Erbery and his friend and colleague, Morgan Llwyd. The sixth tract, *The Idol Pastor* was written to 'the gathered Churches at Lanvaghes', and although Erbery does not mention Walter Cradock by name, there can be no hiding his disappointment with Cradock's ministry.

The Idol Pastor includes an introduction written for the Llanfaches congregation, and a more general treatise on the nature of Christian ministry. Erbery reminded his hearers (for this was a sermon before it was published) that he was a preacher first at Newport. This could refer to his curacy at St Woolos, Newport from 1630 to 1633. It could also possibly infer to the fact that he began preaching in Newport. Was he directed towards a Puritan stance by William Wroth, the founder of the gathered church at Llanfaches?

The letter is written to the gathered Churches at Lanvaghes. Are these conventicles of worshipping Christians, whose mother church was centred on Llanfaches? In November 1639 Cradock played a leading part in the founding of the Llanfaches congregation, and at the outbreak of the Civil War, fled with them first to Bristol and later to All-Hallows-the Great in Thames Street, London.[1]

The scattering of the gathered churches was a sign that the Third Dispensation was about to arrive. The age of the Apostasy was drawing to a close. There had been no faithful ministry during the Apostasy because of the absence of apostles and pastors. Erbery shared this position with the Seekers who believed that the ministry of both apostles and pastors was necessary. Many in the Calvinist tradition regarded the apostles as an extraordinary ministry limited to the Apostolic period. For Erbery and the Seekers, if there were no apostles to ordain, there could be no pastors. For this reason, Erbery no longer regarded himself as a pastor: 'If I should profess my self Pastor of a Church, how could I leave Cardiff without danger of a curse?'

TO THE GATHERED CHURCHES AT LANVAGHES

NEWPORT, THE TOWN WHERE I WAS A PREACHER FIRST

Brethren,

Being called by the Lord to preach at Newport, the Town where I was a Preacher first; It was strong upon my spirit to speak on this Scripture [Jer. 17.16] *(though intending another before) but this I was forced by the Spirit of the Lord to declare. Some of Lanvaghes members there present supposed I had heard of their Pastor's leaving the Flock. Truly, I did not hear of it at all, only that he was Chaplain in the City to a Regiment of Foot; but not that he had left his Church in the Countrey; neither could I believe it, because he was formerly so zealous in Church-fellowship, that himself told me, he should be the most miserable man in the world, if deceived in his Church-way, or drawn away from his Office, as Pastor over them whom he counted his greatest glory.* (p.152)

HOW SHOULD LANVAGHES SAINTS... BE NOW SUCH A DARK & DIVIDED PEOPLE?

Some wonder how the primest Church in South-wales, the Church of Lanvaghes, should be so divided this day...

But how should Lanvaghes Saints, who of old had so much light & love before they went in a Church way, be now such a dark & divided people? The Church of Lanvaghes, that of stones (as they say) is falling down, as a type of the fall of the Church of Saints. Oh blame not your Pastor, as if he did divide you, 'tis the Lord has done it by his Spirit in the man, though the mans flesh may suffer for it. ...the Shepherd shall be smitten, and the gathered Churches scattered [Zach. 13.7], *that the Lord God may gather up the Saints into himself.* (p.152f.)

WHAT I THEREFORE SPAKE AT NEWPORT IN WALES

I know not what power a Pastor has to pick and chuse his members, no more then a private man has to make a Parliament.

What I therefore spake at Newport in Wales, was far beyond my thoughts at first; but if the Lord hath sent me, or led me forth on this subject... (p.153)

THE IDOL PASTOR: OR, FOOLISH SHEPHERD

WHERE GOD CALLED ME A PREACHER AT FIRST

The duty and service that I owe to this place where God called me a Preacher at first, hath commanded my presence here this day; and if none were now present to hear, I would have written these words in the walls and been gone: Wo to the Idol-Shepherd that leaveth the flock, &c. (p.153f.)

GOD WILL GATHER THE SCATTERED REMNANT

And I will gather the remnant of my flock. The flock (as we said before) was scattered by gathered Churches; now God will gather a remnant out of the Churches, though most of the Churches perish with their Pastors; but God will gather the scattered remnant out of all Countrys or Churches, yea rather out of that worldly conversation that many Saints have been carried to, by their Shepherds; God I say will bring them again to their folds, to their spiritual communion, and fellowship with the Father and the Son, and they shall be fruitful and encrease, in all the fruits of the Spirit... (p.154)

APOSTLES AND PASTORS WERE BOTH THE GIFTS OF CHRIST

That all men may see and know how far the present Shepherds are from the Primitive Pastors of Churches give me leave to premise two things.

First, Wherein the Pastors and Apostles were alike.

Secondly, Wherein they differed in their Ministerial Work and Calling.

Apostles and Pastors were both the gifts of Christ, and for the work of the Ministery to continue alike, till the Saints should be perfected, the body edified, and the whole Church come to a perfect man, to the measure of the stature of the fulnesse of Christ.

Therefore that distinction is Antichristian, of Apostles extraordinary, and to cease; Pastors ordinary, Ministers to continue. The Text shews no such difference. (p.155)

SOME TRUTH AND MUCH GOOD HAS BEEN BROUGHT FORTH BY MEN IN A FALSE MINISTERY

...though God in his free grace hath made use of men to minister good to his people, and to feed the woman in the wilderness; yea, some truth and much good has been brought forth by men in a false Ministery, as our old conformists, and honest non-conformists; though many of them since have turned persecutors, or formalists. (p.156)

THE MINISTERY OF THE SPIRIT, SECRETLY, WORKING IN HIS PEOPLE

The Saints will be perfected henceforth by other means, even by the Ministery of the Spirit, secretly, working in his people, who in the midst of confusion, shall be set in perfect order, the people of God in membership with the whole body, when raised out of Babylon. (p.156)

NO APOSTLES, THEREFORE THE CHURCHES SEND FORTH ITINERANTS

The next thing that I am to shew, is the difference between an apostle and Pastor.

First, The Apostolick Ministery was for the world; the Pastor was only for the Church: because we have no Apostles, therefore the Churches send forth Itinerants just like our old journey-priests; for though I confess many of them be godly men, yet they are not good Ministers, nor fit to teach the people, being for the most part no wiser then the foolish Shepherd, who having not the gift of the Spirit, as Saints in common had in the primitive Churches, nor yet studyed gifts of Tongues and Interpretation, as the godly Ministers of the Nation formerly had, will shortly be found such Itinerants, who make a trade of teaching: only what formerly he sold in a shop, is now set to sale in a Pulpit; making merchandize of the word of God, as before of wares.

Secondly, The Apostle was to go up and down the Countrey to preach; but the Pastor was to sit still, and wait on his own Church, Acts 20; Tit. 1.5, therefore for our Welsh Shepherds to turn Itinerants, is not according to rule, nor yet to reason; they'l run at last out of the Church and Country too. (p.157)

THE GOOD SHEPHERD TAKES UP HIS SHEEP ON HIS BACK

Mark the particulars wherein the Pastor is wanting, that is, he is not good in his office; though he preach twice a day to the Church, yet he doth not visit those that be cut off, or hidden, as the margin reads. There's many a poor Saint whose spiritual and temporal state is hidden from the Pastor: How can he visit, when he has left the flock?

Again, He shall not seek the young one; there's many a young beginner that must have milk like Babes; but how can the Pastor seek when he hast lost himself in leaving the flock.

Thirdly, Nor heal that which is broken: there's many a broken heart, that he knows not of because he has left the flock.

Fourthly, Nor feed that that standeth still... when the rest of the sheep are going along, or lead to pasture, some sheep may be so weak, they cannot follow, or so wilful they will not go a foot further; the good shepherd takes up his sheep on his back, and bears him with patience and long sufferance, &c. but how can the Pastor do this, who has left the flock and loves the world?

He shall eat the flesh of the fat and tear their claws in pieces, &c. If there be a fat Parsonage, as they say, a fat place, or preferment, the Pastor follows it, as a dog do's a piece of flesh laid before him. (p.158)

THERE ARE SIX THINGS THE PASTORS SEE NOT

There are six things the Pastors see not, because their right eye, their best sight and light is dark unto.

1. The Mystery of iniquity, the man of sin and son of perdition in themselves, they see not...

2. They see not the end of all Ordinances in the Apostasie... the end of all publick worships in spirit and truth ceased, when the spirit of Antichrist was set up in the Church, and worshipped as God. Common prayers and mixt communions, was counted once by choisest Saints to be the worship of God: so was singing of Psalms and baptizing of Infants, and a blessing after Sermon; also other Ordinances will at last be discovered to end in the Apostasie, when the Apostasie shall more appear in the Pastors.

3. They see not the coming of Christ, and Christ come already into his Temple...

4. They see not Christ in us the hope of glory Col. 1.27.

5. Nor the glory to be revealed in us Rom. 8.18, 21.

6. Nor the glorious resurrection of the Saints, the redemption of the body in this life; the rising of the body of the Church out of Babylon, the Pastors see not, because their right eye is utterly darkned, Ezek. 37.11, 12; Phil. 3.11. (p.160)

I LONG TO SEE AND SERVE ALL THE SAINTS... TO BE MY BROTHERS KEEPER

These were not the things that I then preached, but do now publish for the Pastors sake, that they may repent and return to God from their empty forms and fleshly Church-fellowship, into that Spirit or spiritual communion, where we can never leave the flock. The flock I look upon, not as any particular Congregation, but the Church of the first born written in heaven, whom I am waiting to see and enjoy on earth, even to the spirits of just men made perfect; that is, all the Saints in the spirit, who are with Christ perfectly one and living in God, I would not leave, nor be lacking to. O how I long to see and serve all the Saints, that their souls may prosper; in this sense I desire to be a Pastor, that is, to be my brothers keeper. Cain would not be so, but Abel was a keeper of sheep: so is every Saint to another, and to all the flock: his hearty affections, earnest desires, and delightful remembrance, is of the little flock, of the Lambs, of the least Saints, whom the Lord loves most.

To this most I applyed myself, with many other words to the people of Newport; the Idol pastor was made forth to them as the Idle professor, who is not his brothers keeper. (p.160f.)

TO DO TO EVERY ONE AS WE SHOULD THAT MEN WOULD DO TO US... THIS IS THE SUM OF ALL RELIGION

To do to every one as we would that men should do unto us.

This is the sum of All Religion, that is truly Christian and noble; 'tis the substance of the Law and the Prophets, of Christ and the Apostles writings, Matt. 7.12, Rom. 13.10. This one word will try our spiritual strength, and shew the weakness of Pastors, and of all the people of God. (p.161)

26

The Wretched People 1653

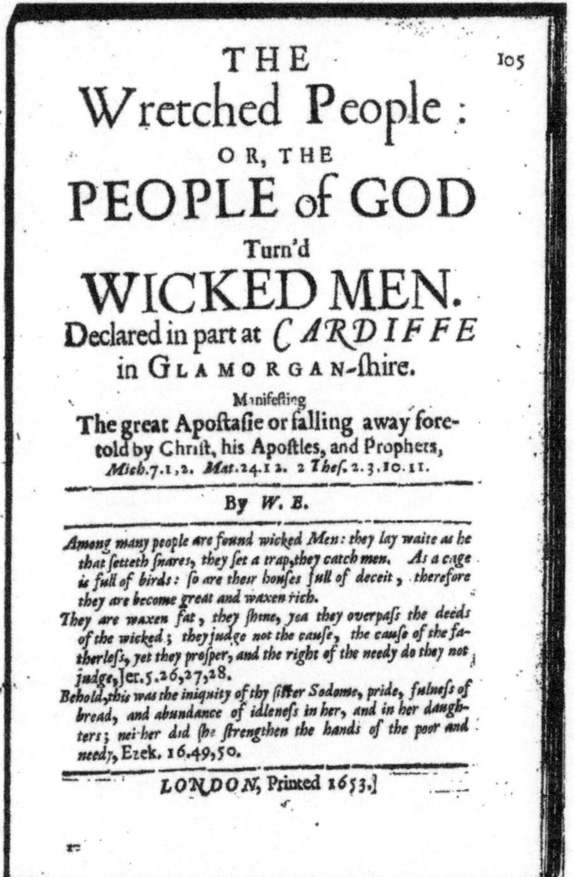

105

THE
Wretched People:
OR, THE
PEOPLE of GOD
Turn'd
WICKED MEN.
Declared in part at CARDIFFE
in GLAMORGAN-shire.
Manifesting
The great Apostasie or falling away fore-told by Christ, his Apostles, and Prophets,
*Mich.*7.1,2. *Mat.*24.12. 2 *Thes.*2.3,10.11.

By *W. E.*

Among many people are found wicked Men: they lay waite as he that setteth snares, they set a trap, they catch men. As a cage is full of birds: so are their houses full of deceit, therefore they are become great and waxen rich.
They are waxen fat, they shine, yea they overpass the deeds of the wicked; they judge not the cause, the cause of the fatherless, yet they prosper, and the right of the needy do they not judge, Jer.5.26,27,28.
Behold, this was the iniquity of thy sister Sodome, pride, fulness of bread, and abundance of idleness in her, and in her daughters; neither did she strengthen the hands of the poor and needy, Ezek. 16.49,50.

LONDON, Printed 1653.]

THE Wretched People: OR THE PEOPLE of GOD TURN'D WICKED MEN.
Declared, in part, at Cardiffe in Glamorgan-shire.
Manifesting the great Apostasie or falling away, fore-told by Christ, his Apostles, and Prophets, Mich. 7. 1,2. Mat. 24. 12; 2 Thess. 2. 3, 10, 11.
By W. E.
LONDON, Printed 1653

The Idol Pastor and *The Wretched People* have certain similarities. The first was preached at Newport and written particularly for the Gathered Churches at Lanvaghes. *The Wretched People* was 'declared in part, at Cardiffe' and then dedicated 'to the scattered Saints at Cardiff, and in the Countrey thereabout'. Llanfaches had been founded as a new-modelled church in 1639, and the Cardiff congregation, inspired by Llanfaches, was established by Erbery during the following year. Because Erbery seems to have maintained the family house at Roath, Cardiff, he was clearly in touch with those who had been part of this Independent cause.

The fact that Erbery addressed his letter to scattered saints suggests that he approved of their ecclesiology, whereas he disapproved of the gathered nature of the Llanfaches church. Was Erbery uncertain about the validity of the church form at Llanfaches and Cardiff when they were being established as Independent causes? Had he been reluctant to form a new-modelled church in Cardiff? Was it only respect for the Llanfaches community that led him to create a congregational cause in Cardiff? Probably, Erbery's reluctance about Independency is an after-thought, written after he has moved away from traditional church forms. That he preached Independency at a sermon in Chew Stoke in 1640[1] suggests that Congregational principles led Erbery to establish the Cardiff church.

The focus of Erbery's preaching in Wales was on the New Jerusalem, the Third Dispensation. This had been a consistent theme since the Oxford Disputations in 1646/7. Even before Oxford, Thomas Edwards had accused Erbery of heresy.[2] Erbery does not seem to have deviated from his dual emphasis on Christ in you, the hope of glory (the immanence of Christ), and the imminence of the Third Dispensation.

Erbery never lost hope in God's purposes. The end would come soon and reveal that no one and no thing was left out. Nothing was disposable. As God was in the beginning, God was in the middle, and God was shaping the end. This proved to be an extraordinary message for Erbery's generation. His enemies accused him of heresy and blasphemy, and when proven innocent of these charges, he was tarred with the brush of madness. That ensured that his life and thought would be dismissed, and that William Erbery would be buried in the unread pages of history.

TO THE SCATTERED SAINTS AT CARDIFFE, AND IN THE COUNTREY THEREABOUT

SO WE WALKED, THEY IN THE LIGHT... BUT I IN DARKNESS, BECAUSE CONTRARY TO MY OWN LIGHT

Beloved,

I Was first your Preacher, then your Pastor; and this last, not out of light in myself, but in love to the Saints of Lanvaghes, who being then gathered into a new modelled Church, never left me, till I and mine came into the same form with them: so we walked, they in the light, because I believe that led them into fellowship; but I in darkness, because contrary to my own light, in love only (as I said) I followed them, because I would not offend; but see the judgment of God lesse love and more offences fell between us after we came into a brotherhood, or combination of Churches, then when we were at first a company of scattered Saints. Well, gathered Churches we must be, and so we were, till the sword scattered us all into England; there they of Lanvaghes continued with their Pastor, &c. Teacher, and Ruling Elder. Since their return to Wales, First, their Ruling Elder was removed, then their Teacher was cast out, and now the Pastor has left the flock, which is now scattered as well as we in Cardiff. (p.162f.)

GOD WILL YET GATHER US AGAIN, GATHER US UP TO HIMSELF

Our first scattering was by coming into gathered Churches; by looking on forms, we lost the Spirit and power of godliness. Here we are scattered again, less godliness appearing, than was in us before. Well, God will yet gather us again, gather us up to himself, to the Spirit of Jesus, which appearing in us with power and glory, will manifest to the world who our Pastor is, even he who keeps us as a Shepherd doth his flock. (p.163)

I AM NO MORE THEN MY BROTHERS KEEPER

Let no man therefore nor Minister pretend he is Shepherd or Pastor: for my part, I am no more then my brothers keeper, whom because I would not lose, I have now lost my self with man, yea with the people of God, but I shall be found again, when quite lost: as yet I am saving my self a little, but I must be wholly lost; that's undone and dead to all but God, in whom (I hope) his people will find me alive at last. (p.163)

THE WRETCHED PEOPLE, OR THE PEOPLE OF GOD TURN'D WICKED MEN

NEW JERUSALEM, THAT'S THE THIRD DISPENSATION, OR GLORIOUS DISCOVERY OF GOD IN MEN

The last time of my being in this Countrey, I was carried forth to speak of New Jerusalem, that's the third dispensation, or glorious discovery of God in men, when God himself shall dwell gloriously in the midst of his people, Zach. 2.10, Rev. 21.2, 3… But that method which God took in bringing forth his people of old from Babylon, the same he takes with his people now, in these three things.

First, Their exceeding sin and wickedness appeared before…

Secondly, Their exceeding bondage and captivity followed…

Thirdly, Their glorious deliverance and liberty to build Jerusalem…

Thus 'twill be in these last daies before the New Jerusalem come down; Almost all the people of God will fall to open wickedness, being partakers of Babylons sins. They shall then suffer without and within a sore captivity… (p.164f.)

THE CROWN OF HIS PEOPLE HAVE NO SOUNDNESS, NO SINCERITY, NO SIMPLICITY AND SINGLENESS OF HEART

We are now in the first part, where the people of God appear so wicked…

…old Christians bred and fed by the Lord for many years, nourished and brought up, as 'twere to years of discretion; yet now they Rebel

against God and men, against their own knowledge, conscience, covenants, protestations, promises, remonstrances, &c. but now they are grown so sottish, and brutish, they know no more than a beast… not only those in lowest office but the highest Officer of them all, the Crown of his people have no soundness, no sincerity, no simplicity and singleness of heart, but putrified: so their sins have been secret and hid, but now break forth into open rottenness and running wickedness, not only in their hearts, but their hands are bloody, that's oppression, cruelty, unjustice, and unmercifulness to the poor Nation… (p.165)

A GOOD MAN IS FOR ALL MEN, GOOD TO THE EVIL, AS GOD IS, AND THE SAVIOUR OF ALL MEN, AS CHRIST WAS

…the remnant shall return… A very small remnant indeed… A good man is more then a righteous or godly man, who is good to himself, to save himself; but a good man is for all men, good to the evil, as God is, and the Saviour of all men, as Christ was, who can dye for the brethren, yea for his enemies, and for whom others would even dare to die… (p.166)

THE WICKEDNESS OF THE PEOPLE OF GOD, WILL FIRST APPEAR HERE TO ALL THE WORLD

And as the spirit of Antichrist and the flesh of the Whore has been most discovered and made bare in these daies, and begun to be burnt up in this Nation, above all the Nations of Christendom: so the wickedness of the people of God, will first appear here to all the world.

First, Because they are now set in power: before, the Parliament was a blank or blind, that men could not see the designs of seeming Saints; but now having all power in their own hands, the people of God are purposely set on high, that every man may see their shame, if they sin, or prove oppressors, as former powers have been.

Secondly… that deliverance & glorious liberty of the sons of God, which good men look for, must have a foregoing iniquity, captivity, and bondage within & without; not only mens spirits, but their states shall be under sore oppression… (p.167)

GOD IS LOVE, HE IS NO RELIGIOUS GOD, BUT A RIGHTEOUS GOD

Laying then aside those four things that an hypocrite may attain unto, I shall deal plainly with all the people of God, who know already, 1. That a man may be a great Professor. 2. Perform all good duties. 3. Be free from all gross sins. 4. Have all those common graces of the Spirit, yet be a gross hypocrite; that's, a wicked man, and the worst of all men, yea more wretched.

'Tis no new doctrine to us in Wales, who have heard it a hundred times of old at Cardiff, and Lanvaghes; but because your English men may hear it too... One asked me after this, What Sir, must we do nothing? neither pray, nor hear the word preached? &c. doth not God say, Up and be doing? True, said I; but all this is not the doing, 'tis but the means to shew us what we are to do, or seek strength to do what we know; but the doing is another thing, 'tis to deny our selves, to do good to all, to think no evil, not to seek our own, to give to every one that asketh, to lend looking for nothing again, &c. If ye know these things, blessed are ye if ye do them... Be ye followers of God as dear children, and walk in love; God is love, he is no religious God, but a righteous God, follow him; God is good to all men follow him; God doth not fast and pray, &c. men must follow him in action, and good works of Mercy and Justice... he hath shewed thee O man what is good: and what doth the Lord require of thee, but to do justice, to love mercy, and to walk humbly with thy God; this is the doing, to do justice; and not only to shew mercy, but to love it, even mercy to all men, mercy to the Nation. (p.167f.)

ARE YOU ACQUAINTED WITH THE FACE OF GOD?

What, no man on earth? no earthly means? no maintenance? no place, no preferment? What, nothing but God do you desire on earth? and none but God in Heaven? do you not look for glory there, and joy here?... What, is your desire so to do, and your delight so in him, that if he withdraw his face from you, you die, your flesh and heart fails? Is your soul and body also insensible of it? but are you acquainted with the face of God, with his secret with-drawings, and your spiritual disertions? Oh! God is a stranger to you, and you are strange from his bosome; you have another beloved now besides himself, some corruption or creature you cleave to, the Lord knows. (p.172)

WHERE'S THE SPIRIT OF CHRIST APPEARING IN ANY CHRISTIAN THIS DAY?

I will not say, What Minister, but what Christian man lives by faith this day? he cannot live without a living or a hundred a year, and we cannot live, no more then the souldiers, without constant pay or a settled place. Oh how many a one fears to come to his calling again? and who abides in his calling with God? who makes use of earthly things in a heavenly manner? who useth the world as not using it? who buys as not possessing it? where's the Spirit of Christ appearing in any Christian this day? where's that self-denying and dying to the world? where's that sincerity, simplicity, and singleness of heart? where's the mouth without guile? who lifts up pure hands? where's the spiritual-minded and merciful man? where's the meekness, the lowliness and love of Christ Jesus? that goodness, that kindness, those bowels of compassion to mankind? who hears the groans of the oppressed, the cry of the poor? If the people of God in power had the Spirit of Jesus in them, they would find a thousand wayes to ease the people, though they should part with half of their pay, or publick salaries. (p.173)

OH GOD, THAT THOU WOULDST ONCE SPEAK THY SELF IN THE SPIRITS OF THY PEOPLE

I will not speak of those who have hasted to be rich, and therefore by God's account cannot be innocent; nor yet those who raise themselves in other mens ruins; who grow rich in the Nations poverty, whose places are supported by the peoples oppression; whose pay, salaries, yea their very subsistence is upon the sighs of the poor and needy. I will not go to mens shops, nor follow the people of God in their dealing; Pray what difference between these and the men of the world in trade, in buying and selling? Oh God, that thou wouldst once speak thy self in the spirits of thy people, and shew all their unrighteousness! (p.173f.)

MENS NATURAL ABILITIES, AND MENS SPIRITUAL EXCELLENCY

The second reason is, That God may bring forth his glory before all men, or that glory may be exalted above grace, the glory of God above the grace of the best men. This is a strange and secret thing, a thing that I never spake of before, nor knew till now. 'Tis written Isa. 40.5. The glory of the Lord shall be revealed, and all flesh shall see it together; that's, all men at once shall see the glory of God. Why so? for the mouth of the Lord hath spoken it; that is, God will do what he sayes, that's more then good men will do; but God alone can do what he speaks, even bring forth his glory before all men, that all may see it: how so? how will this be brought to pass?… All flesh, and the goodliness of flesh also, that is, mens natural abilities, and mens spiritual excellency… mens natural abilities may abide long and encrease, but their spiritual excellencies quickly wither, as we may see by experience in the people of God: their natural gifts in government, in Civil and Martial exploits, are much improved above former Statesmen, or Souldiers; but as for spiritual graces, how soon have they withered in the wisest? good men in Parliament, when come to power, how weak were they? Where was the self-denying Ordinance kept? How were not self-interests followed more then common good? What's become of publick spirits? the freedom of the Nation who speaks of? yea, I could name godly men in the old and new-modelled Army fallen from their first love, their lowliness of mind, meekness, mercy, tender-heartedness; their tears are all dryed up, as withered grass, and as the flower of the field which fades in a month. (p.175f.)

THE WORST OF MEN SHALL BE MADE THE PEOPLE OF GOD

A third reason why the graces of Gods people are soon withering, is, because God has a people to call, in their room… Every prophesie and promise in the Prophets has a double performance; in the first coming of Christ, and at his second in Spirit…

So then as at Christs first coming in Spirit, the Nation of the Jews the only people of God were cast off, and sinners of the Gentiles taken in: so 'twill be at Christs second coming in Spirit… What's the new thing? The Tabernacle of God is with men, and he will dwell with them, and they shall be his people, ver.3. [Revelation 21] *What people are these? God himself shall be then their God: not God in covenant only, as with his people under the Law, nor God in Christ only, as he was with those in Gospel-dispensation; but in this third dispensation called the new Jerusalem, God himself shall dwell in them, and with them, a people whom God hath formed for himself... What people, I pray?... men like beasts, and the worst of men shall be made the people of God... God will form to be his people in such a manner, and in such multitudes, as never was under Law or in Gospel-times...* (p.176f.)

IN SAINTS BY CALLING SHALL THE APOSTASIE... BE FIRST REVEALED

...in Saints by calling shall the Apostasie and falling away be first revealed to the full; there shall Antichrist be found at last; as in the Disciples of Christ appeared first, Luke 9.55 and as the Mystery of iniquity did first begin to work in the Primitive purest Churches: so in the purest Churches the Mystery of iniquity and man of sin shall be last revealed, 2 Thess. 2.7, 8...

We have lookt upon Antichrist once at Rome, but of late we have seen him in Reformed Churches; not only in Popery, but in Prelacy and Presbytery has the man of sin appeared to the Saints. I'le speak no more of the Independent and baptized Churches. God may shew them the mystery of iniquity among themselves very shortly.

'Tis all the people of God and the Saints in general, I now mind; these shall find such an Apostasie and falling away in themselves, such a withering of all their gifts and graces that they shall not need to go far to find the man of sin... (p.178f.)

THIS GLORY, THAT BEATIFICAL VISION, AND FULL POSSESSION OF GOD... BE IN THIS LIFE

Faith may fail, hope and our hearts faint, love grow cold, yea every grace die within us; all will confess it that after death it will be so, grace being swallowed up into glory, faith into vision, hope into possession, and love into the Lord himself fully revealed in us. Now if this glory, that beatifical vision, and full possession of God, even the sight of his face, be in this life, 'tis plain, Rev. 22.1, 2, 3, 4. (p.179)

THE TEMPLE OF GOD ARE YE

The Temple of God are ye, and ye the people of God are the men I speak of; your gifts and graces, you worship as God within you.

I will not speak of your dependance on your faith, as Papists do on Good-works, though their good works do more glorifie God, and do more good to men, then your dead faith without works, which doth no good to men, nor to your selves: that faith which worketh by love, is good and profitable to your selves; but your good works are profitable to all men, and to the praise of God, but where that faith, or love, or good works are, among the people of God, is a question. (p.180)

PRAY, WHAT'S THE LIGHT OF NATURE THEN? IS IT NOT GOD IN MEN TOO?

This is clear, their gifts and graces they make a God: for ask them, how know they that God is in them? for this they grant, but not God in the wicked. Well, how know you then that God is in you? because of our gifts and graces, say they, because the light of grace is in us. Pray, what's the light of nature then? Is it not God in men too? What's that light that enlighteneth every man that cometh into this world? is it not the true light? Is not this light God and Christ in us? is it not the word, and the word of God? read your Bible better, Joh.1.

Again, Do not all men live, move, and have their being in God? and did not Paul present every man in Christ? Was not Christ or God in them the light shining in darkness, though the darkness comprehended it not? and yet the light is there, John 1.5, 9; Acts 1.28; Col. 1.28.

Thirdly, The teachings of God in you, your spiritual knowledge, you confess to be God enlightning and teaching you; but whose that in the Plowman, and in the Thresher, that teacheth him to plow and sow, and thresh in season? is it not God in him that's his God, God in union with him? for 'tis God that doth instruct him to discretion, and doth teach him, Isa. 28.24, 25, 26, 27, 28, 29 verses, yea, the threshers work. This also cometh from the Lord, who is wonderful in counsel, and excellent in working.

'Tis a certain Truth, that most Saints make their gifts and graces to be God in them; therefore when these wither in them, or they wanting in either they question whether they be the people of God; and so godly people have been formerly in a spirit of bondage and fear, through the Teachings of men. (p.180)

PROUD THEY ARE OF THEIR HUMILITY

Again, When these gifts are great, and their graces appear; Oh how pert they are! how they please themselves and despise all others; yea, proud they are of their humility, and humble themselves to their own thoughts and designs, Isa. 2.9. (p.181)

LEGAL RIGHTEOUSNESS [AND] *EVANGELICAL EXCELLENCY... TO BE OFFERED UP AS A DEAD CARKASE*

This is the Altar, the eternal power and Godhead, sacrificing all that is of man to himself, yea all that is of God also, below himself; our gifts of nature and grace, all the goodliness of flesh, or any thing below God, must be offered up as a dead carkase: then comes the coal from the Altar to cleanse us. Yea, I count all things but dung for the excellency of the knowledge of Christ Jesus my Lord: that is, not my Legal righteousness only, but all my Evangelical excellency, my gifts and graces, as Master Perkins well expounds.[3] (p.182)

THEY ARE MINE, AND I AM THEIR'S, THEREFORE I CANNOT GO AWAY FROM THEM

Truly the life of the people of God, and mine also, is so unlike Christ, that I have often wisht my self with the Prophet in the wilderness, and to go away from my self, and from my people; they are mine, and I am their's, therefore I cannot go away from them; though they and I be never so bad, God will make us both better, when we see ourselves the worst of men. (p.182)

READY FOR THE PRESSE

The Petition of the High Court of Heaven, in behalf of the Nation (with the Alarm) was ready for the Presse, but I suppress't it for a time, not only out of fear of man, but in love to the People of GOD (especially those in Power) some of them being honest men; for their sake I am silent, till these be as bad as the rest, or the rest be better.[4] (p.183)

27

An Olive Leaf 1653/4

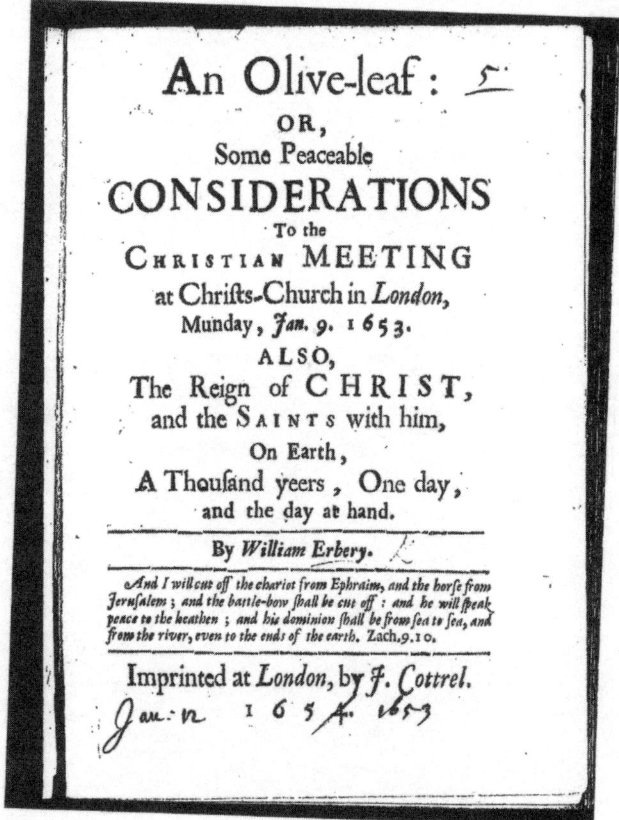

An Olive-leaf: 5

OR,

Some Peaceable

CONSIDERATIONS

To the

CHRISTIAN MEETING

at Chrifts-Church in *London*,

Munday, *Jan.* 9. 1653.

ALSO,

The Reign of CHRIST,

and the SAINTS with him,

On Earth,

A Thoufand yeers, One day,

and the day at hand.

By *William Erbery*.

And I will cut off the chariot from Ephraim, and the horfe from Jerufalem; and the battle-bow fhall be cut off: and he will fpeak peace to the heathen; and his dominion fhall be from fea to fea, and from the river, even to the ends of the earth. Zach.9.10.

Imprinted at *London*, by *J. Cottrel.*

Jan: 12 1654. 1653

An Olive-leaf: OR, Some Peaceable CONSIDERATIONS to the Christian MEETING at Christs-Church in London, Munday, Jan. 9. 1653.
ALSO, The Reign of CHRIST, and the SAINTS with him, On Earth, A Thousand yeers, One day, and the day at hand.
By William Erbery.
Imprinted at London by J. Cottrel, 1654.
(Received into the Thomason Collection on January 12th, 1653/4)

THREE TRACTS WERE written and published during the final months of Erbery's life. Written in January, February and March 1653/4, they responded to specific occasions, and were directed at particular audiences. *An Olive Leaf,* published in January 1653/4 was received by Thomason on January 12th, and *The Man of Peace, or a second Olive Leaf,* entered the Thomason Collection on February 14th, 1653/4. Both were printed in London by James Cottrel – the J. C. who printed for Giles Calvert. Calvert had not been involved with *The North Star*, published in November 1653, nor these tracts of early 1654. Yet he later served as publisher of *The Testimony* in 1658. In 1653 Calvert began publishing Quaker writings, and in 1654 he issued or sold thirty-eight known new titles. Of these, thirty were by Quaker authors.[1] Was this the reason Calvert did not publish Erbery's most political writings?

The titles of *An Olive Leaf* and *The Man of Peace* reflect Erbery's intentions. His long association with the congregation meeting at Christ Church, Newgate, enabled him to empathize with the motives of the Fifth Monarchists. The Fifth Monarchists had believed that the Nominated Parliament anticipated the coming of Christ's Kingdom. However, parliament split over the issue of tithes. The Fifth Monarchist MPs held meetings with Christopher Feake and his congregation at Blackfriars, but on December 12th, 1653, parliament was dissolved and power handed over to Cromwell.[2] In the new constitution, The Instrument of Government, the country became a protectorate with Cromwell as Lord Protector, assisted by a small council. Legislative power was to be exercised by a parliament which would meet on September 3, 1654.

The Fifth Monarchists were furious at this sign of apostasy by Cromwell and his fellow generals. He had betrayed the cause and was an obstacle to the reign of King Jesus. John Rogers,[3] Christopher Feake,[4] vicar of Christ Church, Newgate Street (and lecturer at both St Anne, Blackfriars and All-Hallows-the-Great) and Vavasor Powell[5] were bitter and angry at what they perceived as Cromwell's treachery. On Sunday, December

18th at Christ Church, Newgate, they called Cromwell 'the dissemlingest villain in the world'. On the following evening, at Blackfriars, Feake inferred that Cromwell was the Little Horn and Powell asked the congregation, "Lord, wilt thou have Oliver Cromwell or Jesus Christ to reign over us?" Feake and Powell were taken into custody but remained there for only three days (December 21–24).

Erbery knew he was entering a political and theological maelstrom, a position not unfamiliar to our controversialist! It had been part of his life from his encounter at Lambeth Palace in the 1630s, the Oxford debates of 1646/7 and notably in his trial at Westminster in 1653. Although Erbery understood the motives of the Fifth Monarchists, he also had confidence in The Instrument of Government which had replaced the Nominated Parliament.

An Olive Leaf reported on a meeting at Christchurch on January 9th, 1653/4. Erbery respected Rogers and Powell and the rest of the good people of Christchurch, and he tried to persuade them to understand Cromwell's intentions. He also pleaded with the government to understand the motives of the Fifth Monarchists. Because they shared many convictions, they should seek a compromise. Can they cooperate for the sake of the nation and help fulfill the principles of the Kingdom?

Erbery knew the Fifth Monarchist leaders well. Christchurch, Newgate had been his spiritual home for many years. Who had changed in their millenarian views? Erbery remained convinced that the Third Dispensation was imminent. The Fifth Monarchists were so certain that the Nominated Parliament was the precursor of the reign of Christ, that when it collapsed, so did their millennial dreams.

Their brief imprisonment in late December had no effect on Feake and Powell. The January meeting at Christchurch reveals that they were adamant in their opposition to the new government. Consequently Feake and John Simpson were both arrested and imprisoned in Windsor Castle. A warrant was also issued on January 10th for Vavasor Powell but he escaped to Wales. John Rogers remained at liberty and continued to preach his inflammatory sermons.

FOR MR. ROGERS, MR. POWEL, AND THE REST OF THE GOOD PEOPLE OF CHRIST-CHURCH

FROM BLACK-FRYERS TO CHRISTS-CHURCH

Christian Friends,

I am forced in Spirit to speak, though in much affliction and fear to offend, either to hurt the weak or harden the strong.

'Tis a mercy to you, and a Mystery of Providence to bring you from Black-Fryers to Christs-Church; for as the face of blackness hath lately appeared on your Fellowships: so some have lookt (though I do not) on your actings as Jesuitical, and a Fryerly-Spirit, in your publique speakings against the present Powers: for as Luther himself never declaimed against the Pope as a secular Prince, but as a spiritual Lord: so the people of God ever since have been silent in their sufferings under Civil Governments, though Church Governours, have fallen even by this, their medling with State-matters, and muttering abroad things they know not. (p.184f.)

CHURCH RULERS... FELL BY THEIR OWN BREATH

So Church Rulers being fired by their approaching fall, fell by their own breath: the Bishops or Prelats (whom nothing could throw down, but their own protesting against the House of Lords acting in their absence) were cast and caught in a Premunire against the King. Thus the Presbyters were judged for complying with the Scots and preaching against the English Parliament; This some Independent Pastors also opposed in their publick teachings before; therefore their own Parliament was dissolved, and another power is risen, which because they see not in the Lord, therefore they spake against it, and so their own breath has devoured them. (p.185)

THAT YOU AND I MAY RETIRE INTO THE INNER WORLD

...that you and I may retire into the inner World, and not dwell in the outward Court, which is given to the Gentiles, nor to expect the reign of the Saints with Christ, in outward glory and Government. Rev. 11.2, 17, 18. (p.185)

HE (JOHN ROGERS) INTERPRETED AS THE DISSEMBLING OF SOME IN POWER

'Twas much upon my spirit then to reply to what I heard from you both at Christs-Church, but I would not trouble your publick meeting.

Mr. Rogers spake from Jer. 42.20. Ye dissembled in your hearts, when ye sent me unto the Lord your God, saying, Pray for us, &c.

This he interpreted as the dissembling of some in power, to ask the Prayers of the Prophets and people of God in their troubles, who now act contrary to their own professed purposes of no Personal rule, and contrary to their promises of Remonstrated Liberty to all. (p.185)

NOT TO OFFEND MR. ROGERS

First, It was on my heart to ask you, Are you the Prophets of the Lord, as Jeremiah was, or are ye Ministers of the Gospel, as Paul, &c?

Secondly, Do you speak of the people [of] *God, as confined to your gathered Churches, or the People of God, scattered in the Nation.*

Thirdly, Were your thoughts their's; or were they all taken up with you in the Parliament lately dissolved?

Fourthly, Did not the people of God in general pray, or wait for, not what was to be set up as a Crown on the head of a particular party, or sect, but what might (with God) arise for the good of the Saints, and Nation in common?

Fifthly, Not to make comparisons of parties again, is not the appearance of God as glorious in the 7000 Saints scattered and secret in Israel, as those in gathered Churches...? I King. 19.18.

Sixthly, Not to offend Mr. Rogers; did he speak by a Prophetick or an Apostolique Spirit? were his last proposals to the Parliament, or now to the Lord Protectour, suitable to a Gospel-state, which he professeth? I am sure his former proposals for way of Government were meerly legal, and far below that Glory the Saints are waiting for in themselves, and to the Nation also, Zach. 12.7, 8.

Seventhly, Let me ask, Is it according to the order of the Gospel, for Ministers of Christ to meddle with Civill Government, seeing his Kingdome is not of this World? Joh. 18.36. Luk. 22.25.

Eighthly, Did ever the Ministers of the Gospel speak against Principalities and Powers, though as bad as Nero?

Ninthly, Doth Civil Government concern the glory of the Gospel? is Monarchy in a King any more against the reign of Christ, then Aristocracy in a Parliament? Is not the State of Holland, and Commonwealth of Venice, as much for Antichrist, as the King of France, or Spain?

Tenthly, Will not Christ when he comes to reign, put down all Authority, Power and Rule? Not onely Monarchical Authority but Aristocratical Power, and Democratick Rule? not that Rulers shall not be over men, but God alone will appear to be King over All.

Eleventhly, When God shall be all in all, there shall be but one King in all the Earth, and his name one. Zach. 14.9 then the names of Presbyter, Independent, and Anabaptist shall cease in the Church yea, the names of Cavaleer, Round head, and Romanist shall be no more heard in the Commonwealth.

Twelfthly, Is it not for peace to satisfie all interests, and to coement the divided Spirits of the Nation, that all Englishmen should become as one, when none shall be received before other? You say that the worst of men speak well of the present Government; and is it not well? and a fair way for peace and love? (p.185f.)

MY BROTHER'S (MR POWEL) CONCEITS WERE TOO CARNAL

As for my dear Countreyman, Mr. Powels preaching, I could not but cleave to his peaceable spirit at the end of his Sermon, perswading his brethren to meddle no more with Civil matters, but to speak of spiritual glories, which he held forth in the Reign of Christ, and the Saints with him on Earth.

But because (me thought) my Brother's conceits were too carnal and earthly of this heavenly mystery, and besides he gave me leave to object, I shall in meeknesse and fear, give a reason of the hope that is in me concerning this.

First, 'Tis plain that Christ is a Mystery which he and I do not yet clearly know, nor can manifest unto men; having not the manifestation of the Spirit, given to the Apostles and primitive Churches.

Secondly Christ in us the hope of glory being that mystery of God not to be finished till the seventh Trumpet blow...

Fourthly, Christ in us the hope of glory is this to me, that the glory he had with God before the World (though vailed in his flesh, while living) (yet after that his pure flesh was sacrificed and slain unto God by death) was fully revealed in the Resurrection...

Fifthly, Christ was raised a spirituall body, and though nothing but flesh appeared to his Disciples (not able to behold his glory), yet that he was a spirituall and glorious body indeed, appears by this, that our bodies shall be spirituall also in the mystery of the Resurrection, much more was his body spiritual when raised.

Sixthly, Therefore Christ in us is called the Hope of Glory, because God being in our flesh as in his, we have hereby hope, to be raised up in the same Glory or heavenly Image, and to attain to the Resurrection of the dead: that God even the Father may fully appear in our flesh as in him raised from death; that God may be all in all.

Seventhly... in the fellowship of his sufferings in our flesh, we come to the power of his Resurrection, and appearance of that glory in us...

Tenthly, As Christ when raised began to raign, God exalting him at his right hand to be a Prince and a Saviour, and to give forth the Spirit on the Saints: so the Saints reign with Christ must needs be in the Spirit also...

Eleventhly, 'Tis no Earthly Government or worldly glory is promised to the Saints. (p.186ff.)

THAT HE SHALL COME IN FLESH AGAIN, I QUESTION

Whether Christ shall come to reign personally in flesh, and how, I know not: but that he shall come in flesh again (as you said) I question, if it be not far from that spirituall appearance promised. Zech. 14.5, 9.

1. For if it be now a spirituall body, what's the fleshly one you speak shall appear?

2. If he come again on earth in flesh, how can he appear to all the Saints at once?

3. A fleshly body can be but circumscriptively in one place at once; therefore to meet with all the Saints then on earth, Christ must move swifter then the sun, here and there; not onely from East to West, but every where, North and South.

4. What his spiritual body is, I may shew you (with God) another time; and how in all places and persons, though it appear not as yet.

5. How Jesus came in like manner to the disciples, as they saw him go into Heaven, (Acts 1.11) was told you in the Call to the Churches, the Letter to Mr. Vavasor Powel.

8. ...when that spirit or power of God in me, shall appear in you, ye (though living in the flesh) shall see your life in the Father alone: for, in that day ye shall know that I am in the Father, and you in me, and I in you. Joh. 14.18, 19, 20. (p.188f.)

THIS MONARCHICAL GOVERNMENT OF CHRIST, AND THE SAINTS OF THE MOST HIGH WITH HIM, WILL NOT BE IN WORLDLY GOVERNMENT AND GLORY

Sir, you had three distinctions of the Reign of Christ: I'll tell you a fourth from your own. 1. Providential, over the Nations. 2. Spiritual, over the Church. 3. Monarchical, over the Church and Nations together. Zach. 14.8, 9, 11 compared.

But this Monarchical Government of Christ, and the Saints of the most high with him, will not be in worldly Government and glory...

The Saints of the most High are not those who are falsly accused; as living above Ordinances, for they are far below them; but those who live above earthly things in the Lord alone. These are said, not to be wasted and worried by the last King, but he shall wear them out, wear out their Spirits, in waiting for that righteousnesse which appeares not, for that Truth and peace, pity, tendernesse, mercy, justice, and goodnesse waited for in good men when they come to reigne, but all this will be in the reigne of Christ, when God alone shall reign in Men. Psal. 72.1, 2, 3; 4.12, 13. (p.189f. p.190 is printed as 238)

THE SAINTS... SHALL HAVE A SPIRIT OF JUDGEMENT TO DISCERN ARIGHT OF RULE AND GOVERNMENT

But these two things I observe from Daniel [Chapter 7]... *not that the Saints of the most high shall be in outward Government, and regal Authority, as other Princes have been; but when the greatest and most glorious Kingdoms and Common-wealths shall be so shaken and torn, and tatter'd, so divided and dasht in pieces, that no man will take up a Crown in the Streets; then judgement shall be given to the Saints, (they shall have a spirit of judgement to discern aright of Rule and Government) and the Saints shall possesse the Kingdome, v.20. That poor thing, a Kingdom, which no man would take up or be troubled with, that the Saints shall take, v.18. and possesse in peace living in God above all the powers of man, above all confusions and changes, and above all the trouble on earth, v.25. for Daniels cogitations were troubled, and his countenance changed to thinke of those evils approaching in the last times unto men, and mighty ones, v.28.* (p.190, printed as 238)

SO MANY SAINTS SHOULD INTERPRET THE THOUSAND YEARS, SO CARNALLY

...his Kingdome is for ever: and truely 'tis marvailous to me, that so many Saints should interpret the thousand years, so carnally, when themselves confesse that all the Revelation besides, is a mystery, or spiritual secret. Yet the thousand must needs be ten hundred yeares just. (p.190, printed as 238)

THE MIGHTY GOD, WHO HATH APPEARED SO GLORIOUSLY IN THEM, AND IN FORMER PARLIAMENTS, AND IN ARMY TOO

...because the present Government is judged with so much dissembling and breach of Vowes, let me end with this brief Apology, not for man (as I said before), but for the mighty God, who hath appeared so gloriously in them, and in former Parliaments, and in Army too, that he hath

stained the pride of all glory, and the glory of all flesh, tumbling the earth upside down, and tossing to and fro the Government therof, that nothing but confusion hath appeared; what certainly then can be expected in such changes? what order in confusion? yea what Truth, when God is making man a lye? Isay. 40.6, 7, 13 to 17, what Oaths of Allegiance? what Covenants broken? yet in both, hands have been lifted up to Heaven by honest hearts: what Protestations, Remonstances, and Engagements are gone and vanished? First we were all for the King, then for none, yet for King and Parliament we fought, then for neither: once we professed for the house of Lords, but these were presently laid aside: then for the Commons onely, and yet not for that, but for a Parliament or Representative; this dis-appeares also: and now for King and Parliament again, and yet for neither; for all is nothing because God is all in all. Isay. 40.17. (p.191, printed as 291)

THAT THE PEOPLE OF GOD CAN BE QUIET, AND SIT STILL IN PEACE

And if it be possible, that the people of God can be quiet, and sit still in peace, under their own Vine and Figg tree waiting for the glorious appearance of the great God and Saviour in themselves; that the Nations about may be brought in and saved at last, and joyne to the Lord with them, Zach. 2.10, 11; Rev. 21.24. (p.191, printed as 291)

THE PEOPLE OF GOD ARE IN PRESENT POWER (AS 'TWAS NEVER BEFORE)

And seeing the Princes of Israel begin to appear, and the people of God are in present power (as 'twas never before) I hope they will hear what has been said by their brethren, though carryed forth with much zeal, which (being according to their knowledge, and that knowledge the light of God in them, and they led forth with that boldness and that forbearance appearing in the powers also, and such peace and love still abiding in both, tells me that these wars and wranglings will shortly cease in the Nation, in which God will so appear with power and glory, that all the Nations about shall be broken, or brought in with us at last to the Government of Jesus.

That is, when God alone shall reign in Men, and Men reign in Righteousness, and Righteousness arise in truth, then shall the Royal Law, and Rule of Christ in love be followed: That Men and Magistrates shall do to all as they would be done unto, or rather, do to Men as God would. That's the Reign of Christ, and God in Men. (p.191f. printed as 291f.)

28

The Man of Peace 1653/4

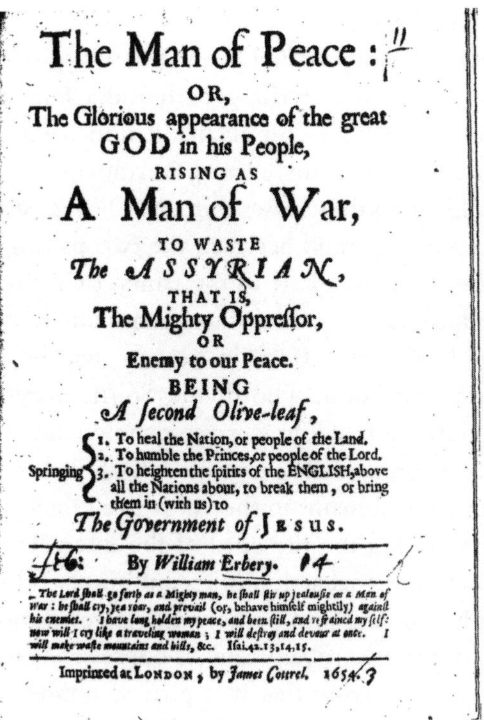

The Man of Peace:

OR,

The Glorious appearance of the great GOD in his People,

RISING AS

A Man of War,

TO WASTE

The ASSYRIAN,

THAT IS,

The Mighty Oppressor,

OR

Enemy to our Peace.

BEING

A second Olive-leaf,

Springing
1. To heal the Nation, or people of the Land.
2. To humble the Princes, or people of the Lord.
3. To heighten the spirits of the ENGLISH, above all the Nations about, to break them, or bring them in (with us) to

The Government of JESUS.

By *William* Erbery.

The Lord shall go forth as a Mighty man, he shall stir up jealousie as a Man of War: he shall cry, yea roar, and prevail (or, behave himself mightily) *against his enemies. I have long holden my peace, and been still, and refrained my self: now will I cry like a traveling woman; I will destroy and devour at once. I will make waste mountains and hills, &c.* Isai. 42. 13, 14, 15.

Imprinted at LONDON, by *James Cottrel*. 1654.

The Man of Peace: OR,
The Glorious appearance of the great GOD in his People,
RISING AS A Man of War, TO WASTE The ASSYRIAN, THAT IS,
The Mighty Oppressor, OR Enemy to our Peace.
BEING A second Olive-Leaf, Springing
1.To heal the Nation, or people of the Land.
2. To humble the Princes, or people of the Lord.
3. To heighten the Spirits of the ENGLISH, above all the Nations about,
to break them, or bring them in (with us) to
The Government of JESUS. By William Erbery.
Imprinted at London, by James Cottrel. 1654.
(Received into the Thomason Collection on February 14th, 1653/4)

ERBERY WROTE *AN Olive Leaf* after attending the meeting at Christchurch, Newgate on January 9th, 1653/4. A few days later, Christopher Feake and John Simpson were arrested and imprisoned in Windsor Castle. Erbery then wrote *The Man of Peace… Being A Second Olive-leaf.* Thomason received it into his collection on February 14th, 1653/4. James Cottrel was again responsible for printing.

Christchurch, Newgate had been Erbery's spiritual home for many years, and he was writing to friends. The treatise has a personal touch. He hopes for reconciliation between the Fifth Monarchists and the Cromwellian government. He reminds his readers that his intention in writing *An Olive Leaf* had been to show the common ground between the two parties. The *Man of Peace* was directed particularly to the saints at Christchurch.

In the Third Dispensation, the Christchurch on earth and Christ Church, the First Born in heaven, will be united. God never abandons creation. The divine Spirit, manifested in the weakness and strength of Christ is also manifested in the weakness and strength of humankind. God in Christ in his weakest and loneliest moments, remains in the saints in all their vulnerability.

From interpreting the presence of the internal Spirit, Erbery turned to God's external action in recent history. His readers had lived through civil war and participated in revolution. God had removed an oppressive royalty and an oppressive parliament, and Erbery warned the Army that if it proved oppressive, it would be overthrown by the Spirit of the Lord, and the sword of his mouth. Erbery reminds the people of Christchurch of how the saints had been persecuted. Puritans had been forced to flee to 'strange Countries', but now for the first time in history, God had ensured that England was to be governed righteously. Erbery speaks with confidence about the present administration. He had never been afraid to speak against the establishment, arguing his case against Archbishop Laud, parliamentary delegates led by Francis Cheynell, and had been acquitted of the charge of heresy by the Committee for Plundered Ministers. Now, perhaps for the first time in his life, he defends the government!

After a decade of civil war, Erbery was confident that Cromwell's concern and administration focussed on national righteousness. This had been one of the motifs behind Erbery's ministry and writings. He was now confident that authority would be exercised wisely and justly. God's people were finally coming into power in England, and this would serve as an ensign for the future of all nations. History was reaching its conclusion with the fulfilment of God's purposes.

The saints should respond to the present government with 'sweet reproofs or strong rebukes'. The sword is to be replaced by pen and tongue and prayer. What of the imprisonment of Christopher Feake and John Simpson? They are like John the Divine at Patmos, and perhaps they too will experience a revelation.

The Man of Peace ends with the following sentence: 'When this is done, the prophesie is finished, and my work is ended.' It may be possible to read too much into these lines, but it is strange that, apart from *Jack Pudding*, probably Erbery's slightest work, this should have been Erbery's final word. There is however a postscript in which Erbery promises that his next publication will be 'That which is to highten the Spirits of the English, &c. shall be next, if God will'. This title was included in the original contents of *The Man of Peace,* but was either not written in time for publication, or a decision was made to omit it. What is certain is that it was never published. Erbery was dead within two months.

FOR MASTER FEAK, MASTER SIMPSON, AND ALL THE MEMBERS OF CHRIST'S CHURCH

THE MEMBERS OF CHRIST'S CHURCH

My Brethren,

I Spake last, for the peace of the State; now I shall a word for yours (and all the Saints with you) in bonds. Heb. 13.3…

The members of Christ's Church, I mean the Church of the

First-born written in Heaven, which I hope to see on earth with you in spiritual glory; when all the scattered Saints, scattered in forms and flesh are gathered up into One, and One in All. (p.202)

MAN IS BECOME ONE WITH GOD IN CHRIST THE GOD-MAN

I shall not preach, but present in haste a few Proposals to your prudent and pious considerations, in certain Queries and Answers following…

Q. *How is this man the Peace?*

A. 1. By taking mans flesh into union with God in himself, and manifesting that Union in us by the Spirit. That is, though the Spirit appear not in men as yet, nor doth manifest their union with God; yet that Man is become One with God in Christ the God-Man, is manifest by this. 1. Because he is Immanuel, God with us, not God with him only, but God with us is Christ. 2. He shall save his people from their sins: that is, not only his people the Jews, that Nation, but the Gentiles, or Nations, that's joy to all people; he being born not only a child to Us, but the Saviour of the World. 3. From the worst of men Christ came according to the flesh: Rahab the harlot was his Grandmother, and Manasseth the murtherer his forefather, as well as Hezekiah and good Josiah: for Christ was not only the son of Abraham the faithful, but the son of Adam the fallen, Mat. 1.1, 5, 10; Luke 3.38 compared. 4. All the sons and daughters of men may therefore see themselves in God with Christ, Isa. 45.22, 5. No son of Adam, but is one with the Son of God, if men had the power to present every man in Christ, Col. 1.28, 6. Not only the Apostles, but the Poet saith, we are the off-spring of God; and the Poets saying is canonized as Scripture by the Apostle: for in him we live, move, and have our being, Acts 17.28. We, that's all men, for no Saints were there present with the Apostle: and the Poet spake not of Saints, but of Men with himself; that we are his off-spring. 7. Our own Catechisms tell us, that not any mans person, but the whole humane nature was taken up with Christ in God. (p.203f.)

CHRIST... PERFECTLY ONE WITH GOD... WE ARE ONE WITH GOD

Therefore God did crucifie and slay that flesh to himself, made it weak as ever mans was, a worm and no man, that God might appear to be all in all. And as Christ in his greatest weakness, and lowest state of flesh, when he fainted, and feared, and cried out as a man forsaken of God, was as perfectly one with God, as when he was in highest glory, in his mighty works of wonder, and most gracious words: so we, though troubled, tempted, sorrowful to the death and sinking to despair, as he, may yet be sure we are one with God: and though his pure flesh in us, our gifts, graces, joy, peace, and spiritual strength, be so weakned and wasted, crucified and slain, that nothing but the face of death appears without and within us; yet we, I say, even in this dead estate of flesh, are as perfectly one with the Father and his love to us, as his beloved, and our life in him as pure, as the Son's was when dying, and as ours appears to us in our highest attainments, and most heavenly enjoyments, &c. Thus is this Man the Peace. (p.204)

CHRIST DOTH APPEAR, AND APPEAR IN US, AS OUR PEACE, AND OUR PEACE PERFECTED IN SUFFERING

Q. But who is the Assyrian?

A. The oppressive power of man, and in man.

First, I say, the Oppressive power in man, is the Assyrian: that is, the weakness of the flesh, besides the strength of corruption, our infirmities, fears, faintings of spirit, spiritual desertions, and seeming forsakings of God, this doth oppress us; but then when Christ doth appear, and appear in us, as our peace, and our peace perfected in suffering, and our sufferings now become his, (for he suffers in us, and in all our afflictions he is afflicted) all this doth refresh, and fully satisfie, yea free us from the inward Assyrian, the oppressor within, being the power of flesh oppressing our spirits, or the weakness of flesh when the Spirit is ready to rise, &c. Matth. 26.41; Rom. 7.18, 23. (p.204f.)

THE KEEPERS OF THE LIBERTY OF ENGLAND WERE KEEPERS INDEED

But as there is an Oppressor in man, so the Oppressor of man is some man (or men) without, called the Assyrian, or King of Babylon who carries us captive, and keeps us in bondage in our spirits and states: but we shall be delivered from both, when we shall rule over our oppressor, Isa. 14.2...

For as Egypt and Assyria were the only two great Powers who kept the people of God in bondage formerly according to the Type: so in Truth King and Parliament, in this Land were the two Powers, who kept the people of the Lord and the people of the Land from their expected and promised freedoms. For the Keepers of the Liberty of England were Keepers indeed, and of our Liberties from us. (p.205.)

THE SPIRIT OF THE LORD IN THEM RAISED A PARLIAMENT... **[AND]** ***AN ARMY... WE SHALL RAISE... SUFFICIENT STRENGTH AND MOST PERFECT ABILITY***

Q. How shall the people of God raise forces against the Assyrian, or Oppressive powers of men?

A. Not by power, nor by might, (or Army, saith the margin) but by my Spirit, saith the Lord, Zech. 4.6.

The people of God under the King, had no power nor might to resist him, but the Spirit of the Lord in them raised a Parliament against him, even seven shepherds and eight principal men, or Princes (as the margin reads) for as the Commons were as the Shepherds, who stood for the Country; so the house of Lords were as the principal men; or Princes of men, which have Crowns in their Arms.

Again when a corrupt Parliament oppress'd the people, who raised up an Army, first to purge, then to dissolve them? The Spirit or power of God in his people in City and Country, and in the Army too.

If this third Power prove to be the Assyrian, we shall raise against him seven shepherds and eight principal men; yea, a sufficient strength and most perfect ability in the Lord to waste Assyria with the sword: that is, the Spirit of the Lord, and sword of his mouth, shall as surely slay them, as ever Kingly power was by the mouth of the Sword. (p.206)

THESE KINGS, WITH THEIR NOBLES, LORDS, AND DUKES, ALL PROCEEDED FROM A CURSED PEDIGREE

But Nimrod was an oppressive power, he was a mighty hunter before the Lord, Gen. 10.9. that's cunning and cruel to destroy both man and beast. So the former Kings of England have been, not only King James, but William the Conqueror, was a mighty hunter wasting all Hampshire to make room for his game: but God met with his son Rufus in the sport, causing a shaft aim'd at the Deer to shoot thorow the Kings heart.

Again, former Kings were mighty hunters before the Lord; that is, hunters of his people, whom they persecuted to strange Countries. Therefore the Kingly posterity is now hunted out of their own Countrey also, and fain to run to and fro in forrain Lands for relief.

Nimrod that Kingly power has been from the beginning, and gone on in a race of oppression over the people of God: yet have these Kings, with their Nobles, Lords, and Dukes, all proceeded from a cursed Pedigree. (p.206f.)

IN THE THIRD DISPENSATION NOW APPROACHING... THE STATE IS TO ACT IN CHRIST

...seeing we wait for a new Heaven and a new earth, wherein dwelleth righteousness, and this righteousness is promised to be on earth as well as in heaven; that is, in the Civil as well as Ecclesiastick state (for our officers shall be peace, and our exacters righteousness), therefore in the third dispensation now approaching (wherein the people of God are in highest power), all things in heaven and earth shall be gathered up into Christ not only the Saints in common, but the State is to act in Christ, and as Christ Jesus would do to men. (p.208)

THOSE ROCKS, WHEREON FORMER KINGS AND PARLIAMENTS WERE WRACKT AND RUINED

Therefore his Members and brethren are bold in the Lord, not to dishonour, but to admonish the highest in power, not to run on those rocks, whereon former Kings and Parliaments were wrackt and ruined. The Parliament's Charybdis was their strangling (by delays) the Petitions of the fatherlesse and widow, of the poor and oppressed ones, while they sought themselves onely. That Scylla which spilt the King, was his setting up the state of his Court and Courtiers, preferring none but the rich, his friends and favorites, a company of fools and flatterers, though the oppressed peeled nation was ready to perish. And yet the King had a revenue of his own to maintain his Royalty: the glory and gallantry of his Palace, his babies and bawbles were no burden to the people. (p.208f.)

FROM THE MIDST OF SAINTS ONE IS RISEN ABOVE US

4. Though the name of Kings be now somwhat suspicious to the Saints, (therefore an Act was made by the late Parliament, that the name of Kingly power, and that unnecessary charge should cease) yet to me 'tis not so ominous seeing the Kings of the earth bring their glory & honour to the new Jerusalem, Rev. 21.24. But 5. seeing the nations are there said to be saved also, I believe ours is the first that shall be saved from all their oppressors and oppressions. 6. The ground of this to me is thus, because our Nobles begin to be of our selves, and our Prince or Governour to proceed from the midst of us, Jer. 30.21 that is, from the midst of Saints one is risen above us, and of the same spirit with us he is though not in Forms of Religion, wherein the Saints do differ, yet in the power of Righteousnesse we all agree: yea, our Prelatick brethren vowed in their Baptism to forsake the devil and all his works, the pomps and vanities of this wicked world; against which, God hath visibly appeared, plagueing the oppressing King and his proud Courtiers; yea, against that pomp and vanity the Saints have always protested, as being not sutable to the Spirit of Jesus, no, nor to the spirit of a Man: for who can see a poor Nation perishing for want of that fulnesse which is spent in meer superfluities? (p.209)

SETTING UP HIS THRONE IN THE HEARTS OF HIS PEOPLE

7. Though Christian Kings and Nobles, bewicthed [bewitched] *with the glory of the Earth have nothing to entertain one another, but their gawdy shews, and simple gallantry; yet are some heathen Kings as much in honour with God and men, though thy sit on a Carpet, and set up their throne in the boughs of trees: and so may an honest Christian Prince be as happy and honourable in a guard of Red-coats, as with the most gorgeous attendance and modes of Nobles.*

8. What a glory will this be for the nations about, to behold a man in the image and likenesse of God, cloathed with the robe of righteousnesse and garments of salvation, saving the Nation under him from all that needlesse expence which may be spared, and setting up his throne in the hearts of his people.

9. Though neither Scripture nor the Spirit of Jesus will suffer any scorn or reproach to be cast on the Powers ordained by him... yet are not Kings unlimited in their power, nor unaccountable to the People, as all the people of God, Parliament and Army, have formerly protested; but even the highest in Power has been curbed and cut off by force, yet still that Force had the face of Authority on it. For the sake of the Saints I believe it was so disposed by Divine wisdom, that fools might not reproach his people for Rebellion against their Prince or Parliament. (p.209f.)

THE POWER BEING NOW IN THE HANDS OF THE PEOPLE OF GOD

10. As the Parliament subdued the King, and the Army dissolved the Parliament, and the People had a hand in each (both Parliament and Army being the Peoples servants, as 'twas commonly voted) so the Power being now in the hands of the people of God, God will truly talk with them, if they offend; yea, trouble them too, if they oppresse...

...Oh! how many widows and fatherless children have perished by the late Parliament! yea men who were averse to War, those who never so much as fought for the King, are for ever undone and rob'd of their childrens portions, called the glory of God. Now as all Oppressions in the Land were charged on the Prince of Israel... the Parliament was a mighty man, by whom the King fell; and the Sword of the Army was as the mean man, by whom the Parliament fell. But there will be an oppressive Power that shall not fall by man, but by God he shall fall, by the sword of the Lord onely, by the Spirit of the Lord; this shall slay the Oppressor, but save the Power... yet the fire is in Zion still, a spirit of righteousnesse is so kindled in the people of the Lord, and in the people of the Land, that

it shall never be quenched, till a King comes to reign in righteousnesse, and Princes to rule in judgement, Isa. 32.1. (p.210f.)

'TIS LIKE THE LORD WILL BLESSE THE PRESENT GOVERNMENT

11. Therefore it is that some speak of a Publick spirit of righteousnesse risen of late in the world. It began first with us in England; it followed in France, though there the fire is fiercer, the flames more furious, and a greater confusion is comming on that Nation for the blood of the Saints that they have shed... [God] *makes the changes of Government in England so milde and peaceable, that the Nations about call it a miracle, to see neither a drop of blood nor a tear shed, scarce a sigh of the people, in the fall of their Princes, Zach. 12.4, 6 compared.*

12. That spirit of righteousnesse, that publicke spirit of liberty and freedom has been embondaged in former Ages by the spirit of Antichrist in the world, as Mr. Goodwin well observed in this Anticavalierism, p.31, 32, 36,[1] *for as the Priest and the Prince, the Mitre and Scepter were both supported each by other: so we read in the Revelation, that the Beast carries the Whore; the Civil state bears up the Ecclesiastick; and this bolsters up the other in all unrighteousnesse, that the Church might rule; for then the Rulers may rant... so 'tis like the Lord will blesse the present Government, because 'tis now as 'twas never before, that is, the Ecclesiastick state is not set up with the Civil power, nor sits in the throne, as formerly, and as 'tis in New-England this day...* (p.211)

YET THE SAINTS... CANNOT CLEARLY SEE THE LORD IN THE CLOUDS

13. Though this spirit of publicke righteousnesse be risen up in the Saints, yet the Saints (lying still in spiritual bondage in Babylon, in much confusion) cannot clearly see the Lord in the Clouds, nor yet men aright in these things, nor the wayes of God in the deep, nor the wayes of men in the dark, nor those crosse providences every day appearing as a wheel in a wheel, nor those whirlwindes without and within, which carry the best of men about so quick, and so high, and then down again in the dirt, as David was, that no Saint can stand or see clearly, what God will do with Man, and with Magistrates in this Nation. (p.211)

ALL THAT WILL BE HEREAFTER (I HOPE) SHALL BE ONELY BY SWEET REPROOFS, OR STRONG REBUKES

But though this publick spirit of righteousnesse, be not come forth so fully in the Saints, as to reprove Kings, and to binde them in Chaines, as it will be (for, this honour have all the Saints; and this will be so, till all the Saints be together empower'd with God, which is the reign of Christ) yet who knows, but that the first fruits of the Spirit begin to appear? some secret breathings after publick righteousnesse, some gaspings for peace, and glimpses of glory on earth... so the Saints begin to raign with God, already, in that sense aforesaid, Olive-leaf p.7.

Now this publike spirit of righteousnesse in the Saints so ruling the Nations, is not by Resisting, but by Reproving the Powers; not yet by reproaching them, but by strong rebukes. Indeed formerly the Saints have resisted (even for outward Liberty) unto blood; both King and Parliament can witnesse it also; but all that will be hereafter (I hope) shall be onely by sweet reproofs, or strong rebukes. (p.212)

THE LORD IN THEM, WHO HATH DONE ALL, AND ORDAINED THEM, AND SET THEM ON HIGH

'Tis true, some spiritual men and Ministers have formerly acted in secret against the Civil Powers, as Prelates with the Irish for the King, and Presbyters with the Scots against[2] *the Parliament; but our Independent brethren never did so, nor would act (I believe); onely they spake conscientiously, as they conceived, in zeal for their God, for the good of men, for the honour of Saints, for the safety of the nation, yea for the glory of the Government and Governours thereof in the reign of Christ, which though they mistake in, and have some misapprehensions in that spiritual mystery, yet (not acquainted with Mysteries of State, nor minde of God in all things) they spake simply plainly, and openly, not intending any secret Design, nor Commotion among men, but discharging their conscience in reproving the untruths and evils of Men. But God will turn all things to good.*

...so I deny not (as I said before) but there may be a beginning of the same spirit of publick righteousnesse and reproof too of Kings in the people of God this day.

Neither do I speak in this against the Powers, but for the Lord in them, who hath done all, and ordained them, and set them on high, not to throw them down again, I hope, but to exalt himself in them, and all the Saints with him, and all the nation with them in Peace and perfect freedom at last. (p.212)

THEY ARE RETIRED FOR A TIME WITH JOHN IN PATMOS

And as my brethren meant no hurt to the Powers, so the Powers intend no harm to them; (all is for peace and love) not to imprison, but onely to restrain them, not from their private liberty, but from the publick concourse and popular salutes which might rather oppress their spirits, then refresh them. Therefore they are retired for a time with John into Patmos, which was not a violent banishment. (p.212f.)

A POWER OF REPROOF SHALL APPEAR IN THE SAINTS, THAT THEY SHALL SMITE AND SLAY MEN WITH A WORD'S SPEAKING

But because we spake of those reproofs and strong rebukes before, let me tell you in a word, There is no way for peace, nor shall War ever cease, but onely by this: he shall rebuke many people; then shall they beat their swords into plow shares, &c. Isai. 2.4.

How will God rebuke but by men? and by what men more, then by the Saints? yea, by the People also, who shall rebuke, their Princes and Oppressors, as 'tis plain Isai. 19.20.

But how will God in the Saints rebuke the Powers of the earth? Why by the Spirit of Jesus in them, which shall make them of so quick understanding in the fear of the Lord that they shall judge, not after the sight of the eyes, nor reprove after the hearing of the ear. Here's a secret, that the Saints in the Lord shall judge men whom they never see and reprove what they never hear of by them. Isai. 11.3. How can this be? 'Tis answered vers. 4. With righteousnesse he shall judge the poor, and reprove with equity for the meek of the earth: that is, the Lord in his people is said to judge the poor. To judge here, is rightly to consider of their cause, or condition. And mark, 'tis with righteousnesse and equity they reprove, and for the meek of the earth, who sit still and are quiet in all their sufferings: yet can they see in God, and speak to God what is done among men, and by men cunning and cruel: therefore he shall smite the earth with the rod of his mouth and with the breath of his lips shall he slay the wicked, vers. 4. that as Christ with the breath of his lips made a band of souldiers to fall down backwards, John 18.3, 6 and as Peter by the word of his mouth slew the wicked hypocrites, even two at once, Acts 5.5, 10, so I believe 'twill be again, that such a power of reproof shall appear in the Saints, that they shall smite and slay men with a word's speaking. (p.213)

NOT NEW FORMS OF RELIGION, BUT A POWER OF RIGHTEOUSNESS IS EXPECTED NEWLY TO ARISE IN THE NATION... THAT'S THE NEW HEAVEN AND NEW EARTH WAITED FOR

So then, 'tis not so much by speaking in publicke unto men, or against men, but the Saints shall so see in God mens estates and spirits, that this shall be not onely a strong reproof, but a sure ruine of such in whom righteousnesse appears not: their rebukes being not verbal, but substantiall and strong, yea so fiery, that all before them shall fall.

I know what I say in this, by experience... but as God is a spirit, so in a spiritual, secret, and unknown manner, men are confounded and killed by some poor souls, who never see nor speak with their adversaries, who neither touch them, nor think a thought of evil against them; yet by those they are killed when once they appear against the Lord in them, and against that publicke righteousnesse so oft professed. Rev. 11.5.

Lastly, 'tis clear by the Word, that Kings and Nobles must be bound in chains at last, that they shall not do what they list, as Kings and Parliaments have done, but what the Saints in the Spirit shall direct and advise, not with command, or contempt to the Powers on earth, but by a heavenly approach to God, and by that appearance of

Righteousnesse in Him, which they wait to be revealed in themselves and in all, for the Nations peace.

'Tis true, the Saints have not been so bold of old, as to bring forth their spirits in publick, because the Power was not in the hands of the Saints, as now; who therefore must not think to play Rex, as they say, and to rant it as they please in all unrighteousnesse and riot, because there is a righteous generation, a pure and holy people left in the Nation, that shall never leave them alone, nor rest from calling upon them in publique, or (which is worst) crying to God in secret against them: yet not against them, but for them they pray, and yet against them those prayers will be, which are for them; never was it worse with King and Parliament, then when so many prayers were made; then all those prayers turned against them, because the Power of righteousnesse could not arise in either.

And this is the last reason, why of late times, some Saints have been taken up into the civil state, and others to speak so much of civil things in their most spiritual discourses, because God is going up now in higher discoveries of himself even in low things of the earth: for as there is a new heaven, and new earth (as I said) wherein dwelleth righteousnesse, so not new forms of religion, but a power of righteousnesse is expected newly to arise in the Nation, not onely in the Ecclesiastick, but in the Civil state, in Church and Common-Wealth, that's the new Heaven and new Earth waited for, when the Civil state shall be wholly spiritual. (p.214f.)

HE IS STARK BLIND WHO HATH NOT SEEN GOD ALREADY, RISING IN THE NATION, IN PARLIAMENT AND ARMY BEFORE; AND I HOPE HIGHER HEREAFTER IN THE PRESENT POWERS

Therefore 'tis a poor low thing what some Ministers talk of, that men must preach of nothing but Faith and Repentance, and run sixteen yeares backwards, (as one phraseth it) into old Puritanism again. This is a pretty thing indeed (whereas the world is on fire like Sodom) to look back with Lots wife, &c. or not forget what is behind with Paul, when the price of the high calling of God in Christ Jesus is not onely before us, but nearer to us then ever (the falling away being full, and Christ ready to come, and the face of God beginning to appear on our foreheads).

...surely he is stark blind who hath not seen God already, rising in the Nation, in Parliament and Army before; and I hope higher hereafter in the present Powers. (p.215)

WHEN THIS IS DONE, THE PROPHESIE IS FINISHED, AND MY WORK IS ENDED

That which follows is of more spiritual and inward concernment, he shall cry like a woman in travail, to bring forth his glory in our flesh: but our flesh (as Christs) must first suffer the pangs of child-bearing, Rev. 12.3 [should be 12.5], *or God in us, vailed in our flesh will cry, yea roare, before his glory be revealed with power; in this he destroys and devours at once all our fleshly strength and weaknesses too in himself, making waste mountains and hills, high men and things; mountains of imaginations, strong holds of carnal reasonings, and every high thought that exalts it self against the knowledge of God. When this is done, the prophesie is finished, and my work is ended.* (p.216)

POST-SCRIPT

That which is to highten the spirits of the English, &c. shall be next, if God will. In the mean while, if the Assyrian (or any forrain Force) shall dare to tread in our borders, we shall raise against him, seven shepherds, and eight principal men, a sufficient strength (in the Lord) by land and sea. However, This Man shall be the Peace. (p.216)

29

Jack Pudding 1653/4

Jack Pudding:

Or, A

MINISTER

Made

A Black-Pudding.

Preſented

To Mr. *R. Farmer* Parſon of *Ni-cholas* Church in *Briſtol*:

By *W. E.*

Ye have ſaid, 'Tis a vain thing to ſerve God, and, What profit is it that we have kept his Ordinance, and that we have walked mournfully, or (as the Hebrew reads) *that we have walked in black?* Mal.3.14.

To *ſerve* God, is not in Forms of Worſhip, *&c.* but in waiting continually on God, & following Chriſt, in the Croſs, or fellowſhip of his ſufferings, *Ioh.* 12. 24, 25, 26, 27.

Printed at LONDON.
1654.

Jack Pudding: Or, A MINISTER Made A Black-Pudding.
Presented To Mr. R. Farmer Parson of Nicholas Church in Bristol:
By W.E.
Printed at LONDON 1654.
(Received into the Thomason Collection on March 17th, 1653/4)

Jack Pudding, THE last of Erbery's tracts to be published in his lifetime (Thomason added it to his collection on March the 17th, 1654), is a kind of literary joke. Although it reminds us of Erbery's alert and humorous turn of phrase, the tract is worth preserving only because it lies within a much larger corpus. On its own, it would be a poor reflection of Erbery's life and work. Giles Calvert neither published nor included it in *The Testimony*. Possibly he did not think it worth preserving, and he wished to preserve Erbery's reputation.

The occasion of the tract was Erbery's visit to Bristol where 'the meer hand of providence having brought us thither', he met Morgan Llwyd. Invited to speak at St Nicholas Church, they were prevented from entering by Ralph Farmer, the vicar. Although they were eventually permitted to speak, Farmer later described the meeting in derogatory terms. Farmer had good reason to fear interruptions. On December 10th, 1653, Elizabeth Marshall, a Quaker, had harangued Farmer as he was about to administer communion at St Nicholas. Three years later, in 1656, Farmer published, *Sathan Inthroned in his Chair of Pestilence, Or, Quakerism in its Exaltation*, in which he expressed his abhorrence at James Nayler's Palm Sunday entry into Bristol. Farmer pointed out that Dorcas Erbury, William's daughter, was one of Nayler's disciples. Farmer had good reason to fear the presence of Llwyd and Erbery.

PROEME[1]

PRIESTS OR MINISTERS, AND THEIR ORDINANCES, WERE CONTEMNED OF GOD

There are two several times, wherein the Priests or Ministers, and their Ordinances, were contemned of God, and of men too at last. 1. When the Church was under Apostacie (as ours is)... 2. Not onely the Apostacie, but the approaching glory, or glorious appearance of the great God in his people, being at hand, doth cast contempt and a curse on the Church-Ministers, and their Ordinances...

This, I thought fit to premise unto the following Discourse, which might seo[e]m ridiculous to some; though serious Truths, both Religion and Reason, may appear therein to many. Farewel.

Thy W.E. (p.1)

JACK-PUDDING: SO HE WAS PLEASED TO CALL ME IN PUBLIKE

Before I come to my Text, I must begin with my Parson, a man at first but a Clerk, not Clerk of a Parish, but to a pettifogging Lawyer, or Committee, as they say; then a Maltster, now a Minister of the Gospel, or John of all trades, that's Jack-Pudding: so he was pleased to call me in Publike, at his Parish-meeting, where he was merry at the Jest; but I shall prove him in earnest to be that indeed, not onely a Jack, but a Black-Pudding. (p.1f.)

MR. MORGAN FLOYD OF NORTH-WALES, AND MY SELF OF THE SOUTH

The occasion of his Scomma[2] *was this: Mr. Morgan Floyd of North-Wales, and my self of the South, meeting together in Bristol, the meer hand of providence having brought us thither, not any particular designe, as some have imagined; we had liberty from God, with the love of men, and the Magistrates leave, to speak in publike, though the Minister Parson Farmer stole away the Keys, and kept the Church-doors fast, till by Authority they were opened for us, I mean for Mr. Floyd though I spake after he had ended.* (p.2)

MR. FARMER… CALLING ME HERETICK BY NAME, OR (WHICH IS WORSE) JACK PUDDING, AS MR. FLOYD MOUNTEBANK

The next day I departed the City, and the Sunday following Mr. Farmer like a coward comes behinde my back, and smites me in my absence, calling me Heretick by name, or (which is worse) Jack-pudding, as Mr. Floyd Mountebank, though he forbore to particularize my friend, who being in the City, sent a sober Chalenge to Mr. Farmer to meet him in publike or private to reason about things controverted, and censured by the said Farmer. But the man was so faint-hearted, he dar'd not appear, but refused the Gantlet, though he be as bold as a Lion in his Pulpit, and roars upon all that cannot conform or crouch to his Doctrine and Discipline. (p.2)

M. FARMER IS A JACK-PUDDING

...I once thought to question him in publike at his Church, but for peace sake I forbore, lest I might offend the worthy Governours and Citizens present.

For this cause, I publish it to the world, that not onely the Parson might repeat of his bitterness, his folly and frowardness but that his people might know, he is no Minister of Christ, nor a Christian man indeed.

This I prove, first, as a Scholar by Reason, then by Scripture, to all rational and religious men, in this short Enchymem:

M. Farmer is a Jack-pudding, Therfore no Minister of Christ (p.2)

But Mr. Farmer is made of fat and blood, and a black coat or skin about him:

Therefore he is a Black-pudding. (p.3)

...the Black Pudding before; for 'tis made of the blood of that: yea, this very Prophet in the same Chapter tels us, that he that offereth an oblation, is as he that offereth swines blood, Isa. 66.3. He that offereth is the Priest or Parson; and that he is the Pudding, is plain by the words, as read in the Original, where those words [as if he offered] *are not; but thus 'tis in the Hebrew: He that offereth an oblation, swines blood; that is, he that offereth is swines blood, or, a black Pudding.* (p.6) FINIS.

30

The Great Earthquake 1654

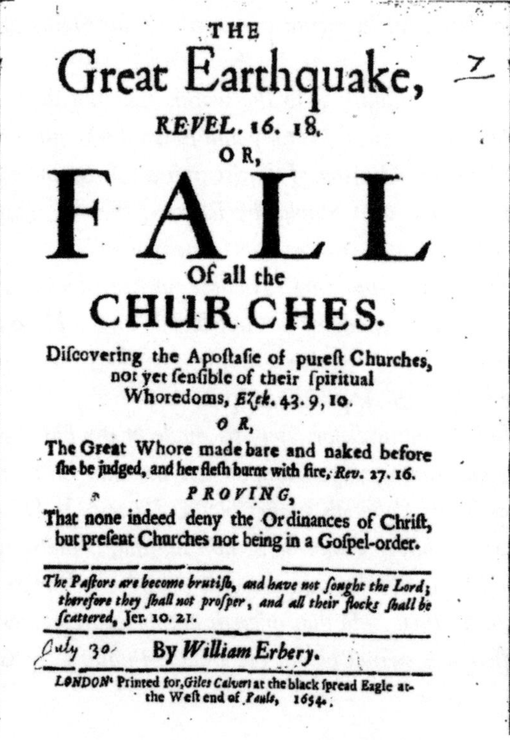

THE

Great Earthquake,

REVEL. 16. 18.

OR,

FALL

Of all the

CHURCHES.

Diſcovering the Apoſtaſie of pureſt Churches, not yet ſenſible of their ſpiritual Whoredoms, *Ezek.* 43. 9, 10.

OR,

The Great Whore made bare and naked before ſhe be judged, and her fleſh burnt with fire, *Rev.* 27. 16.

PROVING,

That none indeed deny the Ordinances of Chriſt, but preſent Churches not being in a Goſpel-order.

The Paſtors are become brutiſh, and have not ſought the Lord; therefore they ſhall not proſper, and all their flocks ſhall be ſcattered, Jer. 10. 21.

By *William Erbery.*

LONDON Printed for, *Giles Calvert* at the black ſpread Eagle at the Weſt end of *Pauls*, 1654.

THE Great Earthquake, REVEL. 16.18. OR, FALL Of all the CHURCHES.
Discovering the Apostasie of purest Churches, not yet sensible of their Spiritual Whoredoms, Ezek. 43. 9,10.
OR, The Great Whore made bare and naked before she be judged, and her flesh burnt with fire, Rev. 27.16. 1
PROVING, That none indeed deny the Ordinances of Christ, but present Churches not being in a Gospel-Order.
By WILLIAM ERBERY.
LONDON, Printed for, Giles Calvert at the black spread Eagle at the West end of Pauls, 1654.
(Received into the Thomason Collection on July 30th, 1654)

The Great Earthquake, published three months after Erbery's death entered the Thomason Collection on July 30th, 1654. The treatise is well planned and carefully written, in contrast to *Jack Pudding* which had been published in March, the month before Erbery died. It is puzzling that Erbery's two most systematic works, *The Great Earthquake* and *The Honest Heretique* remained unpublished during his lifetime. The latter had been written during 1653, and possibly *The Great Earthquake* was completed just before Erbery's death. Both present a careful defence of his convictions.

John Webster's *To the Christian Reader,* in which he passionately defends Erbery, stands in sharp contrast to most surviving contemporary material which had attacked Erbery for insubordination or heresy. The account of his trial before Archbishop Laud is the first of a litany repeated by the Presbyterians, Thomas Edwards and Francis Cheynell, the Independent, Henry Nichols and the Baptist, Edmund Chillenden.

The Great Earthquake is as close as Erbery comes to systematizing his thought. His convictions, founded on a deep Christian experience are expressed carefully and systematically. His other writings of late 1653/4 were written quickly to meet specific occasions: the three tracts which responded to the Fifth Monarchist crisis of late 1653, and *Jack Pudding* in March 1653/4. None of these were published by Giles Calvert. On the other hand, *The Great Earthquake* has a careful introduction by Webster and was published by Calvert. It is as if this tract was produced with a flourish. Here is the thinking of the late William Erbery. Here is the opportunity for all who have misjudged him, even slandered him, to see the man he really was.

The tract is dedicated to the Ministers of the Church of England, and New England. The New England Churches were Independent or Congregational, of the New England Way as Erbery had previously described them. But who are the ministers of the Church of England? If the tract was written during Erbery's final months, he was probably addressing the Independent establishment, now in ascendancy.

Erbery introduced his theological position. Existence can be understood as being in tension between two polarities: the great Mysteries of God, Christ and Godliness; and Antichrist, Man and Iniquity. When God's purposes are fulfilled, God will be All in All. The history of space and time is being directed towards their fulfilment. Erbery divided history into three dispensations. The Second Dispensation, or the Age of the Son was ended by the Apostasy when humankind no longer reflected the image of God. This 'Second Fall' paralleled the fall of Adam when humankind initially failed to fulfill God's intention, and became enthralled by the spirit of Antichrist. The life of the church had been corrupted throughout the age of Apostasy. Erbery condemned both the historic Papal Church and the contemporary churches because all had fallen from Gospel practice. The gifts of the Spirit were no longer manifested.

The Apostasy resulted in the replacement of genuine prayer either by formal liturgical prayer or repetitive extempore prayer. Erbery's exploration of the practice of prayer was rooted in his experience of God in Trinity. Prayer is at the heart of his Christian experience, reflecting the eternal relationship and conversation between Father, Son, and Spirit. At the heart of Erbery's radical interpretation of the Gospel was that no thing and no one is separated from the inward presence, power and grace of God. Nothing is lost. All is fulfilled.

Erbery arrived at this revolutionary position from his experience in the Army and in radical London conventicles. Previously, like his Puritan contemporaries, his preaching had focussed on the preaching of faith and the need for repentance. This might be good news for the few, but was bad news for the majority, who either rejected the message, or had never heard the message. The tectonic shift in Erbery's theology coincided with the revolution taking place in the social and political life of these islands.

Erbery's emphasis on the immanence of God was, as we have noted, paralleled by his sense of the imminence of God. God, hidden within creation and within the saints, will soon be manifested in glory at the Third Dispensation. The age of Apostacy draws to a close and the final age is about to arrive.

During the final days of the Apostacy, Church forms, structures and ministry will inevitably collapse and be replaced by magistrates who will serve as God's instruments to usher in a government of righteousness and peace. Erbery almost eulogizes the approaching Kingdom. His final prophetic words are an expression of hope that God's purposes are being fulfilled.

TO THE TRULY CHRISTIAN READER

THE DOCTRINE OF PERSECUTION FOR CONSCIENCE SAKE... WAS A STRANGER TO HIS SPIRIT AND PRINCIPLES

The Author of this ensuing Discourse, was a person raised up by the Lord, to bear his Testimony against all Formal and Traditional ways of Religion, Ordinances, and Government, in the (so called) Christian World; a Design, though seemingly managed by him, with some eagerness and severity of Spirit (if you abstract some passages in this, and his other Discourses) yet in much love and oneness of Spirit with the Worshippers themselves, that their persons might be saved, but so as by fire, I Cor. 3.15.

The Doctrine of Persecution for Conscience sake (though erroneous) was a stranger to his Spirit and Principles, which owned no compulsion in matters of Religion, but that Scriptural one, viz. the energie, and the effectual working of the Spirit of God over-powring the Soul, and leading it captive by an holy violence to those Divine and Heavenly Discoveries, which our Author bore Witnesse to. (p.258f.)

WE HAVE HEARD THE BRAND OF... INURED UPON HIM

Hence it is, that we have heard the brand of a loose person, or a Ranter, an Apostate and Blasphemer, an Antiscripturist, Antiministrist, an Antiordinancist, an Antitrinitarian, Universalist, and what not inured upon him. (p.259)

HE WAS RATHER A PRESSER FORWARD

1. He was no friend to looseness and prophaneness, either in himself, or others; his own strict, sober, and Christian deportment in the whole course of his conversation…

2. He was rather a presser forward, then an Apostate: Forgetting those things that are behind, &c. 'Tis true, he was formerly as strict and zealous in all literal observations, as any of his equals: yea, he might have boasted herein (as the Apostle Paul) if it had been worth his labour: But it pleased God to raise him up from all fleshly rites to a more near and secret enjoyment, which took him from some outward performances, which many Christians please themselves in…

As for Prayer, he was led into the secret places of the Almighty; to see that it was not to be limited (as the Jews did) to morning and evening Tides… (p.259ff.)

TRADITIONAL CUSTOMS… OUR AUTHOR DID DECRY

…'twas onely the traditional customs which many place their Religion in, which our Author did decry upon which account, Christ himself bore the brand of a Blasphemer before him. (p.262)

THE SCRIPTURES WERE OWNED BY HIM, AS GIVEN BY INSPIRATION

4. The Scriptures were owned by him, as given by inspiration; yet the bare letter not rested in, but the truth and power, being the treasure hid in the field, sought after. (p.262)

BETTER NO MINISTRY THEN A PRETTNDED ONE

5. As is the Scripture, such are the Ministers of it (i.e.) such as act in the truth and power, or in the form and notion onely… The first Ministry of the Apostles, Prophets, Evangelists, Pastors, was not denyed by our Author: but how it could be continued during the Apostasie, or how, and when renewed, are questions and not cases so clearly stated, but that they may well admit of doubts and scruples, especially since the gifts which accompanied the first Ministry are ceased; and our Author was of this mind, Better no Ministry then a prettnded one.

6. After Ministry, follow Ordinances, which our Author acknowledged he ws not against or above, but under and below, as not perceiving the power of those Primitive Institutions… (p.263)

THE DOCTRINE OF THE TRINITY… WAS NOT PERFECTLY OWNED BY HIM

The Doctrine of the Trinity, as explained by the Schools in Personalities, Subsistences, &c. was not perfectly owned by him, One Faith, one Lord, one Baptism, were the Three great Articles of his Belief: Neither did the Lord contain himself within himself, but was made manifest in the flesh of Christ, according to that (God was in Christ reconciling &c.) and doth continually work in the hearts of his people by his spirit. Neither could he see how the Doctrine of these distinct Personalities and Subsistences, could accommodate their Design, who first broached them, in order to the clearing (as is supposed) the Doctrine of Christ's Satisfaction to the Father, in that sense as they define it. For if God were in Christ, that God was the Father, for God is one; it is not one divine nature in Christ satisfying, another in the Father satisfied, but the Father in the Son. And if the essence be the same, how can the personality make a difference?

8. And indeed the opinion of our Author, as to the satisfaction of Christ's death, was accounted none of his lightest errors: (p.264)

HE DISCOVERED LIGHTNESS AND VANITY OF SPIRIT … IN SOMME OF HIS DISCOURSES

If any object, he discovered lightness and vanity of spirit in some phrases and expressions, in some of his Discourses.

I shall answer.

1. It is not good to set up Ones own spirit, as a rule for the spirits of all other men, considering the various out-goings of one and the same spirit in different Saints.

2. No doubt, the Prophets themselves in some of their expressions, did not in all things comply with the gravity of the common dialect, then in use amongst the people.

3. He acknowledged himself to be in Babylon, as well as other Saints; no marvel then, if there were some spots in his Moon, yea, let us consider rather how much he wrote well, as what (we conceive) he wrote amiss. J.W. (p.264f.)

ON MR WILLIAM ERBERY, DECEASED

Thy Spirit, next to Christ's, is Christian School,
Such sweetness, meeknes, such humility
Transcending Mortals, speaks thy Race on high.
If Supream good define it self by Love,
How near to that High Orbe did thy Soul move,
Who didst embrace the Christian, One in all,
Both Presbyterian, Congregational,
And at same time, thou didst the Saintship sever
From the Opinion, This fails, That shall never.
For why? Thy larger Soul took the dimension,
Of every several Sect and Apprehension.
Hammering, refining, purging out the dross
Till Saint was sav'd in the Opinions loss
This work was Thine…
Tis true, uncasing formal righteousness
Which decks itself in strictest letter-dress,
Thou didst some ways prefer the open sinner,
opposing coorse offenders to the finer.
Devotions tim'd from hours and minutes dare,
Speak an embondag'd and a Legal State
Free was thy spirit, pray'd always, always praised,
Prayer is desire not uttered but raised.
(p.265ff.)

TO THE MINISTERS OF THE CHURCH OF ENGLAND, AND NEW-ENGLAND-CHURCHES

THE MYSTERY OF GODLINESS, AND THE MYSTERY OF INIQUITY

The two great Mysteries (read in Scriptures, which the Spirit is now revealing) are Christ, and Antichrist; the Mystery of Godliness, and the

Mystery of Iniquity: Christ is the Mystery of God; Antichrist the Mystery of Man. God manifest in the flesh, Immanuel, Jehovah Tzidkenu, the Lord our Righteousness, God with Us. The wisdom and power of God in us, is the Mystery of Christ, Christ in us; Christ, in a Mystery, men know not; and godly Christians will not acknowledge. This also is the Mystery of Antichrist, Man manifest in us, Man with us, and in us, the righteousness of man: Man magnified and exalted, Flesh and the goodlines thereof set up in us, is Antichrist indeed; for as the number of the Beast is the number of a Man; so Man alone exalted in the goodliness of flesh, is the Man of sin, the Woman upon the Waters, the great Whore: the wisdom and power of Man is the Mystery of Antichrist within us, which men know not yet; but God is now manifest in flesh, and beginning to appear in men, that neither man nor flesh may appear any more, but that all being swallowed up in God, God may be All in All. (p.268)

MAN WAS MOST MANIFEST IN KINGDOMS… GOD… IN CHURCHES

The time was, when Kingdoms and Churches were the two Temples, in which these great Mysteries dwelt and were discovered. Man was most manifest in Kingdoms, when Kingdoms were meerly civil, the wisdom and power of man appeared most in Kingdoms. So God was most manifest in Churches, when Churches were wholly spiritual, the wisdom and power of God was all in all in Churches. (p.268)

WHEN… NATIONAL CHURCHES BEGAN… ANTICHRIST CAME TO BE GREAT

But when Kingdoms came to be Christian, then Kingdoms began to be Churches; yea Churches came to be Kingdoms, and National Churches began; then also Antichrist came to be great… Christian Kingdoms, because they were Christian, would needs appear and act as Churches, to judge of the things of God, and to order all things in the worship of God, whereas they had nothing to do but with the Government, and outward good of Man.

Thus the Man of sin was revealed; for though God be All in All, and there is no wisdom nor power in Man, but the wisdom and power of God; yet man, at his best, being but a Beast, and every man brutish in his knowledge; Man, I say, misapprehending himself to be something, and not God in him to be all, and his Being in God alone, but willing to be wise; and as God to know good and evil, having had his eyes open to see some power and strength in himself, is immediately stript, made naked, and appears nothing, now indeed, but a man of sin, a meer man, made naked, not cloathed with God, nor God All in All: for the man of sin, is man deceiving himself, seeming to be something, to be some body, to have some wisdom and knowledge in himself; whereas God, in truth, is the wisdom and knowledge of Man, and man is nothing but a Beast... (p.268f.)

ANTICHRIST APPEARS MOST VISIBLY IN PARTICULAR CHURCHES

Indeed, the Mystery of Antichrist, the Mystery of Man is manifested in every Saint; but the mystery is most manifest, and appears visibly in every particular Church; for as the Church being in Spirit was thereby called Christ, though a Saint may be so called also, Christ being in every one, and every one in Christ; so Antichrist appears most visibly in particular Churches, or in Saints joyned in that fleshly fellowship, where the Spirit of Christ or Manifestation of the Spirit not appearing, the Church must now be called Antichrist, the man of sin, the great Whore. (p.269f.)

THE BRITISH IN WALES, BEING THE FIRST CHRISTIAN CHURCH IN THE WORLD

...the British in Wales, being the first Christian Church in the World, long before the Papall Church in Rome; I say the Apostacy of those Churches was so visible, the pride of their Ministers so vile, the power of their Synods in Glamorgan and Monmouth-shire so prevailing over the Gentry and petty Kings of that Country, the canons of their Clergy so potent, yea the Churches there and then so carnall in all superstitious Ceremonies both Jewish and heathenish, as never was more grosse in the midst of Popery afterward. (Spelman. Antiq. Britanic.)[2] (p.270)

CHRISTIAN-KINGDOMS... ACT AS CHURCHES, PRELATES, PRESBYTERS, ELDERS OF INDEPENDENT CHURCHES

...Antichrist never came to be great, till Kingdoms began to be Christian; and Christian-Kingdoms, because they were Christian, would needs appear and act as Churches, call Councels and Synods, condemn Heresies, judg of the Truth and Mysteries of God by the gifts of men.

When kingdoms came thus to be Churches, then Churches began to be kingdoms. That is, the Mystery of Antichrist... the very Apostles aspiring to a Prelacy, would needs exercise authority as Kings and Rulers of the Nations, and the Elders (not only to see preheminence as Diotrophes)[3] *but to Lord it over Gods heritage, or Clergy; for so the Church was called, though afterwards the Elders or Ministers appropriated that name to themselves; for they indeed alone would be the Church, as the Pope with his Conclave-Prelates in their Convocation; and Presbyters in their Classis call themselves the Church; yea, the Elders of Independent Churches also have all the power, and do Lord it over their Churches, though the Churches carry the name...*

I will not mention now the Papall Churches, where the Popes have raigned as Kings and Emperours, yea, were called Gods: Neither will I mind the Episcopall Churches, when Prelates domineerd as Lords, not onely Lording it over Gods heritage, but as spirituall Lords in the Civil State.

I passe by also the Presbytery; their Sun being set at noonday, their Directory of Worship, Confession of Faith, Classicall Government, their large and little Catechism, with all those great works, being even at an end. (p.270f.)

THE INDEPENDENT CHURCHES ARE THOSE MY SPIRIT HATH BEEN MOST CARRIED OUT AGAINST THESE TWO LAST YEARS

The Independent Churches are those my spirit hath been most carried out against these two last years, but could not come forth in a publick contest till now they are come to power, carried up in pomp and state, and fleshly glory; whereby they discover themselves by their delicacies, to be indeed the

Great whore, deceiving a world of men, their Forms being more refined, and her flesh fairer, for they are men of great Gifts and Grace too…

I will not repeat all that I have written, but this (with God) I shall make good to the World, that these are no true Churches of Christ; not Zion, but The Whore; though they seem and speak as the Spouse; yet are they not like the Gospel-Churches, neither in Spirit nor Form. No Ordinance among them in the letter, much lesse in spirit, according to the Gospel. (p.271)

THE FIRST GOSPEL-ORDINANCE… WAS THE BAPTISM OF THE SPIRIT

For, indeed, the first Gospel-Ordinance, or that which constituted the Church in a Gospel Order, was the Baptism of the Spirit: this being not the bare presence of the Spirit, for so all the Saints under the Law had the Spirit: but the spirit, in a Gospel-sense, was not yet come (Joh. 7.39); or (as it is in the Greek), The Spirit was not yet, till Jesus was glorified. Again, the abundance of the Spirit was not this Baptism of the Spirit; for the Prophets had thus the Spirit of Christ, and Christ breathed the Holy Spirit on his Disciples after his Resurrection; but the Baptism of the Spirit was not till after the Ascension, Act. 1.5.

The Apostles, with all the Disciples, 120 by name, were assembled together, yet were they not in a Church-state, nor constituted in the Order of a Gospel Church, till they were baptized with the Holy Spirit, Act. 1.15. & 2.47. Yea the Apostles themselves, who had a Call and a Commission from Christ to teach all Nations, and to baptize Believers, could not go forth to perform either till the Baptism of the Holy Spirit was come upon them, Act. 2.38. (p.272)

THE GOSPEL-ORDER WAS IN THESE THREE THINGS

The Gospel-order was in these three things (as the Temple had three parts).

The first is the manifestation of the Spirit in manifold gifts, I Cor. 12.7; Mark 16.18; Jam. 5.14.

Secondly, A Ministry of the Spirit, with gifts given by the laying on of hands,

I Cor. 12.28; Ephes. 4.11; I Tim. 4.14.

Thirdly, the administration of the Spirit in all the Ordinances of the Church, which were not onely Baptism and Breaking of Bread; but a Psalm, a Doctrine, a Tongue, an Interpretation and Revelation. All these also were the Ordinances of Christ for the edifying of the Church... (p.272f.)

APOSTACY... BEGAN, WHEN THE MANIFESTATION OF THE SPIRIT CEASED

The Apostacy foretold by the Apostle then began, when the manifestation of the spirit ceased, when the ministry of the spirit was cast down, and when that administration of the spirit was trodden under foot: and this is a sufficient notoriety or visible signe that all Church-Ordinances were changed into a confusion, or fleshly performances, when the spirit did so visibly disappear, and the Gospel-order to be found no more. (p.273)

THE BAPTISM OF THE SPIRIT

...the Baptism of the Spirit was that manifestation or pouring forth of all the gifts of the Spirit, (not on every believer, but) on every Church of Christ, that the Church came short in no gift, I Cor. 1.7. This was the true constitution of a Gospel-Church, the Baptism of the Spirit, the manifestation of the Spirit in manifold gifts, without which no Church can be in the order of the Gospel, I Cor. 12.6, 7, 28. (p.275, printed as 175)

THE LAYING ON OF HANDS

The laying on of Hands, did concern the Ministery, who received a gift by the laying on of Hands. Independent Ministers make a meer ceremony of this, never looking for any gift thereby, as Papists and Prelates did; but the Presbyterian Ministers of Scotland are a little wiser then ours; for there being no gift, they lay aside the laying on of Hands altogether in ordayning their Elders. (p.275, printed as 175)

THE BREAKING OF BREAD OR COMMUNION

Secondly, The Breaking of Bread or Communion, that was in the primitive Churches, was not as 'tis in the present Churches, by takeing a piece of Bread, or tasting a sip of wine from the Minister's hands, (a meer popish superstition to put such pomp and reverence on sacramentall Bread and Wine) but breaking of Bread was a full Meal, for the word is so; and The supper of the Lord shews the same to be a full Meal, or Feast of Love, for both is one, though old childish Fathers make a difference between the Feast of Love, and Supper of the Lord; so often used, even daily, that is, every First day the Church meeting to break Bread, Feast in Love, to Feast on the Lord together, on the Lord in them; the Bread broken being the Communion of his Body; for the Church indeed was that body of the Lord, the Church was Christ: This the Church knows not, nor confesses how fully the Godhead is embodyed in their flesh, how perfectly one with the Father, as Christ: They are afraid of this; therefore as if there were but a part of God, and part of Christ in them, they take a piece of Bread: thus they discern not the Lords Body, yea, they do not shew forth the Lords death, that is, dying to all things but to God, as Christs purest flesh was crucified to the Father: but this communion and mystery of Christ, and of his death, is not known nor taught by the Churches; alasse, these are heavenly things, too high for them who live in dead Forms: nay, they scarce know the earthly thing, the Form of Breaking bread: this being as I said a full Meal, for they did break Bread from house to house, eating their meat with singlenesse of heart, praising God; yea, they drank also to the full… (p.275f. printed as 175f.)

CHURCH-PRAYERS

Thirdly, the next Ordinance was Church-prayers, these being as peculiar and proper to the Church, and for the Church alone, as Breaking of Bread, Acts 2.42… Christ prayed only in private or with his Disciples apart, Luke 11.1. And the Apostles preaching to the world, never prayed with the world… such Forms of Prayer, praying before Sermon, and after Sermon (a meer popish custome) with the Lords prayer after the first, and a Priestly benediction after the second Prayer. For Blessing the people last of all, is both Popish and Priestly, it being a legal ordinance ending in Christ… (p.276)

ARE MEN THE BETTER TO BE BEATEN FROM ONE FORM OF PRAYER TO ANOTHER, WHICH IS AS BAD

We know the whole power of popish Religion is in their much praying; so Protestants could not be taken from it, till their common Prayer was taken from them by force: I cannot commend this Reformation; for what are Men the better to be beaten from one Form of Prayer to another, which is as bad, if not worse then that before, because seemingly more spirituall, yet having not the power… Besides that long praying which ministers glory in, is both legall and heathenish… The Lords prayer, the prayers of Christ, and the Apostles prayers were very short, succinct, plain, and to the purpose, without such preambles, abundance, and vanity of words, and vain-glorious enlargements… (p.277)

ALASSE, NEW-LIGHTS ARE LAUGHED AT BY THESE MEN

…yet God and their own Conscience can tell how little they pray in their Closets, how loose their petitions are in private, how seldom they retire into their own spirits… they seek not any nearer sight of the Lord, nor any new discovery of God in them: Alasse, New-lights are laughed at by these men, though God indeed be the Father of Lights, there being more Lights then one begotten and brought forth daily by our God and Father. (p.277f.)

THEY FAIL IN THEIR FORMES OF PRIVATE PRAYERS

And as the Churches erre in their Formes of publique prayer, so they fail in their Formes of private Prayers, &c. For they pray not to the Father; nor, secondly, in the name of Christ; nor, thirdly, can they pray in the Spirit. (p.278, printed as 178)

FIRST, THEY DO NOT PRAY TO THE FATHER

First, They do not pray to the Father, but to the first person in Trinity, whom Christ never knew nor acknowledged; for had there been a second

Person or subsistence in the God-head, coessential and coequall with the Father, surely Christ should and would have worshipped him; but Christ never prayed to any Person but to the Father; and no Christian ever prayed to the Spirit till the spirit of Antichrist (Veni Spiritus Sancte) came into the world. Not that I deny the holy Trinity according to Scriptures; But (disclaiming all the Traditions of our For-fathers, and teachings of men) I beleeve that God is Father, Son, and Spirit, and that the Son of God, the Man Christ Jesus is God blessed for ever; yet both in a Mystery, which no man can manifest or reveal but the Spirit, Math. 11.25; Ephes. 1.17. (p.278, printed as 178)

THE FATHER… THE SON… THE HOLY SPIRIT

The Father being none else but the one onely true God, of himself and in himself, inhabiting eternity: The Son being the same God and Father manifest in Flesh, and dwelling among men; That one mighty God and Father powerfully going forth, and exerting himself, or appearing in manifold gifts, and operations in flesh, is the holy Spirit. Which things are not to be carnally understood, according to the letter, as if God sent his Son, and the Son sent the Spirit; but comparing spirituall things with spirituall, we shall perceive that the Son is the Father, and the eternall Spirit is both Father and Son: so the Father is said to send the Son, where he himself appeares in flesh (from the beginning, in the fullnesse of time, or this day: for Christ is the same today, yesterday, and for ever:) And Christ speaking in the dayes of his flesh, that he would send the Spirit, is nothing else, but that he who dwelt with them, should be in them; that is, when God even the Father, who dwelt in his flesh, should be manifest in theirs, Joh. 14.17, 18, 19, 20. (p.278, printed as 178)

THE MAN CHRIST IS GOD BLESSED FOR EVER: GOD EVEN THE FATHER DWELLING IN HIM

Thus also I confesse that Jesus is the Son of God, and that the Man Christ is God blessed for ever: God even the Father dwelling in him, and doing all in him, being all in all to him: His flesh being the form of God, an image in whom the God-head appeared to men; The Son of God being nothing in himself, but the Manifestation of the Father, and could do nothing of himself, but as the Father dwelling in him did all his works and words. (p.279, printed as 179)

THE MAN JESUS CHRIST, THE MAN GOD BEING IN US

Again, I conceive, the Man Jesus Christ, the Man God being in us; to be all in all to us, God dwelling in us as in him, our flesh annointed & filled with the Godhead as his, and we perfect in one with the Father as he. This is the true Faith & Confession of the Son of God (if once revealed in us, Gal.1.16. and 2.20) else how could the Son thus confess'd bring us to God, God dwelling in us, and we in him thereby, I John 4.2, 3, 15 compared. (p.279, printed as 179)

SECONDLY, THEY DO NOT PRAY IN THE NAME OF CHRIST

Secondly, They do not pray in the name of Christ: But, as Saints of the Old Testament knew God in Covenant with them, not God in Christ one with them (that's the Father) So the Churches apprehend God at a distance, standing a farr off, below in the Temple, not able to enter into the Holy of holiest, into the God-head himself; but call upon his Name as great and terrible, glorious and fearful (for so the Law presented God to Men) they have not the spirit of the Son to cry Abba, Father; the Son being not revealed in them, how can the spirit of the Son be sent forth at all? I beleeve the Son is in them, and the Spirit is there, though hid in their flesh: but they conceiving Christ at a distance, Christ without them, as long ago in flesh on earth, and now afar off in heaven from them, as long ago in flesh on earth, and now afar off in heaven from them, not nigh them and in them; They do not pray in his Name, They go not as the Son to the Father, with that neernesse and confidence as Christ did to God; but as strangers and forraigners, or as far off from God being very low in the flesh; They beg the Father still for Christ Jesus his sake, as if Christ procured the love of the Father to them, or merited life and salvation for them; or as if God would not hear them but for his worthinesse sake: words not spoken of in Scripture, neither hath his Intercession such carnall sense. For as the Son is none else save the Manifestation of the Father; so the Son can do nothing of himself, but manifest the Fathers love to us, and our life in God with him: He being but the way to the Father, God even the Father being the end and ultimate object of all our Christian knowledge, confidence, faith; yea, all that divine worship and honour given to the Son is to the glory of God the Father, it tends and ends in God, though by Christ, and through Christ; that is, thus: We beholding in him the glory of the Father, full of grace and truth; I say, we seeing Christ one with the Father, and his flesh full of God, God even the Father being perfect in union with him, and he the beloved of God, living in the Father alone: We see by this the same true in our selves (for he is the truth and life as well as the way) and learning the truth as it is in Jesus, the life of God is thus revealed in us also (God revealing his Son in us first) so we pray in Christs name, we pray as the Son to the Father, as those who are perfectly one with God, the onely beloved, and living in the Father alone. This is indeed to be with Christ; this, to behold his glory, not carnally in heaven, but here in us, in the spirit. (p.279f , printed as 179)

THIRDLY, THE CHURCHES CANNOT PRAY IN THE SPIRIT

Thirdly, the Churches cannot pray in the spirit, not having that spirit sutable to a Gospel state, as we shewed before; at best, all their prayers are legall, as the prayers of Saints under the Law; for though they repeat never so oft the name of Christ, they do but take the name of God in vain not knowing God in Christ, nor Christ in them, nor the spirit of Christ, the Spirit of the Son, which Gospel Saints indeed had, else they had been none of his: But I beleeve many now are the Lords, that have but a legal spirit, but the spirit of bondage, the spirit of a Servant, not the spirit of a Son, much lesse the spirit of the Son: Saints now deceive themselves, in thinking they have the spirit of adoption, the witnesse of the Spirit, the seal of the spirit, the earnest of the spirit. Alas, how little assurance had Saints a while ago?

What long discourses were learned religious men fain to make, and find out what witnesse the witnesse of the Spirit was; yea, best men were scarce sure of their Salvation at last, or must have signes to know the people of God, questioning they might be hypocrites; whereas no

Saint under the Law, even in time of desertion did ever doubt of his salvation: Nor Secondly did they question whether they were the people of God or no: Nor Thirdly, that they were Hypocrites; yet this was usuall with our Gospel-Saints not long since... now Saints... see their liberty and freedom by being in a Church state, as Children of Abraham, and people of God therefore, for some conformity to the Law, or to the Letter of Gospel commands; but I beleeve few have that full assurance to the end: few rooted and established in the Gospel; none know the exceeding greatnesse of his mighty power, which is indeed the Spirit, the Spirit of the Son the Gospel spirit, the Spirit of Liberty; Alas, How can Christians boast of this, that are in Babylon... (p.281)

THE PRIVATE PRAYERS OF GOSPEL-SAINTS, WAS... WAITING UPON GOD IN CHRIST

...yet I conceive, that the private prayers of Gospel-saints, was not in sound of voyce, or forme of words, but waiting upon God in Christ for the supplyes of the Spirit, and of all good things promised, as may appeare, Rom. 8.25, 26, we know not what to pray for as we ought, but the Spirit helpeth our infirmityes with groanings which cannot be uttered. We know what to utter, what to pray for in our formall prayers, yea we have the form and pattern of all our petitions framed in our heads before we utter them, we know what to pray for, besides we have our set times, of our hours of prayers, our duty-times (as we call it). We pray morning and evening as David and Daniel did use to do under the Law: sure such duty times were never heard of in the Gospel-times, therefore praying in the Spirit scarce appeares in these times, much lesse among those who are most zealous for it. (p.282)

THERE IS NO PREACHING IN ALL THE CHURCHES... CHRIST IN US IS THE MYSTERY OF CHRIST, AND OF THE GOSPEL ALSO

Fourthly. There is no preaching in all the Churches, no preaching of that they pretend, no Gospel-preaching; for neither the doctrine of free grace, nor discoursing of Christ after the flesh, is the preaching of the Gospel; the Gospel is a Mystery hid from ages and generations before and under the Law, not manifested to the sonnes of men, till 'twas to the Apostles and Prophets by the Spirit: but the Covenant of Grace, free-Grace, the forgivenesse of sin, &c: was fully manifested by Moses and the Prophets of old. Againe, Christ after the flesh is not the Gospel, for the Apostles would henceforth know Christ after the flesh no more; not Christ without us, but Christ in us is the mystery of Christ, and of the Gospel also; yea, though Christ after the flesh did present the Gospel in part, preaching peace to the Jewes; the Kingdome of heaven being then at hand, yet the Kingdom was not come nor the Gospel fully preached till Christ came againe and preached peace to them that were afarre off, and to them that were nigh, Ephes. 2.17, this comming of Christ was not in Flesh, for that was crucified before, verse 16. (p.282)

PAUL PREACHED NOTHING BUT CHRIST IN HIM

...but he came in spirit, that is, 'twas Christ in the Apostles that afterward preached, seeing you seek a proof of Christ speaking in me saith Paul; he knew Christ living in him, and himself crucified with Christ... we see Paul preached nothing but Christ in him, Christ dying in him, Christ rising in him, not as if I had attained to the Resurrection of the dead... So that all the Ministers of the Churches come too short in these three things which the Ministers of the Gospel had. First they had the manifestation of the spirit in manifold gifts enabling them to preach the Gospel purely, and with power... Secondly, They could clearly manifest the mystery of the Gospel, and preach glad tydings to every creature under Heaven, to every man and woman in the world, presenting every man in Christ, and Christ in every man. (p.282f.)

YEA IN EVERY CREATURE THE APOSTLE COULD MANIFEST CHRIST

Thirdly, the Ministers of the Gosd[p]*el could not onely manifest the mystery by Scripture, but without scripture they could make it forth in the works of creation, from the writings of poets, the mystery of God even the Father and of Christ: For in him we live move and have our being: and we are his off-spring; we, that is man-kinde, for the Poet means that; and the Apostle also, he is not farre from every one of us;*

yea in every Creature the Apostle could manifest Christ, therefore the Gospel is said to be preached in every creature under Heaven, Col. 1.23. The Heavens declare, yea day to day uttered speech, Psal. 19.2 &c. So the Sun, Moon and Stars, their sound is gone throughout all the world, v.4. That is the sound and speech of every creature; and as the Gospel is called the witnesse of God, I Cor. So the rain and fruitfull seasons do fully witnesse God. Thus the Apostles though to the Jewes they spake from scriptures, because the scriptures were owned by them, yet to the Nations, who denyed all scriptures of the prophets, and knew no other then the poets, and their own prophane authors, the Apostle I say never preached to them out of scriptures; for to what purpose was it to tell the heathen of Moses, the prophets and the psalms, or to preach of their sinnes (as our New England Ministers do to their Sagamoores very simply) but as the mystery of the Gospel preached by the Apostles could not be read in Scriptures nor learnt by man at all, but only as it was Revealed in them by the Spirit, so they spake; yea, the Speakings of Christ out of Scripture was onely as a Minister of the Circumcision, First reading a Text out of the Law, &c. as all our Gospel-teachers can do, they cannot preach without a Text out of Scripture, they have not the manifestation of the Spirit. (p.283f.)

THEY CANNOT CONVINCE ANY MAN BY THE LIGHT IN THEM... FROM INWARD EXPERIMENTS, FROM OUTWARD PROVIDENCES

...neither can they manifest the mystery of the Gospel, the mystery of Christ in us, of God manifested in our flesh, they cannot present every man in Christ, and every man living in God, and God the Saviour in all men, &c. these glad-tidings there is no Minister can preach to any people (much lesse to every creature, to all Nations, having no gifts of tongues or interpretation) they cannot preach the Gospel to those who deny Scriptures, they cannot convince any man by the light in them, which is no other then Christ in them, nor hold forth Christ from the appearance of God in the world, from the light of the world that is in them, from inward experiments, from outward providences, from the writings of Poets and prophane Authors; yea, from all the

Creation. Therefore 'tis plaine there is no preaching of the Gospel by any Independent-Church or preacher whatsoever. But still our Ministers cry, Do we not preach as the Apostles? did not Paul and Peter hold forth Christ after flesh? I answer againe, The Apostles indeed did hold forth Christ after the flesh, 1. Because their Ministery was much in the Letter, having but the first fruits of the Spirit, 2. They preacht much of Christ after the flesh to the Jewes, proving him to be the Messias by Scriptures: but to the Heathen who knew no Scriptures, nor expected the Messias thereby, Christ after the flesh is never named to them by the Apostles, but Christ only in the Spirit, God in mans flesh which they manifested, yea God manifest in the flesh of the Creation, as we said before, for this is Christ in Spirit also. 3. Though the Apostles did preach Christ after the flesh, yet not as the end, as the adequate or ultimate object of their ministry, or of mens believing; but Christ being the only way to the Father, by him men were brought to God, and by him did believe in God, that all the Christian knowledge and faith of men might tend and end in God. (p.284)

GOD IN CHRIST WAS THE RECONCILER... GOD IN CHRIST WAS THE REDEEMER OF THE WORLD

...what was the Man Christ Jesus, but God in flesh, the Saviour of men? not the Man, but God in that man was Jesus the Saviour. For as God in Christ was the Reconciler, &c. 2 Cor. 5.29 [should be 5.19] *so God in Christ was the Redeemer of the world: God in him was the Head and Husband of the Church, God even the Father was all in all in that flesh, brought forth of a Virgin; the hypostaticall Union, so called, being not between the person of the Son and the humane Nature: but the humane Nature united to God even the Father was the person of the Son. The preaching of the Gospel was thus to manifest God in the flesh of men, as in the man Christ, and men in union with the Father as that Man, that Man-God being in us, because God was in him; for as God was with him, so God is with us, and God with us is Christ, Immanuel. Without this knowledge taught of God, men preach not Christ, but they preach Man, and themselves.* (p.285)

THE LORD'S DAY IS NO MORE THEN THE DAY OF THE LORD

'Tis too long at present to shew how the Churches (as it was said of the Princes of Egypt) do err in every work of their hand, erring in all their Ordinances, dutyes, dayes of Feasting, feasts of Thanksgiving, conforming in all to the National Churches, but especially in sanctifying the Lords Day. There is nothing, they are more dark in then in this: whereas the Lords Day is no more then the Day of the Lord, the Day of God, when God shall reveal himself to men, and in them clearly... But how comes the Lord day to be the first day of the week; or the fourth Commandment, speaking of the seventh day, prove the sanctifying of the first day? (p.286)

THE LORD'S DAY AND SABBATH

Who can prove the change of the day by Christ; or that the Apostolick Churches kept holy the first day as God sanctified the seventh? especially, seeing the next succeeding Ages, even the primitive Churches of the first 300 yeares, kept the seventh day as the Sabbath; yea, celebrated the Lords day and Sabbath together for a long time; (or the Apostacy presently succeeded the Apostles departure.) Ignatius, being but about 100 yeares after Christ, sheweth the same; After the Sabbath day (saith he) let every one that loveth Christ celebrate the Lords day the Queen of dayes, (for the Sabbath day was King, or chief, as one expounds) Ignat. Epist. Ad Magnes. The celebrating of the Lords day alone was first instituted by Constantine the great, Hosp. cap.9. pag.27. anno 300. Afterward it was established by the Laodicean Councel, an.364. commanding Christians not to Judaize in keeping the Sabbath, but to work on that day, and keep holy the Lords day, Hosp. Orig.Fest.cap.9.pa.27. In all this 'tis observed, that the Eastern Churches, which were the most part of Christendom, did celebrate the Sabbath, as I said, and the Lords day together, Socrates cap.8.lib. 6 and cap.21. lib.6. Mr. Brierwood on the Sabbath, against Mr. Bifield. pag.77. Perk. 1 vol. on the fourth Commandment. But the Romish or Western Churches would not have their Church-Assemblyes on the Sabbath, as in all other Churches of the world: so the Centuryes report, Cent. 4.c.6. p.477.[4] (p.287)

INDEPENDENT CHURCHES MAY SEE THEIR JUDAISME

I am the more large in this, that Independent Churches may see their Judaisme in their strict observance of an outward Sabbath, their simplicity in sanctifying the first day of the week as the Lords day; Their ignorance or connivance not cleering those things which are so certain; Their conformity with Popish Churches, Their carnal complying with the Protestant State-Religion; Their Laodicien condition, thinking they are rich, and have need of nothing, that they need no Order, nor Ordinance, nor Officer; whereas they are so poor, blind and naked, that they have no Gospel-Ordinances, nor a Day at all: but walking in the dark, deceive themselves and others. (p.287)

SANCTIFYING THE SABBATH... (IS) TO SANCTIFIE THE LORD ALONE

This indeed is the sanctifying the Sabbath, not to abstain from worldly thoughts and words, and from working on the seventh day of the week, but to sanctifie the Lord alone, when he onely is our All, when we are nothing, but he is our Being; and our being in Him, when we do nothing, but the Father dwelling in us doth all our works. When we thus find not our own wayes, nor speak our own words, nor speak words as 'tis in the Hebrew. Man neither speaks nor does any thing indeed, but God does all, and is all in us.

...And truly for love and peace sake, I can rest and refrain from labour on that day, not in conscience, but in a civill respect, that men might shew some kindnesse to the poor creature, that in mercy the beast might have some rest, and that labouring servants might have a day to rejoyce in... (p.289f. printed as 189f.)

SAINTS ARE CALLED UPON TO ABIDE FOR GOD MANY DAYES: TO WAIT WITH PATIENCE

But the Church being since fallen away, and lying under the Apostacy having lost that Gospel glory, and manifestation of the spirit in manifold gifts not appearing, The saints are called upon to abide for God many dayes: to wait with patience for the second coming of Christ, and appearance of the great God... all the dayes that men find themselves in the Apostacy, they must abide for God without any Ordinance or sacrifice, without any Church-Officer or King. (p.292)

I AM BELOW ANY GOSPEL-ORDINANCE

Yea, but the discoveryes of God in the Saints in the latter dayes (that's the anointing)... Saints shall be no more enbondaged to fleshly formes, nor burdened with carnall Ordinances, nor yoked to Church-fellowship any more. What some Saints scoff at others, and others say of themselves, that they are above Ordinances, I cannot judge nor condemn; but for my part, I do not professe myself above Ordinances, but far below them in mine own feeling; though I may be above in the favour and knowledge of God, yet as far as I know, I am below any Gospel-Ordinance, having not that manifestation of the spirit that was alwayes with them in the Churches, nor that presence and power of the Spirit appearing in me (as was in them) to carry me up from living in Ordinances, to live in God alone; nor yet that testimony of the spirit to tell me, that in the use of Ordinances as they are, I may be preserved pure from that uncleannesse which sticks upon them through the Apostacy... (p.292)

I AM THUS A NON CONFORMIST STILL

...therefore it is that I am thus a non conformist still, and separate my self from the Churches and their Ordinances as unclean. Common prayers, and the prayers of Churches are both alike to me, the Prelates weekly Friday-Fasts, and the Presbyters monthly Wednesday Fasts, yea the Independent Feastings and dayes of thanksgiving, are but as the holy dayes of Bishops: so is their Order, Ordination, and every Ordinance or work of their hands... (p.292)

THAT LIFE & PEACE WHICH ONCE I FOUND IN ORDINANCES, IS DEPARTED FROM ME

For that life & peace which once I found in Ordinances, is departed from me, and my self dead unto them, as I believe many others are; though some Saints have still satisfaction and sweetnesse in them, and God seems to accept their prayers; yet this is no more then was before, when in our ignorance we used common Prayers, and mixt Communions &c. How sweet and satisfactory was God then unto us, though the use of those carnal Ordinances was as unclean as the high places were of old to the people of God... Thus the Lord God and Father of mercyes, who is free in his grace, abundant in goodnesse and truth, being not bound up to means, might appear for a time even comfortably to his people even in Gibeon, in corruptest formes and fellowship; not that he approvs them, but that in his good pleasure he may manifest his everlasting love the more to his people. (p.293)

TAKE AWAY FROM ME THE NOISE OF THY SONGS

And surely though God may bear awhile with this singing of Psalmes, yet the time is come that he will say, Take away from me the noise of thy songs. Mark it, 'tis but a noise that their singing makes, and 'tis the noyse of Babel, confusion of tongue in all their Psalmes; but God who hath silenced that Prelatick Pricksong, and is now silencing Presbyterian plain-song, will also cause the songs of Independant Churches to cease; now indeed they have a jolly time of it, here Fasts are turned into Feasts, their tears into triumphs; 'twill be quite contrary when their songs shall be turned to lamentation, their mirth to mourning, their fulnesse to famin, and their formes to fire to be consumed by the Spirit. (p.293)

THE GOVERNMENT OF THE CHURCH IS THE ONELY CONTROVERSIE AMONG THE CHURCHES

...the government of the Church is the onely controversie among the Churches, not the great Mystery of Godlinesse, God manifest in flesh, no matters of Doctrine or worship are questioned by them; but the Government of the Church, whether the Church or Elders shall rule: This the Independent Churches deny; though their ruling and teaching Elders be as proud as Presbyters: but sure the time is come that men who are so much for Government and Rule, shall swear they will be no Rulers, nor Ruling Elders any more... (p.295)

PREFERMENTS, PLACES, PRIVILEDGES, AND PARSONAGES

...these three the Prelatick, Presbyterian, and Independant Ministers, are the only men that have been Teachers in this Church and Kingdom; now God will cut off all three in one moneth. How? By setting them one against another, to oppresse and vex, and eat the flesh one of another, for as the Prelates have formerly eaten up the Priests, and all that maintenance for the Popish Church which was in the Land, so the Presbyters have eaten up all the livings and livelihoods of Prelates: The Independent Ministry are now the third that feed on the flesh of Presbyters, whose Preferments, Places, Priviledges, and Parsonages, is now become food for Independent Churches. (p.196, should be 296)

THE LORD IS BREAKING HIS COVENANT

...the Lord is breaking his Covenant that he made with all the people, that is, all the Churches are broken: for their Covenant which once they thought and taught to be essential to the Church, that Church-Covenant is now broken; they are ashamed to call it so any longer: 'Tis now an Agreement or Association. For as Church-fellowship is now called an Agreement of Saints, to walk in the ways of Christ: so when Saints differ, or some great Controversie ariseth, here is an Association of Churches, nothing differing from a Classical or Provincial Presbytery, though the Independent Elders are not pleased to call it so. (p.298)

CHRIST SHALL COME AGAIN IN SPIRIT

Formerly there was a gathering of Churches, but the everlasting Gospel shall be yet preached by an Angel flying in the midst of Heaven, with more freedom and fulness of salvation, with more light and glory then the first Apostles, who preached the Gospel, with the Holy Spirit sent down from Heaven, which the present Churches have not received, yet conceive they can preach the Gospel, having not the gift of the Spirit to manifest the Mystery: but when Christ shall come again in Spirit, when Christ shall appear the second time without sin to salvation: surely then death shall be quite abolished, and that last Enemy destroyed, and utter destruction shall be no more, for sin and evil shall be seen no more, but salvation onely, and life shall be again brought to light with more glory then ever, as I shall shew another time, in another Treatise (with God). (p.298f.)

COME NOT NEAR ME, FOR I AM HOLYER THAN THOU

These whom the Lord God will slay, are the Apostate Churches which separate themselves, having not the spirit, which say (not onely to the World, but to Saints not in fellowship with themselves) stand by thy self come not near me, for I am holyer then thou, ver.5. [Isaiah 65]*... they see not God dwelling with men, the great God appearing in the least and lowest Saints, v.2.* [Isaiah 61] *whom yet they hate, casting out their Brethren for his Names sake; that is, because of God manifest in them: but he shall appear to your joy, and they shall be ashamed...* (p.299)

MAN SHALL BE NOTHING, AND GOD SHALL BE ALL IN ALL

...these servants of God, wait on God onely: who wait for the apearance of God in them: These, that wait thus on God, shall not be ashamed, but God shall appear (in them) to their joy; yea, God shall call them by another name, not the shameful name of a Church, but the name of Christ; yea, the name of God shall appear in them, they shall feast on God, and all the gods of the Earth shall be famished; that is, all men (and members of Churches also) men of highest parts, and purest graces, shall be famished by God, by God's appearance in men; for man shall be nothing, and God shall be All in All. (p.300)

FIRST APOSTLES; SECONDLY, PROPHETS; THIRDLY, TEACHERS

The Church, under the Law, had some gifts of the Spirit manifest among them, as the gift of Prophecie, the gift of Healing, yea raising the Dead, with signs and miracles, and the Angels moving the Waters of Bethesda, wherein all Diseases were healed at an instant, this continued in the Jewish Church to the last: this is more then present Churches have, having less of the manifestation of the spirit then that under the Law... not having one gift of the spirit to continue their Church-state to be of a Gospel-glory, wherein was the Baptism of the Spirit, and all the gifts of the Spirit were poured forth as Rivers of Living-Water on all the Churches of Christ; for though every Believer had not the Baptism of the Spirit... yet every Church of Christ was baptized with the Spirit, and had those manifold gifts manifest among them... his was the Gospel-order which God set up in the Church, is plain, ver. 27, 28 [I Corinthians 12] *now ye are the Body of Christ, and Members in particular, and God hath set some in the Church: first, Apostles; secondly, Prophets; thirdly, Teachers &c.*

This was the Ministry of the Church, and gifts of Christ; not extraordinary, as men say, for that time, as if Pastors and Teachers were the onely Ministers to continue in the Churches to the last. (p.302)

AND IS NOT THE MINISTRY OF APOSTLES AS NECESSARY NOW?

For what Scripture speaks of those as gifts extraordinary? the gifts of the Spirit were as ordinary for the Church, as the Ordinances? Why should Ordinances continue, and not the gifts?...

Where is a Psalm, or a Doctrine, or a Tongue, or Interpretation, or Revelation, all being unto edifying?... What confusion of Tongues must needs be, when there is no gift of Tongue, either to translate Scriptures truely, or truely to interpret them in the gift of the Spirit, or to reveal the secrets and spiritual mysteries in them that have been hid from Ages and Generations since the Apostacy?... And is not the Ministry of Apostles as necessary now to preach the everlasting Gospel to the world, seeing Pastours and Teachers must onely attend their particular Churches? But where are there those Pastors, and Teachers, and Elders, whom Apostles were to appoint and ordain? Where are the Apostles hands, with the laying on of hands of the Presbytery? Was it not the Apostles Office in chief, to ordain Elders in every Church? and were not Evangelists designed by them, to ordain Elders in every City?... What Church then can be in order, without an Apostle? Were not the Apostles the only Speakers, who concluded and did all in Synods? What can a Christian Synod do without them? How can a Church excommunicate, or cast out, but by the spirit of an Apostle, who is still said to deliver to Satan? In a word, what Gospel can be in the World, or Government in the Church, without an Apostle? yea, what Ordinance can be in order without them? (p.303)

LAYING ON OF HANDS

Next to Baptism, the doctrine or Ordinance of laying on of hands follows, whereto as the Apostles hands must be joyned, so the gift of the spirit was ever with it, without which, the laying on of hands is but an empty ceremony, as 'tis in all the Churches, only the Church of Scotland is more subtile and wise, not to use that foolish complement, but to ordain without any laying of hands, knowing no gift is now given thereby, unless it be a good Parsonage, as in the English Presbytery; but, in the Primitive, there was a gift given by the laying on of the hands of the Eldership, with the Apostles, on the Elders to be ordained, who also received the gift of Healing… (p.304, printed as 249)

THE LAST REFORMED AND MOST REFINED CHURCHES OF THE SEPARATION

Presbyterian Churches may justly be condemned of much evil and failing, yet are to be commended that they pretend still Reformation; but the last reformed and most refined Churches of the Separation, say they are rich, and have need of nothing; they need no Order, nor Ordinance, nor Officers of the Church; they see and know all the truths of Christ: therefore by the judgment of Christ they are blind, and men shall shortly behold their nakedness. (p.304, printed as 249)

AS THE CHURCHES ARE NOW DIVIDED BODIES, SO THEIR BAPTISMS ARE DIVERS

…so the Churches in Babylon are, Presbytery, Independent and Baptized Churches: For though in the Primitive Times, there were divisions between brother and brother in the Churches; yet never was there a division between Church and Church, as at this day. All the Brethren walked in one Church-way, worshipping God with one consent, one Church-order, Ordinances, and Officers, were all by the same Spirit alike in all the Churches, who, in this sense at least, kept the unity of the Spirit in the bond of Peace: for as there was one body among all, so

but one Baptism; but as the Churches are now divided Bodies, so their Baptisms are divers: one Church baptizeth the whole Nation; another Church baptized onely the children of Believers; The third baptized onely Believers themselves. (p.305)

THE GREAT GOD SHALL BE MANIFESTED IN MEN, AND MAGISTRATES

If the Honourable Parliament would but be pleased; God so appearing in them, to judge things in the spirit, and see how dead and desolate the Churches are of the gifts of the spirit, how naked they are, not adorned with one spiritual gift, they would no more dote on the Whores flesh, though never so fair, nor on any Forms, though never so oft reformed, but burn her flesh with fire; when thus the powerful appearance of the great God shall be manifested in men, and Magistrates; the Churches shall appear no more. (p.306)

WHEN GOD IN US, SHALL MINISTER ALL LIGHT UNTO US

This is the second apearance of Christ, of God in men: in the first appearance of Christ, the Church appeared, yet cloathed with all the gifts of the Spirit; that is, God appeared in power in the midst of Saints; but when God shall appear now the second time, God dwelling among men, which is the new Jerusalem, then that Church, nor those first gifts of the spirit shall appear any more; but the spirit, even God himself shall minister in his own glory and power, nothing but God shall appear in man, and man shall appear no more: No need of Churches or Ministers when God shall be our Church, and the house we live in; when God in us, shall minister all light unto us. Thus in the new JERUSALEM, there is no Temple, no Church-state, not Ordinance: and the City hath no need of the Sun, or of the Moon, to shine in it; for the glory of God shall lighten it, and the Lamb is the light therof. Sun and Moon are now the Lights of the World; these are the Ordinances of Heaven, and have been the ordinary means of conveying Light to the Earth; the Sun, the Light of the Day; the Moon and Stars, the Light of the Night: so there has been a Ministry by Day and Night, in the day of Christ; and the first appearing of God, there was a Ministry of Apostles, Prophets, Pastors, and Teachers, as the ordinary means of light to the World, and to the Church: When the Church came under the Night of Apostacy, and while the spirit of Antichrist was come in power, darkning the Sun and Air, there was still a Ministry of men, as the means of Light: yet as the Moon to the Night, ever changing in several Forms of Popery, Episcopacy, Presbytery, Independent, and Baptized Ministers, here the Ministry changed as the Moon; yet God in his free grace was pleased in all the times of the Apostacy, still to appeare enlightning the World by the Ministry of men, in some dark discoveries of himself. (p.306f.)

GOD SHALL APPEAR NOT ONELY THY LIGHT, BUT THE LIGHT OF THE WORLD, THE LIGHT OF EVERY MAN, AND THE LIGHT OF EVERY CREATURE.

But when Christ shall appear the second time, when the day of Christ shall dawn after the night of Apostacy is ended, when the day of God shall be again, and God shall appear the second time binding up the breach of his people, and healing the wound that was made by that spirit of Antichrist prevailing in the Church; then the light of the Moon shall be as the light of the Sun, and the light of the Sun shall be as the light of seven dayes, that is, there will be a perfect light, for God shall appear to be the light of men; as Christ was ever indeed the light of the world, and God in truth was the light of men from the beginning, shining in darknesse, though the darknesse did not comprehend it, and though men did not know God in them to be their only light; but as I said, God shall appear in the last dayes to be the light of men, then men and ministers shall be no more the meanes of light; the Sun shall be no more thy light by day, neither for brightnesse shall the Moon give light unto thee, but the Lord shall be unto thee an everlasting light, and thy God, thy glory. Thy Sun shall no more go down, neither shall thy Moon withdraw it self, but the Lord shall be thine everlasting light, and the dayes of thy mourning shall be ended; as mourning was Babylons plague, the judgement of the great whore; so thou shalt never mourn for want of a Minister, for the Lord God, in thee, shall minister light unto thee; Men and Ministers may go down; yea, the Sun may set at Noon-day, and there may be withdrawing of all Light, and all left in Darknesse: but, in Darkness, the Lord will be thy Light, as well as when thou art in clearest light; when thy light shall be the Lord God in thee, then God, thy Sun, shall not go down; and God, thy Moon, shall not be with-drawn: yea, God shall appear not onely thy light, but the light of the World, the light of every Man, and the light of every Creature. (p.307f.)

THOU SHALT THEN CLEARLY SEE THE INVISIBLE THINGS OF GOD, EVEN THE ETERNAL POWER AND GODHEAD IN THE WHOLE CREATION

...thou shalt then clearly see the invisible things of God, even the Eternal Power and Godhead in the whole Creation, and no more Sun or Moon shining in the Heaven, but God himself shining in both, and his glory filling the Earth also, and every thing in Heaven and Earth, as the appearance of God. (p.308)

NOW WE SEE ONELY THE OUTWARD FORMS OF THE CREATION... WHEN WE SHALL SEE GOD ALL IN ALL, WE SHALL NEVER SEE NO MORE FORMS OF CREATURES

This is the fire that burns not onely Churches, but every Creature in Heaven and Earth, God appearing in all.

This is the Fire, which all the Prophets and Apostles speak of, to come in the last days: This Fire came down at the first coming of Christ in Spirit, when the Spirit, when God in power first appeared in the Gospel-Church, then the Church under the Law, the Jewish Church was burnt up, the Sun was turned to Darknesse, and the Moon to Bloud; all the glory and light of the Law was darkned, the Temple, Priesthood, Sacrifices, and all their Ordinances were changed, and became as bloud: So the same signes in Heaven above, and signes on the Earth beneath, shall be again (in Kingdoms and Churches also) Bloud, and Vapour, and Smoak, all this was in Spirit then performed, it shall again be so fulfilled with greater power; when the appearance of the great God shall be, this Fire, even God himself, that consuming fire, and everlasting burnings shall not onely burn up Churches, and the flesh of the Whore, but the purest flesh of men, and pride of all glory, when God our glory shall appear as the glory of Heaven: and his glory the fulness of the Earth, then all the Works on the Earth shall be burnt up with fire (as all the Works of Man shall be burnt up in God) that is, as now we see the Works of men, and not God working all in all: So now we see onely the outward Forms of the Creation, every Creature being that Form of God; but when we shall see God All in All, we shall never see no more Forms of Creatures, or Churches. (p.308f.)

31

The Testimony of William Erbery 1658

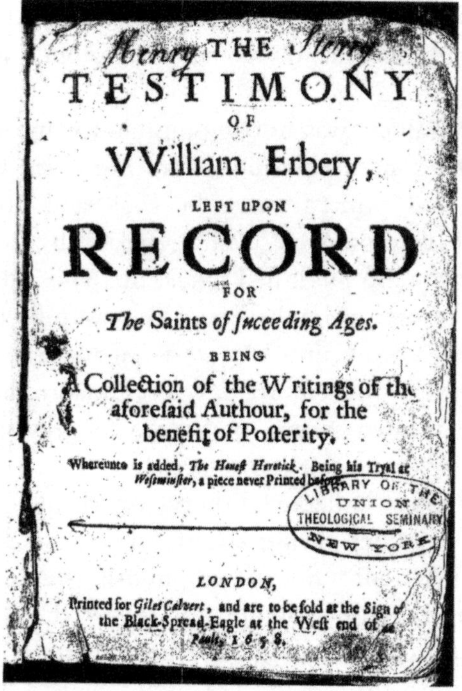

THE
TESTIMONY
OF
VVilliam Erbery,
LEFT UPON
RECORD
FOR
The Saints *of suceeding Ages.*
BEING
A Collection of the Writings of the
aforesaid Authour, for the
benefit of Posterity.
Whereunto is added, *The Honest Heretick*. Being his Tryal at
Westminster, a piece never Printed before.

LONDON,
Printed for *Giles Calvert*, and are to be sold at the Sign of
the Black-Spread-Eagle at the West end of
Pauls, 1658.

THE TESTIMONY OF William Erbery,
LEFT UPON RECORD FOR The Saints of suceeding Ages.
BEING A Collection of the Writings of the aforesaid Authour, for the benefit of Posterity.
Whereunto is added, The Honest Heretick, Being his Tryal at Westminster, a piece never Printed before.
LONDON, Printed for Giles Calvert, and are to be sold at the Sign of the Black-Spread-Eagle at the West end of Pauls, 1658.

What would have happened to the tracts of William Erbery if John Webster[1] had not collected them in 1658? And if Giles Calvert[2] had not sold them at the 'Sign of the Black-Spread Eagle at the West end of Pauls'? *The Testimony* is a collection of most of Erbery's work. The publishing of Erbery's tracts present a fascinating story. The first to be published by Calvert was *The Lord of Hosts* or *The Armies Defence* in 1648. From 1652 onwards he was responsible for publishing seven more tracts, beginning with *The Grand Oppressor* of 1652 and ending with *The Great Earthquake,* published in July 1654, a few months after Erbery's death.

However Calvert was not responsible for most of Erbery's work. His first tract, the orthodox catechism, *The Great Mystery of Godliness* was printed twice in 1639 and 1640 by Rob Milbourne. It was followed seven years later by the radical *Nor Truth not Errour,* also published twice, in 1646/7. It has neither the name of printer or bookseller. This was to be the norm for most of Erbery's work until *An Olive-leaf* and *The Man of Peace* were published by J.C. in 1653/4. Presumably this was James Cottrel who printed several of Erbery's works sold by Giles Calvert.

When Webster collected Erbery's work in *The Testimony* he gathered together all but six of Erbery's works. One can understand his desire not to re-publish the orthodox *The Great Mystery* because that did not reflect the general tenor of Erbery's thinking. But it must be a matter of conjecture why he omitted the others. He might have felt that some, like *Jack Pudding* were too frivolous. He did not publish *The Welsh Curate, Apocrypha, The General Epistle to the Hebrews* (all of which had been published together with *The Bishop of London* in 1652) – for some reason, Webster included only *The Bishop of London* in *The Testimony.* Webster also omitted *The Mad Mans Plea* of 1653 and *Jack Pudding* of 1654. What is also surprising is that *The Honest Heretick* did not see the light of day until four years after Erbery's death when it was published in *The Testimony.*

Webster's *To the Christian Reader* serves as an introduction to *The Testimony,* and is an important apologia for the life and work of William Erbery.

TO THE CHRISTIAN READER

THE AUTHOR OF THESE FOLLOWING TREATISES... MET WITH MUCH OPPOSITION

The Author of these following Treatises, though in the dayes of his pilgrimage, he met with much opposition from the first kind of zeal; yet (I am perswaded) his own Spirit was tipt and seasoned with a pure Evangelical zeal: which though it seemed to break forth into some expressions, which by their flaming, might seem to import a mixture of Legal zeal; yet he was so true a Master of it, and it was so much in its own place, that it did enlighten and warm rather then devour, and by the Light therof did discover the Formal Religion, Ministry, Rites and Ordinances of the earthly Church. (p. ii.)

THE TRUTH OF ALL PROFESSIONS HE DID OWN

This Author did discover a mind much like God herein; The Truth of all professions he did own, and walked up with them by the hand to their head and spring; The mixture and adherencies of Flesh and blood, which carnal spirits had introduced on a fleshly design, pretendedly to beautifie the Truth, he did disclaim and condemn, in which attempt his flesh suffered, and underwent many reproaches, by the litteral Professors of the Formal Church. (p. iv)

THIS FRIEND HAD MUCH EXPERIENCE OF THAT SPIRIT... TO WEAKEN THE CREDIT AND AUTHORITY OF HIS DISCOURSES

Hence it comes to pass, That under pretence of Religion and Holyness, the professors of the Formal Church do persecute and opp[o]*se the spiritual worshippers, casting of them out in the name of the Lord...*

This Friend had much experience of that spirit, which did not only encounter him with all Native and home-bred slanders (that I may so speak) but also levyed in many Forreign and auxiliary reproaches of a strange nature and import, on purpose to weaken the credit and authority of his discourses. (p. v.)

THOSE ACCUSATIONS… ANSWERED… IN THE HONEST HERETICK

Thou hast here many of those accusations charged upon, and answered by this Author, before a Committee of Parliament (in the Treatise entituled, ***The honest Heretick)****, by whom he was required to put his answer in writing, which he did with his own hand, and it is here presented to thee in the forementioned Treatise; Thou hast likewise in the beginning therof, a brief and more succinct answer, which to prevent tediousness and too much offence (such was the tenderness of his spirit), he gave into the said committee with his own hand. (p. v.)*

IN HIS THOUGHTS DID GRASP THE THRONE, AS YOU MAY SEE IN… NOR TRUTH NOR ERROR

If any do desire a further account of this friend, his writings, spirit and principles, Take it thus; His spirit was still working up, to the highest pitch of attainments, though he were sensible of his present frailty, and could say with Paul, not as though I had already attained, or were already perfect, by reason wherof he did serve and groan under present bondage, and was as a servant in the house; yet there was a seed of freedom in his spirit, which was not satisfied, but with the highest enquiries, and did not rest but in the search after, and desire of the fulness of God, to be manifested in him according to his measure: so that he was a Son though under age, and in his thoughts did grasp the Throne, as you may see in the Treatise entituled, ***Nor Truth nor Errour,*** *&c. (p. v.)*

THIS PRECIOUS SEED… WILL ACCOMPLISH GREAT THINGS IN THE WORLD… THIS WAS HIS JUDGMENT IN… THE LORD OF HOSTS

This precious seed of Freedom in the heart of the Saints, now groaning being burdened, yet will in time break forth powerfully and effectually in them, and by them will accomplish great things in the world. The Lord will appear as ***a Man of war****, This was his Judgment in the Treatise called,* ***The Lord of Hosts*** *&c. (p. vi.)*

ALL PRETENDERS TO THIS FREEDOM... READ THE BISHOP OF LONDON

In the mean time all pretenders to this true freedom, and to the fruits and effects of it, being judged by their spirits and waies (of what opinion soever), were decryed by this Author, and their nakedness laid open. Read ***The Bishop of London*** *&c. (p. vi.)*

TO DISCOVER SUCH PRETENDERS... THE SWORD DOUBLED, &c THE MONSTROUS DISPUTE

To discover such Pretenders in that ungospel-like and unapostolike maintenance by Tyths, and in their ineffectual administration of the Letter of the Gospel... is the sum of the two Treatises entituled, ***The Sword doubled,*** *&c. something relating thereunto being contained in that called,* ***The Monstrous dispute.*** *(p. vi.)*

THE FORMALITY OF THE WORLDLY CHURCH; AND PRESSING TO ATTAINMENTS... A CALL TO THE CHURCHES

Yea, That none might be left without excuse, he gave in his Testimony and witness to the Truth of what he did apprehend, discovering the Formality of the worldly Church; and pressing to attainments indeed, in the Paper entituled, ***A Call to the Churches.*** *(p. vi.)*

WHAT THOSE ATTAINMENTS ARE... IN THE BABE OF GLORY

And what those Attainments are, is in some measure held forth by this Author, in ***the Babe of glory****, breaking forth in the broken flesh of the Saints. (p. vi.)*

ENDEAVOURS TO HEAL AND RECONCILE THE BROKEN SPIRITS OF THE SCATTERED SAINTS... A FIRST AND A SECOND OLIVE LEAF

In the mean time, such Christians who were pure and innocent in all appearances, were much owned by this friendl he had a first and a second ***Olive-leaf*** *for them, wherein he endeavours to heal and reconcile the broken spirits of the scattered Saints. (p. vi.)*

THE TRUTH WHICH HE SAW SHALL BE MADE VISIBLE BY THE POWER OF GOD TO OTHER SAINTS IN AFTER-TIMES... THE GREAT EARTHQUAKE AND CALL TO THE CHURCHES

Yet this he did without complyance with their sinful waies and Customs, or giving them the least countenance in any Formal or Ceremonious way of worship whatsoever; His spirit was much drawn forth against this. ***The great Earthquake,*** *and* ***Call to the Churches*** *will be a witness for him, when the Truth which he saw shall be made visible by the power of God to other Saints in after-times; In which testimony as he was faithful in his measure, so doubtless great is his reward. (p. vi.)*

MANY REPROACHES AND MUCH OPPOSITION... THE HONEST HERETICK

So much work of such a nature against such adversaries, managed with so much industry and faithfulness could not but raise up much dust about him, I mean many reproaches and much opposition, of which you may read some in the forementioned Treatise called, ***The honest Heretick.*** *(p. vi.)*

FOUR THINGS IN THE MINISTERY WHICH HE CONSTANTLY HELD FORTH

There were four things in the Minstery which he constantly held forth.

1. That there was a measure of a pure appearance of Spirit and Truth, in the Apostles daies.

2. That about the latter end of their daies, or soon after, a Cloud of Apostacy darkned and Ecclipsed the said appearance; the Spirit of the

Lord withdrawing it self, and men substituting an outside carnal worship in the room thereof.

3. That this Apostacy was not yet removed from the generality of professing Christians, notwithstanding their pretences of deliverance; but that they lay under it, till this very day, and were likely so to do for some time.

4. That when the appointed season came, the Apostacy should be removed and the new Jerusalem come down from God, out of Heaven, of which though some glimpses might now appear in particular Saints; yet the full view, and accomplishment thereof seemed to be farther off. (p. vi, vii.)

THE RESTITUTION OF ALL THINGS IS YET AFARR OFF

And indeed, if we consider the great workes yet to do, and the many prophesies yet to be fulfilled, we may well conclude, That the restitution of all things is yet afarr off; The Saints running from Mountain to Hill, is rather an exchange of one bondage for another then any reall redemption from the Ancient yoke. (p. viii.)

HE FOLLOWED THE ADVICE OF THE PROPHET JEREMY TO THE CAPTIVED JEWES, JER. 29. SEEKE THE PEACE OF THE CITY

During this State of Apostacy and Captivity, this Author was of an excellent spirit in reference to the powers and rulers of this world, He followed the advice of the Prophet Jeremy to the Captived Jewes, Jer. 29. Seeke the peace of the City... He did not calumniate or reproach the King of Babylon, as some of those (called) Prophets had done, who by that meanes brought destruction on themselves, verse 22 but in a darke and captived estate, he perswaded submission, as from the Lord to the rulers of this world. This Author knew that the Creation was made subject to vanity by a greater power then its own, and that it was to rest in that vanity, in hope, till the number of the years were fulfilled: so that it was the Wisdom, as well as the obedience of the Saints, to make their Captivity as comfortable as they could; but to shake off the yoke before the season came, was to rebel against the Lord, Jer. 28.16.

Besides his interests lay not in the powers and priviledges of this world, he was crucified to the world, and the world was crucified unto him. (p. ix)

LET NO MAN FROM HENCE CHARGE HIM AS ONE THAT FELL OFF

Let no man from hence charge him as one that fell off, or complyed with the Caldeans, the Authors of the Saints bondage... No, he had too deep a share in their sufferings, so to do, and his perswasions herein, were not grown dead upon any such fleshly politick design of this world; but upon the true discerning of the seasons. (p. ix.)

SOME FRAGMENTS OF THIS AUTHOR, THAT HIS TESTIMONY MAY NOT BE LOST

To conclude, Thou hast here presented to thee, some fragments of this Author, That his Testimony may not be lost, but may remain upon Record against the backslidings of this age; for who cannot but lament to see professors turned persecutors, the Principles, Designs, and interests of this world, ruling and reigning in the spirits of those, from whom better things were expected, whose judgment lingreth not; Be patient therefore Brethren until the coming of the Lord. As for this friend, his memory will be pretious in the hearts of many, (for that Truth, faithfulness and sincerity which appeared in him) amongst whom is ***J.W.*** *(p. ix.)*

ENDNOTES

SELECT BIBLIOGRAPHY

GENERAL INDEX

INDEX OF THE WRITINGS OF WILLIAM ERBERY

ENDNOTES

PREFACE

1 W.T.P. Davies, *Episodes in the History of Brecknockshire Dissent,* p.14.

2 G.F. Nuttall, *The Welsh Saints, 1640–1660,* p.21.

3 B. Brook, *The Lives of the Puritans*, Vol. III, p.190.

4 Thomas Rees, *History of Protestant Nonconformity in Wales*, p.43.

5 Thomas Richards, *The Puritan Movement in Wales, 1639–1653,* p.182.

6 Christopher Hill, *The World Turned Upside Down,* 1975.
— *The Experience of Defeat, Milton and Some Contemporaries*, 1984.
— *The English Bible and the Seventeenth Century Revolution*, 1993.

PART ONE:
AN INTRODUCTION TO WILLIAM ERBERY

A SKETCH OF WILLIAM ERBERY'S LIFE

1 Brian Ll. James, *William Erbery, Ceisiwr Cymreig,* p.64.

2 *The Terror of Tithes* (1653), see below, Chapter 6, p.102.

3 *The Idol Pastor* (1653), see below, Chapter 25, p.278.

4 James, *Ibid.,* p.65.

5 S.R. Gardiner, *The Constitutional Documents of the Puritan Revolution,* p.100f.

6 Henry Wharton, *Troubles of Laud,* pp.533, 537, 544, 555.

7 There was a severe outbreak of plague at this time. Thomas Richards, *Cymru a'r Uchel Gomisiwn,* p.39.

8 Christopher Love (1618–1651), born in Cardiff was son of a merchant. In 1642 he was appointed chaplain to John Venn's regiment. Venn became governor of Windsor Castle. Having rejected episcopal ordination, Love was ordained a Presbyterian. He opposed the republic, and in September

1649 he was involved in a plot to assist the Scots bring Charles II home from exile. He was beheaded at Tower Hill on 22nd August 1651.

9 Christopher Love, *A Cleare and Necessary Vindication* (1651), p.36.

10 John I. Morgans, *The Life and Work of William Erbery,* Appendix I.

11 E. Arber, ed., *A Transcript of the Stationers Registers, 1554–1640 AD*, p.426.

12 *The Great Mystery of Godliness* (1639 and 1640), see below, Chapter 1, p.46f.

13 *The Wretched People* (1653), see below, Chapter 26, p.286.

14 James, *Ibid* p.72.

15 *Ibid.,* p.72.

16 *Ibid.*, p.73.

17 Lloyd Bowen, *Wales and Religious Reform in the Long Parliament, 1640–42,* pp.36–59.

18 Bowen, *Ibid,* Section II. The Petition claimed that there were only '13 constant preachers, that preach morning & evening or expound the catechisme every Lords day in the Welch tongue.' In Glamorgan there were only five preachers 'all either pluralists, non-resident, slothfull, or scandalous persons, preaching sometimes some of them, some never.' The Petition claimed that 'if the bishop & the book [of Common Prayer] were removed, these reading priests would be silenced, and the people would seeke out for a preaching ministry [as] meanes of their salvacon.'

19 Bowen, *Ibid.,* Section III. This Second Petition, as well as being more anti-episcopal than the earlier petition, included a programme for reform. It requested that the Commons find 'some comfortable redresse for full removal of all grievances... and that there be a freedome without any molestation for any whom the Lord hath fitted with gifts and graces.'

20 *The Honest Heretique* (1658), see below, Chapter 15, p.140. This is testified to by the report of the Commissioners of Array in Glamorgan (under 15 December 1643) that 'a graunt to John Greene of Cardiffe of the house of William Erbury... at and under the yearly rent of £4.' (Llandaff Diocesan Records)

21 Love, *A Cleare and Necessary Vindication* (1651), p.36.

22 Richard Baxter, *Reliquiae Baxterianae* (1696) part 1, p.53.

23 Anne Laurence, *Parliamentary Army Chaplains*, p.124.

24 Thomas Edwards (1599–1648). As early as 1641, Edwards opposed liberty of conscience as dangerous sedition. The London Presbyterian ministers established a weekly lecture for Edwards at Christchurch, Newgate (where ironically Erbery was later to preach). His lectures proved so popular that

he published *Gangraena* in 1646. It was a vicious attack on what he depicted as the dangerous and blasphemous consequences of toleration. Liberty of concience was like a creeping gangrene which must be exterminated.

25 Thomas Edwards *The First and Second Part of Gangraena* (1646), Part 1, Div. 2, p.24.

26 Thomas Edwards, *The Third Part of Gangraena* (1646), Part 3, p.89 f.

27 *Nor Truth nor Errour*, see below, Chapter 3, p.60ff.

28 M. Wynn Thomas, 'Ceisio a Chael: Perthynas Morgan Llwyd â William Erbery', *Y Traethodydd*, Ionawr 1987.

29 Medwin Hughes, 'Llythyrau William Erbery', *Cylchgrawn Llyfrgell Genedlaeaethol Cymru*, XXVI.

30 Anne Laurence, *Parliamentary Army Chaplains*, p.124.

31 At the outbreak of war, Edward Finch was dispossessed as vicar of Christ Church, Newgate by the Committee for Scandalous Ministers. He was replaced by William Jenkyn, a staunch Presbyterian. Thomas Edwards also lectured there weekly. However after the execution of the King, Jenkyn was replaced by Christopher Feake, a leading Fifth Monarchist and Christ Church became a centre of Fifth Monarchist activities.

32 Anthony à Wood, *Athenae Oxonienses, An Exact History of all the Writers and Bishops Who have had their Education in The most ancient and famous University of Oxford,* London, 1692.

33 *The Lord of Hosts*, see below, Chapter 4, p.77f.

34 By late May 1644 Calvert was established as a publisher at the sign of the Black-Spread-eagle at the west end of St Paul's Cathedral. Calvert was a prolific publisher, with thirty-seven new titles in 1646, thirty-one in 1647, thirty-two in 1648. In 1653 Calvert began publishing Quaker titles and of the fifty-two known titles issued or sold by Calvert that year, fourteen were by Quaker authors. In the following year thirty of the thirty-eight were by Quakers. Of the 475 known Calvert publications, 200 were by Quakers. Ariel Hessayon, *Oxford D.N.B.*

35 *The Whitehall Debates*, see below, Chapter 5, p.93f.

36 *The Honest Heretique* (1658), see below, Chapter 15, p.188f.

37 John Webster (1611–1682) was a schoolmaster who enjoyed controversial debate. His sermons preached at All-Hallows, Lombard Street, and at Whitehall in June 1653, attacked the clergy and emphasized that scripture could be interpreted by the laity. The relationship between Erbery and Webster was a close one – Webster published Erbery's collected works in 1658.

38 Anthony à Wood, *Athenae Oxon.*, Vol. II, p.104.

39 Brian James, p.82ff. Christine Trevett, *William Erbery and his daughter Dorcas; Dissenter and Resurrected Radical.*

THE CONTRIBUTION OF WILLIAM ERBERY

1 *An Olive Leaf*, see below, Chapter 27, pp.296ff, and *The Man of Peace,* Chapter 28, p.307ff.

2 Christopher Hill, *The World Turned Upside Down*, p.147f.

3 *A Scourge for the Assyrian,* see below, Chapter 7, p.107.

4 *The Whitehall Debates,* see below, Chapter 5, p.96.

PART TWO:
THE WRITINGS OF WILLIAM ERBERY

Chapter 2: PETITIONS TO THE HOUSE OF COMMONS 1640

1. Lloyd Bowen, *Wales and Religious Reform in the Long Parliament, 1640–42,* pp.36–59.
2. *Ibid.*, p.7 (internet version).
3. William Wroth (1575/6–1641) has a revered reputation as the founder, in 1639, of the first nonconformist church in Wales. His patrons as rector at Llanfaches were the Lewis family of Y Fan, near Caerphilly, a family also linked with the career of Erbery. Both Wroth and Erbery appeared before the Court of High Commission in 1635. It is possible that Wroth resigned his rectory in 1638 and proceeded to found the Puritan congregation in the 'New England Way' in 1639.

4 Henry Walter (1611–78?) was born in Monmouthshire and matriculated at Jesus College, Oxford. He was the principal executor of William Wroth's will. On 28 October 1646, Walter, Cradock and Symonds were appointed as preachers in Wales by the House of Commons. In 1650 he became a commissioner as a result of the Propagation Act. In 1653, he became vicar of St Woolos, Newport, from where he was ejected in 1662. He may well have been the founder of the Independent Congregation at Mynyddislwyn.

5 Richard Symonds (1609–58) was born in Abergavenny. He taught in Shrewsbury where he began a long association with Walter Cradock. He was appointed a schoolmaster to the Harley family at Brampton Bryan,

Herefordshire. He was one of the Welsh Puritan ministers who fled at the outbreak of war to the south-east of England. In 1645 he, Cradock and Walter were appointed by the House of Commons to preach as itinerants in south Wales. They were also among the approvers under the Act for the Propagation of the Gospel in Wales.

6 Walter Cradock (*c.*1606–1659) was born at Llangwm, Monmouthshire. In 1633 he was suspended from preaching for refusing to read the *Book of Sports.* He left Cardiff for Wrexham where Morgan Llwyd was converted through his ministry. In November 1639 he played a leading part in the founding of the Independent church at Llanfaches. On the outbreak of civil war, he moved first to Bristol and then in 1643, to London where he became a lecturer at All-Hallows the Great, Thames Street. In 1646 he, Walter and Symonds were appointed by the Commons to preach as itinerants in Wales. In February 1650, Cradock was again listed as an itinerant preacher under the Act for the Propagation of the Gospel in Wales. He was not attracted by millenarianism and had a positive view of the state-funded ministry. Unlike his colleague, Vavasor Powell, he took a positive line towards Cromwell's religious policies.

7 Ambrose Mostyn (1610–63) was a Puritan preacher. Like Erbery, he was a graduate of Brasenose (1630) and became a pronounced Puritan. Before the wars broke out, the Commons named him as a Puritan lecturer at Pennard in Glamorgan; later, on 27th July 1646, the Committee for Plundered Ministers ordered him to preach in Swansea and the neighbourhood. In 1648, along with Morgan Llwyd and Vavasor Powell, he embarked on preaching missions to north Wales. He was named as one of the twenty-five approvers in the Propagation Act of 1650. In 1659, on the death of Morgan Llwyd, he was appointed pastor of the Wrexham congregation.

8 Robert Hart appears to have been the curate of Moccas which lies between Hay-on-Wye and Hereford on the Wales-England border, around twelve miles south of Brampton Bryan… Hart's patron was Henry Vaughan, almost certainly the squire of Moccas.' Lloyd Bowen, *Wales and Religious Reform,* p.6, internet version.

9 Brampton Bryan in Herefordshire was the home of Sir Robert Harley. It was there that Cradock, Vavasor Powell and Morgan Llwyd first met. This was a centre of early puritanism, and Harley and his wife Brilliana were prominent patrons. Nuttall, *Welsh Saints,* Chapter 1; Lloyd Bowen, *Wales and Religious Reform.*

10 Propagation Act, see Thomas Richards, *Puritan Movement in Wales,* Chapter 6.

11 May-games: 'Merrymakings associated with the first of May… Foolery… trivial.' *The Shorter Oxford English Dictionary.*

12 Relators: 'an informer; one who sullies the materials for an information by the Attorney General.' *Shorter O.E.D.*

13 Commendams: 'a benefice "commended" or given in charge to a clerk or layman to hold with enjoyment of the revenues until an incumbent was provided or for life.' *Shorter O.E.D.*

Chapter 3: NOR TRUTH NOR ERROUR 1647

1 John Hewson was an Army officer and regicide. During the 1630s he was employed as a shoemaker in Westminster. In 1645 he was appointed lieutenant-colonel in the New Model Army. In 1646, while stationed in Oxford, he illegally preached several times in a local parish church. He participated in the Putney debates and in 1653 he represented Ireland in the Nominated Parliament. He fled to the continent when it became clear that Charles II was to return to the throne.

2 Henry Wilkinson (1610–1675) served as a member of the Westminster Assembly. Among the three official sermons he preached before parliament was one with the title 'Miranda stupenda' delivered on 6 July 1646 in thanksgiving for the fall of Oxford to the Army. In 1646 parliament dispatched Wilkinson to Oxford. In 1646 he was chosen senior fellow of Magdalen and deputed a parliamentary visitor. Parliament appointed him, on 1 March 1648, canon of Christ Church, Oxford.

3 Among the visitors sent by parliament were Edward Reynolds, later bishop of Norwich, and Henry Langley who became master of Pembroke College, Oxford, but the key figure was Francis Cheynell. In 1646 and early in 1647 Cheynell was engaged in public debate in Oxford with William Erbery.

4 Sir Thomas Fairfax was appointed commander in chief of the New Model Army in 1645. As his Army approached Oxford, Charles escaped and the city was handed over to the parliamentary troops on 24 June 1646.

5 Sir Richard Ingoldsby (1617–1685). He was stationed at Oxford after the fall of the city. One of the judges at the trial of the king, he only turned up to sign the death warrant.

6 James Cranford (1602/3–1657). On 20 June 1643 Cranford was made one of the parliamentarian licensers for the press. He fiercely opposed religious toleration and he licensed many pamphlets attacking heresy, including

Thomas Edwards's *Gangraena* (1646). He wrote the prefaces to the various editions of *Gangraena.* He was implicated in Christopher Love's conspiracy with the Scots.

7 Thomas Edwards, see above, p.24.

8 Adoniram Byfield (d. 1658/60) was a chaplain to Sir Henry Cholmondeley's regiment in the earl of Essex's Army. He possibly wrote *A Letter Sent from a Worthy Divine* (1642) in which he described the war. On 6 July 1643 he and Henry Roborough were appointed scribes to the Westminster Assembly.

9 George Thomason (*c.*1602–1666) was a bookseller and collector of civil war tracts. His remarkable collection of political and religious tracts between 1640 and 1661 comprised 22,000 items. He added the dates of publication or acquisition on the works' title-pages and this has proved an invaluable resource for the dating of events.

Chapter 4: THE LORD OF HOSTS/THE ARMIES DEFENCE 1648

1 John Lambert (1619–1684), parliamentary soldier and politician. During the invasion of Scotland in 1650–52, Lambert was second in command to Cromwell. Lambert's 'Instrument of Government', introduced on 16 December, was the written constitution that was the foundation of the protectorate. At the installation of Cromwell as protector Lambert had a prominent place in the proceedings. 'He rode with Cromwell in his carriage and it was Lambert who handed Cromwell the sword of state.' D.N. Farr, *Oxford D.N.B.*

2 Anne Laurence, *Parliamentary Army Chaplains*, p.124.

3 *An Olive Leaf,* see below, Chapter 27, p.296ff.

Chapter 5: ARMY COUNCIL WHITEHALL DEBATES 1648/9

1 Sir William Clarke (1623/4–1666). Clark served as secretary to the New Model Army. His knowledge of shorthand was of great value. He was present at key events such as the Army debates at Saffron Walden, Reading, Putney (all in 1647) and Whitehall (December 1648–January 1649).

2 A.S.P. Woodhouse, *Puritanism and Liberty Being the Army Debates (1647–9) from the Clarke manuscripts.*

3 *The Agreement of the People* (28th October 1647) was drafted by the Levellers, both civilian and in the Army. It was an attempt at creating a written constitution. It was discussed at Putney (October–November 1647) and later at Whitehall (December–January 1648).

4 Henry Ireton, an Army officer married Cromwell's daughter Bridget. He took a conservative position in both the Putney and Whitehall debates. He feared that an extension of the franchise would lead to a disregard for the poverty-owning class. He was vehemently opposed to religious liberty.

5 Sir Hardress Waller (1604–1666). In the Putney debates, Waller wanted to separate religious dissension from political reform. He was a member of the court which judged Charles and on 29 January he signed the king's death warrant.

6 George Joyce is well known particularly because he led the troop seizing Charles I at Holmby House and took him to the Army headquarters at Newmarket.

7 Thomas Harrison (1616–1660) fought at Marston Moor and Naseby. He held chief command in England during Cromwell's Scottish campaign in 1650–1. A leading spirit in Barebone's Parliament, he became a leader in the 1650s of the Fifth Monarchists. 'More exciting to him than tedious parliamentary debates were the Monday prayer meetings at St Ann Blackfriars, where the fiery preaching of Christopher Feake and John Rogers furnished heady inspiration. More appealing than boring meetings of the council of state were the Fifth Monarchist gatherings at Arthur Squibb's house in Fleet Street to plot political strategy.' Ian J. Gentles *Oxford D.N.B.*

Chapter 6: THE GRAND OPPRESSOR OR THE TERROR OF THE TITHES 1652

1 See above, *Petitions*, Chapter 2, note 4.

2 *Bron na ellir awgrymu fod y pamffledyn yn un hanesyddol yn hanes y Gymru fodern am mai yma yr ymddengys (hwyrach am y tro cyntaf) briodoleddau'r gydwybod gymdeithasol, Anghydffurfiol.* [It may be suggested that this pamphlet is a historic one in the history of modern Wales, as here appears (possibly for the first time) the attributes of the Nonconformist social conscience] (translation). M. Wynn Thomas, 'Ceisio a Chael: Perthynas Morgan Llwyd â William Erbery', *Y Traethodydd*, p.39.

3 Erbery was probably making reference to the 'Act repealing several Clauses in Statutes imposing penalties for not coming to Church.' (September 27, 1650 – Gardiner, *Constitutional Documents*, p.391ff.) This Act repealed aspects of several Elizabethan Acts which enforced uniformity. Various statutes 'enjoining the use of Common Prayer, the keeping and observing of holy days, and some other particulars touching matters of religion; and finding,

that by the said Act divers religious and peacable people, well-affected to the prosperity of the Commonwealth, have not only been molested and imprisoned, but also brought into danger of abjuring their country, or in case of return, to suffer death as felons…' Gardiner, *Ibid*., p.391.

Chapter 7: THE SWORD DOUBLED: A SCOURGE FOR THE ASSYRIAN 1652

1 Thomas Meredith (*fl.*1747–1770). 'In 1770 selected portions of the works of William Erbury and Morgan Llwyd etc., collected by him, were published under the title *A Scourge for the Assirian the Great Oppressor*'.
(W. Laplain, Salop, G. M. Roberts in *The Dictionary of Welsh Biography*)

2 The name of William Perkins (1558–1602) recurs more often than any other in later Puritan literature. He greatly influenced the early Congregationalists, including those of New England. A fellow of Christ's College, Cambridge, the substance of his preaching was the sin of man and the necessity of regeneration. His doctrine was essentially Calvinistic. Robert Bolton (1572–1631), educated at Lincoln and Brasenose Colleges Oxford, was another early Puritan preacher. Like Perkins, his preaching was based upon predestination, and salvation by faith alone. Nicholas Byfield (1579–1622) of Exeter College, Oxford, was another Calvinist who published theological treatises. John Dod (1555–1645) of Jesus, Cambridge was the chief holy man of the spiritual brotherhood. His exposition was 'plaine and familiar' and he travelled a great deal among the common people. The leaders of the Puritan movement frequently turned to Dod for encouragement. Daniel Dike (d. 1614) of Sidney Sussex, Cambridge, was another of the Puritan preachers with a Calvinist theology whose preaching concentrated upon predestination and repentance.

3 John Preston (1587–1628), fellow of Queens College, Cambridge and chaplain to Charles I; an influential Puritan preacher. Converted by John Cotton, his theology was Calvinist. His influence at Court was counteracted by Laud. Richard Sibbes (1577–1635), master of St Catherine's Cambridge, was responsible for the conversion of John Cotton and Hugh Peter. Volumes of his sermons were published. He was a particular expert in describing the process of conversion and the tactics of the spiritual war. Tobias Crispe (1600–43), educated at Cambridge is usually described as an antinomian, but certainly falls within the Calvinist camp.

4 John Goodwin (1594–1665) of Cambridge produced the most impressive statement of a theological formula for toleration. He set up an independent

congregation in St Stephens, Coleman Street, London. Maintaining an Arminian position, he wrote against militant Presbyterianism, published work in favour of general redemption and wrote tracts against the Baptists and Fifth Monarchists. Thomas Goodwin (1600–1680) of Trinity, Cambridge, was one of the most active preachers and publishers of sermons. He was a member of the Westminster Assembly and joined the dissenting brethren. A leading Independent, he was chaplain to the council of state before becoming president of Magdalen College, Oxford in 1650. He attended Cromwell's deathbed. He set up an Independent congregation in London in 1660.

5 The fourth stage was that of holding forth Christ in the Spirit, represented by Sedgwick, Sterry and Sprigge. All were chaplains in the parliamentary Army – as of course was Erbery and all must have, at some time, been his colleagues. William Sedgwick (1610–69), of Pembroke College, Oxford, was an Army chaplain influenced by millenarianism. Peter Sterry (d. 1672), Cromwell's chaplain and Fellow of Emmanuel, Cambridge, was a Platonist and mystic. He stressed the superiority of the Spirit to Scripture and Reason, and was extremely tolerant. Joshua Sprigge (1618–84), Fellow of All Souls, Oxford, was a chaplain to Fairfax and also went above forms in preaching. Erbery particularly approves of their preaching in this final stage before the Third Dispensation, because they concentrated on the presence of the indwelling Christ and their anticipation of the spiritual imminent return of Christ.

6 William Dell (d. 1669), chaplain to Fairfax, preached several times before the House of Commons. He emphasized the presence of the Spirit as the only essential. Learning could be a hindrance to the preaching of the Gospel.

7 Cromwell, *A Letter from Dunbar,* p.11.

Chapter 8: THE BISHOP OF LONDON 1652

1 All-Hallows the Great became a centre for the Fifth Monarchists who were anticipating the return of Christ and the establishment of his Kingdom on earth. John Simpson was pastor of the congregation which met there, and he and Christopher Feake launched the Fifth Monarchist party at All-Hallows the Great in December 1651.

2 John Simpson (1614/15–1662), Fifth Monarchist preacher. In 1647 Simpson ministered to the congregation at All-Hallows the Great, London. In December 1651 he joined Christopher Feake at All-Hallows to rally

support for the millenarian cause. Feake and Simpson were the first leaders of the Fifth Monarchist movement. When Cromwell became protector in December 1653, Simpson and Feake denounced him at All-Hallows as an apostate. They were arrested in January 1654 and held in Windsor Castle.

3 Christopher Feake had become vicar of Christ Church, Newgate in 1649, and at about the same time was a lecturer at both St Anne Blackfriars and All-Hallows the Great. In 1650 he preached before the Lord Mayor of London in support of the Fifth Monarchy prophesied in the Book of Daniel, and in 1652, Major-General Harrison recommended that he preach before the House of Commons. By the end of 1651, Feake, Simpson and others organized the Fifth Monarchists. He was a vehement critic of Cromwell and his government.

4 In two later tracts, *The Olive Leaf* and *The Man of Peace*, written at the end of 1653 and after the expulsion of the Nominated Parliament, Erbery wrote with considerable clarity about the political struggle.

5 See above, the Preface.

6 William Packer was an Army officer. He fought at Dunbar, commanding Cromwell's cavalry. Although by 1652 he was allied with the Fifth Monarchists, he was not prepared to oppose the protectorate.

Chapter 10: APOCRYPHA 1652

1 Thomas Brightman (1562–1607) was an eminent Presbyterian. In his theology he emphasized that the golden age of the Apostles had been followed by the Apostasy which continued until the Reformation. The progress of the Reformed church in Europe and in England reflected God's action in ushering in the Kingdom. His work had a major influence on millennial and eschatological thinking both in England and New England in the seventeenth century.

2 Sir Henry Spelman (1563/4–1641), a historian and antiquarian recorded the ancient Councils of the church, emphasizing particularly the role of the British representatives.

3 Pharez, son of Judah and Tamar, and twin brother of Zerah. (Genesis 38.29)

4 Morgan Llwyd, *A Call to the Churches*, see below, Chapter 13, p.153ff.

5 'The chiefest of pastors' is probably David Walter, a commissioner appointed by the Propagation Act of 1650. Erbery's letter (*A Dispute at Cowbridge*) to Walter and letters to Llwyd were later published in *A Call to the Churches* (February 1652/3).

6 Possibly Erbery is describing the arrival of Quakers in Wales, who seem to be having their greatest impact upon Baptists. However, it was not until October 1653 that Richard Hubberthorne and John Lawson, both Lancashire Quakers, arrived at Wrexham, although in July of the same year, Llwyd had sent messengers to George Fox.

Chapter 12: WILLLIAM ERBERRY TO THE LORD GENERAL CROMWELL 1652

1 John Nickolls (1710/11–1745) was an antiquary. He possessed 130 manuscript letters addressed to Oliver Cromwell, written mainly between 1650 and 1654. The letters had been owned by John Milton.

Chapter 13: A CALL TO THE CHURCHES 1652

1 The title-page of the original tract was addressed to 'the Baptized Teachers'. However, the first page is addressed 'the Baptized Churches'. *The Testimony* is consistent in that both the title and first page refer to 'the Baptized Churches'.

2 Morgan Llwyd (1619–1659) was born in Maentwrog parish, Merioneth but was probably educated at Wrexham, where he came under the influence of Walter Cradock. He became linked with the Independent congregation at Llanfaches and during the Civil War seems to have had several military postings. Llwyd ministered at Wrexham from 1647 and was later supported as an itinerant by the Propagation Act of 1650. The content of both Erbery's and Llwyd's letters suggest that Llwyd was seeking clarification on various theological issues, and it is certainly possible that Erbery's responses influenced Llwyd's thinking as expressed in his classic works of Welsh mysticism.

3 *At hyn, fodd bynnag, dylid ychwanegu'r awgrym fod gohebu ag Erbery wedi bod o fudd mawr i Forgan Llwyd, a hynny mewn cyfnod allweddol yn hanes ei ymbaratoad i fod yn awdur. Oherwydd mae'n debyg taw wrth iddo ymgomio ag Erbery ar bapur y llwyddodd i roi trefn ar rai o'i syniadau hanfodol, astrus.* [In all probability the correspondence with Erbery had been of great benefit to Morgan Llwyd, at a key stage in his preparatory work as an author. It is likely that by his conversing on paper with Erbery, he was giving shape to some of his integral, critical ideas.] (translation) M. Wynn Thomas, 'Ceisio a Chael: Perthynas Morgan Llwyd â William Erbery', *Y Traethodydd*, Ionawr 1987.

4 *Os mynnwn ddarganfod gwerth cyhoeddiadau cynnar Morgan Llwyd rhaid troi*

at lythyrau William Erbery, oblegid hwy yw cynsail y llythyrau Cymraeg. Na ddibrisiwn y seiat lythyrau hon. Hi a fagodd hyder a chrebwyll barn yn yr awdur Cymreig; rhoddodd gyfle iddo i leisio'r ofnau a'i obeithion a rhoddi trefn ar ei feddyliau. Âf mor bell â dadlau mai amrywiadau cynnar ar y Llythur ir Cymru Cariadus *ydoedd y seiat lythyru rhwng Morgan Llwyd a William Erbery.* [If we wish to discover the value of the English compositions of Morgan Llwyd, we must turn to the letters of William Erbery, because they preceded the Welsh letters. We must not undervalue these letters. They nurtured the confidence and discerning judgment of the Welsh writer. They gave him the opportunity to voice his fears and hopes, and enabled him to shape his thinking. I will go so far as to claim that the correspondence between Morgan Llwyd and William Erbery present us with the earliest variations of *Llythur ir Cymru Cariadus.*] (translation) Medwin Hughes, 'Llythyrau William Erbery', *Cylchgrawn Llyfrgell Genedlaeaethol Cymru* XXVI.

5 Henry Walter, *Petitions,* see above, Chapter 2, note 4.

6 Ambrose Mostyn, *Petitions,* see above, Chapter 2, note 7.

7 Vavasor Powell (1617–1670) was born in Knucklas, Radnorshire. When a schoolmaster at Clun he was influenced by Walter Cradock. In 1642 he became vicar at Dartford, Kent. In 1646 he joined the New Model Army besieging Oxford. In 1650 he was appointed an approver under the Propagation Act, and preached before the House of Commons on the 28th of February 1650. He became known as the 'metropolitan of the itinerants', especially because of his preaching in mid Wales. Powell is still held in high repute amongst Baptists in Radnorshire and Montgomeryshire. His outlook was millenarian and, after December 1653, he spoke disloyally of the protector. He was orthodox in his Reformed theology. During the Restoration, he was imprisoned many times and died in the Fleet, London in 1670.

8 Walter Cradock, *Petitions,* see above, Chapter 2, note 6.

Chapter 14: A CALL TO THE CHURCHES; A DISPUTE AT COWBRIDGE 1652

1 David Walter had been one of the itinerant preachers for Glamorgan, approved by parliament in 1646. He became a Commissioner under the Propagation Act of 1650. He worked mainly in the Swansea and Neath district. Thomas Richards, *A History of the Puritan Movement in Wales.*

2 Henry Nicholls held the living at Coychurch and ministered to a gathered church at St Mary Hill. Thomas Richards, *Ibid,* p.168.

Chapter 15: THE HONEST HERETIQUE 1652

1 William Clarke (1623–1666). *Whitehall Debates,* see above, Chapter 5, note 1.

2 See above, Part One, p.30.

3 Gilbert Millington was clerk of the committee for plundered ministers in 1645 and on the parliamentary committee that discussed ways to preserve the peace between England and Scotland in 1646. He was active in parliament, supporting a Presbyterian settlement and sitting on several parliamentary committees, including one which condemned Socinianism.

4 John Phelps served as clerk to the committee of plundered ministers. He was also one of the two clerks of the high court of justice which tried Charles I.

5 Edmund Chillenden served as a lieutenant in the New Model cavalry. During the Putney debates, his loyalty remained with the Army leadership, and against the more radical new agents selected by some regiments. 'In February he gave evidence of the heretical preaching of William Erbury before the committee for plundered ministers... By 1653 Chillenden was the leader of a General Baptist congregation in London, influenced by the doctrines of the Fifth Monarchy... Initially his congregation met in Aldgate but in June 1653 it was granted the use of the stone chapel at the north end of St Paul's Cathedral where in October a riot ensued between its members and a group of stone-throwing apprentices. By the end of the year, however Chillenden had lost his Army commission and been expelled from his church for getting his maid pregnant... His enemies such as Erbury delighted in his downfall but he was eventually readmitted to the congregation.' P.R.S. Baker, *Oxford D.N.B*

6 Erbery's and Skippon's lives were intertwined from the time Christopher Love found Erbery the position of a chaplain in Skippon's regiment in 1643. Both were at Oxford with the Army during the siege. At Westminster their lives cross again. Skippon served under both the Earl of Essex and under Sir Thomas Fairfax. In 1650 he was appointed commander-in-chief of all the forces near London. He was incensed at the blasphemies of James Nayler.

7 Thomas Grey, Baron Grey of Groby (1622–1657) was a military commander. He signed the death warrant. Although a member of the Council of State (1649–54), he turned against the government and was imprisoned as a Fifth Monarchist in 1655.

8 Probably this was Francis Pemberton (1624–1697). He supported parliament throughout the Civil War. He was called to the bar in November 1654.

9 On July 20th, 1620, Pastor John Robinson preached to members of the Leyden Church who were about to leave for America: 'If God reveal anything to you by any other instrument of His, be as ready to receive it as ever you were to receive any truth by my ministry; for I am verily persuaded the Lord has more light and truth yet to break forth out of His holy Word.' R.G. Martin, *John Robinson,* Independent Press, 1961.

10 Henry Ainsworth (1569–1622), a separatist minister who exercised his ministry particularly in exile in Amsterdam. A fine Hebrew scholar, he translated and annotated a substantial portion of the Old Testament between 1612 and 1627.

11 Jakob Boehme (1575–1624), German Lutheran theosophical author, known as 'philosophus Teutonicus'.

Chapter 16: MINISTERS FOR TYTHES 1653

1 Lazarus Seaman was rector of All-Hallows, Bread Street, London. He played an active role in the Westminster Assembly, and was an active Presbyterian minister in London. He received a DD at Cambridge in 1649. He was vice-chancellor of Cambridge University in 1653 and 1654. He advocated a national ministry and a defence of tithes before a committee of Barebone's Parliament in 1653.

2 Cornelius Burges was an Oxford MA, earning a DD in 1627. In 1634, like Erbery he refused to read the *Book of Sports* in church. When the Long Parliament was recalled, he and Stephen Marshall were invited by Pym to preach the first fast sermons before the House of Commons on 17 November 1640. In December 1643 Burges was appointed lecturer in St Paul's Cathedral with a salary of £400 a year – probably the highest ministerial stipend ever given to any Puritan minister in this period. He must have had other income because he made three purchases in 1649 and 1650 with a total of nearly £6,000 and bought much of the property of the dissolved bishopric and dean and chapter of Wells. A Presbyterian, he was vehemently opposed to the sectaries. Tai Liu, *Oxford D.N.B.*

3 William Strong (d. 1654) was a prominent minister at Westminster and in the City of London. He preached before the Houses of Parliament and the civic leaders of London. In 1645 he was appointed one of the seven preachers to lead worship at Westminster Abbey. As a Presbyterian he subscribed to the Solemn League and Covenant, but by the early 1650s, Strong became a leading Independent divine. On 20 March 1654, when

the Independent church government had been finally established, he was appointed one of the commissioners.

Chapter 17: A MONSTROUS DISPUTE 1653

1 John Webster, see above, Part One, note 37.

2 Walter Cradock, *Petitions*, see above, Chapter 2, note 6.

3 Edmund Chillenden, *The Honest Heretique*, see above, Chapter 15, note 5.

Chapter 18: THE MAD MANS PLEA 1653

1 Anthony à Wood, see above, Part One, p.27.

2 *Ill of his whimsies*, see above, Preface, p.11.

3 Is Robert Blake, 'the great man of the sea'? Blake took little active part in politics and may have favoured the forced abdication of the king rather than his execution. He served the Commonwealth faithfully but viewed the behaviour of Barebone's Parliament with disfavour.

Chapter 19: THE BABE OF GLORY 1653

1 *A Call to the Churches*, see above, p.153ff, and *The North Star*, below, p.236ff.

2 *Proh Tempora! Proh Mores!* by J.N. a Mechanick. It was described as 'an unfained Caveat to all true Protestants not in any case to touch any of these three serpents; Mr Erbery's Babe of Glory, The Mad-mans Plea and Christopher Feakes Exhortations.' J.N. tells his readers that he is reporting on what Erbery 'hath often expressed at Sommerset house in the Strand by word of mouth, in the hearing of many of my friends.' He warns that the book contains 'only a rabble of news from North wales, brought to London by a seduced Disciple' (probably Morgan Llwyd).

Chapter 20: THE NORTH STAR 1653

1 *A Call to the Churches*, see above, p.153ff and *The Babe of Glory*, above, p.231ff.

2 Note the confusion with the use of brackets. It should read 'Thirdly, To be patient (or as the margin reads long-patient, or suffering with long patience), to the coming of the Lord, Jam 5.7. Farwel.'

Chapter 21: A WHIRLEWIND FROM THE SOUTH 1653

1 'For there are three that bear record in heaven, the Father, the Word, and the Holy Ghost: and these three are one.' I John 5.7 (Authorized Version). 'This verse in the KJV is to be rejected. It appears in no ancient Greek MS nor is it cited by any Greek father; of all the versions only the Latin contained it, and even this in none of its most ancient sources. The earliest MSS of the Vulgate do not have it.' Amos N. Wilder in *The Interpreter's Bible.*

Chapter 22: THE CHILDREN OF THE WEST 1653

1 Erbery's description of the various forms of Welsh Baptists is paralleled by Thomas Richards' history of Baptists in seventeenth-century Wales. Thomas Richards, *The Puritan Movement in Wales, 1639–1653.*

2 See Sir Henry Spelman, *Apocrypha,* see above, Chapter 10, note 2.

3 The Donatists were a Christian group in the Early African Church. The theological attack against them was led by Augustine. Erbery could well have sympathized with some of their beliefs because they believed the traditional celebration of the sacraments was invalid.

Chapter 23: A FLASH OF LIGHTNING FROM THE EAST 1653

1 *The Wretched People,* see below, Chapter 26, p.295.

Chapter 24: THE WOMAN PREACHER 1653

1 *The Bishop of London*, see above, Chapter 8, p.127.

2 Christopher Feake, *The Bishop of London*, see above, Chapter 8, note 2.

3 John Simpson, *The Bishop of London,* see above, Chapter 8, note 3.

4 William Kiffin (1616–1701) was a Particular Baptist minister, and cloth and leather merchant in London. He was known as captain because of his service in the London militia.

5 *An Olive Leaf*, see below, Chapter 27, p.296.

6 *The Man of Peace*, see below, Chapter 28, p.307.

7 *Nor Truth Nor Errour*, see above, Chapter 3, p.60.

8 Henry Ainsworth, *The Honest Heretique*, see above, Chapter 15, note 10.

9 The Waldenses survive in Piedmont in northern Italy. Their persecution by the Duke of Savoy led to Milton's famous sonnet, 'Avenge O Lord thy slaughter'd saints'.

10 Erbery is probably referring to the Anabaptist refugees in Munster in 1533–5.

11 Zisca was a Bohemian soldier and reformer. Foxe's book of Martyrs states: 'It is reported, that when he was demanded, being sick, in what place he would be buried; he commanded the skin to be pulled off from his dead carcass, and the flesh to be cast unto the fowls and beasts, and that a drum should be made of his skin which they should use in their battles; affirming, that as soon as their enemies should hear the sound of that drum, they would not abide but take their flight.' Preface, p.256.

Chapter 25: THE IDOL PASTOR: OR FOOLISH SHEPHERD 1653

1 On the outbreak of the Civil War the Llanfaches congregation fled to Bristol (1642), and, when that city fell, to London (July 1643), where along with Cradock, it joined the church of All-Hallows the Great in Thames Street. Cradock was one of the principal originators of the Act for the Better Propagation of the Gospel in Wales (1650). On 25th March 1652–3, Cradock established himself at Usk, thus displaying moderation in his views upon tithes.

Chapter 26: THE WRETCHED PEOPLE 1653

1 Chew Stoke, see above, p.21.

2 Thomas Edwards, see above, p.24.

3 William Perkins, *A Scourge for the Assyrian*, see above, Chapter 7, note 2.

4 *A Flash of Lightning from the East*, see above, Chapter 23, p.265.

Chapter 27: AN OLIVE LEAF 1653/4

1 Giles Calvert, see above, Part One, note 34.

2 'On 12 December 1653 Cromwell accepted the constitution and his own place in it as "the single person", and was installed as my Lord Protector.' (Ivan Roots, *Commonwealth and Protectorate*, p.170.)

3 John Rogers had been ordained as a Presbyterian in 1646 but became an Independent, when he moved to London. By 1653 he had become a millenarian. As soon as the Rump Parliament was dissolved, Rogers proposed on the 25th April 1653 that Cromwell should select godly men to rule through a parliament or Sanhedrin. After the collapse of the Barebone's Parliament and the inauguration of the Lord Protector, Rogers turned against Cromwell, and in turn was rebuked by Erbery.

4 Christopher Feake, *The Bishop of London*, see above, Chapter 8, note 2.

5 Vavasor Powell, *A Call to the Churches*, see above, Chapter 13, note 6.

Chapter 28: THE MAN OF PEACE 1653/4

1 John Goodwin's *Anticavalierism* was published in October 1643.

2 The original publication corrects an error: Page 13, line 3, for *for*, read *against*.

Chapter 29: JACK PUDDING 1653/4

1 Proeme: an introductory discourse to a book or other writing; a preface, a preamble. (*The Shorter Oxford English Dictionary*)
Scomma: A flout or scoff. (*S.O.E.D.*)

Chapter 30: THE GREAT EARTHQUAKE 1654

1 Should be Rev. 17.16: corrected for *The Testimony*.

2 For Henry Spelman, *Apocrypha,* see above, Chapter 10, note 2.

3 Diotrophes, III John 9.

4 It is interesting to note Erbery's use of scholarship in this section on the Sabbath. He seems to have the use of a library. Was it his own in London? In his writings, he usually reflects his scholarship lightly, but in this instance he felt it necessary to prove his point.

Chapter 31: THE TESTIMONY OF WILLIAM ERBERY 1658

1 John Webster, see above, Part One, note 37.

2 Giles Calvert, see above, Part One, note 34.

SELECT BIBLIOGRAPHY

à Wood, Anthony, *Athenae Oxonienses An Exact History of all the Writers and Bishops Who have had their Education in The most ancient and famous University of Oxford*. London, 1692.

— *An Account given to Parliament by the Ministers sent by them to Oxford*. London, 1646.

Anon, *A Winding-sheet for Mr. Baxter's Dead*. London, 1685.

Arber, E., (ed.) *A Transcript of the Stationers Registers, 1554–1640 AD*. London, 1877.

Ashley, M., *England in the Seventeenth Century (1603–1714)*. 3rd ed., 1961.

Barbour, Hugh, *The Quakers in Puritan England*. New Haven, 1964.

Brook, B., *The Lives of the Puritans*. 3 vols, London, 1813.

Baxter, Richard, *Reliquiae Baxterianae*. 1696.

Bowen, Lloyd, *Wales and Religious Reform in the Long Parliament, 1640–42*.

— *Transactions of the Honourable Society of Cymmrodorion*. New Series, Vol 12. pp.36–59.

Bradstock, Andrew, *Radical Religion in Cromwell's England*. London & New York, 2011.

Carlyle, Thomas, *Oliver Cromwell's Letters and Speeches*. London, n.d.

Cheynell, Francis, *Truth Triumphing over Errour and Heresie*. London, 1646.

Chillenden, Edmund, *Preaching without Ordination*. London, 1647.

— *The Inhumanity of the Kings Prison Keeper*. London, 1643.

Cohen, A., 'Two Roads to the Puritan Millennium', *Church History*, Vol. XXXII, 1963, pp.322–342.

Cohn, Norman, *The Pursuit of the Millennium*. London, 1962.

Davies, Gordon, *The Early Stuarts (1603–1660)*. Oxford, 1959.

Davies, Horton, *The Worship of English Puritans*. Westminster, 1948.

— *Worship and Theology in England: From Cranmer to Baxter and Fox, 1534–1690*. Grand Rapids, 1996.

Davies, W.T.P., 'Episodes in the History of Brecknockshire Dissent', *Brycheiniog* III, 1957.

Dictionary of National Biography, Stephen and Lee (eds). New York, 1885–1900.

The Dictionary of Welsh Biography down to 1940. Sir J.E. Lloyd and R.T. Jenkins (eds). Cardiff, 1959. Articles by E. Lewis Evans, R.T. Jones, Thomas Richards, G.M. Roberts.

Edwards, Thomas *The First and Second Part of Gangraena*. 1646, Part 1.

— *The Third Part of Gangraena*. 1646, Part 3.

Feake, Christopher, *A Beam of Light*. London, 1659.

Firth, C.H., ed, *Clarke Papers*. 4 vols, London, 1891–1901.

Gardiner, S.R. *The Constitutional Documents of the Puritan Revolution, 1625–1660*. 3rd ed. Oxford, 1906.

Gwyn, Douglas, *Apocalypse of the Word*. Richmond, Indiana, 1986.

Haller, W., *The Rise of Puritanism*. New York and London, 1957.

— *Liberty and Reformation in the Puritan Revolution*. New York and London, 1963.

Hill, Christopher, *Puritanism and Revolution*. London, 1962.

— *The Century of Revolution. 1603–1714*. Edinburgh, 1961.

— *The World Turned Upside Down*. Harmondsworth, 1975.

— *The Experience of Defeat, Milton and Some Contemporaries* (1984).

— *The English Bible and the Seventeenth-Century Revolution*. London, 1993.

Hughes, Medwin, 'Llythyrau William Erbery', *Cylchgrawn Llyfrgell Genedlaeaethol Cymru* XXVI.

Johnson, G.A., 'From Seeker to Finde', *Church History*, Vol. XVII, 1948, pp.299–315.

James, Brian Ll., 'The Evolution of a Radical', *Journal of Welsh Ecclesiastical History*, 1986, Vol 3, pp.31–48.

Jones, J. Gwynfor (gol.) *William Erbery, Ceisiwr Cymreig, yn Agweddau ar dwf Piwritaniaeth yng Nghymru yn yr ail ganrif ar bymtheg* (1992), pp.63–91.

Jones, Rufus, *Spiritual Reformers in the Sixteenth and Seventeenth Centuries.* Boston, 1959.

Jones, R.T., *Hanes Annibynwyr Cymru.* Swansea, 1966.

— 'The Life, Work and Thought of Vavasor Powell (1617–1670)' Bodleian Library, Oxford, D.Phil thesis, 1947.

Jordan, W.K., *The Development of Religious Toleration in England.* 3 vols, London, 1932–8.

J.L., *A Small Mite.* London, 1654.

J.N., a Mechanick, *Proh Tempora! Proh Mores!* London, 1654.

Laurence, Anne, *Parliamentary Army Chaplains 1642–1651.* Woodbridge, 1990.

Love, Christopher, *A Cleare and Necessary Vindication* (1651).

Martin, R.G., *John Robinson.* London, 1961.

McLachlan, H.J., *Socinianism in Seventeenth Century England.* Oxford, 1951.

Morgans, John I., 'The Life and Work of William Erbery', Bodleian Library, Oxford, M.Litt. thesis, 1968.

— 'The National and International Aspects of Puritan Eschatology', unpublished thesis for Ph.D. at Hartford Seminary Foundation, 1970.

Niccols, Henry, *The Shield Single against the Sword Doubled.* London, 1653.

Nuttall, G.F., *The Holy Spirit in Puritan Faith and Experience.* Oxford, 1946.

— *The Welsh Saints, 1640–1660.* Cardiff, 1957.

— *Visible Saints.* Oxford, 1957.

Oxford Dictionary of National Biography: articles by P.R.S. Baker, Bryan W. Ball, Michael Baumber, Theodore Dwight Bozeman, E.T. Bradley, Bernard Capp, Antonio Clericuzio, Christopher Durston, D.N. Farr, Charlotte Fell-Smith, C.H. Firth, Ian J. Gentles, Richard L. Greaves, Paul D. Halliday, Stuart Handley, Frances Henderson, Ariel Hessayon, Sean Kelsey, Henry Lancaster, Patrick Little, Tai Liu, M.J. Mercer, Michael E. Moody, Roger Pooley, Stephen K. Roberts, Jim Spivey, Timothy Venning, E.C. Vernon.

Paul, R.S., *An Apologeticall Narration*. Philadelphia and Boston, 1963.

— *The Lord Protector*. Grand Rapids, 1964.

Rees, Thomas, *History of Protestant Nonconformity in Wales*. London, 1883.

Richards, Thomas, *Cymru a'r Uchel Gomisiwn, 1633–1640*. Lerpwl, 1930.

— *The Puritan Movement in Wales, 1639–1653*. London, 1920.

— *Religious Developments in Wales, 1654–1662*. London, 1923.

Roots, Ivan, *Commonwealth and Protectorate*. New York, 1966.

Terry, A.E., 'Giles Calvert Publishing Career', *Journal of Friends H.S.*, Vol. XXXV, 1938.

Thomas, M. Wynn, 'Ceision a Chael: Perthynas Morgan Llwyd â William Erbery', *Y Traethodydd*, Ionawr 1987.

Trevett, Christine, 'William Erbery and his daughter Dorcas; Dissenter and Resurrected Radical', *Journal of Welsh Religious History*, Vol. 4, 1996, pp.23–50.

Usher, R.G., *The Rise and Fall of the High Commission*. Oxford, 1913.

Watts, Michael, *The Dissenters, From the Reformation to the French Revolution*. Oxford, 1985.

Westminster Confession of Faith. The Free Presbyterian Church of Scotland, 1970.

Wharton, Henry, (ed.) *The Troubles of Laud*. London, 1694?

White, B.R., 'William Erbery (1604–1654) and the Baptists', *The Baptist Quarterly*, Vol. XXIII, No. 3, July 1969.

Wilder, Amos N. in *The Interpreter's Bible*.

Woodhouse, A.S.P., *Puritanism and Liberty Being the Army Debates (1647–9) from the Clarke manuscripts*. Chicago, 1951.

Yule, G., *The Independents in the English Civil War*. Cambridge, 1958.

GENERAL INDEX

L

M

N

INDEX OF THE WRITINGS OF WILLIAM ERBERY

G

The Honest Heretique is just one of a whole range of publications from Y Lolfa. For a full list of books currently in print, send now for your free copy of our new full-colour catalogue. Or simply surf into our website

www.ylolfa.com

for secure on-line ordering.

TALYBONT CEREDIGION CYMRU SY24 5HE
e-mail ylolfa@ylolfa.com
website www.ylolfa.com
phone (01970) 832 304
fax 832 782